GERARD MANLEY HOPKINS

A VERY PRIVATE LIFE

A Companion to Victorian Literature (with T.M. Parrott)
The Dust of Combat: A Life of Charles Kingsley
Enter Rumour: Four Early Victorian Scandals
The Accents of Persuasion: Charlotte Bronte's Novels
The Triumph of Wit: A Study of Victorian Comic Theory
Tennyson: The Unquiet Heart
With Friends Possessed: A Life of Edward FitzGerald

GERARD MANLEY HOPKINS

HOPKINS

A Very Private Life

Robert Bernard Martin

G. P. PUTNAM'S SONS

New York

G. P. Putnam's Sons
Publishers Since 1838
200 Madison Avenue
New York, NY 10016

First American Edition 1991

Library of Congress Cataloging-in-Publication Data
Martin, Robert Bernard.
Gerard Manley Hopkins: a very private life / Robert Bernard
Martin.—1st American ed.
p.   cm.
Includes bibliographical references and index.
ISBN 0-399-13610-X (alk. paper)
1. Hopkins, Gerard Manley, 1844–1889—Biography.   2. Poets,
English—19th century—Biography.   I. Title.
PR4803.H44Z71727   1991   91-6971 CIP
821'.8—dc20
[B]

Printed in the United States of America
1 2 3 4 5 6 7 8 9 10

This book is printed on acid-free paper.

∞

for C.M.M.

CONTENTS

LIST OF ILLUSTRATIONS

13   a. The Catholic Club, Oxford, 1879
       b. Church of St Aloysius, Oxford
14   University College, Dublin, 86 St Stephen's Green, *c.* 1900
15   a. Hopkins, Oxford, 1879
       b. Hopkins, [Dublin?], 1888
16   'Bathers', Frederick Walker

    Ms, 'Epithalamion', 1888

The author and publishers are grateful to the following for permission to reproduce pictures and/or for furnishing copies:

(Oxford University Press) on behalf of the Society of Jesus: 1b, 5b.

Harry Ransom Humanities Research Center, the University of Texas at Austin: 1c, 9b.

Bodleian Library: 2a (MS Eng. misc. a.8, f. 107); 4a (G.A. Oxon. a.49, p. 22, no. 45); 4b (G.A. Oxon. a.38, f. 27v); 9a (MS Eng. misc. a.8, f. 104); 11a (G.A. Oxon. a.69, p. 116); 13a (MS Top. Oxon. d. 501, f. 111. Minn. Coll. reg. 39/8). With Lord Bridges: 8 (Dep. Bridges 56/1, f. 9). With the British Province of the Society of Jesus: ms on p. 389 (MS Eng. poet. d. 150, f. 7).

National Portrait Gallery: 2b, 7b.

Master and Fellows of Balliol College; 6a, 6b.

Barbara Strachey: 13b.

Walker Art Gallery: 16.

INTRODUCTION

In a BBC broadcast in 1957, Lance Sieveking, a relative of Gerard Manley Hopkins, told of an old man in Dublin who remembered passing the half-open door of Hopkins's rooms in St Stephen's Green on the day after his death in 1889. Although it was June, a huge fire was burning in the grate, and when he turned to investigate, he saw 'an old fellow, all in black', pulling out the contents of a chest of drawers and 'heaping papers on the fire'.

We shall never know what was destroyed that day, although it seems a safe supposition that most of the poet's remaining private papers went up the chimney. It is not certain what happened to many of those that survived the clean-up, nor even who the black-clad figure was, since two different priests in the community claimed to have done the stoking.

Fr Wheeler, who had cared for Hopkins in his final illness, told Robert Bridges some four months later that his patient had had a presentiment that he would not recover, 'but I am sure he took no measure to arrange his papers, gave no instructions about preserving or destroying them. Any suggestion to that effect would be made to me, and he never broached the subject at all.' Fr Wheeler said that after Hopkins's death he looked through the papers hurriedly without reading them. When he saw letters that were obviously from Bridges, he put them aside to return to him, he destroyed many others immediately, and he sent to Hopkins's family what seemed relevant. Later he heard that Bridges wanted anything remaining, and he dispatched to him whatever had survived.

In apparent indignation, Fr Joseph Darlington wrote to Bridges when he heard Fr Wheeler's account, 'After GH's death, it was *I* who went thro' all G.H.'s letters & papers: he seemed to have kept all he ever received. It was *I* who found "Rosa Mystica".' Bridges noted on the back of an undated copy of Fr Darlington's letter that 'Father D's memory went altogether wrong about Gerard Hopkins. It was not he but Father Wheeler . . . who sent me Gerard's MSS at his death.' He dismissed Fr Darlington as a 'pervert', a fierce old-fashioned term of opprobrium for converts.

Who destroyed Hopkins's papers is unimportant today, and if he had realized how much he had inadvertently given away about his lack of knowledge of Hopkins, neither priest might have been eager to claim the distinction. 'From the bent of Fr Gerard's mind and work', wrote Fr Wheeler, 'I should think he would have been glad to leave something permanent in literature or art', but he obviously had no idea he was dealing with the personal effects (insofar as Jesuits have such things) of the most original English poet of the century.

Fr Darlington said that 'There was no sign in any of his diaries or letters etc of any depression or unhappiness, quite the contrary; they were the letters of a man living in another world altogether than this – quite apart from all sordid surroundings; he never noticed them.' It is hard to see how the merest scanning, let alone going 'thro' all G.H.'s letters & papers', could have left such an impression in Fr Darlington's mind, since they are a record of deep depression and heart-breaking misery.

The lack of understanding of Hopkins displayed by fellow priests who had lived in the same house with him for half a dozen years was certainly excusable, since they had no reason to regard him curiously and no idea that his papers might be of interest to the world. Nor was their ignorance of his importance unusual. None of his obituaries so much as mentioned that he was a poet, and even the notice of his death in the private Jesuit journal, *Letters and Notices*, repeated the judgment of an 'old college friend', who thought his conversation too critical in tone: 'If he had not been the victim of a lengthened and overwrought critical education, which makes men subjects of an operation, rather than trained instruments for work, Hopkins had all the elements of an eminent artist or literary man.' The writer is not identified, but it is worth noticing that Darlington liked to be thought of as an old college friend, since he and Hopkins had had the same tutor at Oxford. But his opinion of Hopkins was like that of nearly everyone who met him after his undergraduate years. Getting to know Hopkins has always been difficult.

Hopkins perhaps felt he had no need to give instructions about the disposal of his papers, since in the last years of his life he had begun destroying the records of his life, and before becoming a member of the Society of Jesus, he had burnt the poetry he had composed up to that time. He kept many papers by him, but we know that over the years he had got rid of many others. Even so, the sum of papers Fr Wheeler burned must have been considerable, and one of the ways that posterity gets to know about its great predecessors was diminished.

In 1884 Hopkins himself wrote that only eleven friends had been given his poetry to read, although he recognized that some of them might have let others read it while it was in their possession. It is fairly certain that quite a few more had read it than he remembered at the time, but it was of course unpublished, and the fact is that very few indeed had ever seen one of his works, and he had nothing like a regular group of readers. He even lacked the circle of constant readers among his intimates that most poets have; there were only three other men, fortunately all poets, who saw most of what he wrote. R. W. Dixon admired nearly everything he saw, but he was fairly uncritical, and probably Hopkins did not put too much stock in his generous and unfailing praise. Coventry Patmore said that he admired Hopkins's poems, but he certainly did not like any of them unreservedly, and some of them he actively disliked. Robert Bridges was the best of friends and as good a reader as Hopkins could have expected for his constantly startling poems, but he was far from enthusiastic about many of them, and he said after Hopkins's death that the loss would have been even greater had his friend been a better poet; literally true, of course, but not indicative of unqualified admiration.

Bridges was to be the editor of the first edition of Hopkins's poetry in 1918, nearly three decades after his death. In the intervening time he had probably become more enthusiastic about the poems, but it was surely as much love of Hopkins the man as of his poetry that kept him faithful to the task all those years. Hopkins wrote countless letters to Bridges about poetry and about his own works, but remarkably little about the emotions that prompted them; he was too reserved to lay bare his feelings, and Bridges was too well bred (the term is the right one here) to ask about them. Many previously unknown facts about his life keep surfacing, but they are not what we want to know about Hopkins. Recently there has even been a rumour that the location of his grave was falsified; possibly, but that really tells us little about the emotional, intellectual and psychological makeup of a great poet, which is what most of us want to know.

Perhaps the answers to some of our questions about him were in those letters burning in the fireplace in St Stephen's Green, but the probability is that much of his life would never have been committed to paper. It was noticed by friends how little his face betrayed of his emotions, and he preferred it that way. As he grew older, his reticence increased so that the period we know least about is the end of his life. In his last posting, to Dublin, Hopkins lamented that he was cut off from family, country, and friends, but in part that isolation was of his own choosing, and for all his need of affection, he gave away little of his own private life to his acquaintances.

But perhaps the loss has been less than we might initially think. Most people who fall in love with his poetry continue to read his published letters and journals and the reminiscences of friends, so that Hopkins himself becomes in time a special kind of friend. And we know about Hopkins in the way that we know our other friends, less by the direct content of what they tell us than by the way they speak or write, by their tone of voice. Of that Hopkins gives us plenty, and it becomes our best evidence about the man.

There was one of his friends to whom he might have been completely frank about himself, but he saw that young man only once in his life, and when he was twenty-four his friend died. After that he was never easy about revealing himself to others, even to such an affectionate intimate as Robert Bridges.

My own experience of Hopkins's poetry began many years ago, when I was an undergraduate. Like other new readers of his poetry, even today, I found him extremely baffling, an impression first formed through the difficulty of following the literal sense of his poems, although it always proved to be there when I had been sufficiently diligent. Behind the poems, however, I thought I knew that there was a devout convert priest, an open and spontaneous lover of both the physical and the spiritual world, a man whose moral problems were resolved by the faith he had adopted, whose obscurity for thirty years after his death was finally compensated by commemoration in Westminster Abbey. In the near half-century since I first read 'Thou art indeed just, Lord', I have slowly come to feel that understanding the poems is far less difficult than getting to know the mysterious man who wrote them. He hid his tracks so well that, like Fr Darlington and Fr Wheeler, we may misunderstand him, but, unlike them, we at least begin with the knowledge that he is both adept at evasion and well worth investigating.

Few poets have inspired in others more passionate involvement with their works and lives, and since his poetry, his personality and his intellect were all of great complexity, his admirers are often devoted to discrete facets of them, convinced that their own interests are the important ones. Creating Hopkins in their own image is perhaps a necessity for cultivated readers, scholars or critics in order to come to initial grips with Hopkins. I cannot pretend that my own biographical interest in him exhausts all possible ways of considering a very great poet, or that it will satisfy all those lovers of Hopkins with a specialized interest in his art, but it does set out to discover what manner of man he was.

One last word: we are used to thinking of Hopkins as a Roman Catholic convert and Jesuit priest, but we need to remember too that for almost exactly half his short life he was a member of the Church of England. If we can believe what most psychologists tell us, the psyche is formed early in our existence. When Hopkins was converted at twenty-two, the personality, intellect and spiritual cast of mind that characterized him at his death were well established, and the outlines of the great poet he was to become were already implicit. For that reason, I have chosen to spend a great deal more time than earlier biographers on his undergraduate days, when it had all begun.

CHAPTER I

THE IMPORTANCE OF BEING
MANLEY
1844–63

Even his name is usually wrong. Gerard Hopkins disliked 'Manley', and seldom used it except on official papers, yet today anyone neglecting to put in his middle name is probably met with a look of momentary mystification and an almost automatic correction of 'Oh, Gerard *Manley* Hopkins', so that one soon learns to include it, to save time and avoid confusion. 'Gerard', given in honour of the saint, is appropriate enough, but his second name came from his father and his father's forebears, and his uneasiness with it is equally fitting, since in some ways his life was to be an adjustment to his family and to his father in particular. 'Manley' had a good bit to do with his once lying in bed contemplating the ugliness of his name until he was so mortified that it was a cure to vainglory simply to recall the thought.

The play on 'manly' can hardly have escaped Gerard Hopkins. It is a word ringing with Victorian values, one that sprang unbidden to the lips of headmasters familiar with *Tom Brown's Schooldays* and the works of G. A. Henty and which must equally have set the teeth of a generation of schoolboys on edge. Honesty, chastity, virility, bravery, frankness, clean fingernails and a host of other major virtues are all comprised in its syllables. Above all, for a Victorian, it indicated decent English values. A recent study of Ritualism and sexual deviation is called 'UnEnglish and Unmanly', and the title tells it all. Manliness is precisely what Hopkins's father wanted in his eldest son, and the name was to be his guide: the importance of being Manley.

Manley Hopkins (1818–1897) and his wife Kate (1821–1920) had

1

nine children, of whom the first and best known was born on 28 July 1844 in Stratford, Essex, where the Hopkins family had been settled for a quarter of a century. Stratford was still some way from being the busy part of London that it is today, but it was beginning to lose its rural character. Nonetheless, it was a good place for a young couple, married only a year, to begin a family, for it was inexpensive enough for them to live comfortably on what was still a somewhat overextended income.

Like his father and grandfather, Manley Hopkins was an average adjuster, or marine insurance broker. His grandfather, Martin Hopkins, had prospered and risen to the bourgeois respectability of Master of the Glass-Sellers Company and freeman of the City. Martin's son, Martin Edward (father of Manley), had made a good marriage to Ann Manley, daughter of a well-to-do Devon family of yeomen farmers who had owned their land for six centuries. But Martin Edward was not so good a man at business as his father, and he seems to have had trouble settling to a particular form of insurance and trade. For a time he apparently prospered, since in 1830 he gave a subscription of £30 to the building of two new chapels,[1] but at his death in 1836 he left the family finances in some disarray, with an estate of only £200. His widow, a jolly woman who lived to be ninety years old, with a strong Devon accent to the end, was left with five children, of whom Manley was the eldest son. At eighteen he had already been out of school for three years at the death of his father, and he took over responsibility in providing a home for his mother and brothers and sisters. During the next few years he learned average adjusting, then in the month his first son was born, he set up his own firm, which is still in business.

Chestnut House, 87 The Grove, Stratford, was a pleasant three-storied semi-detached house with big rooms and high ceilings, sufficiently large to accommodate Manley Hopkins, his wife, mother, sister and, for a time, two brothers. They lived comfortably, if not luxuriously, with a cook, housemaid, nurse and nursemaid for the rapidly growing family, and presumably daily women to help with the cleaning. Large though the household sounds today, it was not far off the standard of a rising young businessman and his family. By 1852, when they left Stratford, the Hopkins family had four children besides Gerard (one died the following year at twenty-two months),[2] and the house was bulging.

The family sounds conventional enough, but there were some murky corners in it. Kate Hopkins, the mother of the rapidly expanding family, was the daughter of a London doctor, John Simm Smith, who had a prosperous practice and a somewhat colourful reputation. Among his patients was a Mrs Ann Thwaytes, who had inherited £500,000 on her husband's death. Dr Smith had been attending her since 1832 and had advised her since then on the administration of her property. He had been receiving about £2000 annually for his help, as well as some £50,000 in gifts. As residuary legatees of her estate she named Dr Smith, his brother Samuel and his son John in her will. Dr Smith and his brother were to receive £180,000. In the lawsuit that naturally resulted on her death, it was established that Mrs Thwaytes believed 'that she and Dr Smith were members of the Holy Trinity, that Dr Smith knew all her thoughts, and that she had a special part to play in the Last Judgement, for which event she had prepared the drawing-room of her London house.'[3] Although nothing criminal was proven against Dr Smith, the resultant publicity was painful for the Hopkins family, but the money had been useful in acquiring a fine house for the Smiths in Croydon. It may also have contributed to the running of Chestnut House. Rather less spectacularly but more interestingly for his grandson, Dr Smith had been a fellow student of Keats when walking the hospitals and remembered him well.

Kate Hopkins came from a family that perhaps seemed on the face of it more likely to produce a great artist than did her husband's. Among her connections, admittedly distant, she could boast of Sydney Smith and Gainsborough, while Thomas Lovell Beddoes was the best Mr Hopkins could claim. She was naturally motherly and sweet-tempered, and said to be far better educated than most women of her day. She was certainly interested in music and poetry, and before her marriage had learned to speak German while staying in Hamburg, although that is perhaps an inadequate basis for the statement of her son's first biographer that she was 'a keen student of philosophy, history, and politics'.[4] Gerard's many letters to her suggest that she was loving, a trifle too demanding about affection, and generally willing to be a buffer between her husband and her son. It is only fair to add that the tone of Gerard's letters to her does not support the claims of his biographer about the breadth of her intellect, and that at some periods of his life his letters seem more dutifully filial than spontaneously loving. She was proud of his poems without necessarily understanding them completely. Their correspondence was seldom concerned with poetry.

Manley Hopkins, in spite of having left school so young, was a man of startling breadth of interest, although it sometimes seems spread a bit too thinly; we are reminded of Gerard's apparent belief that he was capable himself of achieving something remarkable in almost any field that attracted his interest. Besides founding Manley Hopkins and Sons and Cookes (a title that suggests he might have welcomed the interest of Gerard), he became a widely recognized authority on average adjusting. He acted as Consul-General for the Kingdom of Hawaii in London for over forty years (of which more later), and in the chinks of his life he was constantly busy writing. He wrote *A Handbook of Averages*; a history of Hawaii that was for a time the standard work because of the way he had read everything about the kingdom he could get his hands on, even though he wrote it in a few months without ever having visited the islands; *A Manual of Marine Insurance*; three volumes of poetry that may be the best ever produced by an average adjuster; a book on the cardinal numbers; and an unpublished novel. In his spare time he wrote literary criticism and poetry for *The Times*, *Once a Week*,* *Cornhill*, and other London periodicals, as well as a series of newsletters about London for a Hawaiian paper, the *Polynesian*, and occasional verses for almost any happening that caught his fancy. The importance of all this activity is not that he was a master of any aspect of it but that it helped create the kind of family atmosphere that nurtures creation in its members by the simple process of taking it for granted. Although there is no record that any of his books was ever reviewed, he certainly assumed that writing was intended for the eyes of others, an inherited attitude towards

---

* One of the illustrators of Manley Hopkins's verse in this periodical was Frederick Walker, and it may be from this source that Gerard first knew the work of the man who was to become his favourite Victorian painter.

publication that made it difficult for his son to go through life entirely unknown to the literary world.

Undoubtedly Gerard was greatly influenced by his father's incessant literary activity, but since he did not emulate him directly, it is difficult to be precise about the nature of the influence. What is more certain is that Manley Hopkins's writings reflected his attitudes to the Roman Catholic priesthood and to homosexuality, both important in his future dealings with what seemed to him a wayward son.

His history of Hawaii has occasionally been praised by scholars for its understanding of Roman Catholic priests and its admiration of their work in the islands, with the suggestion that his tolerance may have inspired Gerard's later conversion. The truth is quite different, for his approving remarks about Jesuits and other Roman Catholics are quotations from other writers (e.g., Richard Henry Dana the younger) and used primarily as a stick with which to beat the Protestant missionaries. The opinions of the Roman Church expressed in his own voice are far from admiring:

> We cannot for a moment praise or defend conduct wherein truth is sacrificed to expediency, or even if it were not blasphemous to say it, to religion; but the priests of the Roman Church look upon their allegiance as inviolable, and as excusing some acts which the clergy of other churches would disdain and detest. They are in the position of privates in an army. When the latter take away the lives of men standing opposite to their ranks, men against whom they have no personal quarrel and whom they have never seen before, they look upon themselves as instruments only, scarcely more accountable for the bloodshed than their rifles are. The responsibility of life remains with the superior authority; their own judgement seems taken away, – the voice of conscience to be suspended.[5]

This was written only four years before Gerard became a Roman Catholic, and it goes a long way to indicate both the attitude of his father and precisely what Gerard was rebelling against.

It is mildly surprising to find that Manley Hopkins's writings for

The Times included such important reviews as those of two major Tennyson poems, *The Princess* and *In Memoriam*.[6] In a heavily jocular consideration of the latter, he raps Tennyson over the knuckles for two serious faults in what he nonetheless recognizes as perhaps the most important English elegy. In the first place, 'the enormous exaggeration of the grief' is responsible for our feeling that 'Instead of a memorial we have a myth. . . . The hero is beyond our sympathy.' The second major defect 'is the tone of – may we say so? – amatory tenderness . . . Very sweet and plaintive these verses are; but who would not give them a feminine application? . . . Is it Petrarch whispering to Laura? We really think that floating remembrances of Shakespeare's sonnets have beguiled Mr. Tennyson. . . . the taste is displeased when every expression of fondness is sighed out, and the only figure within our view is Amaryllis of the Chancery Bar.'[7] Since both aspects of Tennyson on which he lands with such heavy irony were characteristic of his son and at least implied in his poetry, we could hardly expect great sympathy between Hopkins father and son, and indeed they probably felt little.

Mr Hopkins's business was prospering, his family was growing, and they needed more room, as well, probably, as an address with more prestige. Stratford was being overrun by manufacturing, and the big houses on leafy streets were being choked by rows of workmen's cottages. Behind Chestnut House itself was a row of wooden hovels backing on to the Hopkins's garden. It is interesting, in light of his lifelong dislike of the Irish, that Gerard's family should have been forced to move in part by their influx into Stratford. It is hardly surprising that their choice of a new home in 1852 should have fallen on Hampstead, that breezy green refuge from the Victorian city.

Number 9, Oak Hill Park had been built the year before the Hopkinses moved into it. There were a dozen large detached houses in a plot of seven acres, which would have been known in less genteel surroundings as a development; the group had won a first prize at the Great Exhibition for model residences for gentlemen. Each house had a large garden, and number 9 had a tall elm tree. It all lay at the top of Frognal, with an ample view of London through a veil of trees; soon the inhabitants dispensed with the middle-class habit of house numbers, so that the Hopkins's address became simply 'Oak Hill, Hampstead'. A quarter of a mile away lay Hampstead Heath, the portion near Jack Straws Castle, within easy reach of nurses taking the children for an airing. It was the perfection of what was to become known in a few decades as Forsyte territory, middle class and struggling hard to eliminate a taint of Cockneyism.

Manley Hopkins threw himself into local affairs with all the energy of the newcomer and soon was a churchwarden at St John's, the pretty church at the end of Church Walk, a few streets away. He also acted as business manager of the parish school and predictably contributed to the parish magazine. He, like his family, was moderately High Church in practice, dignified but nothing outré, as he might have put it, which is not to indicate that they were anything but truly devout. They held family prayers, and the children were naturally expected to say their prayers before bed. It is not easy to guess how much beyond decent middle-class devotion they felt, although Gerard became a Jesuit priest and his sister Milicent an Anglican nun.

Mr Hopkins had done well for an almost completely self-made man, and he was justifiably proud of how far he had come. He was not rich, but we can get some sense of how well he was doing financially from the knowledge that when he died his estate was valued at £25,000, more than a hundred times what his father had left. In 1856, four years after the removal to Hampstead, he was to take another step up. His younger brother Charles had been in Hawaii since 1844, with a position in the civil service that he owed to his brother Edward, who had preceded him to the islands. Charles's initial appointment was due to his having had experience in 'an attorney's' chambers, and he moved from job to job in the Hawaiian Government, almost all of them to do with the law. He was a breezy and charming man who took easily to Hawaiian life, learned the language, became a citizen of Hawaii, and bought himself a 12,000-acre ranch on the island of Oahu. Like both his brother Manley and his nephew Gerard, he was short and slight, and he had a somewhat effeminate manner that had earned him the nickname of 'Polly', in spite of which he had begun a family in Hawaii, descendants of which still live there. It is a shame that no record remains of what Manley Hopkins thought of the mode of life adopted by his brother, who took part in a ménage à trois with a Hawaiian couple, of which the wife bore him a son. Charles became somewhat notorious in Hawaii for his attacks on the rigid sexual morality taught by American missionaries.

King Kamehameha III took to the young Englishman, called him by the nickname of 'Hopekini' and even paid part of his salary personally in order to have him closely associated with the court. Hopkins was also a good companion to the King's young nephew and adopted heir, Alexander Liholiho. When the Prince and his brother Lot came to England in 1849, Manley Hopkins had called on them in the Tavistock Hotel at the suggestion of his brother Charles. The following spring the young princes came through England on their way home, and went to Stratford to see the Hopkins family at Chestnut House, where Prince Alexander wrote that 'we dined at a very sumptuous dinner, a la Angleterre'. When the ladies had retired, 'we spent some time in conversation and sipping coffee. We then joined the ladys in the Drawing Room. The conversation turned alternately on the Islands, and on Hopkins not writing &c.'[8] It hardly sounds an entertainment to charm a fifteen-year-old, even a prince, but he went away with a very good impression of Mr Hopkins and remembered the visit with pleasure.

By 1856 Prince Alexander had succeeded to the throne as Kamehameha IV. He was a strong Anglophile and had married a young woman who was one quarter English; he was most receptive to the suggestion that Manley Hopkins be the new Consul-General for the Hawaiian Government and their Chargé d'Affaires for Great Britain. His position put Hopkins in touch with many important men in the British Government and in 1859–60 with Samuel Wilberforce, Bishop of Oxford, with whom he corresponded enthusiastically over the appointment of a suitable High Church-man to be the first Bishop of the Reformed Catholic Church of Hawaii, which was connected with the Anglican and Episcopal Churches, in spite of its ominous name. It was all very heady for a man who had been a boy in an average adjuster's office, and Manley Hopkins did not need to be a monster to recognize that it was all threatened a few years later when his eldest son, on whom he had counted heavily, threw away everything his father had painstakingly achieved, in order to become a Roman Catholic and live outside the social pale.

However, all that lay in the future when the Hopkins family moved to Hampstead. By 1860 the family had increased until there were eight children in the household. Cyril, next in age to Gerard, was the only member of the family to enter their father's profession, and, like Gerard, he attended Highgate School. The two brothers got along well enough but seem never to have been close; when they were young, Gerard tended to make fun of Cyril and to be a touch patronizing to him, as befitted his age. It tells us something of his innate fastidiousness that his disparagement of his brother is often couched in physical terms, as in the family story that when they were both in the nursery Gerard was found crying over his smaller brother who had been ill; when asked the reason for his grief, he said, 'Because Cyril has become so ugly!'[9]

Arthur and Everard (youngest of the family) both became illustrators and commercial artists; Arthur was one of Gerard's favourite companions all his life, and they often went to galleries and museums together or exchanged letters about painting. Lionel was, like most of the family, mildly eccentric, resembling Gerard in both build and face, sharing with him a quiet humour and a gift for stating plain truths; he became a distinguished Chinese linguist, served as a Consul in China, and retired in 1908, to live on a full pension until his death forty-four years later at the age of ninety-eight.

None of Hopkins's sisters married. Milicent, with whom Gerard seems often to have been on uneasy terms, became an Anglican nun and died at ninety-seven. Kate, perhaps Gerard's favourite of all the family, was the daughter who devoted herself to the care of her parents, tending her mother until she died at ninety-nine. Grace, a talented musician who helped her brother with his efforts at composition, died a mere child among the family at eighty-eight.

Before Gerard went off to Oxford and the family began dispersing, they had great fun from games and entertainments, charades and dressing up. The twelve-year-old Gerard is shown in one photograph, by his Uncle George Giberne, somewhat overwhelmed by a hat with sweeping plume and a courtier's coat with big collar.[10] The programme still exists[11] of one of their dramatic evenings, at the home of his grandparents, Dr and Mrs Smith, in January 1863. There were fifteen speaking parts for the family in the 'Xmas story of true love', in which the main role was played by 'Mr Gerard M. Hopkins', who had the role of 'Prince Carmoisin ("with joyfull eyes"), "lighter-footed than the fox"'. All the descriptions of the roles and plot are full of the puns that so amused the whole family.

Most large families, unless they are deeply dissatisfied, sound as if they have a great deal of fun together, and no doubt the Hopkins tribe did. Gerard, as eldest of them, was in the curious position that a child in his place often has, looked up to by the others at the very time that he feels cut off by the arrival of new children. For all her motherly instincts, Kate Hopkins probably had too little time to lavish affection on each child separately, and Manley Hopkins was in the City until after the children were in bed, and too busy to take long holidays with them in the summers. In any case, he seems not to have had the gift of being at ease with the young.

Before he went to school Gerard was taught at home by his mother and his 'Aunt Annie' Hopkins, his father's sister who made her home with them. Miss Hopkins was quietly talented at painting and drawing, which she taught to Gerard; none of his paintings has survived, although many of his drawings have. He was sufficiently talented to consider a life as an artist. His method was unusual, but it shows how internalized art was for him: according to his sister, he learned to sketch by 'making himself his own model, by throwing himself into the attitude he wanted to depict first & then drawing . . .'.[12] Aunt Annie apparently also taught him to share her own interest in archaeology and encouraged him to use it as the subject of some of his juvenile verse. He was said to have an exquisite voice as a boy, and it was probably his mother who taught him to sing; she certainly implemented his Aunt Annie's fostering of his early poetry.

It is possible that the largely feminine influence under which he lived as a small boy was responsible for the manner that was described variously as graceful or effeminate when he was grown. Certainly, no one could have been further from a tough. He was very short of stature, slight, and quick of movement; what is probably the first of his letters extant indicates his family's worry about his size: 'Uncle Marsland says if I dont eat more meat Cyril will come home bigger than *i* – He says suppose, Cyril were to come home a little man with whiskers and turned up collars!!'[13] His face was narrow and unusually long, making his head look almost too large for his body. A small mouth, fair hair and light-brown or hazel eyes completed the picture. One of his relatives described him as a beautiful small boy, but the effect of the few photos and sketches that have survived is rather of delicacy verging on over-refinement. But it was, as it remained in maturity, an arresting face.

His nervous grace, according to relatives, concealed a total fearlessness that manifested itself in a love of climbing to the top of tall trees, where he would remain balanced for hours, gazing with wonder at the landscape and, incidentally, preserving the distance between himself and his family that was always so important to him. The tall elm in their Oak Hill garden was his usual platform, but he would often go to Croydon to stay with his Smith grand-parents in Blunt House, their dignified country mansion, set in the middle of eighteen acres of well-timbered park. On the lawn by the house were two cedars of Lebanon and a large old beech, on which he practised his climbing skills. All the children seem to have gone there frequently, in part no doubt to relieve their parents of their care but also for the pleasure of the Smiths in their grandchildren. As their first grandson, Gerard was a particular favourite.

He was also the favourite nephew of his mother's sister, Aunt Maria Giberne, and her husband, Judge George Giberne, and he often stayed with them in Epsom. Mrs Giberne would take him sketching, and Uncle George shared with him his experiments in photography, showing him how he built his own cameras and made his own plates, which he had to put into the camera wet. During his schooldays Gerard posed for the photographs that are the chief source for our knowledge of his appearance before he went to Oxford.

At Epsom Gerard probably came unwittingly on a connection to one of the most important persons in his adult life. Certainly he would have met another frequent visitor to the house, Judge Giberne's eccentric sister Maria (who wrote her surname as de Gibèrne), a beautiful woman of extravagant religious passions who was much given to falling in love with intellectual persons of both sexes. When she was young, Francis Newman had proposed to her, then repeated the proposal five or six years after her refusal. But she could not marry him, for the truth was that she was in love with his brother John Henry and continued to be so for many years before she settled for the calm of friendship with the Cardinal. As a result of her feelings for him she had become a Catholic convert, and in 1863 she took the veil as Sister Maria Pia. At Epsom the voluble Miss de Gibèrne was perhaps the source of Gerard's first knowledge of the man who was to become his model, even his religious father, admiration for whom played a strong part in Gerard's own conversion.

By 1854 Manley Hopkins knew it was time to choose a school for his eldest son, now eight. As the son of a man hovering uneasily between trade and profession, Gerard would not automatically be accepted at any of the great public schools, so his father's sights had to be lowered. Either by luck or because he had chosen Hampstead for that very reason, just across the Heath was Sir Roger Cholmley's Grammar School, usually called Highgate School, perhaps because of the uncertain spelling and pronunciation of its founder's name. It had been founded in the sixteenth century, five years after Westminster and six before Harrow, chiefly for the free education of boys and young men from Highgate. In the intervening centuries its standards had slipped so far they had become almost invisible, and like so many other old schools, it had been almost finished off by the eighteenth century.

In 1838 the Governors called in the Revd John Bradley Dyne, D.D., Fellow of Wadham College, Oxford, as a reforming Headmaster. Dyne believed in the primacy of Evangelicalism, the classics, and the birch. Or, to be more accurate, the whip, for he beat the boys with the riding whip he used to control his horses. In a day of flogging headmasters, Dyne was a formidable rival for the honours of Dr Keate of Eton. All the same, he caused a remarkable change in the reputation of his school: in the twenty-five years between his becoming Head and Hopkins's leaving the school, he had raised the enrolment from nineteen boys to more than 130, the standard of classics was very high, and the teaching was reputed to be among the best in the London area. Hopkins hated it.

During his time there, Highgate had eighty day boys and

approximately fifty boarders. The school was still committed in theory to free places for forty boys, but in spite of the intentions of the founder, most of the pupils came from professional families living within a few miles of the school: sons of lawyers, clergymen, bankers, and army officers, many of them from homes resembling number 9, Oak Hill Park, whose occupants, like Mrs Hopkins, were anxious to move up the social scale but wanted their sons well educated at a moderate cost. At just over £18 a year for day boys and £91 for boarders, the school was considered rather expensive but worth it. During most of his nine years there, Hopkins was a boarder, living in Elgin House in the High Street, but he lived at home as a day boy for a short period at the end of his time at the school.

On entering Highgate he and his fellow eight-year-olds were expected to be able to read and write and to have studied arithmetic. They were then plunged into a curriculum that included English, Latin, history, arithmetic, and the principles of religion. Most of the boys also studied either French or German, at £3 p.a. extra; Hopkins studied both, as well as drawing, which cost £4. Later they undertook Greek and advanced mathematics. Dyne put an unusual emphasis on the ability to write English well, and he made the boys translate the classical poets into acceptable English, which was the reverse of most translation taught in schools of the day. In that way, he may have furthered Hopkins's poetic talents. It is worth noticing that another Highgate boy, a decade Hopkins's senior, was the great philologist W. W. Skeat, who had also studied with Dyne.

Of the games he played as a schoolboy, Hopkins preferred cricket, in part no doubt because his size was no handicap to him, but team sports were always less attractive to him than those he could do on his own. One of the latter about which we might like to know more during his schooldays is swimming, which was to be his favourite physical recreation as an adult. The boys from High-gate were given free access for bathing in the ponds in the park of Ken Wood, the great Adam house of Lord Mansfield, which stood only a short distance from the school. Some of the boys, like Hopkins's friend Marcus Clarke, found these among the most enjoyable moments of their schooldays. Presumably those who were unable to swim when they arrived were given instruction, but

Hopkins was not comfortable out of his depth until he was an undergraduate. Bathing was in some ways the Victorian male recreation that most clearly marked out its participants as members of the upper classes, or at least aspirants to them. Practically every school with any pretension arranged for its boys to stand in shivering rows before they launched themselves into weedy streams. It was understood that there was a vaguely Greek cachet about it that no other sport could match. Since it was exclusively male, the bathers were always nude, so that there was an undercurrent of unspoken sensuality about it, as well as the associations of the classical gymnasium that made it respectable. 'Epithalamion', written near the end of his life, was Hopkins's closest equivalent to the scenes of boys bathing that were dear to Victorian painters, but it demonstrates adequately his fascination with the recreation that began for him in the secluded ponds of Ken Wood.

The academic load was heavy for most of the boys, but Hopkins took to it easily, and soon he was the wonder of the school. Most poets have been clever enough to do well at school if they wished, but Hopkins was surely unusual; the problem is not to determine whether he won prizes but to find out how many. One investigator of the records at Highgate says that he won 'as many as five', while another lists prizes for classics annually for seven years until he left the school; the prize for English verse in his first year in the sixth form; the prize for Latin prose the following year; the Southampton prize for classical history in each of his three last years; a School Exhibition in 1862; and the Governors' Gold Medal for Latin Verse in his last year, when, to cap his efforts, he also won an Exhibition to Balliol College, Oxford.[14] Curiously, he seems to have been at the top of his form only twice, probably because he was often dragged down by his lapses in mathematics and handwriting.

On the whole, however, his work was almost unparalleled, and one can only feel sorry for his brother Cyril, who entered Highgate in 1856, two years after Gerard, had an absolutely consistent record of never winning a prize, and left in 1861, two years before Gerard, to take a place in his father's business. After that, none of the Hopkins boys attempted either Highgate or Oxford.

Gerard's spectacular success had an effect precisely the reverse of what one might expect: it only served to make him more popular with the other boys while it thoroughly alienated Dr Dyne, presumably as a result of hidden jealousy, since he must have known that his pupil was considerably more intelligent than he. In spite of disliking the boy, Dyne could not so completely ignore the record as to keep Gerard from being a prefect when he was a sixth-former.

Hopkins had few of the attributes that normally make schoolboys admire their fellows. He was brilliant at his studies. He was not bad at games, but he clearly did not like them much. He never got into trouble with anyone except Dr Dyne (although the spectacular quality of their mutual dislike probably increased his popularity). He was unostentatiously religious, and in the middle of the horseplay in his house at night, he would sit calmly reading his New Testament, in compliance with a promise to his mother. As an adult he remembered himself as 'a very conceited boy', but he was actually, in the simplest and most profound sense of the word, good, although he was seldom sanctimonious. He should have been disliked thoroughly for all these reasons, but he was respected and liked instead, in part, as one of his contemporaries remembered, because 'he was full of fun, rippling over with jokes, and chaff, facile with pencil and pen, with rhyming jibe or cartoon'. One suspects that there was another reason: the fact that just under the surface of his mild behaviour there lurked a profound rebelliousness that he allowed to surface only a few times during his nine years at the school. One of his primary reasons for choosing the discipline of the Society of Jesus years later was that it demanded absolute obedience of the sort that he knew he should have and was deeply aware he could never achieve unaided: the most difficult course always seemed the natural one to him.

But however clever and good he was, Hopkins was a real, live boy, not a saint in school uniform, and the fact should not be forgotten if we are to understand him. Individual goodness probably came easily to him at this point in his life, but the social virtues like charity, humility, calm temper and obedience were not an innate part of his makeup; however hard he worked to cultivate them, their mastery eluded him all his life.

It was not only Hopkins who was victimized by Dyne. One of his friends, Marcus Clarke, left what seems a scarcely exaggerated record of the Headmaster in a thinly disguised account of his own schooldays:

> When I was at school I was flogged twice a week, and did not like it. The gentlemanly headmaster – he was cousin to an earl, a D.D., and strictly orthodox – was noted for his use of the birch, and used to smack his lips over a flogging with intense glee. He was a left hander (there was a legend extant to the effect that he had broken his right arm in flogging a boy, but I always doubted it myself), and the way he used to 'draw' the birch was astonishing. He used always to stop after ten strokes, if the victim cried out, but as I was under the impression that he flogged me from purely personal motives, and wanted to show my indifference and skey-orn, I would have died rather than whimper.[15]

Much of what we know about the personal aspects of Hopkins's school career comes from two very long letters, one written before he left Highgate, the other three decades later by the recipient of the first letter, his schoolfellow C.N. Luxmoore. Both have been examined often, but it is worth being reminded of them because they suggest patterns in his later life that have been ignored by writers more intent on hagiography than biography.

In the first of these letters, written in the spring of 1862, Hopkins tells how he had been studying hard for the examination for the Exhibition he won to Balliol and had asked for a private room in which to study. At first all went well, and Dyne even suggested he be given a fire every evening. For some misdemeanour, 'the most trifling ludicrous little thing' (Hopkins could be maddeningly vague about the nature of his own offences), the room was taken away from him, he was 'degraded to the bottom of the prefects', and deprived of the testimonial he needed to try for the Exhibition. As Hopkins told it, 'Dyne and I had a terrific altercation. I was driven out of patience and cheeked him wildly, and he blazed into me with his riding-whip.'

When peace had been restored and Hopkins was allowed his private room once more, there was another explosion when he refused to let his reading candle be extinguished at lights-out. This time he was 'in a worse row than ever about absolutely nothing'; when he had provoked the Headmaster still further, Dyne deprived him of the room again, sent him to bed at half past nine, threatened him with expulsion, and said that he hoped Hopkins would not be at the top of the school in examinations. It is hard to judge the matter fairly when we have only Hopkins's own account of it, but he sounds as provoking as Dyne was hasty and easily provoked, and there is certainly a touch of something uncomfortably close to self-righteousness in his attitude to the row.

There is no profit in censuring the priggishness of a schoolboy a century and a half later, but recognizing it may help us to understand Hopkins as an adult by ridding ourselves of the notion that he was an unnatural angel as a boy. In this case his method of final protest seems to have been to move home as a day boy and resign as prefect, since he could obviously not serve unless he was living in the school. Many years after his death, his sister, who had heard about the episode from her mother, indicated that she felt he was completely innocent: 'when he was made prefect at school he made himself so unhappy over things that he saw going on wrong & could not stop, that my Father took him away from being a border [sic] & he became only a day boy & was no longer a prefect'. [16]

Luxmoore, to whom Hopkins wrote the letter just mentioned, recorded his memories of Hopkins the year after his death. He still remembered with delight that 'Skin', as Hopkins was known from the transposition of the last letters of his name, was 'one of the very best and nicest boys in the school, with his face always *set* to do what was right'.

One story Luxmoore told was of how Gerard had totally abstained from all liquids for three weeks, 'the pretext being a bet of 10/ to 6d, the real reason a conversation on seamen's sufferings and human powers of endurance'. According to this account Hopkins's tongue had turned black, but he persevered to the end of twenty-one days, at which time Dyne swooped down and made Gerard return the money he had won. Hopkins pointed out with reason that this 'really rewarded the other boy, and only punished him, who had endured the suffering and exhaustion of the effort'. The result of his remonstration was, of course, punishment by Dyne. The story was intended by one who knew him well to show

Gerard's fortitude and stoicism about physical suffering, which it certainly does, but at this distance one suspects that it inadvertently demonstrates something more, a trait not too unlike spiritual pride. The point, once more, is that he was nearly as mixed in his motivation as other boys. 'If a fault be chargeable to your brother', said Luxmoore to Arthur Hopkins, 'it was the being unable to suffer wrong silently, the insisting on arguing his case . . .'. Cyril Hopkins put the position mildly but accurately when he said that the beauty of Gerard's moral courage was marred by his eccentricity.[17]

The tender vulnerability that underlay his sometimes brittle exterior is also shown in Gerard's letter to Luxmoore, in which he tells of his disappointment over a romantic schoolboy friendship. It is useful in understanding the grown-up Hopkins, for it shows nakedly how much he wanted intimate companionship without always knowing how to attract it or even being willing to bend his standards gracefully in order to accommodate his friends; on 13 April 1862 he wrote an account of the incident in his journal:

After prayers Alexander Strachey came up to the bedroom at my request to have a last talk at the end of the quarter. I had found out from Clarke who had walked to Finchley with him the day before that on Clarke making some mention of me as 'your friend Skin', he said, 'He is not my friend'. 'O yes he is' said Clarke, and afterwards asked why he went no walks with me. 'Because he never asks me' said Strachey. Not wishing to compromise Clarke, I first asked him the same question, to which he gave at once the same ungrateful answer. Being thus master of the situation, I told him I had not expected so ungrateful an answer. He knew, I said, the reason; at least he might have appreciated the sacrifice; that he had not spoken except on the most trivial subjects and on some days not even that, that he had taken no notice of me, and that I had been wretched every time I saw or thought of it, was only what I had bargained for, I sowed what I now reaped; but after this sacrifice to be told he did not walk with me because I never asked him was too much.

Hopkins told him that he might have 'friends more liberal than I had been but few indeed who would make the same sacrifice I had', but he could not make the other boy see his point.

They were interrupted by the arrival of the other boys who slept in the same room; later Hopkins asked if Strachey would have said anything more had they not come in. '"No, I don't think so" he said with a cool smile, and I left him. Perhaps in my next friendship I may be wiser.'

Hopkins was not very specific about the nature of his own sacrifice, but it seems to have been keeping away from Strachey when the other boy did not want to be approached.

When the announcement was made that he had won his Exhibition to Balliol, Hopkins's mother thought he might in civility write to tell Strachey. He did, but there was no answer, and, 'with the exception of a cold "How do you do?", we have not spoken this quarter. Yet it is still my misfortune to be fond of and yet despised by him. If ever hereafter you should have any intercourse with him *experto crede* and do not believe in his unselfishness, his sincerity, or his gratitude, for he has little of either.'[18] Gerard's disappointment was a rehearsal in small of his desolation three years later over Digby Dolben, but Dolben's rebuffs did not bring the same bitterness of reaction, probably indicating much more profound emotions about him than about Strachey.

Whatever difficulties there may have been for Hopkins at Highgate, most of them were made up for by a general atmosphere of respect for literature, including Dyne's insistence on writing well. The continuing tradition of the place into this century is shown by the presence there of John Betjeman, who was a pupil and wrote about the area, and of T. S. Eliot, who taught there for a short time. In Hopkins's day one of the junior masters was a young clergyman, R. W. Dixon, who fell ill after a few months and had to resign. Dixon had been intimate with the Pre-Raphaelites, he could quote Keats by the yard, and he was a poet himself. He scarcely knew Hopkins except by sight at Highgate, but from several of the other masters he heard that the boy was one of the outstanding pupils in the school. Hopkins in turn read and admired Dixon's verse, and though they did not meet again for some years, each remembered the other clearly and retained the memory of him as someone special.

Hopkins was writing poetry before he came to school, but none of it has survived. The first verse we have is the poem with which he won the School Poetry Prize at Easter 1860, when he was nearly sixteen. The assigned subject was 'The Escorial', also the set topic that year at Oxford for the Newdigate Prize. Entries had to be anonymous, and Manley Hopkins wrote out the poem to conceal his son's identity. Perhaps he also helped on the hard bits; if we can judge from his own poetry, he would have been exigent on rhyming and rhythm. What seems more certain than Manley Hopkins's help is that the poem is obviously descended from Tennyson's 'The Palace of Art', with which it shares a love of gorgeous catalogues of art objects and an almost completely static quality. Like that poem, it is essentially a guided tour of the palace, and the visitor can join in any room. It may also remind us that Tennyson, at the same age, had felt himself descended from Byron. Keats and Spenser (the poem is in Spenserean stanzas) also echo through it, but all of them are to be expected in a young and sponge-like poet just learning his craft. Some of the images seem bought by the job-lot, but we feel that he at least patronized the best shops, run by the best Romantic poets:

> Then through the afternoon the summer beam
> Slop'd on the galleries; upon the wall
> Rich Titians faded; in the straying gleam
> The motes in ceaseless eddy shine and fall
> Into the cooling gloom; till slowly all
> Dimm'd in the long accumulated dust;
> Pendant in formal line from cornice tall
> Blades of Milan in circles rang'd, grew rust
> And silver damasqu'd plates obscur'd in age's crust.

With the charming swank of the young, Hopkins appended foot-notes to make clear both his meaning and his reading. The poem is very pretty stuff indeed, and there were fifteen stanzas of it; one of them has since disappeared, but it hardly matters, since the number seems totally arbitrary. It is nonetheless an astonishingly self-confident poem for a fifteen-year-old, quite unlike what we could expect of his age.

Like many young poets, Hopkins at times thought of verse as almost synonymous with colour, an idea that suffuses his long (143 lines) poem of two years later, 'A Vision of the Mermaids', written his last Christmas before going to Oxford. It is a curious poem for Hopkins, and a reader's first reaction may be that something is missing; it takes a moment to realize that it is drenched in sensuous images without ever suggesting the sexuality that lies behind almost all of his mature poetry. At least superficially, it is Keatsian but emphatically not Hopkinsian, if that term may be used to describe the intensity of his greatest poems:

> A mile astern lay the blue shores away;
> And it was at the setting of the day.
>   Plum-purple was the west; but spikes of light
> Spear'd open lustrous gashes, crimson-white;
> (Where the eye fix'd, fled the encrimsoning spot,
> And gathering, floated where the gaze was not;)
> And thro' their parting lids there came and went
> Keen glimpses of the inner firmament . . .

One has the feeling that here he is writing dutifully, even intelligently, without ever becoming engaged, and we have to content ourselves with the knowledge that it was good practice and that its composition kept him too busy to quarrel with Dr Dyne. A poet lay waiting for discovery, but so far he was well hidden.

'Winter with the Gulf Stream' takes as its subject the unusually warm winter of 1862–3. It is written in competent *terza rima*, showing that he was developing technical proficiency, although the landscape of the poem shows none of the symbolic energy we associate with Hopkins's nature poetry of little more than a decade later. Probably through his father's association with the magazine, it was accepted for publication in *Once a Week* and became one of the very few of his poems published in his lifetime.

Some of his interest in exotic places in his early poetry may have begun on the trips he had made with his father and his brother Cyril to Germany and the Low Countries during the holidays of 1857 and

1860. Probably the trips were intended to help the boys' fluency in German, which they studied at Highgate. In later years Gerard did not display much ease with German, but at the time he felt confident enough about Goethe and German literature to write an amusingly pompous letter on the subject to Herr Müncke, the German and French master at Highgate, in which he implied, without actually saying so, that his German was excellent.

So far Hopkins had all the background for a young poet except perhaps emotional experience, and that was to come. In the meantime, in April 1863, he left for Balliol College, Oxford. His one distinction so far was that he was probably the only newcomer to Balliol to arrive with a poem already published in a national magazine.

There is no evidence that he ever again went inside Highgate School.

CHAPTER II

MY PARK, MY PLEASAUNCE
1863

'The truth is I had no love for my schooldays and wished to banish the remembrance of them, even, I am ashamed to say, to the degree of neglecting some people who had been very kind to me', Hopkins wrote long after leaving Highgate. 'Of Oxford on the other hand I was very fond.'[1] When he went up to the University, he was ebullient, eager to make new acquaintances, with little or none of the reserve that was to become characteristic of him. V.S.S. Coles remembered more than half a century later how, when he was sitting for Scholarship examinations at Balliol with his Etonian friend Vincent Cracroft-Amcotts, 'Gerard Hopkins used to sit near us, and smile at our remarks before we had properly made his acquaintance.'[2]

In those days Hopkins was trailing clouds of the antic from Highgate, and he still had the buoyancy and sense of fun that were later to be partially knocked out of him by what he took for hostility to his conversion to Catholicism. Coles and Amcotts were among the first of many at Oxford to be attracted by his openness and spontaneity. He bubbled with uncomplicated humour, much of it verbal, as one would expect, but in a young man who was to become such a scrupulous poet, it is surprising to see how clumsy and schoolboyish it could be, endearing but hardly more subtle than the puns with which the Hopkins family loved to amuse each other. Robert Bridges, who understood and forgave so much in his friend, seems never to have found Hopkins as funny as he found himself. But Bridges's standards were not those of most undergraduates, who were immediately taken by Hopkins's quirkiness, so that from the beginning he was a social success at Balliol.

Of the twenty new men at Balliol in 1863 at least a quarter were

Etonians, and inevitably they initially formed their own clique. But even in an institution as self-contained as Victorian Oxford there were some advantages to coming from outside the charmed circle. When Hopkins arrived in April from a thoroughly unfashionable school, he knew few men in College well, but he was at least unencumbered by a ready-made coterie and in no danger of being thrown into the shadow of one, nor was he reticent about making new acquaintances, as he might have been had he arrived with an established set.

Both the young men who had noticed his amiable manner during the Scholarship examinations became friends of his. Only a month after he arrived at Balliol, Hopkins was seeing a good bit of Amcotts at 'wines' given by other undergraduates or as his own guest, and by the end of May he was already referring to him genially as 'the Genteel Skeleton' and praising him for the brilliance of his piano-playing and for being 'the greatest *dilettante* in the college. He also writes very good poetry.' The ease with which he made the acquaintance of Amcotts was a pointer to the quality of new friends he sought, but in this case they never progressed to greater intimacy.

To Coles, who did not come up to Oxford until the following year, he became much closer and to him owed his introduction into many of the High Church circles in Oxford, and perhaps the speed with which he got to know Coles's two closest friends from Eton, Robert Bridges and Digby Dolben, who in turn became, in their different ways, Hopkins's own best friends.

Both Amcotts and Coles were among the declared High Church party in Oxford spiritual life and both derived from backgrounds of country gentry: Amcotts from a Lincolnshire family of consider-able antiquity, noted even in their remote corner of England for being somewhat stiff-necked about their position in county society; Coles from Somerset, where his squarson father held a family living at Shepton Beauchamp. Both young men were members of Oxford circles in which the feelings between the members were rather more fervid than elsewhere. In all these ways they were typical of a good many of the friends Hopkins was to make at Oxford.

'I do not suppose that life holds anything more enjoyable, except perhaps a successful honeymoon, than an undergraduate's first summer term at Oxford', wrote one of Hopkins's contemporaries at Balliol.[3] By coming up in the Easter term, Hopkins had the best of the University year, and he set out at once to make up for his comparative unhappiness at Highgate.

In 1863 Oxford had changed little visually in the half-century since Rudolf Ackermann's romantic prints of the city and University were published. Dusty trees still lined the mostly unpaved lanes, even such narrow ways as the Turl, and the gowns and robes of undergraduates and senior members of the University out of their colleges gave the drowsy streets the look of aquatints. The 'river-rounded' little city was almost as self-contained physically as it had been when its limits were set by medieval walls. True, the countryside no longer lapped up to the grey stone of the colleges, but the city was distinctly marked out like an understated English Carcassonne, its perimeter uninsistently guarded on three sides by the Thames and its tributaries, to be crossed only by toll bridges. To the south, like a gateway to rural England, was Folly Bridge, over which undergraduates had little reason to pass except for riding on the Berkshire Downs, for running with the beagles, or for the lengthy perambulations with which they filled their afternoons. To the east, Magdalen Bridge, the entrance from the London Road, was still only a single track wide between Magdalen tower and the toll booth in the Plain, but it kept at bay the squalid slums of St Clement's across the Cherwell. Beyond the old city limits on the way to Woodstock or Banbury, the Victorian exuberance of north Oxford was in its infancy, and past Canterbury Road little broke the flat plain between the Cherwell and the Thames except interminable fields of vegetables. To the west, past the new station of the Great Western Railway, was the toll bridge at Osney, where once the monastic centre of Oxford had been, and beyond that lay the straggle of houses that now blurred the clear line between country and town.

The railway station, which still seemed at a safe distance from the centre of the University, was symbolic of the industrialization that was to overwhelm this most romantic of English cities and that was to gobble up much of the countryside that Hopkins feared for. The University had fought successfully for a decade and a half to keep the station out of the city, so that passengers for London had to get on one of the eight coaches that daily drove ten miles south to Steventon to meet the train for Paddington. From 1842 to 1852 a train had been permitted to come to a new station built at Grandpont, just beyond Folly Bridge; then the Corporation of Oxford, envisioning a new prosperity for the city, independent of the University, agreed to a station on the site of the present one. It was inconvenient enough to satisfy the opponents of the railway, but emblematically it was at last situated within the semicircle of toll bridges, in Oxford itself. For years it was to provoke bitterness in Oxford, and it seemed to the undergraduates, including Hopkins, a particularly offensive example of what was happening to ancient England. Snorting, noisy, dangerous, above all ravenous in devouring rural land, it was as obnoxious as it seemed to Dickens in *Dombey and Son*.

It would have taken a far more hard-hearted man that Hopkins to resist the grace and symmetry of Oxford as it was when he first went up; his volatile affections, which inclined him to love at first sight, instantly claimed the University and the city in which it was planted: 'This is my park, my pleasaunce', he wrote in a love poem to the *genius loci*. For the remainder of his life it was to remain earthly perfection, a delicate poise of intellect, affection and beauty from which he could feel alienated but for which he never had anything but love.

'I can not go on describing all Oxford, its inhabitants and its neighbourhood,' he told his parents, 'but to be short, everything is delightful, I have met with much attention and am perfectly comfortable. Balliol is the friendliest and snuggest of colleges, our inner quad is delicious and has a grove of fine trees and lawns where bowls are the order of the evening. Sunk below the level of the quad, from which it is separated by a pretty stone parapet, is the Fellows' garden, kept very trim, and abutting on it our graceful chapel . . . .'.[4]

Taking up residence in Oxford in the spring rather than in the autumn meant that there was not the normal gap of a term between matriculation and moving into college. The acceleration of social activities habitual to Oxford in the spring and early summer had already begun. Hopkins moved into his rooms at the end of the first week in April, at the beginning of the Easter term, then he

matriculated on the 19th of the month. Three days later, in the first
long letter to his parents from Balliol that has survived, he was
happily and somewhat loftily explaining the arcane slang and habits
of undergraduate life as glibly as if he had been in Oxford for years.
It inevitably seems premonitory of the pleasure he was to take much
later in explaining the cant and customs of the novitiate when he
became a Jesuit.

Like many undergraduates, he was full of himself in his anxiety to
discourse on his new surroundings, his pleasures and his duties,
charmingly jamming his pages with the names of new acquaintances of whom his parents had never heard, particulars of his living
arrangements, and details from the timetables of his daily scholastic
obligations, to allay the worries of his family that he might not be
taking his studies seriously enough. Besides recording his own
pleasure, however, in these early letters, he often seems to be
stroking his parents' apprehensions, as if there were a slightly
nervous truce beneath the affectionate surface. Gerard was to be the
only one of their children who went to the University, and one
wonders whether they still had lingering doubts about whether it
had been wise to let him do so; his conversion to Roman Catholicism at Oxford three years later must have seemed justification for
any misgivings.

Hopkins's rooms were on the top floor of his staircase, so that
the shape of the roof made his 'cieling' a sloping one. The incon-
venience of running up and down the stairs between lectures was
compensated for by the fact that 'from four of my six windows I
have the best views in Balliol, and my staircase has the best scout in
the college, Henry'. He had a bedroom, a sitting room, and a cellar,
which was useful in giving 'wines', but there was neither scout's
pantry nor outer door (the 'oak') to 'sport' as notice to callers when
he wanted to be alone. Rooms were assigned arbitrarily, although it
was recognized that wealthy parents could employ 'methods of
corruption with the College butler' to secure better lodging for
their sons.[5] (It is almost impossible to imagine Manley Hopkins
'corrupting' the butler even if money had been more plentiful in the
Hopkins family.) Each new inhabitant took over the battered
furniture left in the rooms by the previous resident, paying the
scout an exorbitant price for the contents. The standard was about

£35 to £40, but Hopkins got his for £18, since it was more than ordinarily decrepit.

According to a writer in *Cornhill* in 1865, 'the actual necessary cost of an university education *need* not exceed 130*l*. a year; but we must at the same time candidly avow that we should never recommend a young man to go to the university with less than 200*l*. a year'.[6] Hopkins's Exhibition was worth about £75 annually, which he presumably kept for his own use, since his father paid his college expenses as well as giving him extra money from time to time, although Gerard apparently felt that he received too little and had to resort to heavily joking letters to get more from home.

John Henry Newman, who was in so many matters Hopkins's arbiter, had written that 'Almost everything depends at Oxford, in the matter of acquaintance, on proximity of rooms. You choose your friend, not so much by your tastes, as by your staircase.'[7] Perhaps out of a slight sense of envy because he had only an Exhibition, rather than a Scholarship, Hopkins turned up his nose at the pair of Scholars living on his staircase. One of them, Edmund Martin Geldart, eventually became one of Hopkins's best friends, but initially he could see nothing but the physical ugliness of the 'dreadful and ghastly man'. In his shock at finding him a neighbour, Hopkins described him to his family: 'His grey goggle eyes, scared suspicious look as though someone were about to hit him from behind, shuddering gait or shuffle, pinched face, in fact his full haggard hideousness, are even now only breaking on me.' One senses in Hopkins's final comment the real reason for his initial dislike of Geldart: 'I would not have had twenty Balliol scholarships to change places with him.'

All his objections to Scholars melted, however, when he met Courtenay Ilbert, who lived below him on the staircase. Ilbert, who became one of the best-known parliamentarians of the late nineteenth and early twentieth centuries, was 'the cleverest man in Balliol, that is in the University, or in the University, that is in Balliol, whichever you like'. He had already won the Hertford and Ireland Scholarships, and he was to win both the Craven and the Eldon Scholarships; two years later he was elected a Fellow of the College. 'He is also handsome and in fact is an admirable Crichton.' Best of all, one spring Sunday he shouted up the staircase to ask

Hopkins whether he 'felt inclined for a walk. Of course I was only too much honoured, and we had a pleasant walk to some heights that overlook Oxford and past . . . Bagley Wood.' For Hopkins it was the equivalent of the feelings of Ernest Pontifex in *The Way of All Flesh* when he is taken up by Towneley, the golden, negligent hero of the University. Although there is no indication that their intimacy progressed beyond that first long walk, Ilbert was the personification of what Hopkins held most dear in other men: intelligence, moral fervour, and good looks. Physical beauty was not more important in others than character, but the one often seemed to him a reflection of the other.

Naturally, his first enthusiasms were for the social occasions on which he was meeting his fellow collegians. 'Wines' were the commonest form of entertainment: a group of half a dozen men gathered in the rooms of one of them after dinner for an hour or two of conversation and wine. It was rare for anyone to have too much to drink, and more than one of Hopkins's contemporaries said that he had never seen drunkenness within the walls of Balliol itself. Hopkins suffered agonies of undergraduate embarrassment when one of his aunts was so ill-versed in Oxford usage that she referred to a 'wine-party'.

Wines were more frequent among undergraduates than breakfasts; usually the latter were 'commonized', with several men having their 'commons', bread and butter, taken to the rooms of one undergraduate so that they could eat in company without extra expense. A more elaborate breakfast entertainment might consist of hot dishes, omelettes, fish, even roast fowl, served in an undergraduate's rooms, with the host passing out the food. Breakfasts were also a usual way for the senior members of the College to entertain their pupils. Shortly after he arrived Hopkins was invited to the Master's lodgings for a '"perpendicular," e.g. a "wallflower" evening' with stiff conversation, a form of entertainment indigenous to 'Owsenford'.

The invitations came in so fast that a fortnight after the beginning of term Hopkins was telling his mother with forgivable complacency: 'At the present rate it appears likely I shall know all Oxford in six weeks. I have not breakfasted in my own rooms for 10 days I think.' It is pleasant to see that his own rush of social scrambling did not blunt Hopkins's awareness of the loneliness of some other freshmen. At the very time that he was breakfasting out every morning, he called on an acquaintance, Richardson of Magdalen, 'whom I found remote, unfriended, melancholy, slow; no one at Magdalen or indeed I think in the whole 'Varsity, as it is called, had called on him. Afterwards I found him in Ch.[rist] Ch.[urch] meadows. We strolled together by the Cherwell.'

Hopkins's poetry is the plain record of the atavistic appeal he felt in rivers like the Cherwell, in pools, wells, or the sea itself: water, preferably moving, became, as much as for Heraclitus, the symbol of mutable beauty masquerading as permanence, and, conversely, of form transcending decay. As Robert Frost was to say of the motion of contraries in a brook,

> It is from that in water we were from
> Long, long before we were from any creature.[8]

At Oxford Hopkins most often recorded his pleasure in the quiet Cherwell or in the Isis, to give the Thames its local name, as he certainly would have done. Only two days after his matriculation, he made his first expedition on the river with James Strachan-Davidson, who had entertained him the previous evening at a 'wine'. Hopkins and Strachan-Davidson (who became Master of Balliol over forty years later) went to the upper river, where they 'took a sailing boat, skulled up and sailed down. We then took canoes. I know nothing so luxuriously delicious as a canoe. It is a long light covered boat, the same shape both ways, with an opening in the middle where you recline, with your feet against one board, your back against a cushion on another . . . The motion is Elysian.' Strachan-Davidson's canoe had shipped so much water that he had to go ashore to bale it out; Hopkins, after congratulating himself on being dry, then found himself 'washed onto the opposite lee shore', where he was 'comfortable but embarrassed, and could not get off for some time. Altogether it was Paradisaical. A canoe in the Cherwel[l] must be the summit of human happiness.'

Hopkins haunted the beautiful rivers around Oxford during his first three years at the University. Canoeing (one of his drawings shows a man stretched out reading a book in a boat; see Plate 5a); endless walks to Iffley or Godstow or Binsey or more far-flung settlements along the rivers; crossing by ferry at Bablockhythe or Marston; sketching the buildings beside the placid streams; swimming at Parsons's Pleasure, the men's bathing place ('I think I could save my life by swimming on the river now', he hazarded that summer after he had been practising): all were testimony to his love of water.

As an undergraduate Hopkins was active physically, but, as at Highgate, he played few games, since he was so small, nor did he even take part in some of the sports on the river that might have been expected. One of the favourite pastimes in the University was rowing. His friend Samuel Brooke of Corpus Christi lamented shortly after he had come up to Oxford of the division of the University into those who rowed and those who did not: 'At Oxford most of the men boat. The minority are considered fools. . . . "Are you a boating man?" is the question; if the rejoinder is in the affirmative it is "Hail fellow, well met". If in the negative, it is scowls and dagger-glances. . . . There is no sympathy for the calm inoffensive being who harms nobody, and does good to many. However great his charity or his goodness, if he cannot handle a boat or a gun, or eat a good dinner with ease, or talk without stammering, these excellent qualities profit him nothing.'[9] Much as Hopkins loved the river, there is no indication that he ever rowed seriously, although his initial delight in canoeing would suggest that he would follow up that occasion. Certainly, he loved swimming, once he felt proficient.

Rugby football was just becoming popular as a University game, and probably he played that a little, in spite of his size, since he knew it well enough after leaving Oxford to play at the Oratory and be injured on the field. According to his contemporaries, there was a good deal of cricket at Balliol, as well as real tennis, racquets, and fives, but again there is no indication that he ever took part in any of them. He was, however, a formidable walker and went for three- or four-hour excursions throughout the Thames valley, not infrequently making an interesting old church or manor house his destination.

In Oxford itself there were less innocent diversions, reflecting a vicious side of undergraduate life often conveniently forgotten. Near Folly Bridge in Christ Church Meadow there was usually a sleazy group of loungers with terriers to whom the undergraduates would pay 6d. to watch the dogs destroy a rat, or slightly more to have a polecat torn to pieces. One of Hopkins's contemporaries told him of seeing 'three Ch.Ch. men laughing loudly at a rat with back broken, a most ghastly sight, flying at the dog. He kicked away the dog, put his heel on the rat's head and killed it, and drove away the crowd of cads.' It inevitably made Hopkins wonder 'what would be the just statement of the effects of cruelty to animals, cruel sports, etc.'.[10] But he may have been unusual in his concern, for Matthew Arnold appears to have frequented dog fights, and even such a mild man as Sam Brooke recorded without comment having attended a public execution in front of the Oxford gaol 'to see the sight' of the hanging.

'Except for much work and that I can never keep my hands cool, I am almost too happy,' Gerard wrote to his mother in the middle of his first term at Oxford, then in fear that he might offend her, he added contritely, 'I hope you will not consider it unkind to say how happy I am, but in fact there are so many companions of my own age and so much liberty to see and do so much, that it ought not to make you think it unkind.'

His prickliness about family criticism was still evident a month later, when he wrote to 'Dearest Mama' from the Oxford Union, of which he was a brand-new member: 'Then if Aunt Katie has not got the letter it is no fault of mine, but the Union's or the Post Office's. I posted it like any other letter, here, and put it in a foreign paper envelope directed to Warrington Terrace. If it has gone astray it is a thousand pities, but that is really no fault of mine. After this I cannot write an interesting letter; you have so put me out by your gratuitous blame.' In the same letter he made enquiries about his aunt Maria Giberne, whom he had failed to meet when she came to Oxford: 'She is another of the people that make out I do not comply with little requests etc.' One understands his aunt's annoyance, since he had failed to think about meeting her until after the College gates had closed for the night, and then had neglected to call on her the following morning. Whether his mother was interfering in his Oxford life or whether his was simply the normal reaction of an undergraduate shaking off home influences, there was clearly some basic lack of understanding between parents and son, a fact worth remembering when considering how he lashed out at his family on the occasion of his conversion three years later. At this early age he was already allowing a glimpse of that slight lack of sympathy with others that is often a component of a morally intense personality.

On first becoming a member of the Union, he used it primarily as a writing room for the sake of sending letters on its notepaper; he never took part in its debates, and gradually he seems to have appeared there less and less. In any case, it was part of an innocent Balliol affectation in those years not to take part in Union debates, reserving that kind of activity for College societies in which the level of intelligence was thought to be higher.

When Hopkins went up to Oxford, Balliol was a college undergoing profound change. There was already no doubt of its intellectual eminence, and nearly everyone who attempted the difficult task of ranking colleges put it at the top of the heap; New College, Christ Church, University and Corpus Christi were usually among the runners-up, but there was a startling unanimity about the preeminence of Balliol, and nowhere was its superiority more evident than in the study of 'Greats' (*Literae Humaniores*). In the seven years beginning in 1860 there were approximately 150 men in residence in the College, and of those 99 read Greats, and 35 took Firsts in Finals.[11] The tutors of Balliol were generally regarded as the intellectual élite of the University and completely devoted to teaching. The result was that 'a small Oxford College, with slender resources and undistinguished buildings, produced year after year in numbers disproportionate to its size men who were outstanding in the most varied walks of life: philosophers, historians, statesmen, ecclesiastics, ambassadors, viceroys, civil servants, lawyers, writers, headmasters and heads of colleges, athletes and sportsmen'.[12] To tell the truth, the last two categories were far from outstanding, but there was good intellectual reason why its matriculation examinations were generally known as the most difficult of all those in Oxford.

In 1863 it also had a fame, almost notoriety, for its theological position, since it was the wellspring of Broad Church or Liberal religious ideas. Although most Victorians were only too aware of the dangers to conventional religion of Broad Church thinking, it is not easy today to be specific about its content, for it was more a negative idea than a formulation of tenets. Its essence was a defiance of traditional definition or categorization, and the exemption of no subject, however sacred, from examination in the light of reason. Modern advances in scientific and critical investigation were to be applied to dogma and Scripture. Traditional teaching of the Church Fathers was finally of less value than the test of recent human experience: postulations about eternal damnation, for example, were not to be taken literally since there was no proof of them, and common sense about such matters was more important than faith. In its denial of the numinous as a guide, it was, of course, the ultimate refutation of the sense of unbroken historical continuity of truth from Christ's lifetime to the nineteenth century, which the Oxford Movement had worked hard to promote. Broad Church thought was so concentrated in Balliol that its very name seemed like a pun on the site of the College in Oxford's Broad Street.

At the heart of the College was Hopkins's first tutor, Benjamin Jowett, the best known of the classicists in the College, perhaps in the University, and certainly the outstanding member of the Broad Church party, who thus united in his own person two of the most prominent aspects of Balliol. A decade earlier he had been defeated in the election for the Mastership of the College, and he had not yet quite consolidated a working majority of the Fellows, but he was easily their most conspicuous member. (It was the election of Hopkins's acquaintance Courtenay Ilbert as Fellow in 1865 that finally gave Jowett the majority in College meetings that he needed to wield undisputed power.)

Jowett was Regius Professor of Greek, but his religious opinions had made him seem so dangerous to the High Church party, centred in Christ Church, that for eight years he had been shamefully kept from receiving more than about a tenth of his proper stipend by his opponents, who were responsible for its payment. To a few close friends Jowett displayed a dogged fidelity, but to the world he often turned a glacial imperturbability, an aspect of his manner that was no doubt responsible for much of the antagonism and mean-spiritedness he raised in his opponents. It was not until two years after Hopkins arrived at Balliol that some financial reparation was made to Jowett for the withholding of his stipend.

What had contributed most to the odour of brimstone that hung around Jowett was his contribution to *Essays and Reviews*, a volume of Liberal theological essays that appeared in 1860, only a year after *The Origin of Species*, and that seemed to complete the destruction of the bases of traditional Christianity begun in Darwin's book. Two of the other seven contributors had been formally charged in the Court of Arches with heresy, and though their original conviction was reversed, the mud stuck. Jowett himself was denounced to the court of the Vice-Chancellor of the University on the same charges, which were dismissed within a month or so after Hopkins's arrival. It was understandably a difficult time for Jowett, but his misleadingly unemotional manner apparently kept Hopkins from appreciating what was going on in his tutor's mind.

With his natural inclination to High Church beliefs, Hopkins would not seem the ideal pupil for Jowett, but they appreciated the excellence of each other's intellects behind beliefs with which they could not sympathize. Jowett must have admired the single-mindedness of his new pupil when he applied himself to his studies. In turn, Hopkins could hardly have helped being impressed by the devotion of Jowett to the instruction of his pupils; he made a practice of seeing each of the approximately ninety members of the College individually at least once a week, even those undergraduates who were not his pupils; it must have seemed to their tutors that he was exceeding his mandate. He was almost single-handedly responsible for the importance of Plato in the classics curriculum, he brought a passion to the study of Greek that made most of his colleagues seem pedantic by comparison, and he introduced Hopkins to Hegel and Kant.

A particularly lively account of the life of a typical Oxford undergraduate contemporary with Hopkins says that the 'day after his arrival he has an interview with his tutor, who talks about his reading, puts him into some lectures, and gives him a little general advice, which he probably does not adopt'.[13] Shortly after his own arrival, Hopkins breakfasted with Jowett: 'when you can get him to talk he is amusing, but when the opposite, it is terribly embar[r]assing'. Jowett outlined what he expected each week of his new pupil: 'There is service in chapel at eight; at nine or ten lectures begin; these are over at one, and the afternoon is free; then, at four or five, there is chapel again; and after that dinner.'

Hopkins was told to go to lectures by James Riddell on Aeschylus and Homer, by Edwin Palmer on Aeschines and Virgil, by 'Oily' Smith in algebra, by Jowett himself on Thucydides, by E.C. Woollcombe in divinity, and to two evening classes a week devoted to the composition of his weekly essay, 'alternately Latin and English . . . When I called on Jowett, he advised me to take great pains with this, as on it would depend my success more than on anything else.' Jowett warned him in dismissal, 'to be careful to have no debts beyond at latest the end of term'. Hopkins carefully copied down the formidable timetable in his diary, but when he wrote on his schedule the following year, there was a noticeable omission of many of the earlier morning lectures.

The combination of academic and highly practical everyday advice was characteristic of Jowett, who had a shrewd idea of the value to the College of both pupils whose intelligence marked them out for academic success and those born to positions that made it worthwhile grooming them for a larger life outside Oxford. He was said to have as sure an eye for a promising undergraduate as a Yorkshireman has for a fast horse. In his own defence Jowett said that 'anyone who tries to get hold of young men of rank or wealth must expect to be accused of snobbishness, but one must remember how important it is to influence towards good those who are going to have an influence over hundreds or thousands of other lives'.[14] He apparently thought well of Hopkins but made no special efforts for him except in his studies; in the event he was proved correct in his estimate of his pupil's future when he became an obscure Jesuit priest, a name not to be remembered out of the College.

Despite respecting his own father, Hopkins clearly did not feel close to him and occasionally became artificial in manner when they had to communicate: one of the sins that he recorded for confession was his mockery of Manley Hopkins, and it is quite possible that he was in part seeking a surrogate father in his tutor. If so he was disappointed. One suspects that Jowett found it particularly difficult to be close to his pupils and that the chill of his manner was adopted to conceal the hauteur of heart that underlay it. After his death Thomas Arnold wrote of the first biography of Jowett: 'It is touching to observe how much he was beloved by a host of friends, to all of whom indeed, so long as they did not make what he called "a mess of life", he was truly affectionate and "serviable". On the unfortunate and perplexed he turned a cold unpitying eye; failure, or what he deemed such, awakened not his censure only, but his dislike.'[15] Indeed, W.H. Mallock thought that one poor pupil, a Scotsman, had lost his faith through Jowett's scepticism and cut his own throat with a razor in Port Meadow, and that Jowett, unperturbed, preached the funeral sermon.* There is no evidence that Jowett either censured or disliked Hopkins, and he recommended him enthusiastically many years later to University College, Dublin, for a chair in classics. All the same, he had always maintained that it was a man's duty to remain in the Church of his birth, an opinion he regarded as particularly appropriate in the case of young Oxonians contemplating submission to Rome. It is unlikely that Hopkins's conversion moved his position on the matter.

To maintain his timetable of seeing each undergraduate once a week, Jowett would entertain at breakfast, or at solitary wines where the younger man sat on the opposite side of the fire from the silent tutor, or by taking long walks. There are many stories told of how during the latter, as well as in tutorials, he would let hours pass without making a single spontaneous remark to his terrified companion, which of course provoked an intolerable desire on the part of the undergraduate to say something, anything, no matter how banal. Jowett was reputed to listen in silence to the babblings of the young man, then on reaching Balliol once more, he would fix a stare on him and advise him to cultivate his conversational powers. It is small wonder that many junior members of the College would go to extreme lengths to avoid being alone with him. In his obituary in the Jesuits' private periodical, *Letters and Notices*, it is said of Hopkins that 'the views of . . . Dr Jowett, seem to have contributed to his abandonment of Anglicanism',[16] but it is improbable that either Jowett's theology or even his manner had much to do with it.

Hopkins's first contact at Balliol with Broad Church principles

---

* It is worth remembering that Mallock so disliked Jowett that he skewered him as Dr Jenkinson in his mordantly witty 'novel', *The New Republic*. Probably the story is an embroidery of Jowett's tactless sermon on an undergraduate who had committed suicide, in which he said that there were times in a man's life so hopeless that it was perhaps better to leave it than to continue one's misery. Not that it is a much more attractive aspect of Jowett revealed, but there is no suggestion in it that the unfortunate young man was driven to desperation by Jowett himself.

presented him with serious problems, since they were so different from the High Church ones of his family, as well as from his own innate conservatism. Nevertheless, he seems to have been attracted to them for at least a short time. Few details remain of what was surely a not too serious flirtation, but a year after coming to Oxford he warned a friend of the dangers of Liberalism, of 'doing what I once thought I could do, *adopt an enlightened Christianity*'.[17]

What was far more consistent with his temperament as we know it was his reference in his first weeks in Oxford to having wine with half a dozen other young men who were more traditionally minded than most of the College. Their host on the occasion was Frederick Gurney, whose family was friendly with that of Hopkins; he was an attractive man some three years older than Hopkins and a leader of an undergraduate High Church society, the Brotherhood of the Holy Trinity. Among the others in the rooms that evening was Amcotts, A.E. Hardy, whose father became first Earl of Cranbrook, and William Addis, who was to be one of Hopkins's closest friends at Oxford (after Hopkins's death he claimed to have known 'him in his undergraduate days far better than any one else did').[18] 'These,' Hopkins wrote, 'and some others (among whom I humbly hope to be enrolled), represent the High Church section at Balliol.' Addis had a remarkable later religious career full in equal part of conversions and recantations, but at this time he had gone no further than to put aside the non-conformity of his boyhood for Anglican principles, which were to be changed in turn for Roman Catholic ones immediately after Hopkins's conversion. One of Gurney's friends, Samuel Brooke of Corpus, came in after the wine had begun, 'and played the piano gorgeously'; this was apparently Hopkins's first meeting with Brooke, a nervously High Church young man who was to become closely associated with him in several undergraduate Anglo-Catholic societies. Disillusionment with Brooke soon set in, and Hopkins said that in spite of seeing him a great deal, 'He is of course a very clever man, but very strange and bigoted.' Brooke's diaries of this period are among the most detailed, if slightly detached, records we have of the undergraduate life of Hopkins.

After the wine had broken up, 'Gurney and several others went to Liddon's lecture (one of a series on the first epistle to the Corinthians) delivered at S. Edmund's Hall. Gurney took me. The lecture, I need scarcely say, was admirable. Liddon, perhaps you do not know, is Pusey's great *protégé* and is immensely thought of. After lecture, tea and coffee, while Liddon goes round chatting. Gurney introduced me, and I shall now go every Sunday evening. Is not that "exceeding one's most sanguine expectations"?'

Henry Liddon, whose acquaintance Hopkins made that evening with such satisfaction, was more influential on the younger man and his faith than any other priest in the Church of England. At the time he was Vice-Principal of St Edmund Hall and he had also retained his Studentship at Christ Church, where he was closely associated with his mentor, Dr Pusey. He was a good theologian whose real contemporary reputation derived from his spell-binding lectures and sermons. Decades later one of his auditors remembered his series of Lenten discourses in the University Church as clearly as if they had been delivered only a few weeks before:

> Can we ever forget them? The swarms of undergraduates, herded in galleries, in deep rows, or crowded into every nook and corner on the floor . . . the mighty hush of expectation; and then the thrill of that vibrant voice, vehement, searching, appealing, pleading . . . we lived on the memory of it till next Lent came round, and then we were all there again; the same scene enacted itself, the same voice pleaded with us for our souls. So from year to year in our weak, boyish hearts, the flickering flame of faith was saved from perishing under the gusty tumult of the perilous times.[19]

It is hard to imagine oneself back into the company of those who were so compelled by his talks, for most of the adjectives used to describe him have lost their urgency in our century: thrilling, impetuous, beseeching, hypnotic. The slight distaste for him that a modern reader may feel comes less from what he was than from the feelings he inspired in others, and inevitably the easiness of their praise makes its object faintly suspect. As the chronicler of his career wrote reverently in the *Dictionary of National Biography*, 'He bent himself in his sermons to exclude originality of idea; he spent himself in the effort simply to prove and to persuade. And to this effort everything in him contributed – his charm of feature, his exquisite intonation, his kindling eye, his quivering pose and gestures, his fiery sarcasm, his rich humour, his delicate knowledge of the heart, and his argumentative skill.' But perhaps it is not fair to hold a man responsible for his admirers.

Liddon was one of the most popular men in Oxford, and the crowds of undergraduates who 'stood ranked thick on each other's toes, in huddled S. Mary's, to catch every word of the ringing voice' were attracted as much by his flamboyant personality as by his theology. One of his young followers wrote a series of sonnets to him, and there was a general jostling for invitations to accompany him on his long afternoon walks, on which he would discourse earnestly of Christian morality as it applied to his undergraduate companions. The Sunday chapel requirements of most colleges could be met by attending services elsewhere, and many of his congregations were made up of High Church enthusiasts from all over Oxford, Hopkins among them, although in time the charm began to wear thin for him.

It was even more exciting to talk to Liddon privately than to hear him on the podium or in the pulpit, for he brought the whole force of his personality to bear upon undergraduates, treating them like equals intellectually. While most Oxford clerics indicated their calling simply by wearing a white stock, Liddon dressed the part. With his 'face of almost faultless beauty', dark eyes glittering above a dazzling white Roman collar, a black cassock, and broad belt, he resembled a handsome and worldly Latin ecclesiastic more than a provincial Anglican clergyman. In his diary he wrote his own account of the evening on which Hopkins was first introduced to him: 'My lect in evening very full attended indeed. Much interesting talk afterwards. The Balliol element steadily increasing'.[20] Since Hopkins was apparently the only newcomer to the lectures from Balliol, we can assume that Liddon had noticed him especially and marked him out for the intimacy that was to characterize their future friendship. It was not a bad beginning for a young man making his way in the High Church world.

CHAPTER III

MY RITUALISTIC FRIEND
1863

The Anglo-Catholic wing of the Church of England, the direct descendant of the Oxford Movement, had changed considerably from its immediate ancestor of two decades before, when Newman, Keble and Pusey as young men were issuing the *Tracts* that ruffled Oxford and frightened all England with the prospect of a deep division in the Church. What had been a closely knit group had disintegrated: Keble had been living in retirement in Hursley since 1836, and Newman had gone over to Rome in 1845. Only Pusey, saddened and embattled, stayed on in Christ Church as the leader of a far less robust body of believers, splintered in their beliefs, shaken in their unanimity. The group was still very conspicuous in Oxford by its presence, but it was less important intellectually than it had been twenty years earlier.

One of the best historians of the whole phenomenon has summarized the shift that took place in it over a quarter of a century:

The movement's partisans, under the leadership of John Henry Newman, E.B. Pusey, and John Keble, became known variously as Tractarians (after the series of 'Tracts for the Times' produced under Newman's editorship), as Newmanites, and (after Newman's secession to the Roman Catholic Church) as Puseyites. Initially the movement sought to shore up the autonomy of the Church with respect to the state and it claimed a place within the historic High Church wing of Anglicanism, but its agenda soon expanded to include the revival of a great many 'Catholic' doctrines and practices abandoned by the English Church at the Reformation or thereafter. By the time young Tractarian clergymen began to

41

move out from the universities to serve parishes and missions, they were calling themselves Anglo-Catholics, and the most extreme were coming to be called Ritualists, in reference to the most visible – and, for many critics, the most disturbing – of their innovations.[1]

To hostile observers in the 1860s it seemed that the energy of the Tractarians that had once gone into reaffirming the continuity of the Church from the days of the Apostles to the present had diminished into a puerile obsession with externals, and that the intellectual rigour which had once demonstrated the familial ties of Roman Catholicism and Anglicanism as two independent bodies of equal validity had dwindled into a weak-kneed aesthetic preoccupation with ancient rites and ceremonies, with the authentic cut of vestments and the proper use of incense. Sam Brooke, Hopkins's new friend from Corpus Christi, was typically worried about the concern of the High Church set with liturgical details and about 'too much talk about Crosses and Candlesticks'.[2]

Hopkins was certainly never on the wilder fringes of Ritualism, although he was concerned with decorum in the Anglican liturgy and occasionally went to London from Oxford to attend services at All Saints, Margaret Street, and St Alban's, Holborn, two of the most ritually extreme of London churches. More typical of his deepest concerns was the letter he sent to Ernest Coleridge, a friend from Highgate, urging him to come up to Oxford as soon as possible, since it was 'the head and fount of Catholicism in England and the heart of our Church . . . The great aid to belief and object of belief is the doctrine of the Real Presence in the Blessed Sacrament of the Altar. Religion without that is sombre, dangerous, illogical, with that it is – not to speak of its grand consistency and certainty – loveable. Hold that and you will gain all Catholic truth.'[3] The letter, written more than two years before his conversion, is an indication of how early he had settled on the essentials of his faith rather than the externals, of how little his mind ran naturally on ritual. When he was at last converted to Roman Catholicism, one of his first anxieties was that his father might believe that his change of religion was due to aesthetics rather than theology.

But since Hopkins was so much concerned with the historical

truth of his Church, it was natural for him to be interested in its ceremonial and what it indicated of the truth of its teachings. At Oxford, for example, we know that he frequently attended the most extreme of High Church parishes, that of St Thomas, near the railway station, an old church whose Vicar took pride in having first worn a chasuble in 1854, so that he was one of the two first Anglican clergymen to resume Eucharistic vestments since the Reformation. All the same, at this time it would have seemed to Hopkins sacrilegious to concentrate on the first term of the religious symbols rather than on the second term, their metaphorical significance. It took him years to be comfortable in his poetry with the thought that the evidence of his senses was not sinful, or even inferior, in the apprehension of the Divine, and to the end of his life he seems to have felt that the externals of the Church were useful and attractive without being important in themselves: a curious attitude in a poet so devoted to the sanctity of the physical world.

To the new breed of High Churchmen, the Ritualists, the older generation of Tractarians seemed dated and dowdy. Even Pusey himself, always given a token nod as surviving leader of the Movement, probably had less direct influence on Oxford religious life than his associate, Liddon, who had allied himself with the Ritualists. The exception to the feeling that the Tractarians were passé was one of them who had himself left the Movement long before, John Henry Newman. In the nearly two decades since he had become a Roman Catholic, he had not appeared in Oxford, but his thin, elongated shadow lay over much of the city. To the Broad Church and Low Church parties he was still a silent warning of the dangers of the High Church, which could only too easily serve as a prelude to Roman Catholicism. To the young Ritualists, on the other hand, he was the departed leader who had brought the Church of England to a state of such dignity that they no longer needed to follow him and become converts in order to feel part of the Catholic, Universal Church. Undergraduates still emulated his distinctive, graceful manner of walking with a gentle incline of the body, and they affected tail-coats worn with long, high-buttoned 'Mark of the Beast' waistcoats in memory of his stork-like appearance, so that his presence seemed still to haunt the city he had left unvisited for so long.

One of Hopkins's first expeditions after he came up to Balliol was to the austere little church in Littlemore that Newman's family had built and where he had served as a young clergyman, there preaching his last sermon 'before the exodus'. Newman had a particular significance for him as a priest for whom the formal address of 'Father' had a good bit more meaning than mere conventional usage, and time after time Hopkins seems to have been deliberately stepping like a dutiful child in Newman's tracks. Jowett and Liddon were both temporary father figures for him, but of them all it was Newman whose influence persisted. It would be simple-minded overstatement to say that in his own spiritual journey Hopkins was from the first consciously following Newman from Oxford and High Church to Rome and the priesthood, or to say that in so doing he was deliberately rejecting Manley Hopkins, Jowett, Pusey, and Liddon and settling on Newman as surrogate father, but there is a striking similarity in the paths they chose, of which Hopkins must have been aware.

Like other enthusiastic religious groups, the Ritualists could seem remarkably silly to those who did not share their views. A.G.C. Liddell, who was a Balliol undergraduate from 1865 to 1869, told of 'an unpopular character, who was given to Ritualism and held services in his chamber with incense, vestments, and lights. These were an abomination to the other dwellers on the staircase, who used to express their dissent by occasionally smoking out the performance, by means of damp squibs thrown into the man's lobby inside the "oak" or outer door.'[4] (Curiously enough, the unlucky Ritualist occupied desirable rooms that had once been Hopkins's, which suggests that the group may have practised a discreet bit of nepotism in College matters.) Hopkins himself appears never to have been the object of ragging, although he was gently satirized by Martin Geldart in a humorous recollection of Balliol in the 1860s called *A Son of Belial*. In the book Jowett makes his appearance as Professor Jewell, Liddon is called Canon Perry, and Hopkins is known as 'my ritualistic friend Gerontius Manley'.

In real life Hopkins adopted many of the manners and practices of the Ritualists. By 1865 he was apparently using the scourge to flagellate himself during Lent, he habitually declined to eat meat on Fridays and on at least one occasion refused a dinner invitation on a

Friday. The previous year he had written to a friend that 'My mother does not let me fast at all, and says I in particular must never do it again, and in fact I believe I must not. I feel like the Hindoos when the Suttee was abolished; but that is to me almost greater mortification of the spirit than fasting of the flesh.'[5] In spite of her prohibition, he often fasted and had to be warned away from doing so because his strength gave out.

Liddell and his friends in Balliol were not the only 'hearties' who disliked the Ritualists and their habits. One college, known for its hostility to the group, refused to give a pair of High Church undergraduates fish for dinner on Ash Wednesday, although it did relent to the extent of allowing them a box of sardines. In an Oxford church known for its elaborate liturgy, an undergraduate deliberately stood up in the middle of a service, craned on tiptoe at the prettiest girls in the congregation, and generally did all he could to disrupt the service. At its worst the friction was only a particular manifestation of a far older quarrel between the sporting men and the reading men, between the toughs and the aesthetes, but it could make an undergraduate's life unhappy.

It was characteristic of Hopkins that he should espouse unpopular views, suffer for them, and so become even more attached to them. It is difficult to label this aspect of Hopkins, for it is part of the same character trait that led him at Highgate to fast and go without water until his tongue was black. What one person may see as admirable resolution may be perceived by another as merely stubborn; courage is another name for what some might think was masochistic behaviour. It was a problem that cropped up constantly in Hopkins's life, and perhaps it is wisest simply to recognize that a man's character is not determined by the names applied to it. Certainly, Hopkins was never positive about his own motivation, and the remaining records are scant help to us in making up our own minds on the matter.

What seemed to most Anglicans the Puseyites' final betrayal of Protestantism was the adoption of auricular confession. Liddon and Pusey were both adroit in hearing confessions and advocated penance for those under their spiritual direction, although Pusey felt lingering reservations about suggesting it to undergraduates, since he realized that it was such a Rubicon for Broad Church or

Evangelical Anglicans. On 8 February 1864, in his first year in Oxford, Hopkins finally had a chance of a long private conversation with Liddon, with whom he walked the wintry roads near Oxford. 'Walk with Hopkins of Balliol, a long talk about Eternal Punishment', Liddon wrote in his diary. In the evening he had another 'long talk with Dr. P[usey]', but there is no indication whether it concerned Hopkins, who was already known to the older man. On the 11th of February, Ash Wednesday, Liddon noted simply, 'Hopkins of Balliol conf. at 7'. Many years later Hopkins said that even as a Roman Catholic he had never experienced truer contrition than he did that evening in Christ Church. Thereafter Liddon's diary mentions three or four occasions on which he heard Hopkins's confession, and Hopkins's own journal indicates that he went at least once, and probably more often, to Pusey for confession, but he may have made other confessions that neither he nor Liddon recorded, since once the practice had become habitual it was less likely that either of them would take special notice of it. And he almost certainly went to confession elsewhere, probably at All Saints, Margaret Street, or St Alban's when he was with his family in London.

His friend William Addis, who was also High Church in his beliefs, wrote that when he first knew him, Hopkins was 'a little tinged' with liberalism, by which he meant an inclination to scepticism about eternal punishment. 'All changed after his first confession to Liddon (that kindest and best of men).'[6]

When he was only twenty-one Liddon had taken a vow of lifelong celibacy. It was a particularly High Church dedication, and as in the case of most other Ritualists marked the fact that he no longer thought of himself as specifically Protestant. It would not have escaped Hopkins's notice that his model, Newman, had taken a similar vow at an even earlier age than Liddon, and a surprising number of Hopkins's friends had done so too. Among those he met at Oxford who expected to remain celibate were Stuckey Coles, Digby Dolben, and even Robert Bridges, whose plans for living unmarried with his favourite brother were thwarted by the early death of that brother. Coles was typical of the group in thinking that the normal state for priests was celibacy, and most of the vows were taken with the intention of ultimate ordination within the

Catholic tradition, whether that was Roman or Anglican. It is not clear when Hopkins first decided to take Holy Orders, but his fascination with details of doctrine, Church practices and the life of the clergy suggest that it was an early decision, probably made in the first year or so of his undergraduate life.

Inevitably, one asks today whether a commitment to celibacy is not a way of hiding from one's self or others a psychological disinclination to marriage that stems from instincts having little to do with religion. After acknowledging the elements of religious idealism and self-sacrifice that prompted many men in the Anglo-Catholic movement to vow celibacy, a present-day historian of the movement comes directly to the point: 'Did it also, in many cases, have a homosexual motivation? It seems inherently possible that young men who were secretly troubled by homosexual feelings that they could not publicly acknowledge may have been attracted by the prospect of devoting themselves to a life of celibacy, in the company of like-minded male friends, as a religiously-sanctioned alternative to marriage.'[7] Or, as seems even more probable, was not celibacy a way of avoiding the admission even to himself of the intensity of a young man's homoerotic feelings, since a renunciation of sex did not need to specify what particular expression of it was being given up? In the case of Newman, for example, it has long been known that his emotions about other men, and Ambrose St John in particular, were considerably more intense than are usually considered normal. Behind the humour of his description in *Loss and Gain* of the meeting of Charles Reding with a newly married young clergyman and his bride lies a glimmer of the truth about Newman's own reactions: he felt 'a faintish feeling come over him: somewhat such as might beset a man on hearing a call for pork-chops when he was sea-sick'.[8]

There is no evidence that Hopkins ever considered marriage, and he was probably determined on celibacy long before he had even taken his Oxford degree. In 1884 he told Robert Bridges that the reason he liked his friends to marry 'is that a single life is a difficult, not altogether a natural life' and that he felt 'a kind of spooniness and delight over married people, especially if they say "my wife," "my husband," or shew the wedding ring'.[9] But loneliness or even delight in the marital happiness of others was not quite the same thing as wanting to marry himself, and we have plenty of other evidence to show that Hopkins's most intense physical attraction was to men. The tight Anglo-Catholic circles in which he moved in Oxford were in part substitutes for family life.

No one should be surprised if Hopkins was briefly attracted by a young woman, even if his propensities did not usually lie in that direction. The pretty young wife of his friend Frederick Gurney upset him sufficiently to cause a mention in his spiritual journal of his 'Temptation to adultery of the heart with Mrs. Gurney',[10] but his unconscious insistence on the heart rather than the body suggests that the temptation may have been less than compelling physically. It is almost the only indication of his ever considering a woman sexually, and she was safely married.

It is easy to forget how limited the sexual opportunities were for middle-class young men in the 1860s, largely because of the strictness with which girls or young women of their own class were watched or chaperoned. In the lower classes, where appearances, or even conventional morality and respectability, were far less important, the men were freer to act out their natural impulses, and for men of the upper classes, with many available young girls acting as servants in their houses or as workers on their estates, there was also a greater opportunity for sexual expression. Since almost the only other alternative was the sleazy world of prostitution, it is not surprising if neither Hopkins nor the majority of his scrupulous friends ever slept with a woman.

It is a commonplace that Victorian boys in public or other boarding schools were constantly exposed to sex, often of disturbing crudeness. John Addington Symonds, who preceded Hopkins at Balliol by five years, wrote of his time at Harrow that the 'talk in the dormitories and the studies was incredibly obscene. Here and there one could not avoid seeing acts of onanism, mutual masturbation, the sports of naked boys in bed together. There was no refinement, no sentiment, no passion; nothing but animal lust in these occurrences. They filled me with disgust and loathing. My school-fellows realized what I had read in Swift about the Yahoos.'[11] Such activity revolted sensitive boys and at the same time it set the patterns and limits of their sexual imagination, so that, like Symonds himself, they had a complicated response made up of disgust at their own animal nature and a strong sexual desire aggravated by the very acts that had excited their abhorrence. The majority of Hopkins's High Church friends came from public schools, and one suspects that their reactions to sex were deeply complicated, predetermined by their schooling.

Geoffrey Faber, the authority on the personal life of the earlier members of the Oxford Movement, showed in *Oxford Apostles* how that group often drew on the energies of relationships that hovered somewhere in the undefined area between friendship and love, probably sexual in inspiration but usually without physical expression; it was an affection that could be tolerated because the labels of homosexual and heterosexual had not yet been imposed, so that feelings were uninhibited by definition.

It is hardly to be expected that men within two or three years of the age of twenty will be able to sublimate their sexual energies completely, and the sentimental friendships of Oxford in the middle of the century were a middle-class attempt to deal with the crude facts of sex and to refine them by the application of love: hardly a revolutionary idea, as they could see in the Greek literature in which they had all been educated. David Newsome has written that 'In the nineteenth century, the normality of both men and women forming highly emotional relationships with those of their own sex, of the same age or sometimes older or younger, as the case might be, was neither questioned as necessarily unwholesome nor felt to inhibit the same relationship with the opposite sex, leading to perfectly happy marriage.'[12] To show affection openly and to speak in terms of endearment were not abnormal but the spontaneous accompaniments of unembarrassed affection; we are in danger of misunderstanding the century if we try to look at it from a wholly post-Freudian viewpoint, or even if we assume that the inevitable result of such affection was its physical expression; there seems to have been little actual sexual contact in the group around Hopkins, almost as if they had seen too much of that in their schooldays and needed to move to a less coarse way of indicating love between males.

Hopkins was certainly moved deeply by his sexual feeling for other men, but there is no proof, or even responsible suggestion, that he ever had sexual relations with anyone else. It is not impossible that he did so, of course, either in school or at Oxford, but it seems most improbable because of his piety, his generally fastidious nature, and his extreme dislike of even speaking of crude subjects. We know from his diaries how much he lamented far less serious lapses from virtue, and it is probable that he would have been deeply shocked at the reality of sexual intimacy with another person.

There is a further complication about Hopkins's sexuality about which we naturally have little information, which is that he seems to have matured physically at a very late age. If we are to trust their position in his notebooks as evidence of a firm date, his notes on nocturnal emissions indicate that they did not occur regularly until he was well over nineteen years old.[13] Since he achieved sexual maturity so late, it is possible that as an undergraduate he was still passing through the phase of homosexuality that we are told is normal in early puberty.

What is certain is that Victorians separated deeds from personality; a man whose sexual impulses were aroused by other men was not to be called homoerotic unless he actually committed homoerotic acts. As J.S. Reed has written of the matter; 'Until late in the century, to ask whether a man known to be chaste was homosexual would have been almost meaningless. The Victorians certainly knew about homosexual *acts* (the death penalty for sodomy was on the books until 1861), but the idea of homosexuality as a *condition* was not widespread until later – and, one might add, that of anything like a homosexual *sensibility* had currency only in some very rarified circles.'[14] Since the very word homosexual had not yet been coined in Hopkins's lifetime, to apply it to him is to be guilty of both verbal and psychological anachronism.

All the same, the Victorians knew as well as we that some forms of behaviour indicate basic truths about personality, and in the case of the Oxford Movement, that there were dangers in the fervour of the romantic friendship that flourished under its aegis, blocking out, at least temporarily, the facility for forming emotional relationships with women, and perhaps making the physical expression of affection between the men in the Movement more probable. Hopkins's friend Stuckey Coles, for examples, recognized while he was still a schoolboy that a 'beautiful and ennobling love for his friends might co-exist with much that is faulty and ill-regulated, and even with much that is corrupt, and that, like all passionate enthusiasms, it has untold capabilities for good but also carries within it possibilities for evil'.[15] They were possibilities discernible within the circles in which Hopkins moved, and one suspects that his vow of celibacy was ultimately more a rejection of his own impulses towards other men than it was a renunciation of marriage.

The Fellows of Balliol were such a distinguished lot intellectually that some modern Hopkins scholars have found it strange that he recorded so few of his opinions about them. Perhaps only academics would find the omission odd, for undergraduates take far less personal notice of their teachers than is flattering to admit. In any case, the senior members of Balliol were probably somewhat removed personally and emotionally from their pupils, however scrupulous they were about their instruction.

As we have seen, Hopkins wrote to his mother about his initial impressions of Jowett, and a few months later he was so enraged at the destruction of a beautiful beech tree shading the rooms of two Fellows that uncharacteristically he wrote of one of them, T.H. Green, that he had 'a rather offensive style of infidelity, and naturally dislikes the beauties of nature'.[16] But that was probably only momentary pique expressing itself rather than settled disapproval, however true it was that Green's growing scepticism about Christianity was difficult for Hopkins to stomach. In 1868, after he had become a Jesuit, Green wrote of him, 'I never had his intimacy, but always liked him very much',[17] the coolness of which is an accurate reflection of his own distant manner. When he returned to Oxford years later, Hopkins made a point of calling on his old tutor, and after his death he wrote that he 'always liked and admired poor Green'.[18]

On the whole, however, he wrote a good deal more about his contemporaries than about his seniors. In the majority of memoirs of Balliol at the time, there is more respect than love expressed for the Fellows, although even that was sometimes missing. Sir William Anson wrote that when he was a contemporary of Hopkins's there was a good bit of inefficient shuffling among the distinguished Common Room. Collections at the end of term, when the young men's work was assessed, seemed to him to be designed 'for the glorification of [E.C.] Woollcombe', another of Hopkins's tutors, 'who writes down minute entries in a book the size of a dining-room table, and thinks himself the pillar of the College'.[19] There is a sting in Anson's remark that would have been very unlike Hopkins, but it has the ring of truth, typical as it is of the thoughts of undergraduates through the centuries about their elders.

Hopkins was an exceptionally intelligent young man and studious enough to justify the high opinion of his tutors, but there is little evidence that hard work at his books engulfed his emotions. A great many of his undergraduate essays have survived and are preserved, chiefly in Campion Hall, Oxford. They are the work of the kind of undergraduate pupil every university teacher would like to have: well informed, crisply and even elegantly written with the enviable command of language that seems not to have been uncommon a century ago, occasionally witty, and often demonstrating unobtrusively their relevance to his own experience. As reference materials they are invaluable, for they show in close detail what Hopkins was reading and considering for four years. Finally, however, one must admit that they would scarcely be compelling reading if they were not the juvenilia of a great poet, pointing to accomplishments much beyond themselves.

Like the rest of his contemporaries reading Greats, Hopkins was expected to study Latin and Greek for four years, and for three he studied Scripture. The burden of his studies of the classics was philosophical rather than literary; there was, for instance, no lyric or pastoral poetry in his readings, and in the study of drama or narrative art a great deal more attention was paid to logic and the analysis of argument than to aesthetic appreciation. It was for this reason that Jowett had stressed how important his weekly essays would be in his studies, for they were direct preparation for his examinations, in which he would be tested for both his knowledge of logic and exposition and his ability to use them. '[T]here is no sign anywhere else that Hopkins' imagination was aroused and stimulated by his studies for Moderations. Neither Homer nor the tragedians spoke directly to his lyric sensibility as did the poetry of his native language.'[20] There was of course no English poetry in the

Oxford syllabus for Greats, but that was not an unqualified defect for Hopkins, since the study of Greats made him at home with other languages, so that however idiosyncratic his own poetry sometimes seems, it is never provincial.

By the end of Michaelmas term in the autumn of 1864, Robert Scott, the Master of Balliol, noted rather surprisingly in his Report Book on the progress of the undergraduates that Hopkins had done work that was *'Fair, very Fair except in Divinity'.*[21]

There is no Master's entry for Hopkins's first term in Balliol, the Easter term 1863, but during its course he took Responsions, a set of exams largely intended to gauge a man's preparation. Highgate had equipped him so well that he sailed through, but other first-year men could not afford to take them so lightly. 'We all got through Smalls', he wrote to his new friend A.W.M. Baillie in the summer of 1863. 'Hardy, after the seizure of his *testamur* [certificate of having passed the examinations] became light-headed, light-hearted, light-heeled. He, Brown and I proceeded to booze at the Mitre, and I forgot to pay my share, but I believe Hardy meant to feast us, in his delight.'[22]

Mowbray Baillie, a Scot who had attended Edinburgh Academy, became acquainted with Hopkins during his first term at Oxford. Baillie was described as having 'a genius for friendship', he was learned for his years, intensely rational, and so near being an atheist that one would not have expected him to become intimate with Hopkins. He outlived Hopkins by many years, absorbed in study, living in London on an inherited income, never flagging in his long affection for his friend. Near the end of his life he said that one of his greatest regrets at not believing in personal immortality was that he wanted so badly 'somewhere, somehow, to meet Gerard Hopkins again'. Among the large collection of Hopkins's letters that he carefully preserved are the first ones, written in the Long Vacation of 1863, when Hopkins went with his family to stay in Shanklin on the Isle of Wight for more than two months.

Typically, Hopkins spent a good bit of time dutifully studying during the holidays, as he told Baillie, but Virgil, Tacitus and Cicero took second place in his imagination to the well-scrubbed pleasures of that demure island resort. 'The sea is brilliantly coloured and always calm, bathing delightful, horses and boats to be obtained, walks wild and beautiful, sketches charming, walking tours and excursions, poetic downs, the lovely Chine, fine cliffs, everything (except odious Fashionables). My brothers and cousin catch us shrimps, prawns and lobsters, and keep aquariums.'[23]

The drawings he made on the Isle of Wight are as charming as he jokingly claimed, and they reflect both his delight in the natural beauty of the island and the composure of his mind that summer. The small, self-contained sketches are often of miniature landscapes framed in meticulously draughted trees; here there is little of the pleasure in profusion that was so characteristic of his later poetry, but the drawings demonstrate his intense preoccupation with nature. At the same time, it is only fair to say that they show too little imagination to make one regret that he did not become a visual artist, as he had thought for a time of doing.[24]

To Baillie he described his sketches as having 'a Ruskinese point of view . . . I have particular periods of admiration for particular things in Nature; for a certain time I am astonished at the beauty of a tree, shape, effect etc, then when the passion, so to speak, has subsided, it is consigned to my treasury of explored beauty, and acknowledged with admiration and interest ever after, while something new takes its place in my enthusiasm. The present fury is the ash, and perhaps barley and two shapes of growth in leaves and one in tree boughs and also a conformation of fine-weather cloud.'[25] The passage presages two important aspects of Hopkins in later life. The first is his intense concentration on the individuality of objects in nature, a directness of attention that contributed greatly to his theories of inscape. And, of course, the passage also reflects the speed with which he could tire of a subject, which was in part responsible for the unfinished artistic projects that littered his mature life, discarded in boredom or fatigue as his interest was drawn elsewhere.

CHAPTER IV

GERARD MANLEY TUNCKS
1863–4

When he left the Isle of Wight in 1863 Hopkins had a sojourn of two or three weeks in London with his family before returning in October to begin his second academic year at Balliol. Only six months before, he had been a freshman in College, excited by all the possibilities of a brand-new society, but now he was returning to what was already more a home than Hampstead, a home filled with friends who had only recently been strangers with whom he had to make his way.

His quarters at the top of a staircase no longer seemed so desirable as they had when first he saw them, and his greater seniority gave him the chance to make a change to pleasanter rooms on his return. It was customary for Balliol men to be allowed only one such change during their undergraduate career, but Hopkins liked the new set in the Garden Quad of bedroom, sitting room, entry, and scout's hole, all contained within an 'oak', as the old ones had not been, and he moved in October, sure that he would enjoy the rooms for the rest of his time in Oxford.

The furniture was of better quality than that in his old rooms; with the addition of 'a cloth and fringe of the colour of stewed pears' to cover the chimneypiece, new carpet and wallpaper, it became a quiet, pretty set. On the walls he hung portraits of Raphael, Tennyson, Shelley, Keats, Shakespeare, Milton, Dante, and Dürer, a list that characteristically says more of his literary preferences than of his taste in painting. Even with a present from his grandfather in hand, he was so behind with his bills that he had to postpone framing his pictures, a fact he mentioned to his mother as a hint that more money would be welcome.

Living on the ground floor allowed him to run in and out

between lectures, and made it far more convenient for his friends to drop in. His airy bedroom with iron bedstead overlooked the street behind the Church of St Mary Magdalene and the Martyrs' Memorial, too high to be looked in by casual passers-by but convenient for friends to shout through its protective iron bars when they were passing and wanted to get his attention. During the day their voices mingled with the noise of workmen building the Randolph Hotel across the street. So much of the physical world Hopkins knew has disappeared since his death that it is hardly surprising that his bedroom should now have its windows glazed with ribbed panes suitable to its use as a lavatory.

His sitting room looked out at the Garden Quadrangle, where he continued to lament the felling of the great beech tree merely to make more light for the rooms of the Fellows. His sorrow at the destruction of trees was to remain as fresh at the end of his life as it was when he was an undergraduate, for it seemed to symbolize all that he hated about the eradication of the past. When he returned to Oxford as a priest his emotions on the subject provided the inspiration for one of his most haunting poems.

Martin Geldart, whose features he had deplored initially, had also moved to Staircase 6 (now Staircase XVI), and Francis de Paravicini, another close friend, lived on the next staircase. Notwithstanding Newman's dictum, there was more than mere contiguity to friends that recommended the location. Balliol was then undergoing some severe architectural changes, but the quadrangle remained much the same a decade later, when Arnold Toynbee wrote that it was 'where one walks at night and listens to the wind in the trees, and weaves the stars into the web of one's thoughts; where one goes from the pale inhuman moon to the ruddy light of the windows, and hears broken notes of music and laughter, and the complaining murmur of the railroad in the distance. . . . The life here is very sweet and full of joy; at Oxford, after all, one's ideal of happy life is nearer being realised than anywhere else. . . .'[1]

Hopkins still wrote to his parents about the wines and breakfasts he was attending, and his photographs show that he was now wearing his hair in a fashionably long cut, but his letters reveal a new seriousness in what he was writing home, an increased interest in matters theological. Even the buildings he was most pleased to see in Oxford itself were almost always the chapels of colleges, not in itself surprising for anyone with architectural interests but somewhat new for him. In writing of his architecturally minded acquaintances, Hopkins mentioned a freshman, Lionel Muirhead, who was 'said to spend his time in reading Art subjects, so Baillie and I are thinking of "assuming" him'.[2] Muirhead was an Etonian whose family lived at Haseley Court, east of Oxford, a country house with long Recusant associations. His High Church inclinations as well as his artistic concerns were to be important to Hopkins, for Muirhead was a member of the Brotherhood of the Holy Trinity, the most extreme Anglo-Catholic undergraduate organization in Oxford.

With little more continuity of prestige than other undergraduate clubs, the BHT, as it was known, alternated between popularity and decay. It had been founded a decade earlier on the ruins of the Oxford Architectural Society, which had run out of old churches to study and was on the verge of dissolving. Since most of the members were devout, 'It was thought that these men might be gathered up, and that they might find in a body of sympathizing elders a strength to resist the various temptations to which they were exposed.' Pusey was approached for advice and saw an opportunity to found an Anglican lay brotherhood. 'Full of the notion that he had taken up, Dr Pusey first proposed that the members of the new body should make a rule of always walking with their eyes turned to the ground, to avoid temptations and as a mark of humility.' One of the Brethren suggested that such a practice was not natural for young men, nor good for them. 'Instead, Dr Pusey suggested that as a mark of membership we should all wear round our loins a girdle of flannel or other material as a token of self-restraint.' Not surprisingly, Pusey's suggestions did not catch on, but the undergraduate members did strive to rise early, pray, and be moderate in food and drink.[3]

In the autumn of 1863 Hopkins was invited to join the Brotherhood. He already knew three or four undergraduate members, as well as Liddon, who was an active senior member of the group, of which R.C. Benson was Master and Pusey the spiritual inspiration. Hopkins dutifully informed his parents of his invitation to join the Brotherhood and of his subsequent refusal, which clearly fitted in with his mother's feelings. Aside from her worry about Gerard's fasting, there is no indication at the time that his parents felt he was becoming too High Church in his outlook, but the fact that his beliefs were changing may have excited her alarm. We know from the diaries of Sam Brooke that a little earlier he too had received an invitation to become a member, about which he felt 'extremely doubtful. Besides the fact that such Society's [sic] are invidious to the University, I am unwilling to compromise myself by entering into a body wh. is not only in itself a secret one, but wh. is also to some extent connected with certain Oratories in Oxford of doubtful fame. From what I saw to-night of the Members of this brotherhood, I can scarcely suppose that those *exceedingly stringent rules* wh. are supposed to bind the members are in very active force.'[4] In deciding to decline the invitation, Brookes said that besides being devoted to 'religious sentimentalism', the Brotherhood was 'fraught with every kind of ill-famed notoriety'.

Precisely what the unsavoury repute was of the oratories to which some of the confraternity belonged was never made clear by Brooke, but his shock suggests that it may have been sexual in origin, as does the slightly seedy reputation of some of the members, whose religion was tinged with something less than spiritual. In any case, Hopkins never became a member, but he did adopt Pusey's suggestions about a penitential girdle and about accustoming himself to the 'discipline of the eyes', a peculiarly difficult penance for one so curious about the external world as he was. When he became a Jesuit novice it was one of his most habitual forms of penance, and it indicates something of the rigour of his personality that he had to be cautioned against adopting it too stringently.

In spite of not joining the Brotherhood, Hopkins spent a great deal of time with its members, including Muirhead and his best friend and fellow Etonian, Robert Bridges, who had been proposed for membership the same day that Hopkins was. It is probable that had he never met Bridges, the world would never have heard of Hopkins.

Like so many of Hopkins's Oxford friends, Bridges came of an upper-middle-class landed family who sent their sons to Eton, where he distinguished himself in sports and games, particularly as a formidable oarsman. But there were several aspects of his personality, hidden behind a courteous, well-bred exterior, that belied his conventional appearance and background. For one thing, he was deeply religious in what was to become an increasingly unorthodox fashion; his moderately High Church background had been fanned at Eton into enthusiasm for Anglo-Catholic beliefs that lasted him through his schooldays before beginning to crumble when he came into residence in Corpus Christi College in the Michaelmas term of 1863. By the time he took his degree he appears to have been more interested in the musical tradition of the Church of England than in its theology, but, true to his background, he never formally left the Church. When Hopkins met him, his disbelief was tattered but Anglican for all that.

He was later sorely tried to maintain his friendship for Hopkins at the same emotional pitch after Hopkins had been converted to Roman Catholicism, but as the account of his life in the *Dictionary of National Biography* notes sagaciously, Bridges remained respectful of the religious instinct in other men, whatever the form, his innate courtesy inclining him to remain alive 'both to the beauty of holiness and to the holiness of beauty'. Bridges came from a family sufficiently prosperous to ensure that he never needed to work for a living, but he intended to become a doctor, largely for the sake of the knowledge of the physical world that it would provide. After the age of forty he planned to give up the practice of medicine and devote the rest of his life to the composition and study of poetry.

It was typical of Bridges's self-effacing relations with his friends that Hopkins did not suspect for more than ten years that his Oxford companion had any poetic ambitions or instincts, and that he should discover for the first time that Bridges wrote poetry when he accidentally saw a review of his friend's first volume in 1874. Bridges seems to have recognized without pain that he was a poet who wrote by theory while Hopkins was a naturally lyric poet for whom theories frequently acted as bonds rather than illumination.

The fact that he never mentioned his own poetry to Hopkins at Oxford suggests a rather curious question about Bridges: was his natural reticence true modesty, or was it a particularly refined kind of disregard for the opinions of others? The question would be an artificial one if it were not that he has so often been criticized for waiting nearly thirty years before publishing the poems of Hopkins. It is probable that it would have been intolerable for him, both personally and on behalf of Hopkins, to publish works that would not be taken seriously by their readers, readers for whom he might not have complete respect but whose condescension would have been doubly difficult to swallow for that very reason.

Even when one considers their common interest in literature and religion, it is startling that Hopkins and Bridges should so easily have become friends, since one was a 'hearty', a member of the College crew at Corpus, apparently not much interested in aesthetic matters, while the other was a slight, faintly effeminate young man already marked out as a thoroughgoing Ritualist, with a background quite unlike Bridges's own. But, like many men with vaguely embarrassing aesthetic concerns encased in the bodies of athletes, Bridges was much attracted to Hopkins's scholarly but eel-quick intelligence and artistry, which gave him an example of how to handle his own poetic talents.

For his part, Hopkins's pleasure in knowing Bridges is perhaps easier to understand. As the writer of Bridges's obituary in *The Times* said, 'His extraordinary personal charm . . . lay in the transparent sincerity with which every word and motion expressed the whole of his character, its greatness and its scarcely less memorable littlenesses.' Behind the physical presence 'was always visible the strength of a towering and many-sided nature, at once aristocratic and unconventional, virile and affectionate, fearlessly inquiring and profoundly religious'.

A photograph of Bridges taken a decade after he first met Hopkins shows a face that one might expect of an athlete who had neglected to take care of himself: heavy, mustachioed, looking as if he were more interested in beer and bulldogs than in poetry. But the testimony of those who knew him is of someone who looked very different. Two of his friends, who were probably not unusually affected by good looks in other men, recorded that they could hardly take their eyes off him and thought him 'the possessor of the most *beautiful* face ever seen in a man'.[5] One of my own friends who knew him as an old man said that he had the singular elegance of appearance that comes from intelligence rather than genes, and that he resembled no one else so much as the elderly George Meredith.

It is no wonder that a man who was so responsive to physical beauty as Hopkins should have been attracted to Bridges. A few years before his death he indicated obliquely how much he admired the grace of both body and mind in his old friend when he was trying to reassure him about the quality of his poetry:

> I am not the best to tell you, being biassed by love, and yet I am too. I think then no one can admire beauty of the body more than I do, and it is of course a comfort to find beauty in a friend or a friend in beauty. But this kind of beauty is dangerous.

Greater than that, however, and without its attractive dangers was beauty of mind, genius, and still further beyond, 'beauty of character, the "handsome heart" '. And for Hopkins in 1879 it was true, as it had been in 1863, that Bridges's beauty of body, mind and character all came from the soul.[6]

When they met in the autumn of 1863, neither Hopkins nor Bridges could have guessed that each would become the other's closest confidant about poetry and Bridges was to remain Hopkins's most loved friend as an adult. It seemed almost ordained that what was probably Hopkins's last poem, on the subject of 'The fine delight that fathers thought', should be dedicated 'To R.B.'. Bridges, in addition to his own poetry and his position as Poet Laureate, was to be Hopkins's first editor, the man who saved his friend's poems and presented them to the world.

Another member of the Brotherhood, considerably more devoted to its functions than Bridges, was Edward William Urquhart, who was a curate at SS. Philip and James, Oxford, then a new High Church parish on the northern extremity of the old city limits. Neither an undergraduate nor yet quite a senior member of the BHT, he had taken his degree in 1861 and after a year or two in Bristol had returned to Oxford both as priest and as hanger-on to the University in that vague capacity of the recent graduate who is unable to sever his ties. He was still hoping to convert his first-class degree into a Fellowship, ideally at All Souls, although he failed in the elections of 1864. Hopkins presumably made his acquaintance through his friends in the Brotherhood, and they were soon intimate, but their friendship was a curious one, for Hopkins was often scornful of Urquhart, laughed at him, and was unkind about him to others. In spite of all this, Urquhart was much taken with the charm of Hopkins, and, according to his diary, on at least one occasion Hopkins was disturbed by his own sexual reaction to Urquhart. It was to him Hopkins confided when his own conversion to Roman Catholicism was imminent. Urquhart flirted briefly and not very seriously with taking Holy Orders in the Roman Catholic Church, but he finally married and remained an Anglican.

Not many records persist of Urquhart's personal life except a brief reference in the *Memoirs* of John Addington Symonds, who came to Balliol a year after Urquhart. At that time Symonds had not yet overcome his distaste for the attractions of other men, as he was to do so successfully a short time later. His acquaintance with Urquhart he described as 'unwholesome and relaxing. Urquhart, a Scotchman of perfervid type, developed a violent personal affection for me. He had High Church proclivities and ran after choristers.' In company with Urquhart and another friend, Symonds 'frequented antechapels and wasted my time over feverish sentimentalism. But when I perceived that Urquhart was making a dead set at me, I broke off the connection', in fear of being 'made love to'. Another friend took it upon himself to warn Symonds how easily he 'might be compromised by Urquhart's attention. There was no harm in the man. On the contrary, I have every reason to believe that he grew up a good clergyman and excellent husband. But he had acquired the unpopularity which attached to awkward excitable enthusiasts in a mixed society of young men.'[7]

Chorister-watching was among the most noticeable habits of the steamier High Church undergraduates, and the favourite spot for the activity was in Magdalen, where the choirboys were said to be unusually attractive. Sam Brooke, whose meticulous recording of the peccadilloes of his fellow undergraduates betrays his ambivalent attraction to the practices he most disapproved of, wrote earnestly of how 'radically unwise' it was to frequent Magdalen antechapel, even though it was an indulgence of some of his friends and 'others of pure intentions'. It would, he thought, be a 'good ideal to make men thus prove that they came to hear the music, not to see the choristers'.[8] It was presumably his own pianistic talents that made it permissible for him to haunt the chapel, with which he seemed to be so familiar; later he tried diligently, although unsuccessfully, to have his own brother entered as a chorister at Magdalen.

Hopkins, who wrote to his mother about a visit to Magdalen Chapel in 1864, said he 'had never seen it well before and thought it very grand'. We know from his 1865 diaries that he was attracted to choirboys and had to reproach himself for 'Looking at a chorister at Magdalen, and evil thoughts'.[9] That he ever became an *habitué* seems doubtful. Certainly, it would be completely unwarranted to judge him by the proclivities of Urquhart or other friends, but they do suggest the nature of his circle, one that did not encourage the growth of heterosexual responses.

The antiquarian and ecclesiastical interests of the Oxford Architectural Society, on whose remains the Brotherhood of the Holy Trinity was founded, point towards the yearning for historical continuity inherent in High Church thinking. On the face of it, there was a simple desire to show the immediate descent of the Anglican Church of the nineteenth century from its pre-Reformation forebear, the recognition that, if the Church of England were in truth part of the Catholic Church, it must share in the Apostolic Succession. But there was also a somewhat more complicated wish to show that it was Catholic *and* English, a Church that was national in character as well as international in descent. As either Anglican or Roman Catholic Hopkins was as far as possible from being ultramontane in his views; even when he finally accepted submission to Papal authority, he remained completely English, although in philosophy, poetry and language he liked to extend himself backwards in time to the place where there had been no incompatibility between things English and those Catholic. He was in the simplest sense patriotic, and occasionally he expressed himself in ways that today sound more jingoistic than perhaps they were. The strong sense of always being English, almost before he was Catholic, lay behind much of his alienation as a priest when his pastoral and academic duties were among the Irish of Oxford, Liverpool, or Dublin.

As undergraduates he and his friends roamed the Oxford countryside in search of the England of antiquity, so that the names of ancient villages and topographical features lie thickly scattered through his correspondence and journals: Cumnor, the medieval view of the city from Shotover, Sandford, the weir and Norman church at Iffley, the manor house at Wood Eaton, the huge old elm at Fyfield, Stanton Harcourt with its memories of Pope, or Bagley Wood. On the edge of the Berkshire Downs, a long day's walk from Oxford, stood Hendred House, since 1450 the home of the Eyston family, where the sanctuary lamp had not been extinguished for five centuries. Like generations of undergraduates, he loved the Thames above Oxford in the countryside where Arnold dreamed of the Scholar-Gipsy watching the men bathing near the Perch and the Trout, then quiet country inns near the ruins of Godstow nunnery and the tomb of the Fair Rosamond. One wonders whether two of Oxford's greatest poets of the century ever passed one another along the river banks, in what Hopkins called 'that landscape the charm of Oxford, green shouldering grey'.[10]

Hopkins was particularly attracted by the isolated little settlement of Binsey, hidden on the Berkshire side of the Thames (although actually in Oxfordshire), reached from Port Meadow through ponies and geese wandering free. The horses and cows pastured there still came down to the bank to stand in the water in summer, as they had for centuries, switching their tails at flies. Before the Reformation Binsey was a great pilgrimage centre, and the nearby lost village of Seacourt once had twenty-four hostelries to lodge the pilgrims to St Margaret's Church, standing half a mile from Binsey at the end of a causeway across the swampy meadows. Next to a decaying farmhouse, the minute twelfth-century church was almost drowned in greenery, and the surrounding fields were drowsy with grazing animals. It was hard to believe that he was no more than two miles from the bells, the throng and hum of modern Oxford, whose towers were easily visible from the river banks.

In the medieval glass in the church was a figure of St Margaret, to whom St Frideswide, patron saint of Oxford, prayed for the cure of Agar, who had pursued her and been struck blind for his lust. In answer to her prayers a well sprang forth, and its waters healed Agar. When Hopkins first went there, the trickle of water from the well was blocked up, but the legend was easy to imagine in that setting. It combined many things that Hopkins held dear: a deep and almost inborn love of water; his sense of the simple, literal truth of miracles, which never left him; deep devotion to chastity; an identity with distant English history; perhaps most of all his feeling of immediacy with the landscape.

Along the river stood a long line of aspens, dense and quivering, the living symbol of all that Binsey stood for, a 'sweet especial scene', timelessly evoking the English countryside before it was soiled by the Industrial Revolution. As Hopkins walked, he was constantly reflecting upon what he saw, trying not only to imprint it on his vision but to discover what was individual about it, to capture its essence as well as its appearance. On the Thames, near Binsey, he pondered over the weir at the junction with a canal. It is significant that the term he used for weir was 'lasher', a country word that according to the *O.E.D.* means 'the body of water that lashes or rushes over an opening in a barrier or weir; hence, the opening'. The nearer he could get to the basic meaning of a word, stripped of modern accretions and sophistications, the nearer he was to primitive, almost prehistoric thought. 'Lasher from a canal at Wolvercote', he wrote in his diary:

> The water running down the lasher violently swells in a massy wave against the opposite bank, which, to resist its force, is defended by a piece of brick wall. The shape of wave of course bossy, smooth and globy. Full of bubble and air, very liquid. – For the rest of the lasher, all except the shoulder where it first sweeps over it is covered with a kind of silver links. Running like a wind element at the shoulder.[11]

There is a kind of Ruskinian scrupulosity and accuracy of external observation of the lasher here, but beyond that is an attempt to convey at the same time the sense of being within it, of being both the observed and the observer. Such words as swells, resist, defended, shoulder, running, all invoke an anthropomorphic force projecting the reader into the very sensation of being part of the weir itself. This is a blood relative of the immediacy that most readers feel in his poetry.

Hopkins's notes on his walks read as if he were attempting to pack all nature into words. But he had a modesty about his observation, for he did not try to change nature or trim it to the size of his comprehension, only to find its form and shape, both internal and external. It is easy to understand how he wanted to be a graphic artist, then found the Pre-Raphaelite detail of his drawings inadequate because they finally remained on the surface of vision, rather than penetrating into an imaginative interior understanding of the objects he was recording.*

Just as Hopkins tried to insinuate himself into the interior of experience, to inhabit it, so he constantly wanted to go beyond the barrier of mere communication in language to discover from what impulses the language itself sprang. In his undergraduate years he made up innumerable lists of words linked by meaning and sound (more often by consonants than by vowels); he was clearly working on the notion that sound and meaning are yoked by a psychological association considerably deeper than mere onomatopoeia or alliteration, and that perhaps they are also linked by the visual appearance of the words on the page.

> *Crook, crank, kranke, crick, cranky.* Original meaning crooked, not straight or right, wrong, awry. A crank in England is a piece of mechanism which turns a wheel or shaft at one end, at the other receiving a rectilinear force. Knife-grinders, velocipedes, steam-engines etc have them. *Crick* in the neck is when some muscle, tendon or something of that sort in the neck is twisted or goes wrong in some way. . . . *Cranky*, provincial, out of sorts, wrong. The original meaning being *crooked*, cf. *curvus* and for derivation see under *horn*.[12]

In his diary he made a small drawing of a wheel and crank to illustrate his meaning. His love of getting back to the origins of words was less an archaeological exercise than a real attempt to scrape clean the bones of language and restore its purity, which seems in retrospect to have a good deal to do with his attempt to go back in religion to the period when modern habits of thought had not contaminated it.

* Probably the most famous use of 'lasher' in English poetry is the description in 'The Scholar-Gipsy' of 'Men who through those wide fields of breezy grass . . . / To bathe in the abandoned lasher pass.' The poem is set in the same countryside, perhaps remembering the very weir 'above Godstow Bridge' of which Hopkins wrote. We know that Hopkins went to Matthew Arnold's lectures, and the use of the same dialect word in the same setting suggests that he also knew Arnold's celebration of the Thames countryside in his 1853 poem.

To readers who know his later poetry, such lists seem recognizable origins of the poems, but, curiously, aside from fairly conventional alliteration, his linguistic speculation and his verse remained nearly separate for a long time. This meditation on 'crook' seems to have been written shortly after his arrival in Oxford in the Michaelmas term 1863, but it was to be some years before his speculative attitude to language found its way into his poetry.

Hopkins's diaries – notebooks is perhaps more accurate – were kept in an unsystematic fashion, but to the modern reader they are all the more valuable because of their startling juxtaposition of discrete orders of experience. His jottings are like a voluminous portmanteau into which he packs everything that catches his interest, even momentarily. On his walks he made notes on sunsets or blown clouds as if preparing to paint them when he returned to his rooms; a snake gliding in loops through a hedge; squirrels on a branch; or a precise little drawing of a 'dead (water-?) rat floating down Isis. The head was downward, hind legs on surface, thus–'.[13] The cost of his haircut is there, sketches of church architecture, and of course notes for poems and the first drafts of the poetry he composed as an undergraduate.

In the midst of the informal matter of the diary there are entries that seem to have been written down after he returned to his Balliol desk or to his family home in Hampstead, where the passages take on the air of set pieces, as in an early version of his consideration of the limitations of the 'Parnassian' style, that level of high competence that never quite touches the inspired:

> Poetry at Oxford.
> It is a happy thing that there is no royal road to poetry. The world should know by this time that one cannot reach Parnassus except by flying thither. Yet from time to time more men go up and either perish in its gullies fluttering *excelsior* flags or else come down again with full folios and blank countenances. Yet the old fallacy keeps its ground.[14]

Such entries seem mannered and self-conscious, but their tone is noticeable chiefly because they are set against the informality of the rest of the diary; in essence, however, they are really a kind of stretching of his wings as the young writer works his way towards a more public style.

There is self-consciousness of another sort in the diaries, too, as Hopkins seems to be searching for his own identity. Delightfully, however, he damps down his own seriousness, as in the little drawing he made in the summer of 1864 of 'Gerard Hopkins, reflected in a lake Aug. 14'. Feet on the gunwale of a boat, round hat clapped firmly on his head, he peers between his outspread knees at his own image in the water of the lake, its outline clear enough but his face and expression left mysteriously shadowy (see Plate 5b). It is obviously connected to the kind of control he maintained over his features, so that photographs of him seldom hint at what is going on beneath a taut, perhaps deliberately unexpressive face.

On another, more overtly joking occasion, he felt that sudden vertiginous dislocation of self from name that most of us have experienced, and half seriously he tried on another name for size:

> Tuncks is a good name.
> Gerard Manley Tuncks. Pook Tuncks.[15]

If the content of the diaries is in any way a fair guide to Hopkins's mind, it is pleasant to see how frequently humour, wit or simple good nature surfaced in his notes. His reflections on language often led to the kind of play with sound and meaning that he was familiar with in the family addiction to punning: 'Fast days I have found slow days; you do not know how long short commons will last.'

Occasionally, in the course of an ostensibly comic passage, the diary entries become unexpectedly stinging, often at the expense of his family, as if the habit of punning and teasing were inextricable from carefully buried familial resentment that Hopkins could express only by pretending to joke. It is, for example, impossible to miss the hostility to his father latent in the unfinished draft of a poem recorded in the diary, which he called 'By Mrs. Hopley', scarcely bothering to conceal the combination of Manley and Hopkins in the name:

> He's wedded to his theory, they say.
> If that were true, it could not live a day.

> And did he on the children of his brains
> Bestow but half the . . . pains
> The children of his loins receive instead
> There would not be a whole place in his head.

An even more bitter reference to Mr Hopkins's dominance hides in the words of Mrs Hopley 'On seeing her children say Goodnight to their father':

> Bid your Papa Goodnight. Sweet exhibition!
> They kiss the rod with filial submission.[16]

In judging the apparent harshness about his father, and also what sometimes seems condescension to, almost dislike of, his brothers in his journals, the reader should remember that Hopkins probably never quite recognized what he was revealing of his feelings and certainly never intended his squibs for the eyes of others.

With the exception of a brief period, chiefly ten months in 1865, when he specified what seemed to him trangressions requiring confession, Hopkins seldom recorded excessively intimate matters in his diary. It is, nonetheless, deeply personal because its focus is so uninterruptedly on his own life, with few reflections on public affairs of any kind. Indeed, there is seldom even any mention there of birthdays, examinations, illnesses, family gatherings, social occasions, the end of academic terms, or the many other observations of persons or relationships that usually mark the passing of a life; such matters as dates or days of the week are relatively infrequent, as if the entries of the diary were one unending cocoon of personal experience of which the significance was purely internal.

His diaries and journals served Hopkins as storehouses for ideas, phrases, even words, that had taken his fancy, to be tucked away there to mature until he needed them. In 1864, for example, he jotted down two lines notable for their wording:

> A star most spiritual, principal, preeminent
> Of all the golden press.[17]

Twenty years later the most striking part of the passage re-emerged in 'Spelt from Sibyl's Leaves' with 'earliest stars, earlstars, stars principal'.

He also used the diary in trial flights for ideas ripened only considerably later. The passage previously quoted on the Parnassian style gradually evolved during the course of 1864 from the initial journal entries in the spring to an extended letter to Baillie that in turn became the basis of a paper he prepared for the College essay society the following autumn.

His consideration of the Parnassian has become one of Hopkins's most famous contributions to literary criticism, but it might equally well be viewed as a formulation of his own poetic aspirations. It attempts to distinguish between the 'first and highest' form of 'poetry proper, the language of inspiration', and that written by great poets when inspiration has failed them although their habitual level of high competence remains. Typically, he begins his letter on the subject by telling Baillie that a horrible thing has happened to him: he has 'begun to *doubt* Tennyson'. He then proceeds to a consideration of the difference between true poetry and Parnassian in 'Enoch Arden', saying that the latter is the work of a poet who is relying on his learned habits, habits still far above the common level of poets, even when unguided by inspiration.

In reading Hopkins on the subject, one is always aware that he is a poet not a critic, for he is clearly far less interested in orderly classification than in the inner state of compulsion that a great poet feels in maintaining a high level of emotional intensity and technical energy, rather than relying upon a previously achieved manner. It reads like an admonishment to himself instead of a clarification for Baillie or the reader: '. . . it is a mark of Parnassian that one could conceive oneself writing it if one were the poet'.[18]

Like any good Romantic, Hopkins saw that what Wordsworth had called poetic diction was not enough, and that its use 'is no more necessarily to be uttering poetry than striking the keys of piano is playing a tune'. He felt that the greatest offenders in the Parnassian were Pope and his school, and that it was 'common in professedly descriptive pieces. Much of it in *Paradise Lost* and *Regained*. Nearly all *The Faery Queen*'. Hopkins never quite managed to hit it off poetically with Spenser; in spite of a limited admiration for the older poet, he counted 'the lost books of the Faery Queen' among the fortunate losses of literature.[19] The judgement shows us considerably more about him than about Spenser.

Hopkins had a sound distrust of criticism, although he turned his hand to it on many occasions. Much of what he wrote was healthily egocentric, reflecting what he thought his habit should be, rather than being true theory about the work of others. 'The most inveterate fault of critics', he wrote to Baillie, 'is the tendency to cramp and hedge in by rules the free movements of genius, so that I should say . . . the first requisite for a critic is liberality, and the second liberality, and the third, liberality.'[20] And since his own practice was still more personal than his theory, it is dangerous even now for other critics to approach his poetry with rigid criteria if they hope ever to understand it.

As an undergraduate Hopkins progressed steadily in his confidence in his own poetry. In the spring of 1864 he felt so secure that he considered competing for the Newdigate Prize, the most important award for undergraduate poetry at Oxford. Whether he actually submitted a poem is not clear, since the University Archives understandably keep records of successful candidates only, but his diary shows that he went to the trouble of securing all the detailed information he would need for submission. The prescribed subject was 'The Three Hundredth Anniversary of the Birth of Shakespeare', with no limitations on the manner of treatment. If Hopkins attempted a poem on the subject, it has since disappeared, with not so much as a fragment embedded in another poem. The prize was won that spring by W.J. Courthope of New College, with a dutiful work that perhaps depended too much on 'methought'.* What is most intriguing about the competition is

---

*As an undergraduate Courthope had migrated to New College from Corpus Christi, where he probably knew Bridges. His somewhat perspiring prize poem concludes with lines that indicate the sort of pastiche he had cobbled up from Shakespeare, certainly with a nod to Tennyson and perhaps one in the direction of Keats:

> . . . Down the dells is borne
> Departing music, like the beetle's horn;
> And lamps of Elfland fade, and fade, and seem
> A Winter's Tale, or a Midsummer Dream.

that one of the judges was the Professor of Poetry, Matthew Arnold. One would give a great deal to know what he may have made of Hopkins's work. Hopkins was very much aware of Arnold and attended his lectures in a dreary semi-basement room in the Taylor Institution, when all the rest of the younger members of the University were playing games in the golden springtime. Some of his diary notes appear to reflect the older poet's vocabulary, particularly that in 'The Scholar-Gipsy', but we do not know for certain that he read any of Arnold's poetry as an undergraduate, however probable it seems. 'Much that he says is worth attention,' he wrote of one of Arnold's essays, 'but, as is so often the case, in censuring bad taste he falls into two flagrant pieces of bad taste himself.'[21]

One poetic meeting about which there is no doubt took place in July 1864 at a grand literary party at the London home of his Balliol friend Frederick Gurney. Hopkins wrote to Baillie of being introduced to Christina Rossetti and her mother, as well as to the Scottish poet and novelist George MacDonald, Holman Hunt and – somewhat surprisingly – Jenny Lind. His diary indicates that among the other guests were the Brownings, Dante Rossetti, and R.W. Dixon, whom he had not seen since Highgate.

It was heady company for an undergraduate with poetic ambitions, and perhaps as a result of the meeting he was preoccupied with the Pre-Raphaelites all that summer, reading their poetry and going to see their pictures. He was briefly inspired to tell Baillie, 'I have now a more rational hope than before of doing something – in poetry and painting.'[22]

Because of this brief attempt to unite his skills in the two arts,

---

He was to become a literary historian of modest reputation who also published poetry from time to time, occasionally comic but more often pastoral with a vaguely Shakespearean flavour. In 1895 he became a successor to Arnold as Professor of Poetry at Oxford.

The pedestrian subject announced for the competition in 1864 was typical of those during the decade; the preceding year the topic had been 'Coal-Miners' and in 1865 the announced subject was 'Mexico'. Both produced poems of the quality one might expect. In 1860 John Addington Symonds had won the prize with his poem 'The Escorial', in the year that Hopkins won the school prize at Highgate writing on the same subject; one suspects that the school had taken its lead from Oxford.

Hopkins has often been compared to the Pre-Raphaelites or claimed as one of their disciples. He was certainly interested in the unity of the arts, and his early poems and drawings have what might be roughly described as Pre-Raphaelite attention to literal accuracy in the phenomenal world, but he soon gave up serious application to drawing, and his poetry displays a kinetic energy that seems to have little to do with the static quality that was so distinctive in the work of the Pre-Raphaelites in both media. There is also some indication that he was worried about being too stimulated sexually if he were to paint from live models.

He was attracted to Christina Rossetti's poetry,. particularly when it intersected with his own ecclesiastical preoccupations in such poems as 'Heaven-Haven', 'The Habit of Perfection', and 'A Voice from the World', which he claimed was 'An Answer to Miss Rossetti's *Convent Threshold*'. Several years later, he asked his mother to remember him to Miss Rossetti; when he heard that she was 'thrown rather into the shade by her brother', he said that 'for pathos and pure beauty of art I do not think he is her equal: in fact the simple beauty of her work cannot be matched'.[23] With the exception of her works, however, the religious manifestations of the Pre-Raphaelite circle were not likely for long to attract Hopkins, who was too shrewd and too honestly devout not to see through the pasteboard ecclesiastical trappings of most of the group.

The cloistered pattern of Hopkins's later life meant that he was thrown into contact with few other important poets. Besides those at the Gurneys', he met Swinburne and Yeats briefly; he knew R.W. Dixon and Coventry Patmore through a considerable correspondence, and he was of course a close friend of Bridges, even if they seldom saw one another and had to keep up their intimacy through the post. The truth is, however, that there were very few occasions after Oxford on which he had a chance to talk about poetry with an equal or even with a 'Parnassian', and one can hardly help feeling that his artistic insulation accounts in part for both the strangeness of his poetry and its originality.

In the spring of 1864 much of Hopkins's time when he was not studying was taken up with undergraduate societies. With Sam Brooke of Corpus he helped organize an essay group devoted to conservative principles in the Church; the original impetus had begun with Brooke, who attended a meeting of the Old Mortality Society, at which Walter Pater read a paper denying the possibility of a future existence and advocating instead of piety a doctrine of 'self-culture'. It was, said Brooke, 'one of the most thoroughly infidel productions it has ever been our pain to listen to'. A week later the Old Mortality met again and resumed discussion of the subject; a paper attempted to 'shew the absurdity' of Pater's beliefs, but 'the sight of the Old Mortality', according to Brooke, 'is not the sight of ordinary beings and consequently its members failed to appreciate what should have been thoroughly convincing'.[24] In disgust that the society should be so easily persuaded to error, Brooke resigned his membership.

To counteract the dangerous tendencies of Pater and the Old Mortality, Brooke at once revived the idea of the essay society he had been thinking of several months before. Hopkins was not on Brooke's initial list of possible members, but he was so enthusiastic when invited to join that he became one of Brooke's most useful helpers. Together they approached Liddon to become a senior member, and he took up the idea with characteristic energy; before the month was out, he was speaking of it as his own brainchild. Some of the names suggested were the Churchman's Essay Society, the Conservative Society, the Catholic Essay Society, then several others that one or other of the group found unsuitable until at last they agreed upon the Hexameron Society for the unassailable reason that 'there will be 6 meetings in each term'. Hopkins adopted the cause with surprising energy, writing papers, delivering them to the Society, and frequently entertaining the group in his Balliol rooms. It was ironic that he should devote so much time to a group originally intended to nullify the teachings of a man who was to become both his tutor and his friend.

The Hexameron was a University-wide society, but Hopkins also threw himself into the affairs of the Friends in Council, a debating society that was almost exclusively Balliol in membership and hence considerably less Catholic in orientation. He was less at home in debate than in composition, but he was a useful member of the FIC, as the group was usually known, and in April 1864 he was elected secretary.

On the surface Hopkins seemed to be cultivating the debonair manner of a second-year man who spent most of his time on undergraduate activities and little on his studies, but the negligence was no more than a façade. The Master's note on his work for the spring of 1864 was only 'satisfactory', but by the autumn of that year it had become 'Extremely satisfactory', presumbaly as a result of hard work over the Long Vacation. Classical Honour Moderations hung over his head all that summer as still another set of examinations, to be taken when he returned to Oxford in the autumn, and to Baillie he complained semi-jokingly that 'life is a preparation for Mods'.

At the beginning of August he went for a holiday in Wales with two other undergraduates, his friend Hardy and Edward Bond, a St John's man whose parents knew the Hopkins family. In spite of a difference in college and a complete unlikeness in their religious views, Bond and Hopkins were intimate with each other and particularly liked to travel together. Hopkins trusted what he thought of as Bond's severe critical judgement about his poetry, and he confided to him many of his religious problems. In Wales the three young men lodged in Maentwrog at the house of a Miss Roberts, in company with 'four Miss Storys staying in the house, girls from Reading. This is a great advantage – but not to reading.'[25] Their fellow lodgers are worth mentioning because this is one of the few occasions on which Hopkins seems to have been even pallidly interested in the opposite sex.

To get to Maentwrog Hopkins took the train to Llangollen, then walked most of the fifty-odd remaining miles. 'I have had adventures,' he told Baillie:

> I was lost in storms of rain on the mountains between Bala and Ffestiniog. It really happened what is related in novels and allegories, 'the dry beds of the morning were now turned into the channels of swollen torrents', etc. At last a river ran across the road and cut me off entirely. I took refuge in a shepherd's hut and slept amongst the Corinthians. They, I mean the shepherd and family, gorged me with eggs and bacon and oaten cake and curds and whey. Thus I did what old gentlemen tell you with a sort of selfish satisfaction that you must learn to do,

ROUGHED IT;

I believe it means irritating the skin on sharp-textured
blankets. These old gentlemen have always had to do it when
they were your age.

Something of Hopkins's innate fastidiousness shows in a letter to
Baillie about the Welsh holiday, when he confessed that he had 'a
hard time of it to resist contamination from the bawdy jokes and
allusions of Bond and Hardy'. He then obliterated more than four
lines of his letter and pasted a piece of paper over the cancelled text,
which originally said, 'Hardy is always talking of debauching too,
well-dressed girls but when he has introduced himself to them oh
then he is very, very sick.'[26]

When he left Wales Hopkins divided his time before the beginning of Oxford term, half with his grandparents in Croydon, half
with his parents in Hampstead, and he likewise spent part of his
working days in reading for Moderations and part in the composition of poetry. He made good use of his hours, but his letters give
the impression of a man marking time rather than working out of
love of the task. That spring he had written airily, rather like a
character in a second-rate Wilde play:

> Be it ever so homely
> There's no place like home for losing what you have and
> not getting what you want. I always find home so uncivilized;
> they seem never to be acquainted with the ordinary luxuries or
> necessaries.[27]

His work paid off, however, and in December his name was among
those of the three Balliol men who won first-class honours in
Moderations. 'I have had many letters of congratulation', he wrote,
'and have fallen into that state which comes when you have thought
or heard a great deal about something that has happened to you –
that you make an effort to think what the original cause of all the
consequences was.'[28]

There were other serious matters besides examinations on which
his thoughts were running, and though he mentioned them seldom
in either his journals or his letters, they were even more absorbing

to him. It would always have been accurate to describe him as Catholic in outlook, but in 1864 we find the first hints of more than random considerations of his own compatibility with Roman Catholicism, largely prompted by his reading in Savonarola, who had became a hero to him.

Curiously enough, Savonarola engaged the attention of many Victorians who were innocently pleased to find in fifteenth-century Florence an example of the kind of Puritan they thought was known only to Protestantism in their own century. For Hopkins the attraction was more complex, since he seems to have recognized a good many of his own problems in the person of the Florentine Dominican, who, like himself, was both deeply attracted to poetry and painting and repelled by the recognition of how dangerous the arts could be to his own soul.

It is almost a truism that only the deeply passionate make good ascetics, a qualification which Hopkins amply fulfilled. He was both in love with the phenomenal world and aflame with fear of it. If the poetry he wrote at all his odd moments in the summer of 1864 was distracting from his studies, how much more it detracted from his spiritual growth. And painting was still more disturbing. 'You know I once wanted to be a painter,' he wrote some four years later, in a statement that goes far towards establishing a link between his fears of his own sexuality and his distrust of physical beauty in art. 'But even if I could I wd. not I think, now, for the fact is that the higher and more attractive parts of the art put a strain upon the passions which I shd. think it unsafe to encounter.'[29] It was a Victorian cliché that the nude was the highest (and presumably the most attractive) subject in painting, and that idea seems to lie unrecognized behind the statement, covertly indicating to him the sinister temptation of pictorial art. His repressiveness about physical beauty was surely connected with his painful awareness of his own sexual nature, which had constantly to be doused with cold water, disciplined, refined almost out of existence.

Although poetry had its own dangers, it was not necessarily an occasion for sin, and before he became a priest he indicated that religious verse would not be inconsistent with his vocation. One would like to think that he was also obeying a quiet inner artistic sensitivity warning him that his talents lay in poetry not painting.

One of the most attractive aspects of Hopkins's overworked moral consciousness is that in all his renunciations he was seldom motivated to legislate for others. A lesser man would have been chiefly concerned with the behaviour of those he saw around him, but Hopkins was too blazingly honest, too little hypocritical, to think that moral reform began elsewhere. His poems are strewn with agonies of remorse over his own nature, seldom with any censoriousness of others. Certainly, in spite of his awareness of how easily he might be carried away by emotion, he was, as has been said of Savonarola, no foe to either art or learning.

In early January 1865, just before the end of the Christmas vacation, Hopkins caught a bad cold while still at home in Hampstead. During his recovery in bed, he told Urquhart, 'I finished *Romola* and made myself wretched over the fall of Savonarola.' Before reading George Eliot's novel, he had been familiar with the first volume of Villari's *History* of Savonarola's life and A.F. Rio's *De l'Art Chrétien*, but *Romola* provided an immediacy that the other, more factual works failed to give him. 'I must tell you he is the only person in history (except perhaps Origen) about whom I have a real feeling, and I feel such an enthusiasm about Savonarola that I can conceive what it must have been to have been of his followers. I feel this the more because he was followed by the painters, architects and other artists of his day, and is the prophet of Christian art, and it is easy to imagine oneself a painter of his following.'

It was as much Savonarola's Catholicism as either his attitudes to art or his asceticism that attracted Hopkins. 'How strangely different is the fate of two reformers, Savonarola and Luther! The one martyred in the Church, the other successful and the admired author of world-wide heresy in schism.' At first he 'made an effort not to accept' *Romola* because it 'is a pagan book', but he finally capitulated and thought it 'a great book'. Neither George Eliot nor Savonarola probably did much to change Hopkins's mind on the relations between art and religion, but he did recognize in them what he was already considering.[30]

On an emotional level, it was more important that his reading predisposed him to sympathy with another young admirer of Savonarola whom he met shortly after he returned to Oxford at the beginning of 1865. Either as a result of his cold or, more probably, because he was suffering from a natural listlessness after the success of his First in Moderations, he had been complaining of having little on which he had to work, 'unless it be, as it is, hard work to answer my flood of correspondence'.[31] He was in the mood of ready receptivity for a wholly absorbing addition to his life, one which had the advantage of fitting into his own growing interest in Roman Catholicism.

CHAPTER V

DIGBY DOLBEN
1865

In February 1865 Bridges had a guest at Corpus, a distant cousin named Digby Mackworth Dolben, who had just turned seventeen. He had left Eton at Christmas and was eager to come up to the University the following autumn, if possible to his father's old college, Balliol. Bridges introduced him to Hopkins, no doubt thinking that he could help Dolben with getting into Balliol, or at least familiarize him with it. Their meeting was, quite simply, the most momentous emotional event of Hopkins's undergraduate years, probably of his entire life. Two and a half years before this, Hopkins had written resolutely of his disappointment over Alexander Strachey, 'Perhaps in my next friendship I may be wiser.' Any intention of investing his emotions more prudently deserted him when he met Dolben.

A century after his death it is difficult to reconstruct a balanced picture of Dolben, for portraits and photographs, letters, even the enchanted memories of friends, seldom resurrect the compulsion that some golden young men exert over their intimates, particularly if, like Arthur Hallam or Rupert Brooke or Digby Dolben, they die in youth and beauty. The cold judgement of posterity necessarily leaves out much of their charm and may assess moral or intellectual character accurately enough without accounting for their magnetism. When, in his seventh decade, Bridges came to write about his cousin and his poetry, he could remember wryly how maddening, even silly, Digby had been, but in his youth he seems to have been little more proof against his attraction than other friends were, for Dolben was intelligent, funny, and singularly sweet-natured. Henry James, although repelled by Dolben's religiosity, was so bouleversé by Bridges's account of his 'wondrous young' cousin that he lapsed into ardent Jamesian inversion in recording his enthusiasm: 'Extraordinarily interesting I think the young genius himself, by virtue of his rare special gift, and even though the particular preoccupations out of which it flowers, their whole note and aspect, have in them for me something positively antipathetic.' The memory of the young poet, he wrote, 'touches and charms the imagination'.[1]

Like most of Hopkins's Oxford acquaintances, Dolben was well connected in county society and the minor aristocracy of generals, baronets and divines with whom his family was liberally provided, but his connections meant little to him. His father, whose name was originally Mackworth, was the son of a well-to-do baronet whose family fortunes came from Wales; he had married a remote cousin, a Miss Dolben (they were both descended from the fifth Lord Digby), co-heiress to Finedon Hall in Northamptonshire, where her family had lived for centuries, and after their marriage he annexed his bride's name and fortune to his own. Mr Mackworth Dolben then settled down to country life, indulging his taste for the revival of medievalism that seems to have been a family trait. For a quarter of a century he continued to add to the old house until the original was swallowed in what has been called a 'Gothic-cum-Tudor fantasy', a picturesque welter of gables and towers, all with his intertwined initials conspicuously displayed. Part of his energy went into the enhancement of the extensive park that had been designed by Humphry Repton in the previous century. In the midst of Repton's carefully Romantic lake, undulating slopes, and ancient avenues of trees approaching the house on all four sides, he planted beautiful but fussy geometric flower gardens that became famous all over England. Since Mr Dolben was not a hunting man, he passed in Northamptonshire for a scholar.

On his first visit to Finedon, Bridges was clearly overwhelmed by Digby's mother, 'a fine example of one of the best types of culture, the indigenous grace of our country-houses, a nature whose indescribable ease and compelling charm overrule all contrarieties, and reconcile all differences . . . such a paramount harmony of the feminine qualities as makes men think women their superiors'.[2] Bridges obviously intended his description to be complimentary, but somehow a whiff of the inhuman comes willy-nilly through the polysyllabics. Perhaps it is the reference to her ability to 'overrule all contrarieties', for Mrs Dolben, despite the grace and charm, was something of a gorgon, implacably petrifying anyone who disagreed with what she knew to be right. Above all, she knew that the Almighty had from the beginning intended His earthly agency to be the Evangelical branch of the Church of England, relentlessly devoted to the extirpation of either High Church practices or Romish leanings. In politics her innate conservatism led her to keep Finedon from passing at her death to the cousin who normally 'would have inherited the manor and estates, but whilst at Oxford he became a Liberal and Mrs. Mackworth-Dolben had disinherited him as a matter of principle'.[3]

In the nineteenth century an interest in Gothic buildings was often allied to a tendency towards Ritualism or Rome, but not in Mr Dolben's case, for he was as devotedly Evangelical as his wife, and between them they waged war for decades on the Rector of Finedon (still another cousin) for what seemed to them his extreme Roman inclinations.

In spite of the rigour of his beliefs, Mr Dolben was far more indulgent than his wife to their only daughter and three sons, of whom Digby was the youngest. Perhaps because of that very lenience, the boy had become a rebel against most of what his father held dear, not least the rigidity of his family background, which was reflected in his own jaw-breaking full name, Digby Augustus Stewart Mackworth Dolben. He disliked using any part of it, and said he was sure he would die young, since 'Digby' had always been an unlucky name in the family.

But besides the obsession with pedigree, there was an improbable strain of the poetic in his family, for among his relatives were three poets of distinction: Winthrop Mackworth Praed, Arthur Hugh Clough, and Bridges.

Digby's first school was at Cheam, where the religious instruction was of the same Evangelical complexion as that he had received at Finedon. It was described by one of Digby's contemporaries as 'a very popular and comfortable school . . . ultra-Protestant; the boys are encouraged to hold public prayer meetings in the schoolroom, and Catholic truths (e.g. to my knowledge Baptismal doctrines) are flatly denied'.[4] Apparently the school failed in its intended effect, for by the time he arrived at Eton in 1862, Digby was already wholly committed to Ritualism, 'Catholicism' (whether Roman or Anglican), and the insistence on thrusting his own religious beliefs down the throats of those around him. None of this promised well in the house that had been chosen for him because of the 'staunch Protestant bias' of the scholarly cleric in charge of it.

Bridges, who was three years his senior, had never met his young cousin before he arrived as a new boy in the house, where Bridges was captain: 'I enrolled Dolben among my fags, and looked after him.' Dolben was tall for his age, slight, pale, and delicate in appearance; 'though his face was thoughtful and his features intellectual, he would not at that time have been thought good-looking'. He was abstracted in manner, short-sighted (which gave him an expression commonly interpreted as dreaminess), 'a boy who evidently needed both protection and sympathy'. Bridges was severe in his judgement of his looks, for the pictures from his Eton days show him as handsome. His short sight kept him from playing games or even from boating, but he was fond of riding and of open-air bathing, as Hopkins was. Despite the differences in their ages and temperaments, Bridges and Dolben became close friends immediately, united by their love of poetry and their position as two of the dozen or so boys in the school who thought of themselves as High Church in outlook. At this time both Bridges and Dolben intended to become priests; Bridges's enthusiasm for ordination was to wane considerably at Oxford. Dolben's religious enthusiasm was so excessive that it is tempting to believe that Bridges's subsequent lapse from Christian orthodoxy was in part a reaction against his cousin's overwrought devotions.

Dolben's poems often remind the reader of Crashaw in their combination of fulsome religiosity and an improbable sincerity that nearly keeps the overblown imagery from being meretricious. He loved Tennyson, the Brownings, and the prose of Ruskin, but above all, the poetry of Frederick Faber, 'a Romanized clergyman' whose verses excited Bridges's disgust. Dolben was not much interested in Shakespeare, and 'Milton was to Digby as Luther to a papist.'

His poetry was an accurate reflection of his life. At Eton he ostentatiously crossed himself at meals, genuflected in chapel, and carefully left 'Romish Popish and Idolatrous books' about the school in the expectation of their being discovered. At 'Sunday-questions', when the boys were allowed considerable freedom in discussion, he delighted in airing his medieval convictions and in asking awkward questions about dogma in order to provoke the masters. Worse still, at every opportunity he would steal off to Ascot to the Anglican priory run by Miss Sellon of the Society of the Holy Trinity, to Beaumont College at Old Windsor, acquired by the Jesuits a few years before, or to the House of Mercy at Clewer for confessions to Father Carter, who was in charge of the 'full-fledged high-church establishment'.

Bridges gives the distinct impression that ritual and a devotion to haberdashery rather than doctrine attracted Dolben, who was equally comfortable in Anglo-Catholic and Roman Catholic churches, so long as they were filled with candles and hazy with incense. He prided himself on his knowledge of vestments and could hardly curb his enthusiasm for the revived Ritualist practice of wearing chasubles in the Anglican Communion service. By the time he wrote about Dolben, Bridges felt little sympathy with any form of Catholicism, which may have increased his asperity about Dolben's devotions. Even Henry James, in the midst of his glowing appreciation of the young poet, admitted that 'the so precocious and direct avidity for all the paraphernalia of a complicated ecclesiasticism' suggested 'a kind of implication of the insincere and the merely imitational, the cheaply "romantic"'.[5] There is no proof that Dolben's religious opinions were shallow, but the speed with which he changed them suggests that at best they were inconstant. Frequently he sounds as if he had been reading too many novels about Ritualism and was unable to decide on which of their heroes to model himself.

Dolben was clearly the kind of boy who most exasperates his elders, but his contemporaries found him delightful because he had 'plenty of humour and wit, and was possessed with a spirit of mischief as wanton as Shelley's'.

Fortunately, cheerfulness was always breaking in on Dolben's excesses. Once he and some other boys decided to have a retreat at Eton; as V.S.S. Coles remembered, 'We had come to know that there was such a thing as a "Retreat" though how to set about it rather puzzled us. We had reduced our food, and had settled down to devotions consisting eminently of prayers for the soul of K. Henry VI, but "after four" our constancy broke down, and . . . some one was sent for ices.'

When he was not quite sixteen Dolben met the Revd Joseph Leycester Lyne, better known today as 'Father Ignatius' of Llanthony, where he established an Anglican Benedictine community. In spite of his self-conferred priest's orders, Lyne had been unable to have them confirmed in the Church of England, as his bishop sensibly feared that he might not be a proper example to most parishes; late in life he did receive rather obscure orders 'from a Bishop who derived his consecration from some Eastern source'. In January 1864 Dolben wrote to Bridges with joy about Lyne, 'I am to have an introduction to Brother Ignatius of Claydon!!!'

Within a month Dolben had become a member of 'the iij Order' of Lyne's English Benedictines, telling Bridges that he was now called 'Br Dominic O.S.B.iij, under which name you are *not* to direct to me'. For the rest of 1864 he signed his letters with his new name, including with them tracts about the Benedictines with exhortations to Bridges to join them at once. Bridges, who knew Lyne only 'by a *carte de visite* portrait with extravagant tonsure and ostentatious crucifix', refused to take the matter seriously and said he supposed Lyne was delighted to have caught a live Etonian. When he gave in so far as to address a letter to Brother Dominic, Dolben reverted at once to his normal signature, primly reminding Bridges not to use that style: 'It is only Brothers O.S.B. who should do so.'

Best of all, from Dolben's point of view, was that he felt his monastic vows entitled him to a monk's habit, which he immediately procured, correct in every detail, and took with him when he left Eton, changing into it when safe from school supervision and removing his shoes and stockings. He particularly liked the reactions of rural people on seeing a barefoot sixteen-year-old monk in full monastic garb. In the country he would put on his habit at night, slip out of a window, and prowl the countryside on chilly feet in the hope of meeting passers-by. To suit his clothing, he changed his handwriting into an imitation of the script of

Savonarola, whose works he had been reading, like Hopkins at Oxford, and for whom he had conceived a headlong admiration.

Much of the early poetry he wrote was poor stuff, according to his cousin, who had seen most of it at Eton, but the poems written after he was eighteen, Bridges believed, 'will compare with, if they do not as I believe excel, anything that was ever written by an English poet at his age'. Henry James shared Bridges's opinion of the poetry, although he had characteristically to hedge his agreement with qualifications and hesitant negatives. Bridges, he said, need have, 'in respect to the poor boy's note of inspiration . . . no shade of timidity at all – of so absolutely distinguished a reality is that note, given the age at which it sounded: such fineness of impulse and such fineness of art – one doesn't really at all know where such another instance lurks – in the like condition'.[6] Many modern readers would be hard pressed to support the admiration of Bridges and James.

In his religious poetry Dolben's chief object of devotion was the human (and masculine) aspect of Christ, whom he praised so extravagantly and on whom he dwelt with such fervour about His physical beauty as to make the reader vaguely uncomfortable, since it is not always certain how precisely Dolben recognized what he was saying. In 'Homo Factus Est', addressed to 'Thou, the Man Christ Jesus', he asks:

> Thou, my own Belovèd,
> Take me home to rest;
> Whisper words of comfort,
> Lay me on Thy Breast.

The traditional aspects of religious poetry as love poetry seem somehow extended beyond their legitimate bounds by Dolben. Years later Bridges wrote more tartly than usual, 'The reading of these poems makes one see why schoolmasters wish their boys to play games.'

To perplex even further the complicated tissue of religion and poetry in Dolben's life was what Bridges called 'the most romantic of all his extravagancies', his passionate attachment to another Etonian, Martin Le Marchant Gosselin, for whom he felt the 'idealization and adoration' that he confided to his poems and to at least one friend. Intimates usually called Gosselin 'Marchie' because of his second name. Bridges, who was not given to superlatives about his schoolmates, said that he 'attracted me personally as much as any one whom I ever met' and that he was 'a person whom it was difficult not to idolize, if one had any tendency that way'. The note of hesitation lurking behind the latter statement was amplified elsewhere when Bridges indicated that he was fairly shallow: 'he had not the artist's profound insight, and lacked appreciation of the severer excellences'. However true this may have been, it was generally agreed that Gosselin had charming manners, good sense, modesty, a sense of fun, superb technique playing the piano or the organ, and 'features of the uncharactered type of beauty, the immanent innocence of Fra Angelico's angels'.

Presumably Dolben had Gosselin in mind when he wrote his poem 'On the Picture of an Angel by Fra Angelico'. Certainly, Gosselin was the inspiration for a group of poems written after 1863. Dolben was often intensely literal in translating the details of his life into poetry, and the fact that so many of the verses are set by the river's edge in scenery reminiscent of the Thames Valley suggests that he was recalling actual idyllic summer days at Eton bathing with Gosselin. The opening of one of his Eton poems is characteristic of the sensuousness, even sensuality, that informs them:

> On river banks my love was born,
> And cradled 'neath a budding thorn
> Whose flowers nevermore shall kiss
> Lips half so sweet and red as his.
> Beneath him lily islands spread,
> With broad cool leaves, a floating bed. –
> Around, to meet his opening eyes,
> The ripples danced in glad surprise.
> I found him there when spring was new,
> When winds were soft and skies were blue;
> I marvelled not, although he drew
> My whole soul to him, for I knew
> That he was born to be my king,

And I was only born to sing,
With faded lips, and feeble lays,
His love and beauty all my days.

Even after he had left Eton, Dolben continued writing of

. . . the river of my dreams,
The lilied river Thames.

Were it not for Bridges's complaints about the too-close correspondence between Dolben's experiences and his transmutation of
them into poetry, we might be tempted to think of these poems as
wishful constructions of the imagination; as it is, they seem like
fancifully embroidered versions of real events.

Another poem, 'Oh Love, first Love', written at about the same
time as 'On river banks my love was born', seems explicit enough
about the sentimental relationship, even if the circumstances may
be heightened:

Ah Love, first Love, came gently through the wood,
Under a tree he found me all alone,
Gently, gently, he kissed me on the cheek,
And gently took my hand within his own.
. . .
The golden radiance is faded from our path,
And that sweet wood we can enter nevermore;
No flowery carpet lies beneath our feet,
But a waste of thicket and of dreary moor.
But still his hand is clasped within my own,
So, whether we wander through desert or through brake,
The sharpest briars and the roughest stones
Are ever dear to me for his dear sake.

One of the most curious aspects of Dolben's attitude to his verses
was that immediately after he had finished writing them, he would
send them off to his father, whose religious convictions did not
prevent him from reading them aloud to the family, love poems and

all, apparently with no trace of shock. Many years later his daughter wrote that he did not consider them '*wrong* in sentiment'.[7]

According to Bridges, Gosselin never saw the poems and had no 'suspicion that his friend was making an idol of him'. Certainly, Gosselin was never at Finedon, and Digby never visited Gosselin's home. Nonetheless, since Bridges compares the intensity and loftiness of Digby's feelings for his friend to those of Dante for Beatrice, it is hard to believe that Gosselin, in the hothouse atmo-sphere of the Eton of those days, could remain totally unaware of Dolben's emotions. Coles was probably the only Etonian to whom he confided the depth of his involvement, but as an old woman Digby's sister said he had told her of his emotions, too.

Even a schoolboy infatuation could not be straightforward for Dolben, and his feelings for Gosselin disturbed him profoundly, not out of fear that they were abnormal but because they made Gosselin into a spiritual and physical rival of Christ. In his verses 'My love, and once again my love', addressed to Gosselin, he asks the other boy to measure his affection by the fact that he 'had loved him with the love which he had before devoted wholly to Christ, and had thus for his sake lost his love of Christ'. The deep pain of his disturbance about the nature of his feelings for Gosselin comes out in 'Pro Castitate', in which he prays to Christ ('Virgin born of Virgin') to help him consecrate his physical desires to Divine Love. Not surprisingly, even here his invocation is in strikingly physical terms:

> By Thy Flagellation
> Flesh Immaculate –
> By Thine endless glory,
> Manhood Consummate.

The agony of being torn between erotic and spiritual longings makes Dolben seem far more immediate to us than do all his fustian verses in direct praise of Christ – or of Gosselin.

How much physical intimacy there was between the two boys is not certain. Bridges's assertion that Gosselin knew nothing of Dolben's feelings suggests that there was little or none, and one of Dolben's friends said that 'a more pure minded nature than his could not have been'.[8] On the other hand, one of his poems begs Gosselin to repent with him, an invitation not easily explicable in other terms. When Bridges was writing of Dolben forty years after his death, he was so concerned that Gosselin might be embarrassed if the truth ever came out that he still felt compelled to conceal Marchie Gosselin under the pseudonym of 'Archie Manning'. He went so far as to substitute 'Archie' for 'Marchie' in the manuscript of one of the poems, digging at Gosselin's name in the original so vigorously that he left deep gouges in the paper. But perhaps he felt undue consideration for the reputation of Gosselin, who had long since left all that behind him for marriage and a career in the diplomatic service that led eventually to a knighthood. One lasting effect of Dolben on Gosselin's later life was an interest in Roman Catholicism: a decade after Dolben's death he became a convert.*

It was not his sexual morality but his inclination to 'Romanize'

---

* The story of Bridges's troubles in editing the Dolben poems and in writing his memoir is an amusing vignette of post-Victorian reticence. All Dolben's surviving friends agreed that his love poetry to Gosselin and to A.T.T. Wyatt-Edgell could hardly be printed without emendation, and Alick Yorke 'expressed great fear of the poems being misinterpreted by a censorious or evil-minded world, & suggested that they shd. be made to appear to have been addressed to a girl'. It was finally agreed that the substitution of 'Archie Manning' for 'Marchie Gosselin' would suffice to preserve Gosselin's reputation, even if it did nothing to help Dolben's. When Bridges asked Lady Gosselin if he might consult her late husband's Eton diary, she replied that Dolben's name did not occur in it, and that therefore she would not let him see it. A year later she told Eric Barrington that Dolben had been mentioned only once in the diary, on the occasion of his death, when Gosselin wrote something to the effect of 'Poor fellow, I think he was really fond of me.'

By 1910, when Bridges was collecting information for his edition of Dolben's poetry, Wyatt-Edgell had succeeded to the title of Lord Braye; he had also, like Gosselin, become a Roman Catholic convert. According to the Hon. Henry Robert Scott, Dolben had often spoken of Braye as a close friend, both at Eton and after, and Braye had been so fond of Dolben that in 1873 he published Amadeus, an elegy on him. But when Bridges consulted him, he was 'reticent and cautious', then insisted that his name should not be mentioned in the memoir, adding that he would not even accept the substitution of a dash for his name.

Although they scarcely constitute positive proof, Lady Gosselin's refusal to let Bridges see the diary, and her subsequent change of mind about whether Dolben was mentioned in it, as well as Lord Braye's skittishness about being remembered as Dolben's friend, strongly suggest what we might have guessed in any case, that Bridges told a great deal less than he knew about Dolben and his attachments. It all makes one wonder what he may have concealed when writing about Hopkins.[9]

that had caused Digby to be thrown out of Eton in July 1863 when he was caught in a stealthy visit to the Jesuits at Beaumont to attend Benediction. Mr Mackworth Dolben, who had been unperturbed by the poems to Gosselin, was deeply shocked at the possibility of his son's becoming a convert. All that summer Digby was carefully watched to be sure he was not in contact with the Romans, and when he proved surprisingly amenable, his father interceded for him at Eton, convincing the authorities that he was completely reformed, so that he was allowed to return that autumn. He did so without enthusiasm, nonetheless seeming content to remain an Anglican and even apparently happy at being confirmed. Some of his old mischief still remained, and to encourage the boys in his house to fast before Communion, he would steal their breakfast rolls.

By the end of 1864, however, he was bored with Eton, and since his health there had never been good, his father agreed that he could better prepare himself for Balliol by studying with a private tutor before attempting matriculation. On a brief holiday from the constant watch kept over him, he came to Oxford in February 1865, and then it was that he and Hopkins met.

The general outlines of their meeting are clear enough, and its effect on Hopkins is patent in his poetry of the time, but the specific details of what they talked about, how they explored Oxford and how their intimacy developed so rapidly are not recorded. Any reconstruction of those few days must be speculative, based on passing remarks made later in letters, diaries, or poems, and on our considerable knowledge of the characters of the two men. Yet, much as we should like more detailed evidence, there is little doubt of the intensity for Hopkins of that brief period and of its continuing influence for years after. More abundant records would fill out the details but surely not the substance of our knowledge of this friendship.

Years later Bridges said he had little 'but a hazy remembrance' of Dolben's stay, although it was he who had suggested the trip, both to make up for their separation for a year and a half, and so that Dolben might see more of the college and university he intended to enter later that term. Digby had several Etonian friends at Oxford, but most of them were busy with their own affairs and Bridges was unable to give much time to his guest, so that Dolben's stay was spent largely with Hopkins and probably with Coles and Muirhead, his old schoolfellows from Eton. Bridges could see nothing new in his cousin after their long separation, which 'shows that he had not changed much in the interval; and we no doubt spent our time in matters as familiar to me as they were new to him'. But if Bridges had 'no special impression of him', the same could not be said of Hopkins, who met him shortly after his arrival. In their few days together, Bridges wrote with considerable understatement, 'Gerard conceived a high admiration for him'.

Dolben and Hopkins had so many interests in common that it would have been surprising if they had not become close immediately. In Dolben, as we have seen, enthusiasms easily slid over into magnification and distortion, so that they might have seemed almost parodies of Hopkins's interests. But he was an attractive young man, and though to us he stands as an example, almost a warning, of what Hopkins might have become if he had not had so much common sense, to Hopkins he was a new and close friend who shared nearly every idea and emotion that was dear to him. It was not so evident to him as it is a century later that on almost every common interest they stood at the opposite poles of emotional excess and of self-denial.

To two new acquaintances, poised on the brink of intimacy, there is always something startling, nearly miraculous, in the discovery that both have had similar experiences before their meeting and that, unknown to each other, their lives have been running on parallel tracks. For Hopkins and Dolben there were so many likenesses that they are surprising even to an outsider, and the parallels range from the most profound emotions to mere coincidence, such as their both having been deeply influenced poetically by maiden aunts living in their family homes, their both having read Newman's *Loss and Gain*, and the fact that Hopkins's spiritual mentor, Liddon, had been in charge of the parish at Finedon for a short period in the early summer of 1853, when Dolben was a small boy and presumably when his parents had dropped their guard against Ritualism.

One particular bond was that Hopkins that year published his poem 'Barnfloor and Winepress' in the *Union Review*, where the previous year, 1864, six of Dolben's poems had been published.

It would be misleading to say that Dolben and Hopkins coincided in their religious views, since their personalities were different enough to affect their enthusiasms, but certainly both were Tractarian in belief, Ritualist in practice, and so devoted to the Virgin that either might have incurred the charge of Mariolatry that Bridges had levelled at Dolben. Both had pushed the limits of Anglicanism without having yet decided that their consciences could be at rest only with a conversion to Rome, but there is good evidence that during their conversations in Oxford they nudged each other nearer and nearer to a formal change of faith.

Dolben's professions as one of Father Ignatius's Benedictines may have seemed premature to Hopkins, but the idea of taking Holy Orders had occurred seriously to him before he met his new friend, even if he was still uncertain in which Church to take them. At this time Dolben was inflamed with the prospect of founding his own order of monks, apparently of English Benedictines. In letters he referred to it as 'the Establishment', but he had determined to call it the Canons and Brothers of the Holy (or Sacred) Name, and he was busy trying to convince his friends that they should become novices when they had enough money to undertake its foundation. He spoke somewhat grandly of converting Finedon Hall into a monastery if he inherited it, although that possibility was remote for a youngest son.*

Dolben had been making confessions to Father Carter at Clewer, as well as to several startled and ill-prepared parish clergymen

---

* His elder brother had already been drowned at sea while on duty with the Navy, and the second son was to die a short time after Digby, so that on the death of Mrs Mackworth Dolben, Finedon Hall passed on trust to Digby's sister Ellen, who managed her inheritance unwisely and exhausted the family fortune in the upkeep of the house and grounds. When she died in 1912 at the age of 75, the estate was sold in parcels, according to her mother's will, which was designed to prevent the cousin of Liberal tendencies from becoming the heir. A brother of the offending Liberal was also cut out of the proceeds of the sale because he had become a Roman Catholic. Surely, if Digby had outlived his parents, they would have set up safeguards against Finedon ever becoming a monastery, since they preferred that the fine old place be divided up rather than go to heirs of whose principles they disapproved.

elsewhere, and Hopkins had made his first confession to Liddon a year before Dolben's Oxford visit.[10] Both of them habitually fasted and practised various forms of penitential asceticism. We know that Hopkins wore either hair shirts or other extremely uncomfortable garments, and he had already experimented with self-flagellation, if we take at face value the confessional tone of 'Easter Communion', written a few days after Dolben had left him:

> You striped in secret with breath-taking whips,
> Those crookèd rough-scored chequers may be pieced
> To crosses meant for Jesu's . . .

None of these practices was extraordinary for High Church adherents, but their coincidence in two new friends was striking.

Much as both young men loved writing poetry, on this matter at least there is some room for doubting that Hopkins thought of Dolben as his equal. At this stage in his career Hopkins was still writing chiefly about the externals of religious observance, as Dolben often did, but there the resemblance ends, for even in his early poetry there is a toughness, a strangeness and an attempt at finish that one never finds in Dolben's poems, which too often give the reader the feeling that the writer has cleaned up his rough copy and let it go at that. Even more seriously, Dolben's poems are wildly self-indulgent in matter and manner. As Bridges felt compelled to say in the midst of praise for his cousin's works, 'he liked poetry on account of the power that it had of exciting his valued emotions', and in its composition he 'imagined poetic form to be the naïve outcome of peculiar personal emotion'. It was an artlessness of which Hopkins would never have been guilty.

No doubt on this first meeting Hopkins found that Dolben 'was readier to turn symbols into flesh than flesh into symbols; and his sacramental ecstasies [were] of this colour'. In spite of his admiration of Digby and his affection for him, Hopkins never discussed his poetry in writing about him, and at his death, when he wrote to Bridges of Dolben's beauty of body, mind, and life, he conspicuously neglected to praise the poetry that Bridges felt was his claim to lasting fame, although he did ask whether the family intended to publish it. It is an odd little omission that seems to indicate how comparatively strictly Hopkins divorced poetic standards from personal friendship.

Two years before his Oxford visit, Dolben had burnt all the poems he had so far written. The reason Bridges gave for their destruction was Dolben's fear that the poems might be read by the wrong person, since their subject was his affection for Gosselin, but that hardly seems an adequate explanation, because he continued writing his love poems and was still at it when he came to stay in Oxford. What is at least as likely is that he was suffering one of his periodic and short-lived fits of remorse over his feelings for Gosselin (and perhaps some of the other Etonians for whom he felt inconveniently ardent emotions) and that he was emulating his beloved Savonarola, who in 1497 had attempted to eliminate frivolous art in Florence by the 'burning of the vanities'. It was a reason that Hopkins, fresh from his excited reading of *Romola*, would have respected completely. One of the first books he put on his projected reading list after Dolben's departure was the second volume of Villari's biography of Savonarola, and he sent off to London for a copy of a portrait of Dolben's hero (a word he had used in describing Savonarola's importance to himself). Far more important than the loss of Dolben's poems or the reasons for his burning them is that Hopkins was following his example two years later when he set fire to his own poetry before entering the Society of Jesus.

Whatever the feelings of sacrifice of both young men, and there is no doubt that they were sincere, it is worth noticing that neither of them destroyed much of value: Bridges had seen Dolben's early poems and even he thought them poor things. It is probably not irrelevant that Savonarola himself is believed to have destroyed little of great worth. Many, perhaps most, of Hopkins's poems had been copied elsewhere, so that they were not lost irretrievably.*

It is impossible to know how much of their emotional natures Hopkins and Dolben confided to each other, but the rapidity of

---

* Shortly before Dolben's pyromania, Rossetti had thrown his early poems into the grave of his wife Lizzie, to be buried with her; a year after Dolben's death he had them exhumed and published. However much poets love a dramatic gesture, they seem to have an equally sure instinct for preservation of their work.

Hopkins's sense of intimacy with him would suggest that Dolben at least was frank about his feelings for Gosselin. To be sure, he seems not to have told them completely to Bridges, even after a close friendship of three years, for he knew perfectly well that his cousin felt a mild conventional disapproval of his relationship with Gosselin. However, with a boy of the same mind like Coles he kept nothing hidden. For all his occasional silliness, he was perceptive about his friends, and it is probable that he sensed sympathy in Hopkins.

What Hopkins revealed to Dolben in turn is even more conjectural, not least because he was so deeply reticent about his own feelings. But Dolben was his mirror image in so many ways that it would be surprising if he had not voiced that likeness, as well as admitting it to himself. Certainly, within a fortnight he was examining his own emotions for culpability and committing them to paper: they were of the same sort as Dolben's and directly connected with him. Although he must have known their nature, Dolben was in any case still too involved with Gosselin to reciprocate. He greatly admired Hopkins and even used him as a model when he was vacillating on the edge of conversion to Catholicism, but nothing warmer than casual friendship is apparent in his response.

During the few days they were together Hopkins was inspired with a deep sense of his own sinfulness, more probably from recognizing the nature of his own feelings than from committing any specifically culpable act. Nonetheless, much of what he had to face was a strong physical attraction to Dolben, as is made clear by the poetry he wrote after Digby had left Oxford and by the entries in his private diary.

One perceptive Hopkins scholar believes that there was a deep breach between Hopkins and Dolben for some months after their meeting, and that 'there was apparently something in Hopkins that Dolben feared'.[11] If she is correct, the only conjecture that makes much sense of both Dolben's fear and Hopkins's sharpened sense of sinfulness is that he had made his desires clear to Dolben and had been rejected. It is hard to imagine how Hopkins, so sensitive about his own sexual nature, could have got himself into a situation that invited rebuff, but it is the explanation for his continued baffled affection and Dolben's apparent shying away from him that fits the facts better than any other.

Dolben, of course, had other business in Oxford, other friends than Hopkins, who may have found this difficult to accept. In particular Dolben was anxious to meet Liddon, whose sermons he had been reading at Finedon, marvelling over the fact that Liddon had actually assisted the Rector there for a time some years before. 'They are most wonderful – & beautiful –,' he wrote, 'I long to hear and see him – To think that he was Curate here for ever so long; when I was too juvenile to appreciate any advantages!'[12] Hopkins and Coles and Muirhead were all better situated to introduce him to Liddon than was Bridges, who had become increasingly disenchanted with the High Church group in the University.

Hopkins was no use, however, in helping Dolben with admission to Balliol, for his preparation in classics was inadequate, and he was sent away until Michaelmas term of 1865. 'I hate to hear the very name of Oxford, now there is no chance of my seeing it before the Autumn,' he wrote.[13] In the meantime he planned on studying with a tutor, preferably as close as possible to Oxford, although he was afraid that the connection of that city with the Tractarians might make his father reluctant to let him stay in the vicinity. But autumn came and went in 1865. A year later, in the autumn of 1866, the possibility of Oxford had receded until January 1867, and at his death in the summer of 1867 Dolben was still hoping to come up to the University.

Although they could not expect to see each other at Balliol again for some time, the two young men exchanged poems and Dolben promised to send his picture to Hopkins. In their ensuing separation Hopkins planned on keeping in touch by letter.

CHAPTER VI

DEAD LETTERS
1865

In recent years there has been a discernible movement among a few Hopkins scholars to minimize the importance of his feelings for Dolben, but it is an attitude that would have found no recognition among Hopkins's Oxford friends. More than half a century after Dolben's death Coles was trying without success to find records that would help Bridges in writing a preface to his edition of the poems of Hopkins; his memory had begun to slip, but there was one aspect of Hopkins's personality that stuck ineradicably: 'What I should like to remember, but it is only dim in my mind, were his relations to D.M.D. his poems and his proceedings.'[1] Clearly, Dolben had brought out the finest part of Hopkins's character unforgettably.

Not long after Dolben's departure Hopkins made one of his few cryptic references to him in his published diary, recording without comment the receipt of the promised photograph, a *carte de visite*. The laconic manner should not blind us to Hopkins's preoccupation, for Dolben was, as Humphry House first noted, 'closely bound up with the religious crisis of that March', so much so that Hopkins tried hard not to mention Dolben unduly in either conversation or writing. What lay behind his resolution was not a paucity of emotion but an excess.

On the 12th of March Hopkins uncharacteristically wrote the date beside an entry in his journal, as if to indicate its importance: 'A day of the great mercy of God.' The entry uses a verbal formula that was associated in his mind with Dolben: nearly eight years later, when he was still deeply concerned with the memory of his friend, he wrote, 'I received as I think a great mercy about Dolben.' In the latter case he was apparently referring to the conviction he had

98

received about Dolben's salvation. In 1865 he seems to have felt that he had been given assurance of the sanctity of his feelings for Dolben. But his equanimity was not to last long. House was correct in saying that the nature of the spiritual crisis is not totally clear, but it was obviously enough concerned with feelings of guilt, contrition, and forgiveness, and they were in turn connected with Dolben. It may also be true, as has been suggested, that this was the date of his first conviction that in time he must inevitably become a Roman Catholic, but if so, even that conviction seems in part derivative from his preoccupation with Dolben.

After Dolben had gone, Hopkins, went for what Liddon's diary indicates was his fourth confession to him. In his own diary Hopkins meticulously recorded the date, 'Saturday, Lady Day, March 25', a deliberate linking of his confession and the feast of the Virgin, to whom both he and Dolben were devoted. There is no reason to believe that the feast held its central position in his poetry for the rest of his life because Dolben had so loved the Virgin, but the memory added a further resonance to Hopkins's own devotions.

Three days later Liddon wrote in his diary that he 'Saw Hopkins for 1.30 hours from 11 o'clock–'. The length of their talk suggests that Hopkins was much exercised about the subject of their discussion, which would seem reasonably to have been his feelings for Dolben.

On the day of his confession to Liddon, presumably at Liddon's suggestion, Hopkins began keeping notes for his own guidance in further penance, a practice he faithfully continued for nearly a year, perhaps longer. Curiously, he wrote the notes in the same journal that he used for recording more impersonal minutiae of his daily life: addresses, titles of books to be read, nature notes and sketches, even drafts of poems. In spite of the random nature of his jottings, it is often possible to understand his overriding concerns by the repetition and contiguity of the entries. In mid-April 1865, for example, he noted that he intended to read Dr Pusey's sermon 'on the Remedy for Sins of the Body' and shortly after that comes a characteristically understated reminder to himself of things to do: 'Little book for sins. Necktie. Boots to see after. Slippers? Bath. Letters to Aunt Annie, Aunt Katie, Geldart. Trousers.' The third entry thereafter is a record of Dolben's new address in Leicester-shire, where he had gone to study with the Revd Constantine Prichard.

At first glance the reference to the 'Little book for sins' suggests a place in which to record transgressions. If that is what Hopkins had in mind, he evidently never bought the book, or at least never used it for its intended purpose, since he continued to document his spiritual shortcomings in his regular journal. Probably he was referring instead to a flimsy little pamphlet of twelve pages with the title of *Questions for Self-Examination*, of which all copies seem to have disappeared except one in the Liddon papers in Keble; Hopkins's purchase may have been at Liddon's suggestion. Guides to penance necessarily have a family resemblance, but Hopkins's entries in his journal often sound like direct responses to the questions of this booklet.

Hopkins's notes to himself about his transgressions make a fascinating record of the private thoughts of the young poet but not wholly for the sins of commission listed there. In part they are what one might expect of any physically healthy young man with a too scrupulous conscience and a low emotional flash point. The less conventional things he felt bound to confess were often matters that careful readers would guess from his poetry in any case. What is more interesting is the kind of personality revealed by his method of recording them. Most of the diary is in a clear and easily legible hand of fair size, but the entries in preparation for confession are in pencil and so minute that they are at best difficult to decipher. At some later date, perhaps at his conversion, more probably im-mediately after confessing his sins, Hopkins drew a pencil line through these entries but without obscuring them; he seems to have wanted to be able to review them after he had been forgiven for them, and even after becoming a Roman Catholic he kept them. Over the years the pencil script has deteriorated and has been so rubbed that it will probably never again be wholly legible.

It is impossible to predict where his eruptions of guilt will occur, and often he interrupted a passage or even a sentence on other subjects to insert a brief note about something for which he felt contrition. The occasion for the sins seems to have occurred to him so much against his will and so insistently that he was compelled to intrude upon less inflammatory matters. The whole process is a curious one, showing two strongly opposed drives: the intense need for privacy and the recognition that the proper place for the record of his sins was in the context of his ordinary life, as easily available as the addresses of his friends.

Naturally enough for a young Victorian, he thought of sins as largely sexual, and the most recurrent he recorded were concerned with masturbation.[2] Few modern readers could avoid wishing that he might have been spared some of the weight of his guilt by benefiting from the twentieth-century view of the act as perfectly natural. So painfully did it nag at his conscience that he used a repetitive abbreviation, 'O.H.', to indicate when he had fallen into old habits; the phrase seems to have been used both for completed masturbation and for stimulating acts not followed by climax. Even nocturnal emissions seemed sinful, particularly when, as he indicated, they occurred in half-sleep or in the morning, 'not without sin'. At the end of his journal he made a recapitulation of his involuntary emissions, obviously not quite believing they could be innocent. The obsession would verge on the comic if it were not so patently agonizing to him. Ruefully he realized that the occasions for sin lay all around him: a risqué story; looking up the meaning of words he suspected of being obscene; being late to bed or tardy in rising; washing himself. All were dangerous, and Dr Pusey's 'Remedy for Sins of the Body', a liberal use of the sign of the cross, was obviously not enough help. Hopkins was ruthless in his self-examination, and the reader frequently wishes that he had been able to follow the self-counsel in a late sonnet:

> My own heart let me more have pity on; let
> Me live to my sad self hereafter kind,
> Charitable; not live this tormented mind
> With this tormented mind tormenting yet.

In some ways for those who lived in a pre-Freudian world the burden of sexuality was considerably lighter because so few labels existed. Love between persons of the same sex, for instance, could exist happily because they had not been taught to examine their affections for covert sexual motivation or even to believe that their feelings were atypical. In other words, it was the state of innocence to which some modern writers suggest we could return if we were only to realize that there are no such things as heterosexual or homosexual persons, only heterosexual or homosexual acts. It was probably a considerably more perplexing state than this would suggest for those Victorians who could not help displacing their guilt about basic attitudes to an undue emphasis on the enormity of particular acts. Even without labels Hopkins could see clearly the direction in which his inclinations led him, and he was tormented by his temptations, what they indicated about his personality, and what they might lead to in the future.

Sometimes it seemed as if almost anything served to arouse his passions: desirable men glimpsed in church or walking in Christ Church Meadows; 'Looking at face in the theatre'; a glance from another man that lingered too long by the blink of an eye; a particularly good-looking chorister in Magdalen Chapel; the urchin charm of organ boys or shop boys seen from the hidden vantage point of a shop door; letting his friends stay too late in his rooms at night, when the talk inevitably turned to sexual subjects; an affectionate word to Baillie without removing his arm from the other man's; a glimpse of another friend in the negligent state of nudity common among undergraduates. It is indicative of Hopkins's obsessive innocence that he worried about each of these temptations, although none of them seems very serious today and most of them a great many men have felt fleetingly at one time or another. All the same, in totality they indicate that his susceptibility was largely homoerotic. More significantly, they serve as evidence of the intense sensuousness of his nature, if not necessarily of deed, a luxuriance that frightened him and that he was at last able to turn into acceptable channels in religion and poetry.

It was seldom that Hopkins could joke, however wryly, about his own attraction to other men, but in 1866, a year after he had met Dolben, at the very time he was most concerned with conversion, he wrote to Bridges about seeing a handsome Oxford man serving at Mass in St Alban's, London: 'His face was fascinating me last term: I generally have one fascination or another on.' Sometimes his own disgust with himself led him to dislike the faces that attracted him physically, but sometimes 'much the reverse', as he found in this case.

It may seem, when Hopkins was so frank in his spiritual diary about his feelings, that Digby Dolben's name should occur oftener if he were actually thinking of him most of the time. Humphry House's expurgated edition of the journals made a whole generation of scholars believe that Dolben's name was seldom mentioned there. Even in the original the comparative rarity of its appearance gives a wholly false impression of its significance to Hopkins. Either independently or on Liddon's advice, he seems to have decided that his feelings for Dolben were responsible for his spiritual crisis and that the very mention of his name was dangerous to his own emotional and moral equanimity; when he spoke of Dolben by accident to his friends or even thought of him, Hopkins would at once back nervously away from 'the forbidden subject'. In October 1865, many months after Dolben had left Oxford, he guiltily acknowledged 'Running on in thought last night unseasonably against warning onto subject of Dolben', and the following month 'Going on into a letter to Dolben at night agst. warning.'[3] It seems reasonable to suppose that the warning was Liddon's.

Sensibly, Liddon seems to have tried to reassure him that his feelings for Dolben were not innately sinful so long as he neither dwelt nor acted upon them; he also made it a matter for Hopkins's conscience to avoid any unhealthy absorption in Dolben. From what we know of Liddon's own feelings, it is easy to see that he would understand and be sympathetic to temptations such as Hopkins's, when another priest might have condemned them completely. His sympathy and kindness in the matter are probably the reasons Hopkins came to him for confession in 1864 and 1865 more often than to the sterner Pusey. In his spiritual diary Hopkins recorded what he was sure were sins, or at least the occasion for them, and even his own doubting 'scruples' about them, but he was too reserved, probably too worried, to analyse his emotions on paper beyond reminding himself that at least they required clarification in the confessional. Yet the thought of Dolben, interdicted as it was, underlay all of that sexually turbulent spring of 1865.

For many adolescents and young adults the burden of sexuality can be eased by talking of it with their contemporaries and realizing that its pressures are not unique to them. For Hopkins such confidences seemed attractive initially but soon went rancid. Like most undergraduates, he talked a good bit about his emotions to chosen friends, but his reliance upon such conversation began to seem sinful because it was a substitute for confession and dangerously titillating in itself. In particular he felt that his long exchanges with Martin Geldart were ill advised on the late evenings when they talked of intimate matters over a dying fire.

Hopkins's emotions were further complicated by the fact that in response to his own frequent letters, Dolben replied irregularly if at all. Perhaps he was simply a bad correspondent, but more probably he was deliberately damping down Hopkins's feelings, since Marchie Gosselin still occupied the centre of his own. Hopkins's anguish at this time was surely the source of the deeply moving metaphor he used twenty years later in 'I wake and feel the fell of dark, not day' to describe his inability to communicate with God:

> . . . And my lament
> Is cries countless, cries like dead letters sent
> To dearest him that lives alas! away.

Here, and occasionally elsewhere in his poems, Hopkins seems deliberately to blur the dividing line between persons and Deity by withholding the capital letter of the pronouns most Victorians used in referring to Christ, as if to indicate the difficulty of distinguishing between his feelings for other men and those for Christ; we are inevitably reminded of Dolben, who often followed the same practice in his poems to Gosselin/Christ.

'I have written letters without end,' Hopkins told Bridges that August, 'without a whiff of answer.'[4] It may be that Dolben was feeling betrayed by Hopkins after he heard that Bridges had been reading some of his poems without express permission and assumed that he had been given them by Hopkins. 'I certainly should not have selected them to show you', he wrote somewhat petulantly, although he told Bridges he was 'very welcome' to see them. 'Did Coles, or Hopkins give them you – and why? Please remember to tell me.'[5]

At last, on the 6th of November, two days after writing to Dolben in spite of being warned against doing so, and more than eight months after Dolben had left him in Oxford, Hopkins wrote in his diary, 'On this day by God's grace I resolved to give up all beauty until I had His leave for it; and also Dolben's letter came for wh. Glory to God.'[6] It tells us a good bit about Hopkins that the two statements occur in the same sentence. The first part has usually been taken as a prediction of his determination to quit writing poetry, but it also sounds remarkably like an attempt to renounce Dolben, the second part like an inadequately strangled gasp of relief and hope. In any case, Hopkins seems to have associated Dolben and poetry until they became almost indistinguishable. Unfortunately, Dolben's letter was to prove no more a harbinger of regular correspondence than had his *carte de visite*, and before long Hopkins was once more lamenting his negligence in writing. Nor was he able to renounce his feelings for the absent friend.

As one would expect of Hopkins, only the faintest air of hurt at Dolben's lack of response was allowed to show in his diary and correspondence. A truer index of his stifled feelings is found in the series of poems he wrote after Dolben had first visited Oxford. Probably other poems from that spring have been lost, but what remain are enough to chart the course of the gradual collapse of his hopes of intimacy with Dolben.

Modern readers are so used to being reminded that imaginative works of literature are not to be confused with the lives of their creators that we automatically shy away from any overt similarity between the two. All the same it seems obvious that a critic or biographer would be singularly pig-headed if he were to ignore a clear parallel between a poet's preoccupation at a particular time and the poems of the same period, if they reflect a like concern. Only in this limited sense can we confidently connect Hopkins's poetry of the last ten months of 1865 and his deepening sense of rejection by Dolben during that period. The connection, however, seems valid, even necessary. One has only to be familiar with the whole body of Hopkins's poems to recognize how often he dealt with pain in his own life by imaginatively re-ordering it into poetry, although sometimes he was apparently unconscious of the dependence of one level of experience upon the other.

Reading his early poems, one immediately notices a sharp break between 'For a Picture of St. Dorothea', written in 1864, probably in November, and 'Easter Communion', written the following March, only a few days after Dolben left Oxford. Before that break the poems are remarkably accomplished for a young man, with that high level of uninspired competence that Hopkins called 'Parnassian'. There is little of the individuality so characteristic of his later works; some of them might have been written by the young Keats, or Tennyson, or Christina Rossetti, or even an apprentice Hardy. With one poem, however, we have arrived in recognizable Hopkins territory, and though it is not mature work, there is little question of the distinctive stamp of his personality, both in style and in the characteristic sense of transformation, even transfiguration, of the physical into the spiritual. The subject is that of monastic flagellation and self-discipline which so occupied Dolben, the manner is Hopkins's own:

> . . . you sergèd fellowships,
> You vigil-keepers with low flames decreased,
> God shall o'er-brim the measures you have spent
> With oil of gladness; for sackcloth and frieze
> And the ever-fretting shirt of punishment
> Give myrrhy-threaded golden folds of ease.

In March he also translated a Greek epigram that seems to show only the slightest flicker of apprehension behind his headlong love:

> Love me as I love thee. O double sweet!
> But if thou hate me who love thee, albeit
> Even thus I have the better of thee:
> Thou canst not hate so much as I do love thee.

It is, of course, risky to identify his own feelings with those underlying a poem written by another, but it is even more perilous to assume that a translated poem has no deep meaning for anyone but the original author, as at least one recent critic has done in trying to downplay the importance of Dolben to Hopkins. The relevant question is not 'Who wrote the original version?' but 'Why was it important to Hopkins at this time?', for the stubborn fact remains that the quatrain struck Hopkins so forcibly that he was inspired to translate it and copy it into his journal. It was the first time he had been moved to record either original or borrowed love poetry, and there was a compelling reason for this, the intensity of his feelings for Dolben.

The muted, somewhat qualified happiness of these two poems of March 1865 was followed by two sonnets 'To Oxford', on Low Sunday and Monday, the 23rd and 24th of April. Both brim with love so ecstatic that the poet must admit all other lovers of the place to share his joy:

> This is my park, my pleasaunce; this to me
> As public is my greater privacy,
> All mine, yet common to my every peer.
>
> . . .
>
> And all like me may boast, impeachèd not,
> Their special-general title to thy love.

The second of these Oxford sonnets may have been written under the walls of either Balliol Chapel or Butterfield's restoration of Merton Chapel, looking up at the dizzying parapet and sky: in it Hopkins plays with the curious view of the world come from looking at things from an unexpected angle. It is the same pleasure in the topsy-turvy that he brings to his drawing of his own reflection as he looks down into a lake (see Plate 5b). And, for that matter, it is the unnerving new perspective on the world that love brings. But, singular as his view is, he recognizes that it is a slant he unknowingly shares with 'many unknown men' who have not been moved to poetry by the pleasant sight:

> The shapen flags and drillèd holes of sky,
> Just seen, may be to many unknown men
> The one peculiar of their pleasured eye,
> And I have only set the same to pen.

The beauty of town and university, which had always touched him, had taken on a strange and lovely new face as he showed them to

Dolben, and his affection made him want to assert his kinship with other men, to admit other lovers to his own haunts.

It is a shock to move from these sonnets, reflecting a happiness so intense that it must be shared, to the painful renunciation of a third sonnet, dated only one day later, on the 25th of April. There is no dedication, but clearly it was written about Dolben, of whom his mind was full, and who is mentioned in the two entries just preceding the poem in Hopkins's journal. On the 21st Hopkins had jotted down his name and address, and on Low Sunday, the 23rd, he recorded for confession, 'Dangerous talking about Dolben'. Presumably something had happened on the Tuesday following Low Sunday that made him aware that there would never be the bond of intimacy with Dolben that he had anticipated:

> Where art thou friend, whom I shall never see,
> Conceiving whom I must conceive amiss?
> Or sunder'd from my sight in the age that is
> Or far-off promise of a time to be;
> Thou who canst best accept the certainty
> That thou hadst borne proportion in my bliss . . .

The poem initiates the reverberation of misery sounding in Hopkins's poems throughout the rest of the year.[7] The most tranquil state that any of them reaches is a stoic acceptance of man's inevitable unhappiness, capable of resolution only in Christ.

Shakespeare's inescapable presence breathes heavily over the shoulder of most nineteenth-century sonneteers. Although Hopkins was to exorcize himself of the ghost in his later works, he nowhere seems more haunted by Shakespeare than in the sonnets of disillusioned love in 1865. In such poems even the reversion to seventeenth-century verbs and pronouns suggests his conscious indebtedness to the sonnets to Mr W. H.

The natural suspicion that his sudden plunge into sadness was caused by a gesture of rejection from Dolben is heightened by the trio of sonnets that he wrote ten days after 'Where art thou friend'. To them he gave the general title of 'The Beginning of the End' with the transparent subtitle of 'A neglected lover's address to his mistress'.* They are unique in Hopkins's poetry in displaying both sexual jealousy and an I–don't–care bravado:

> My love is lessened and must soon be past.
>   I never promised such persistency
>   In its condition. No, the tropic tree
>   Has not a charter that its sap shall last
>
> Into all seasons, though no Winter cast
>   The happy leafing. It is so with me:
>   My love is less, my love is less for thee.
>   I cease the mourning and the abject fast,
>
> And rise and go about my works again
>   And, save by darting accidents, forget.
>   But ah! if you could understand how then
>
> That *less* is heavens higher even yet
>   Than treble-fervent *more* of other men,
>   Even your unpassion'd eyelids might be wet.

This ineffectual stab at bravery is given the lie in the manuscript of the poems by an abandoned fragment written immediately after the first sonnet, revealing the poet's shame over his jealousy and glancing at the presence of Gosselin half hidden behind the emotion:

> Some men may hate their rivals and desire
> Secretive moats, knives, smothering-cloths, drugs, flame;
> But I am consumèd with my shame
> I dare feel envy scarcely, never ire.
> O worshipful the man that she sets higher.

Rather unconvincingly, in the last of this trio of sonnets the poet assures his 'mistress' that he has already recovered from his loss:

---

*Not all readers have recognized that the poems are written to a man. Jean-Georges Ritz, for instance, was worried at his inability to discover 'la jeune fille' behind the 'crise sentimentale'.

You see that I have come to passion's end;
This means you need not fear the storms, the cries,
That gave you vantage when you would despise:
My bankrupt heart has no more tears to spend.

Bridges, who understood perfectly well both Dolben's role in 'The Beginning of the End' and Hopkins's autobiographical emotions in writing it, noted on the first and third poems in Hopkins's autograph copy: 'These two sonnets must *never* be printed.'[8]

Almost all the rest of the poetry Hopkins wrote in 1865 shows his coming to terms with what he realized was to be a solitary life. Probably most lovers who feel rejected go through the same stage, but for Hopkins it was to be permanent. He certainly continued to feel sexually attracted to others (only to men so far as we can tell), and in the future he was to have brief feelings of emotional intimacy with other persons, but by then he had recognized the necessary transience of such intervals. From this time, too, there is an increased saturation of his poetry with sexual images that sometimes startle the reader in his religious works. They are perhaps most noticeable in his poems of despair, in detailing his frequent sense of impotence and sterility. His recurrent description of himself as a eunuch was already anticipated by the end of December 1865, when he wrote of himself in a mixture of pity and contempt:

Trees by their yield
Are known; but I –
My sap is sealed,
My root is dry.
If life within
I none can shew
(Except for sin),
Nor fruit above, –
It must be so –
I do not love.

It is perhaps only after reading a poem as explicit as this that we can fully appreciate the more deeply buried sexual content of a sonnet

Hopkins had written the previous 26th of June while the hurt of
Dolben's apparent neglect was still new:

> See how Spring opens with disabling cold,
> And hunting winds and the long-lying snow.
> Is it a wonder if the buds are slow?
> Or where is strength to make the leaf unfold?
> Chilling remembrance of my days of old
> Afflicts no less, what yet I hope may blow,
> That seed which the good sower once did sow,
> So loading with obstruction that threshold
> Which should ere now have led my feet to the field.
> It is the waste done in unreticent youth
> Which makes so small the promise of that yield
> That I may win with late-learnt skill uncouth
> From furrows of the poor and stinting weald.
> Therefore how bitter, and learnt how late, the truth!

The most patent reference here is of course to the parables of the
sower in *Matthew* 13, and since Hopkins himself wrote that at this
time he was beginning to think seriously of becoming a Roman
Catholic, it has been suggested that the sonnet refers to his unfruit-
ful years as a Protestant, now bitterly regretted.[9] It may be,
however, that his sense of a coming conversion supplied the overt
content of the poem while his emotional upheavals of that disabling
spring unconsciously provided the language, the imagery, and the
urgency. Certainly, with 'Trees by their yield' in mind, a reader
coming freshly to the poem cannot avoid the sexual implications of
the seed expended to no purpose, which threatens, by its squandering, any yield or crop and ultimately becomes quite as barren as the
seedless eunuch, whose more striking presence informs other
poems. Nor can one ignore the implications of 'waste done in
unreticent youth / Which makes so small the promise of that yield',
particularly when aware that waste was a Victorian euphemism for
masturbation.

It is not easy to escape a reading of the poem suggesting that its
whole substructure is a reflection of his sense of lost opportunities,

of emotional and spiritual sterility after his parting from Dolben. It was a sudden revelation of the terrible literality that lay behind his use of the metaphor of barrenness. Without further evidence it is, of course, useless to argue whether or not Hopkins himself recognized the hidden content of the sonnet, however striking it is for the reader.

In this sonnet, as elsewhere, it is not surprising that his deepest religious emotions are expressed in sexual metaphors; but what is perhaps surprising is the strength with which they asserted themselves, an intensity surely far beyond his conscious volition. To understand his poetry fully, one must always be aware of the urgency of his physical nature and how it constantly bubbled up unbidden into his language.

It is improbable that any but his closest friends noted much change in Hopkins in the months after Dolben's visit to Oxford. In his rooms he hung a portrait of Savonarola, and he put up statuettes, presumably ecclesiastical, in green and purple silk, as Dolben had done at Eton, but his usual routine remained much the same. He continued active in College functions, and on the 20th of February there was a meeting of 'Hexameron at 9 in Muirhead's rooms. Hopkins read an Essay on "Science of Poetry". Very crowded attendance.'[10] He still went to the Union to write his letters, he played chess with Brooke and accompanied him to the river or to the newly planted University Parks, which promised to be a splendid place to walk, and he kept up a constant attendance at wines and breakfasts with his friends.

In 1865 he stayed up at Oxford during the spring vacation for the first time. On the 30th of March he went to hear Fr Vincent, one of the priests connected with Fr Ignatius's (and Dolben's) Benedictines, who was speaking at the Clarendon Hotel on the subject of the Reformation. There was a big crowd, for the Order had attracted a good deal of unpleasant notoriety the previous autumn over the eruption of a scandal in the monastery at Norwich, involving 'a nice-looking chorister and a sentimental young monk'.[11] To the disappointment of Fr Vincent's audience, the 'kind of Anglican monk' made a poor showing because both his logic and his elocution were inadequate.

There was one man in the audience, however, for whom the poor performance mattered little: W.L. Lechmere, who there met Hopkins for the first time. Both men were friends of Martin Geldart, who had told Lechmere that Hopkins wanted to meet him. In 1912 he still remembered keeping his eyes on Hopkins during the lecture, his memory informing the most arresting word portrait we have of the poet's appearance: 'At this moment, looking back over forty years, I seem to be gazing upon some great portrait of a face rather than upon a face. What high serenity, what chastened intellectual power, what firm and resigned purpose, and withal what tranquil sadness or perhaps seriousness suffusing the features, rather than casting a shadow upon them. I have no likeness to assist me; but I continue to see the face.'

The next time they met was at a luncheon party given by Geldart, and once more Lechmere had eyes only for Hopkins. 'He said but little. Indeed, I only remember his saying something about one of the Articles. I saw him but once again, and that only as we passed in the High . . . Of all I came across at Oxford, there was not one whose superfineness of mind and character was more expressed in his entire bearing.'[12] Neither the shortness of his stature nor the lack of virility in his movements detracted from his presence, because of the patent inner distinction of the man.

The quiet assurance of Hopkins's outward manner, which was so striking to others, covered a deep, over-sensitive awareness of his own sins, which to his chagrin had not been mitigated by getting to know Dolben nor blunted by his own attempts to live a reformed life. He worried that he spent too much time on the river, he was 'intemperate' in food and wine at dessert parties, he was inattentive in chapel, he had a 'disrespectful feeling towards Jowett', he began teasing Urquhart in ways that seemed friendly but that he realized acted as a cover for basic hostility, he could not help jotting down verse when he was supposed to be studying, he felt envy when he found that Liddon had called on Coles but not on him, and in his most uncontrollable moments he gave way to 'despondency'.

Worse still, the urgency of his animal nature had not been lessened by his affection for Dolben; indeed, it seemed to have been sharpened. He had to reprove himself for 'Looking at and thinking of stallions' (it shows how perceptive he was in some ways about his own personality that he recognized the sexual content of the image

so long before stallions became standard jargon in modern psychological interpretation of such matters), he found himself 'Looking
with terrible temptation at Maitland', he had 'Evil thoughts, especially from Rover lying on me', and his language had now become
so intemperate that he said 'Sh--' to Urquhart. The long rambles
along the Thames he was accustomed to take were in danger of
becoming occasions for him to meet other men, and he recorded
'Looking at a man who tempted me on Port Meadow', as well as
'Temptation in meeting man at Godstow'. Even more serious was
that his carnal feelings were so closely connected with his devotions
that he despondently found he became excited at thinking of
Christ's Passion or at examining His body on a carved crucifix.[13]
And always his temptations about his own body lay in wait for him
like some feral beast.

Hopkins was surely no more sensual than the average run of men,
but he was out of the ordinary in the scrupulousness with which he
kept track of his temptations, and he was certainly unusual in his
awareness of how engrained was his sexual nature, colouring nearly
everything he did. Sensuality was the enemy, but it seemed to him
that it often concealed itself behind the mask of beauty, either of
man or of nature.

During his summer holidays in 1865 he returned to Hampstead,
as he had not done in the spring break, but after a short time he left
on a trip of some five weeks to see Geldart in Manchester, then on to
the West Country to visit his grandmother's birthplace in Devonshire and pay respects to family friends, and finally to stay with the
Gurneys in Torquay. There are few letters to his family remaining
from that period to show the state of his relations with them, but it
must have been simpler for him to be separated from them during a
period when he was in such a disturbed state of mind.

Geldart's father was 'secretary of the Manchester City Mission'
with an office 'in what they have the face to call Piccadilly, if I
remember right', but the family lived outside the city in Bowden.
Geldart's younger brother was distracting, and Hopkins wrote of
his regret at 'Looking at temptations, esp. at E. Geldart naked',
ruefully recognizing the difficulty of changing his nature.

While Hopkins was with the Geldarts, Bridges sent him an
invitation to Rochdale, where he had made his home with his

mother and her second husband, the Revd Dr Molesworth. Unfortunately, his letter went to Hampstead and Hopkins did not receive it until after he had left Manchester for Devon. 'Else nothing cd. have been so delightful as to meet you and Coles and Dolben', he wrote to Bridges. One or two other half-formed plans to meet Dolben in the next two years came to nothing, and he was never to see him again. 'I wish you . . . wd. have written so that I might have heard while in Manchester, and seen you', he told Bridges regretfully.[14]

Hopkins's disappointment at missing Dolben was probably not fully reciprocated, as is indicated by Dolben's letter to Bridges about being unable to accept the initial invitation: 'I should like to have seen Coles for some things very much, but it was quite impossible for me to come about his time'.[15] Of Hopkins there is no mention, which is hardly proof that Dolben was not excited about seeing him, although that prospect was obviously not uppermost in his mind. A few weeks later he was able to get to Rochdale to see Bridges, but there is no record of Hopkins's having been invited with him.

In Devon Hopkins stayed alone at the Lamb, which 'was about the worst inn at Tiverton I suppose but it was very cheap', and had to rebuke himself for 'Looking at a boy'.[16] He walked to Halberton, and just out of the town he 'met an old man driving a donkey-cart, who spoke in pure Devonshire (surprisingly reminding one of Grandmamma) and talked about the Manleys'. When asked about the event, the old man could not remember the marriage of Hopkins's grandparents, but he directed him to 'Manley wh. I found after some trouble. . . . I was surprised to find it is but a farmhouse.' From Tiverton he went to Exeter, thence to Chagford to walk on Dartmoor.

One remote cousin he met in church took him 'to Broomfield where I was introduced to her two daughters. They are such pretty lively girls. I had lunch there and then they played duets on the piano and harp, Miss Patch taking the harp. . . . They were all very kind, and the Miss Patches walked with me into the town, shewed me my road, and left me under a pleasing sense of what charming country cousins I had. They are my third cousins.'[17]

While he was away his family had been entertaining royalty: the widowed Queen Emma of the Hawaiian Islands, who was on a trip to England in connection with the new Anglican diocese of Hawaii and the proposed cathedral in Honolulu. According to her journal, at three o'clock on the 29th of July the Queen 'drove to Manley Hopkins's Oak Hill to lunch & it was excellen[t] lunch & very sociable'.[18] It would have provided a satisfactorily literary symmetry to her English trip if Gerard had been at home, for she met several other distinguished writers and actually stayed in the houses of Charles Kingsley and Tennyson. Since she could apparently make little of the works of the Poet Laureate, however, it is improbable that she would ever have enjoyed Gerard's poetry.

His holiday seems to have made Hopkins more resigned about Dolben that autumn without appreciably lowering the warmth of his feelings. They were made more complicated when an unexpected letter from Dolben caused a resumption of their correspondence. Hopkins wrote in his confessional notes that he was guilty of 'Spiritual pride abt. Dolben'. Then, as a gift for him, he set about recasting a poem he had begun the previous year, in response to Christina Rossetti's 'Convent Threshold'. Although the poem had languished for a long time, under such a stimulus it soon became so vivid for him that it was a dangerous temptation: 'Scrupulosity over *Beyond the Cloister*'. When he went home for Christmas a month later, he was still working on the poem and realized that he felt 'Dangerous scrupulosity abt. finishing a stanza of *Beyond the Cloister* for Dolben'. The following day he was 'Repeating to myself bits of *Beyond the Cloister*'. Unfortunately, no poem with that name remains, although there has been speculation that it was 'a revision in stanzas' of 'A Voice from the World'.* But Hopkins knew that his interest in Dolben was far from strictly poetic, for he also admitted to jealousy in 'Looking with evil curiosity at a picture of Gosselin.'[19]

Running all through his confessional notes about his sensual

---

*The poem may seem an odd one as a present for Dolben, since the narrator is addressing a young woman on the verge of becoming a nun. MacKenzie believes 'that some intense (even if perhaps shortlived) heterosexual experience provoked it'. Since there is no record of such an experience (not that we could expect there to be) and since Dolben was demonstrably so much in the forefront of his mind at the time, it seems far more probable to me that Hopkins is here changing the sex of the person addressed, just as he did in the trio of sonnets addressed to Dolben under the title of 'The Beginning of the End'.

concerns are concurrent worries over his increasing doubts concerning the Church of England and his growing feeling that he must in time become a convert to Rome. But he knew that it would be extremely unwise, both spiritually and practically, to talk about religious matters to others. For some time he had been less close to Liddon, and now even speaking to his confessor about his problems was to be avoided. A comparison of their private diaries shows that on some occasions Hopkins waited until Liddon was away from Oxford before going to confession to Dr Pusey, whose austere, somewhat removed manner made complete frankness more attractive than once it had seemed. On the 15th of December, for example, Liddon left for the Christmas vacation and the following day Hopkins wrote in his diary, 'I confessed to Dr. Pusey Dec. 16, 1865.'

The reasons for Hopkins's increasing coolness towards Liddon are not wholly clear, but when he finally left the Anglican Church, they had become so estranged that he no longer felt the need even to consult the man who had been his first confessor and spiritual adviser. Liddon himself continued his usual assiduous attention to Hopkins, and probably his interest had become too personal, even stifling, for the younger man, making it necessary to assert his independence.

In any case Liddon had begun to exude that self-importance which some observers so disliked in his later life. One impression of him was left by Thomas Arnold, brother of Matthew, who heard him preach this same year. At the time Arnold was in one of his recurrent religious tergiversations, having just decided he could no longer remain a Catholic, although he could not bring himself to become an Anglican again. To help clarify his mind, he attended two University Sermons in St Mary's on one day: in the morning to hear Mark Pattison, in the evening to observe the other side of the coin:

It was to be the famous Liddon. I was punctual, but there was not a seat to be had, the ladies mustered in overwhelming force. It was strange: but sermon and preacher were now everything most opposite to those of the morning. Liddon is a dark black haired little man – short straight stubby hair – and with that singularly shiny glistening appearance about his sallow complexion which one so often sees in dissenting ministers, and which the devotees no doubt consider a mark of election. Liddon's whole sermon was an impassioned strain of apologetic argument for the truth of the resurrection, and of the church doctrine generally. It was very clever certainly, but rather too long, it extended to about an hour and twenty minutes. The tone was earnest and devout; yet there were several sarcastic, one might almost say irritable, flings at the liberal and rationalizing party.[20]

Arnold was far from an impartial judge, but Liddon hardly sounds the man to whom Hopkins would remain close, although some of his friends did.

By September 1865 Hopkins was at least half certain that he was destined to become a Roman Catholic. To Baillie he wrote about his own 'extravagances (and perhaps also my pugnacity)', expressing himself 'more unreservedly and effusively' than he was used to do. In discussing his failings, he appealed to the awareness of sin he was sure Baillie must feel too:

> You will no doubt understand what I mean by saying that the *sordidness* of things, wh. one is compelled perpetually to feel, is perhaps . . . the most unmixedly painful thing one knows of: and this is (objectively) intensified and (subjectively) destroyed by Catholicism. If people cd. all know this, to take no higher ground, no other inducement wd. to very many minds be needed to lead them to Catholicism and no opposite inducement cd. dissuade them fr. it.[21]

Hopkins was not yet prepared to distinguish fully between Roman and English Catholicism, but his inclination to do so was already perceptible.

At the beginning of Michaelmas term, only a fortnight later, he was fully aware that he was unwisely speculating 'about leaving our Church', although the pronoun suggests that he was not yet ready. Such speculations were part of a process he called 'forecasting'. Three days later, on the 8th of October, he recorded for confession 'Repeated forecasting about Church of Rome. Talking about Dr. Newman at dinner etc in a foolish way likely to produce unhappiness and pain.'[22]

The example of Newman was clearly in the forefront of his mind, as it probably was in that of most Oxford converts of the time. The next day when he had been guilty of 'Dangerous forecasting', his remedy was to copy out the hymn 'Lead, kindly light'. And even that was Newman's composition.

In mid-October he was one step closer to conversion, as his journal indicates: 'Note that if ever I should leave the English Church the fact of Provost Fortescue . . . is to be got over.'[23] It is not clear exactly what 'fact' was Hopkins's stumbling block about the High Church Mr Knottesford-Fortescue, Dean of Perth, since he had a number of brushes with his own Church before his conversion to Rome a few years later. What is important here is the near-certainty Hopkins seems to have felt about leaving Anglicanism. Even more telling evidence about his feelings on the subject are the notes he made in his journal about his Christmas holidays in Hampstead, when he knew he could not yet tell his parents the state of his mind but equally could not refrain from bringing his favourite subject into the conversation. On the 22nd of December he was guilty of 'Foolishness at Grandmamma's with talk abt. Catholicism' and the day after Christmas he came near ruining the holiday by making his mother cry when he introduced an 'argument about the saints'. It may be worth noticing that there is no record of his discussing religion with his father.

Reasonably, Mr and Mrs Hopkins thought they were kind, perhaps indulgent parents, and with equal good sense Gerard knew that their ideas were inadequate for him. When he was so aware of his Roman Catholic inclinations, he could hardly help realizing that they would grate on each other if they were to discuss religion, and during the next nine or ten months he seems to have avoided both the subject and their company, so far as that was possible without outright rudeness. To judge from the remaining evidence, his parents were less tactful about their differences with Gerard, but since they could hardly believe that he was serious about his attitude to Rome, they were unaware that their cautionary advice would drive him even further away from their own views. However unhappily the Christmas holidays passed, open conflict was avoided until the following year.

On Christmas Day Gerard had written a limpid little plea for purity that perhaps was not only aspiration but a half-articulated recognition that 1866 was to see a complete change in his spiritual condition:

> Moonless darkness stands between.
> Past, the Past, no more be seen!
> But the Bethlehem star may lead me
> To the sight of Him Who freed me
> From the self that I have been.
> Make me pure, Lord; Thou art holy;
> Make me meek, Lord; Thou wert lowly;
> Now beginning, and alway;
> Now begin, on Christmas day.

CHAPTER VII

A PROVISIONAL LOYALTY
1866

The possibility of conversion involved a great deal more for Hopkins than a simple switch from Anglo-Catholicism to Roman Catholicism, for that would finally hinge almost entirely on whether he was willing to accept Papal authority and the concomitant recognition of the Roman Church as the only valid connection with the mission of Christ: there were few other Roman dogmas that an Anglican could not swallow if his beliefs were sufficiently High Church, but many social and political aspects of conversion were finally far more visible than a change in one's profession of faith, and those aspects could have profound emotional effects upon a convert. They were probably hurdles as hard to leap over as any doctrinal difficulties.

In 1866 a man was shaken loose from his position in the rigid English social structure if he became a Catholic. Although it was often said, partly in joking, that the only two Churches to which gentlemen could profess their allegiance were the Roman and the Anglican,* the only Catholics who were thoroughly acceptable were those born into the Church, preferably into Recusant families, or, failing that, into backgrounds from which the taint of conversion had been removed by time, at the very least a generation or two. Hopkins was not a snob, but he knew that he was risking ostracism by his family and the possibility of being dropped by many of his University friends, with no guarantee of acceptance within his new Church.

Few Protestants went so far as J. W. Black of Brasenose who had

---

*Exceptions might be made in the case of Quakers, particularly those conspicuously successful in banking or the manufacture of chocolate.

recently said bluntly in a Union debate 'that all Roman Catholics were an importation from the Devil', but Hopkins's friend Sam Brooke noticed 'that people fear Roman Catholics a great deal more than they fear heathens'. The local dislike of Catholics was not based on much personal experience, since in the years 1854–63, there had been an average of 'two [Catholic] students a year passing through Oxford', and as late as 1872 there were only eight in the University.[1]

But feeling in Oxford was only a pale reflection of the hatred of Rome elsewhere, which was perhaps strongest in the families and close friends of converts. Even after Stuckey Coles had reached the age of twenty-six, his father still felt he was in such danger from unwise friendships that he must withdraw 'from any thing more than *quite general* acquaintance with those who have left the Church of England'.[2] Mrs Thomas Arnold, whose husband was intermittently a Roman Catholic, refused to meet any of his co-religionists, even Newman, and at her husband's first conversion had expressed her outrage by heaving a brick through a window of the church in which he was being received. The Hopkins family had a less dramatic sense of occasion than Mrs Arnold, but Gerard could not count on their High Church beliefs being elastic enough to encompass his conversion.

We have no absolute proof that he was already determined on ordination, but his close association with Dolben and Coles and their Ritualist circles suggests that he felt as enthusiastic as they did about the matter, and in 1866 his parents 'believed he had lately resolved on taking orders in the English Church'.[3] If he were to change his Church, it would mean giving up his chances of the comfortable social position of the higher Anglican clergy, as well as the financial advantages that went with it. Certainly, no matter how distinguished his degree, he would not as a Catholic be eligible for a Fellowship in an Oxford college, which otherwise seemed his natural destination. Even his choice of other occupations in which no profession of religion was formally required would be severely limited by a change of faith.

At the very time that the difficulty of his own conversion was coming home to Hopkins, there was another on the horizon that suggested Catholicism might become at least socially respectable in the University. At Christ Church the nineteen-year-old Marquess of Bute was already wavering on the edge, although Liddon, his spiritual adviser in the same college, was doing all he could to keep him in the Church of England. (His excessive reverence for Bute's rank may well have contributed to Liddon's decline in Hopkins's estimation.) All through 1866 and 1867 Liddon wrestled for Bute's soul, but the best he could manage was to extort a promise that Bute would wait until he was twenty-one. Actually, the young man waited until some three months after his birthday before he was finally received.

Liddon's rival for Bute's allegiance was a Roman Catholic priest who was even better known for his agility at scaling the social ladder, for his worldly manners, and for his intimacy with the Scottish and English aristocracy, over whose younger members he was said to exert a sinister influence. In theory T.J. Capel was based in Pau, but he frequently returned to England and went to Oxford, where Pusey once complained he was 'making a raid upon our undergraduates'.[4]

Liddon and Capel were in competition for the same followers, and they disliked each other with an intensity suggesting that each recognized something of himself in the other. They exchanged barbed letters about the validity of orders in their respective Churches, and when Liddon was driven to extreme measures by his distaste for Capel he 'issued a peremptory mandate prohibiting the undergraduates from making his acquaintance'. Precisely how the prohibition was to be enforced was not clear, but Liddon may have had a point, since Capel (who became Msgr Capel in 1868) later became involved in financial scandals connected with his attempt to found a Catholic university in Kensington, was suspended from the Westminster diocese for 'grave moral offences', and was told by Cardinal Manning that he must leave England, since each day brought 'fresh evidence and new proofs of great scandal'. To make his own position quite clear, Manning threatened to resign his See if Capel returned to England. The controversial, not to say un-savoury, prelate ended his life at the head of the Roman Catholic Church in northern California, living on his memories of the heady days in London society when he had been the model for Msgr Catesby in Disraeli's novel *Lothair*.[5]

The whole Bute–Liddon–Capel affair, although it perhaps added social *ton* to Oxford Catholicism, was no help in giving assurance to a young man as strait of conscience as Hopkins, nor in making his family and friends understand his eventual conversion, however much they might love a marquess.

Balliol had a reputation for greater toleration than most colleges, but it was not clear to Hopkins what its official position would be if he were to become a Roman Catholic. There were precedents for dealing with conversions in the College, but none of them was precisely parallel to his case. A decade earlier, when W.G. Ward became a convert, he had forfeited his tutorship and was practically forced into resigning his Fellowship. In 1857 H.N. Oxenham had been received into the Church of Rome, and the College had voted that it did not 'intend to remove Mr. Oxenham's name from the books without his own consent'. But Oxenham had already taken his degree and so would not be living among undergraduates. What seemed more relevant to Hopkins's own case was that in 1858 the College had rejected an 'Application made by Mr. Noel Wellman that his son, being a Roman Catholic, be admitted as an under-graduate without being required to attend Chapel or Divinity Lectures'.

Although it may not have seemed so to Hopkins, the College since then had become increasingly lenient. There was no way for him to guess that within a few months the College was to pass a resolution admitting Catholics and actually take a Catholic into residence. An additional problem was that as a Catholic Hopkins could not in good conscience attend required College chapel. As recently as 1864 the governing body had resolved 'that undergradu-ate members of the College who are certified by their parents or guardians to be Nonconformists shall be excused attendance upon any of the Chapel Services and Divinity Lectures to which their parents or guardians shall object'.[6] Obviously, there was no reason for Mr Hopkins to object to his son's attendance at the College Chapel, and it was nearly impossible to imagine his saying that he did so, even to oblige Gerard. Besides, there was the vexed question of whether Roman Catholics were Nonconformists; certainly, they were not in the popular usage of that term, although it could be argued that technically they were, since they did not conform to the doctrines of the Church of England. It had always been a bad Protestant joke to refer to Roman Catholics slightingly as Nonconformists, but to invoke the name in support of his own conscience would have been very unlike a man as obdurate as Hopkins.

Since he was so convinced that no one with Broad Church principles could understand his feelings, it would have been difficult for him to seek guidance from the Fellows, even if he had thought them more approachable on the subject. Had he done so, he might have been saved a good bit of worry. But he was fiercely independent. It would have been particularly difficult to go to Jowett, since Hopkins would have known in substance, if not detail, Jowett's conviction that 'almost under any circumstances it is our duty to remain in the Church', even when one's belief in the Articles was as attenuated as his own.[7] Besides, Hopkins's reiterated statements in his confessional notes about having made fun of Jowett or of having been disrespectful about him suggest that he would not have sought his advice on an intimate matter.

So far as Hopkins could be sure at the time, there was at least a possibility that a conversion to Rome would mean losing the chance of taking a degree that promised to be brilliant. His spiritual decision cannot have been made easier by the temporal considerations that weighed so heavily on his parents, but he was the most improbable of persons to tailor his actions to fit his prospects. Actually, he seems at times to have taken a defiant pleasure in finding difficulties to face, making one wonder whether he would ever have become a Catholic if the path had been easy. He was far too serious a man to undertake such a commitment simply for the sake of its difficulty, but that difficulty may have helped make a conversion attractive to him, or at least to have drawn his attention.

With his problems revolving in his head, in 1866 Hopkins went back to Oxford for term on the 21st of January, and two days later wrote down his resolutions for Lenten penance. It is a well-known document, but it bears repetition because it indicates so much of his austerity of mind:

For Lent. No pudding on Sundays. No tea except if to keep me awake and then without sugar. Meat only once a day. No verses in Passion Week or on Fridays. No lunch or meat on

Fridays. Not to sit in armchair except can work in no other way. Ash Wednesday and Good Friday bread and water.[8]

On the same day he wrote the last of the confessional notes in his diary, and, almost immediately afterward, the volume ends with a rueful recapitulation of his 'old habits'. There is an air of finality about the entry that suggests he was deliberately giving up keeping notes for confession.

It has been guessed that after this he wrote his jottings for confession in another volume, keeping them separate this time from his journal. We do know that after his conversion he told Newman he was somewhat uncertain as to how to continue with penance: 'Monsignor Eyre seemed to say that I ought not to make my confession by means of a paper as I have been used to do. Will you kindly say whether you wd. prefer it so or not?'[9] This suggests that in the months intervening between the end of the old diary and his conversion in October he had continued confessional notes of the same sort he made while still an Anglican. If so, the notes have since disappeared. Whatever the reason, he did not start writing in his journal again until the beginning of May. The manner of the new volume is more literary, perhaps more studied, and it is far less personal, so that the reader often feels as if a shade had been drawn.

For all his whiplash energy, Hopkins 'was far from robust', and the austerity of his Lenten practices frightened his mother, who insisted on his giving them up. After his conversion, he allowed a little of his resentment over the matter to show: 'Strictly I owed no duty whatever to the Church of England, because it is not what it claims to be, a lawful church, but I did pay a provisional loyalty and even to the extent of keeping its fasts, until you induced me to give them up, which I said I wd. do for a little time: I cd. not otherwise have obeyed you.'[10] All the confusion of love and resentment that he had been feeling for some time about his family was intensified, all the misunderstanding magnified. While he was still keeping penitential notes, he had more than once admitted to spiritual pride in his own sacrifices. A touch of it was probably required if he were to keep up his resolution for the long process of conversion, and perhaps the fear of losing the directness of his intentions made it impossible for him to act with his normal compassion towards those he loved. On another occasion he would probably have taken a more understanding attitude to the affection behind his mother's worries.

It was peculiarly difficult for him to know what to do about the sacraments to which he was accustomed in the Church of England. If it were in truth not a lawful Church, he could not believe he was behaving morally in receiving absolution and Communion from schismatic clergymen. But until he had worked out a decisive answer for himself, he needed all the help he could get from the sacraments in case they should turn out to be valid. For the moment the dilemma was insoluble, so he picked a careful way down the middle, hedging his bets. He continued going to confession until mid-summer, presumably about once a month, as he had done before. On the 13th of June, after waiting until Liddon had been gone from Oxford a few days on his summer holiday, Hopkins wrote the single word 'Confession' in his journal, although he did not give the name of his confessor. His last Anglican Communion was in September of that year, only the month before he was received into the Church of Rome.

According to his friend William Addis, Hopkins spoke to a Roman Catholic priest for the first time in the summer of 1866, but he had been going to Roman Mass for some time before that, of course without confessing or communicating. He was in the un-satisfactory position of attending one church and receiving the sacraments in another. At the time the only public place of Catholic worship in Oxford was the little mission chapel of St Ignatius, across Magdalen Bridge at the beginning of the Headington Road, which had a particular appeal for Hopkins because it had been the scene of Newman's first appearance in public after he had made his submission to the Church, when he and his companions in the Littlemore community walked down through the fields to the plain little building to attend Mass.* And it was there he had heard his last Mass before leaving Oxford in 1846. Hopkins's attendance at the chapel was a silent indication of how closely he followed in the footsteps of Newman, but in later years St Ignatius's was to have additional meaning for him from his own close association with it.

---

*Newman disliked the little church and wrote of it, 'nor is it a slight trial, as you may suppose, except as faith overcomes it, to go to what to outward appearance is a meeting house'.

Most of the trickle of recent Oxford conversions had been funnelled through St Ignatius's, which had served Catholics in both the city and the surrounding countryside since 1793. Until 1859 it had been cared for by the Jesuits, but all during Hopkins's undergraduate years it was served by secular priests, who returned it to the Society of Jesus in 1871. When Hopkins first attended services there, the incumbent was a secular priest, Fr Alexander Comberbach. The congregation had always been small, composed chiefly of domestic servants from Oxford and a few country communicants, most of them the descendants of old families who had, in earlier years, gone to Mass in the chapels of Catholic country houses: Waterperry, Milton Manor, Haseley Court, Mapledurham, Stonor, Brightwell and East Hendred among others, and still earlier to Holywell Manor in Oxford itself. In 1866 it was still the habit of those who drove into Oxford for Mass at 10.30 to go to breakfast afterwards at the Port Mahon, the nextdoor public house.

St Clement's (the area took its name from the Anglican parish), in which the chapel was located, was extremely rough, 'sordid by day, by night oil-lighted', stretching from Magdalen Bridge to Harpsichord Row at the foot of Headington Hill; technically, it was not a part of Oxford. The chapel itself was simple, with round-headed windows that made it easy for detractors to say that it might be mistaken for a dissenting chapel or a workhouse, but its very removal from Oxford had a certain attraction for members of the University who wanted to attend Mass without being seen by friends. The University Proctors were quite aware of this and often sent their 'bulldogs' to stand on either side of the chapel door to identify undergraduates who were coming to Mass without permission from their colleges.[11] There is a tradition that Hopkins and a friend had their names taken by the Proctors some time in 1866–7 and had to pay a fine in consequence.*

---

* If true, the story is useful in establishing the time when Hopkins began attending Mass; after his conversion he would probably not have been fined by the Proctors, since he had permission from Balliol to attend religious services elsewhere. This suggests that the incident occurred before 23 October 1866 and probably before the beginning of Michaelmas term. Unfortunately, the office of the University Senior Proctor has no record of such an event. What appears to be the most authoritative account is in Crehan, p. 210.

In May of 1866 Hopkins moved out of Balliol into lodgings in New Inn Hall Street, sharing them with William Addis. When he had gone into new quarters in College in the autumn of 1863, it was with the expectation of remaining in them for the rest of his time at Balliol, since undergraduates were required to live in College and were allowed only one change of rooms while there. That spring, however, part of the quadrangle in which Hopkins lived was torn down in the great rebuilding scheme of Balliol.[12] Rooms were scarce, and, unusually, permission was given to a few undergraduates to live in lodgings. Addis was already a good friend of Hopkins, and the fact that they were both so close to conversion makes it probable that they volunteered to be among those staying out of College that year, in order to 'live a more Catholic life', as Dolben liked to say he was striving to do. Whether or not it is true, as Addis said, that he knew Hopkins better as an undergraduate than anyone else did, what can hardly be questioned is both his closeness to him during 1866 and the mutual strength they derived from their common attraction to Catholicism. Addis, like Hopkins, belonged to the High Church Hexameron Society, and he read papers to the group when it met in their shared lodgings in New Inn Hall Street. Also like Hopkins, he fasted during Lent, apparently too rigorously, and since his parents were less observant than Hopkins's family, he carried on until he had made himself ill.

Although Addis's religious devotion may have seemed extreme to other friends, to Hopkins he seemed in most matters a model of moderation: 'more and more I reverence the balance, the heartiness, the sincerity, the *greatness*, of Addis', he wrote. On another occasion he told Baillie, 'I have heard fr. Addis: it is wonderful how good he is.'[13]

Together the young men roamed the Oxford countryside, which seemed more than usually beautiful that spring, as they walked and talked of their religious urgings and of their difficulties with their families. The companionship sharpened Hopkins's artistic sensitivity to the gentle landscape, and his journals are filled with arresting notes of what he saw, constantly reminding us that he was knee-deep in the landscape Arnold had celebrated: the blue Cumnor hills, the great elm at Fyfield, the Binsey meadows 'yellow with buttercups and under-reddened with sorrel', all drenched with the sound of cuckoo, woodlark and corncrake.

One long warm day in May they walked to Cumnor, then back to the meadows west of Oxford, noting the change from town to country:

> Over the green water of the river passing the slums of the town and under its bridges swallows shooting, blue and purple above and shewing their amber-tinged breasts reflected in the water, their flight unsteady with wagging wings and leaning first to one side then the other. Peewits flying. Towards sunset the sky partly swept, as often, with moist white cloud, tailing off across which are morsels of grey-black woolly clouds. Sun seemed to make a bright liquid hole in this, its texture had an upward northerly sweep or drift from the W, marked softly in grey.[14]

It is probably more than coincidence that his descriptions of nature became so intense just at the time that he stopped writing of the young men who had filled his aesthetic considerations the previous year. It is as if he had given up his devotion to one aspect of beauty because of its danger and had settled on another, a safer manifestation of the munificence of Heaven.

The whole problem of the moral quality of beauty had been forced on his attention by his absorption in Dolben, and it became more philosophically pressing that spring of 1866 when he went for extra tuition to his new 'coach', Walter Pater, who already had a local notoriety for saying that beauty needed no moral justification save the intensity with which it was experienced. It was a doctrine that struck at the roots of Christian belief. Pater was a new and very young Fellow of Brasenose College (he was only five years older than Hopkins), but he was well known in the University and had already caught Hopkins's attention. A few years before, Pater's own coach had been Jowett, who recognized his brilliance but doubted his steadiness of purpose and the morality of his principles. Nonetheless, he seems to have been the intermediary who arranged for Hopkins to have tuition from Pater.

Jowett surely suggested Pater in the hope that he would act as a counterbalance to the dangerous influence of Liddon, whom he knew Hopkins had seen frequently in the past year or two and whom he rightly suspected of undermining the possibility of Hopkins's accepting Broad Church principles.[15] Although Jowett prided himself on being current with his pupils' interests, in this case he was slightly out of date. What he had failed to notice was that Hopkins had already begun avoiding Liddon, and that in any case the influence of Pater would be far more dangerous than Liddon's because Pater openly voiced doubts that bubbled up in Hopkins but seemed never to trouble Liddon.

As we have already seen, Hopkins had been very much aware of Pater for at least two years, having heard from Samuel Brooke about the essay that he had read to the Old Mortality Society in 1864, advocating beauty as the standard by which to judge morality. Hopkins himself certainly recognized the dangers of such a position, as well as its attractions, and he had joined Brooke and Liddon in founding the Hexameron Society in reaction to Pater, but he was apparently far less alarmed by what he had heard than either of the others. One attractive aspect of Hopkins that brings a modern reader up short is the lack of shock he exhibited at the belief and behaviour of others just when one would expect deep disapproval. In particular, rationalism or disbelief ('neology' in the cant of the day) in his acquaintances worried him far less than his own failings. In making friends he was naturally drawn to those who shared his beliefs, but he seems never to have held scepticism or even outright atheism against any of them. In 1866 he was apparently quite unperturbed, perhaps even amused, at the differences between Pater's beliefs and his own. On the 2nd of May he wrote in his journal, 'Coaching with W.H. Pater this term. Walked with him on Monday evening last, April 30. Fine evening bitterly cold. "Bleak-faced Neology in cap and gown": no cap and gown but very bleak.' By the end of the month he noted, apparently as a mere matter of plain record, not as something startling, 'Pater talking two hours against Xtianity'.[16] We are denied knowning what Brooke thought of the friendship between Hopkins and the young don of whom he so disapproved, for by this time he had run out of steam and had ceased writing in his diary.

As coach and pupil took their windswept ramble, they were a

bizarre picture: Hopkins moving along with the delicate, effortless pace that his friends remembered as typical of him, Pater seeming to lag behind with a heavy, halting step suggesting partial lameness. But Pater was as observant as Hopkins himself of the landscape, and they talked of it as they walked. One friend remembered Pater's love of walking in Christ Church Meadow and along the banks of the Cherwell and how especially attentive he was to 'the movement of light in grass and among leaves, of all fragrances, of flowing water; but with this he was, I presume willfully, blind to human passers-by'.[17] At least the first part of the description might have been written of Hopkins himself.

Pater was not an easy man of whom to be fond, but, curiously, he seems to have been the teacher for whom Hopkins retained the most affection after he left the University. No doubt the fact that they were so close in age made their friendship easier, but even more important was the likeness of reaction in the elegant-minded atheist, as Pater then was, and the palpitatingly serious young religious enthusiast. For very different reasons one of the most important things in both their lives was the moment of perception of beauty. To Pater that moment was given its own validity by its unique intensity, for Hopkins it took its meaning from the fact that it became a revelation of Divinity. To be sure, that meaning was evanescent for him, no matter how hard he tried to keep it in the forefront of his mind, but its importance for him is clear in the single-mindedness with which he tried to perceive and to understand, as well as to savour, the uniqueness of each moment of revelation. However, in his excited setting forth of the meaning he sensed, he sometimes seems to have approached the vehemence of assertion that is a clue to a tiny cloud of covert doubt.

Hopkins, as we have seen, had always been fond of painting, but with Pater as guide he constantly refined his taste, and they went together to look at the splendid pictures scattered so negligently through the Oxford colleges. As they talked their way through long tutorials in the serenity of Pater's pale green rooms in Brasenose, which were furnished with porcelain, bronzes, and a few etchings, looking out over the architectural perfection of Radcliffe Square, Hopkins probably learned as much from his tutor's asides and from the atmosphere of aestheticism as he did from formal instruction. It is striking, if perhaps quite unimportant, that to reach those rooms Hopkins had each time to pass the carved stone features of Duns Scotus, the Subtle Doctor, who had walked that square more than six centuries earlier, and whose philosophy was in time to help him recognize in a flash his own relationship with nature.

The general quality of what Hopkins recorded in his journals was beginning to give way to the particular; more and more his attention was turning from clouds and hills to the details of a tree, a plant, or a leaf, and, curiously, the more minute and painstaking his regard became, the more abstract the description. The more familiar he was with the specifics of what he looked at, the more impersonal became the principles of identification that lay behind it. 'It is the tufts of bloom on Spanish chestnuts, crowning the round tufts in which the leaves are thrown which make those wavy concentric outlines this tree has at twilight,' he noted on the 29th of June, and a week later he wrote in his journal, 'Carnations if you look close have their tongue-shaped petals powdered with spankled red glister, which no doubt gives them their brilliancy: sharp chip shadows of one petal on another; the notched edge curls up and so is darked, which gives them graceful precision.' Somewhere in the minute examination the observer himself seems to have disappeared, as if Hopkins's own reactions were not to be trusted, and the focus has shifted to an abstraction of chestnuts or carnations. 'Oaks: the organisation of this tree is difficult', he wrote wonderingly soon thereafter; when he had pondered the problem for nearly a week, he could at last say, 'I have now found the law of the oak leaves.'[18] Almost instinctively, he was groping his way to a formulation of a symbolic universe, in which both the individual and the generic had their own validity. It is in part this alternation between what is observed and what it signifies that gives such a dizzying, almost hallucinatory quality to much of his later poetry.

Even persons sometimes receded from individuality into pattern. That year he attended Encaenia in the Sheldonian Theatre, both to hear Matthew Arnold deliver the Creweian Oration as Professor of Poetry and to see the father of his friend Hardy receive an honorary degree. But instead of mentioning either of them or the other eight recipients of degrees or even Keble, whose recent death was being eulogized by Arnold, Hopkins wrote in his journal, 'Was happily able to see composition of the crowd in the area of the theatre, all the heads looking one way thrown up by their black coats relieved only by white shirt-fronts etc.: the short strokes of eyes, nose, mouth, repeated hundreds of times I believe it is which gives the visible law: looked at in any one instance it flies.'[19] The entry is a foreshadowing of the way that in some of his poetry he seems to have dehumanized the world, so that persons are less important than perceptions. The characterization of human features as brush strokes is much akin to the way in which painters are often much more interested in technique than in subject.

If we read only his journal, we might have trouble remembering that Hopkins was going through the agony of conversion that spring, for almost none of it percolates into its pages, just as his feelings for Dolben had been largely denied expression for a year without diminishing their intensity. It is startling to read his entry for the 1st of June, when he describes being caught in a thunderstorm on Port Meadow, then without transition says, 'I read today the journal I kept in 1862, burning parts.'[20] Suddenly it is apparent that even if he had not yet consciously recognized his intentions, he was already clearing the decks for his conversion, but a clear statement of the momentous decision had not yet made its way into anything he had written.

CHAPTER VIII

CONVERSION
1866

Instead of going back to Hampstead after Encaenia in the summer of 1866, Hopkins went for a week's walking in the West Country with Addis. They took it in slow stages, for Addis silently tried to make the trip easy for Hopkins, who was far from strong but said little of his health. Although it rained most of the time, they went as far as Bristol, Glastonbury, and Wells, then made a stop in Bedminster for a High Church service at the Sailor's College and 'heard a delightful Gregorian there'. A boat to Chepstow followed, and a visit to Tintern Abbey, where Hopkins paid the ruin the highest of compliments by saying it reminded him of the work of Butterfield. Then came Ross and Hereford, where they went two miles up the river to Belmont and the Benedictine Cathedral Priory of St Michael. Although it was apparently the real reason for their trip, Hopkins seemed shy of going there in Addis's company, so he waited until his friend had made his visit alone, then walked up the river himself.

According to Addis, Hopkins had never spoken to a Roman Catholic priest before this visit. Dom Paul Raynal, Hopkins said, 'was very kind and showed me over everything'. He spoke to both men about the 'doubtful validity' of Anglican orders and gave as his opinion that it would be unlawful to communicate in the Anglican Church. 'I think he made a great impression on both of us,' said Addis years later, 'and I believe that from that time our faith in Anglicanism was really gone.'[1] Whatever Hopkins may have said to Addis on the matter, he was still undecided about his own relation to the sacraments, and he continued communicating in the Church of England even after he had decided to become a convert.

In contrast to the excitement of Belmont, their visit to the cathedral in Gloucester the following day was a disappointment and they found that 'everything is very sadly done'. Anglicanism seemed overfamiliar and tame, and indeed this may have helped Hopkins make up his mind.

Hampstead was equally dull when he returned from Gloucestershire, and a pall hung over the family because financial disaster seemed imminent. Gerard's grandfather Smith had put most of his money in the Agra and Masterman bank, which on the 6th of June suspended payments after a month of rumours about its stability. With a splendidly quixotic generosity, Mr Smith went to the bank when he first heard of their troubles and gave them a further £2500 to help them out of their difficulties, saying that they had been kind to him years before. Now it seemed it would all be lost. Two years later the re-opened bank paid off all its creditors, but in 1866 that seemed highly improbable. Perhaps in response to her husband's troubles, Grandmama Smith had fallen seriously ill and was also a great worry to the family.

Gerard restlessly marked time, awaiting a chance to get away from Hampstead. He walked endlessly in the parks and commons of the city, made comforting visits to his grandparents in Croydon, took careful notes on the pictures in the art exhibitions he visited, and occasionally went with his family to dinner parties. Above all, he tried to work at his books, but as he later confessed, he was unable to accomplish much. We do not know how often he brandished theology at his unwilling family, but the impression gained from his letters and journals is that he was trying hard to avoid any quarrels with them as he worked the problem out in his mind.

In the middle of July he set off for the Sussex Downs for a long fortnight, to walk out his problems in the intervals of what he planned as a concentrated rush of study to make up for his failure to work in London. His two companions were High Church friends from Oxford, W.A. Comyn Macfarlane and A.W. Garrett, both of them, like Hopkins, flirting with conversion. Their original intention had been to go to the Lake District, but at Hopkins's suggestion they stayed in southern England, within reach of a weekly celebration of a Roman Mass. He was still in the uncomfortable position of not knowing whether he was more at home in an Anglican or a Roman church, so he continued attending both.

Hopkins's first choice of location in Sussex would have been near West Lavington, but Macfarlane talked him into staying in the neighbourhood of Horsham, apparently because he had heard of the 'stately' services with vestments in the main church of that town. In spite of his own proclivities, Hopkins could not resist teasing him that 'a rag of popery' should lead him and Garrett 'so palpably by the nose'.[2]

The fortnight was to be the watershed of his life. On the 10th of July he took a train to Midhurst, then walked to West Lavington and back to see Butterfield's church, built there some fourteen years earlier for Manning, when he was Rector of the parish. The parallel of Manning's conversion to his own situation was surely much in his mind. The following day he walked through the great park at Petworth and took a train to Horsham, where he met Garrett. They made enquiries about a place for the three of them to stay cheaply and were told of Mr Ings's farm off a lane leading from Horsham to Nuthurst. 'We walked over to the farm,' he reported, 'had tea with Miss Ings, and finally agreed to take the place for a fortnight.'[3] They found the farm 'as ugly as can be', but the countryside pretty. The terms were 30s. 'a week for lodging, cooking, etc. and to board ourselves', he told Macfarlane:

> You will perhaps not object to Garrett and me planning out our time and work and you will of course make what alter- ation you wish: you remember it is absolutely necessary for me to read hard and for Garrett too. Will you kindly carve? He is going to cater and I shall take the Hours and give you copies of the responses for some wh. we might perhaps say at the beginning of the week.[4]

As it turned out, Hopkins was considerably more successful at arranging for nightly compline at 10.45 than he was on the few occasions when he helped Garrett with the catering, for he was inclined to be forgetful about buying provisions, and once they had to have their 'Tea delayed till past 8 owing to non appearance of Garrett & Hopkins not providing eggs.'

Several times the first week the three young men went to services together, either in the big parish church in Horsham or the 'rather more catholic' and smaller new church of St Mark in North Street. As the days passed Hopkins accompanied the others less frequently and became less open in manner. One evening Garrett and Macfarlane went to Evensong without him and afterwards looked in on 'a fair going on in the Town. Hopkins who had been rather disagreeable in the day had tea ready for us when we returned.' The next day, a Sunday, Garrett and Macfarlane went to St Mark's again, but 'H. deserted us.' After a long choral service they went back to the farm: 'Tea on returning and we had a serious talk with Hopkins about his manners etc.'[5]

This is probably the only time that anyone outside his family ever wrote of Hopkins's manners being bad. He was not reading as much as he should, and walking in the beautiful countryside was clearly doing little for him. It was obvious enough to him what had been wrong for a week, but he felt he could not tell his companions.

His journal entry of the 17th of July is a typical understated coupling of his observance of external nature and his internal wrestlings: 'Dull, curds-and-whey clouds faintly at times. – It was this night I believe but possibly the next that I saw clearly the impossibility of staying in the Church of England, but resolved to say nothing to anyone till three months are over, that is the end of the Long, and then of course to take no step till after my Degree.'[6] As abruptly as notes on his religious feelings intrude on the weather, they stop again, and a week later he made his final entry in his 1866 journal. We know that he began another volume, but it is lost, probably destroyed by Hopkins himself. Whatever the reasons, we have to depend on letters and the records of others for his life in the succeeding year, during which he was received into the Roman Catholic Church.

Presumably he felt conscience-stricken about his graceless behaviour to his friends, mulling over it until the 24th of July, when Macfarlane wrote that he had 'Walked out with Hopkins and he confided to me his fixed intention of going over to Rome. I did not attempt to argue with him as his grounds did not admit of argument. Went to Evensong alone.'[7] Although Hopkins had been moved to talk to Macfarlane in partial apology, afterwards he regretted having done so, for he knew it was advisable to keep his convictions to himself. In his journal he recorded that he 'Spoke to Macfarlane foolishly.' It shows something of his confusion that it was on this evening that he forgot the eggs for their tea.

Later he admitted that he had also let Garrett know of his plans 'through my incaution'. The truth is that all this summer, although he was constantly enjoining strict silence on his friends, he was extremely leaky with his secrets.

The mood of fellowship with which the walking party had begun was disturbed, and after that he seems to have gone his own way more frequently, even tacitly failing to read compline with the others on two or three evenings. Once they went to the photographer in Horsham and recorded their visit in one of those stiff, posed little groups that make the Victorians seem so formal as they wait breathlessly for the slow film. Seemingly somewhat hesitant, Hopkins leans on Macfarlane's shoulder, his hat in the crook of one arm, a stick in the other hand. Adding to his anxious expression is a tentative little moustache, looking home-grown for the occasion and apparently abandoned soon after (see Plate 10a).

When the three men said goodbye at Horsham station, Hopkins went on to Shanklin on the Isle of Wight, to join his family, with whom he was committed to spending three weeks before their return to Hampstead. He was of course unable to talk to his parents about his decision to become a Catholic, although he was clearly brimming over with his plans. One of his brothers, probably Arthur, guessed what was happening and made Gerard confess to it: 'he forced it from me by questions'.[8] In spite of his protests, it was probably a relief to have a confidant in the family, particularly one who felt no compulsion to tell his parents what he had found out. It is improbable that they had no suspicions of what was afoot, especially when Gerard went off to Mass on their return to Hampstead, but he wanted to avoid a direct confrontation, and they no doubt felt that the longer they closed their eyes to his intentions the less probable it was that they would be implemented.

As in Sussex, Hopkins proved a difficult companion. He had, of course, given up the idea of being a painter, but to occupy himself he sketched in the neighbourhood of Shanklin, where he had often filled his sketch pad in previous summers, and he continued trying to get on with his reading for the autumn, with little more success than in Horsham. As most of us do occasionally, he took out his disappointment at his failure to work by complaining of his time being usurped by others.

The one person to whom he might have told everything, with some confidence in being understood, was Dolben, but he had not seen him since their single meeting in Oxford. The previous summer, after refusing two invitations from Bridges, Dolben had at last gone for his only stay at Rochdale, but he hoped to go again in 1866. When Bridges invited Hopkins for the same period, he replied with pleasure, 'I should like nothing so much as to stay at Rochdale, more especially . . . when you hold out the possibility of Dolben being there.' He salved his conscience at leaving Hampstead for two or three weeks by asking if he might spend some time on his still-neglected work during the visit: 'You are kind enough to speak of reading: it would be impossible for me now to take any more holidays, my work is in such a state.'[9] Neither Dolben nor Bridges yet knew about his plans for conversion, but he expected to tell them in Rochdale.

With good reason, Mr Mackworth Dolben thought his son became too excited about religion when he was with his Etonian friends, so he kept Digby from going to Rochdale by the simple expedient of taking him to the West Country. Actually, Bridges was almost the least likely of Dolben's friends to encourage him in his religious antics, which were becoming more and more bizarre.

After leaving Hopkins and Bridges in Oxford in early 1865 Dolben had been sent to a succession of clerical tutors in parts of England seemingly chosen for their remoteness from Eton, Oxford, or anywhere else too exhilarating, although Mr Mackworth Dolben's declared intention was only to find an 'ideal Protestant in a bracing Rectory' to teach his son. Understandably, Digby was somewhat less than enthusiastic about the choice of tutors. Since the beginning of 1866 he had been studying with the Revd Henry De Winton at Boughrood, just over the Welsh border near Hay-on-Wye.

Dolben hated being a year without a confessor and with only monthly Communion. The lack of 'Catholic advantages', he said, 'may be a good way to get into Balliol, but not, I think, into Heaven'.[10]

With two of his companions at Boughrood Dolben was happy, although they probably did not displace Gosselin in his affections. The first of them was his old friend Alfred Wyatt-Edgell (later Lord Braye), already mentioned, who had been at Eton with him and who was so devoted that he published an elegy on Dolben after his death. Years later, in a belated grasp at total respectability, he decided that, after all, Digby had meant little to him; the burden of Dolben's poems does not support that judgement.

Digby's other close companion at Boughrood was H.R. Scott, to whom, twenty years later, Ellen Dolben sent a copy of a poem Dolben had written to him suggesting he had supplanted Gosselin in Dolben's regard:

> Then on another arm I leant,
> And then once more with him I went
>   Through field and wharf and town, –
> And love caught up the flying hours,
> And eyes, that were not calm as your's [sic],
>   Were imaged in my own.[11]

'He used to speak of you as the one of his companions at Boughrood who was most to him,' Miss Dolben wrote in the accompanying letter, 'and I think being with you made him see some beauty & good in manliness, which he was before disposed to underrate, & to confound with mere masculinity. He began rather to wish he could do those things you did, while up to that time, he admired nothing of the kind excepting boating, which was always a delight to him.'[12] Clearly, even if their course had been diverted in another direction, Dolben's impetuous affections had not been tamed by either ideal Protestant or bracing rectory.

If Dolben's father intended his stay at Boughrood to eradicate his Catholic tendencies, he invested the fees unwisely, for Digby asserted his religious preferences by decorating his room with crucifix, candles, and flowers on the dressing table, before which he would prostrate himself in prayer, wearing his monk's habit. Even more disastrously, Mr Mackworth Dolben had not noticed that Boughrood was only a few miles through the Black Mountains from the monastery in the vale of Llanthony where Father Ignatius, the founder of the Benedictine community in which Digby had his minor orders, had removed from Suffolk. At the beginning of his summer holidays, Dolben put on his habit and rode to Llanthony, causing a sensation among the country people he passed that was not unwelcome to him.

Although Dolben did not come to Rochdale, he just missed meeting Hopkins in Birmingham. Hopkins's initial proposal to Bridges had been that he come to Rochdale on the 1st of September, staying the previous night in Birmingham, where, he said somewhat evasively, 'I have some business I must manage to do at some time while I am in the north, most conveniently I think then.'

What he had in mind was a secret visit to the Oratory to see Newman, and the same day that he answered Bridges's invitation, he wrote to Newman asking for an interview with the intention of being received into the Church. Newman, however, was abroad when the letter arrived, and he did not answer until the 14th; Hopkins postponed his visit to Rochdale until he could make an appointment at the Oratory.

Ironically, Hopkins and Dolben, almost certainly without communicating on the matter, had both planned on being in the Oratory on the 1st of September, and had they met, it would have been for only the second time. It was typical that Hopkins should write ahead to make an appointment, while Dolben sent no warning, expecting to be welcomed on arrival. Probably Hopkins never knew how near he had been to seeing Dolben again.

J.T. Walford, who knew Dolben when he was a junior master at Eton, had become a convert and was now taking refuge at the Oratory while considering his future. Absence from Eton, however, had not lessened his spiritual concern for the boys of his old school. Years later he remembered Dolben's arrival, interrupting his own rather specialized devotions:

I was in the chapel of Our Lady in the church of the Oratory praying for the conversion of my Eton friends, when the Sacristan called me to the parlour. There I beheld Dolben, whom I had not seen since his Eton days. Eton! What would it have thought of him now! – he was in such a state – bareheaded, muddy and torn. He was wearing the habit of the Anglican Order, he had been hooted in the streets, mud had been thrown at him, he must have been pelted, in short, I don't know how he came to be in such a state. But his face was radiant, I can never forget it. It shone with joy and peace and seemed to light up the room. He said little of his adventure, but that he had come to consult Newman. Newman was away, but I hastened to call Father Ryder.[13]

Dolben's own version of the incident was unexpectedly low-key: 'I visited the Oratory – Newman was away – but Fr. Ryder was most civil and not at all contemptuous.' The surprisingly subdued tone is probably attributable to the fact that it was his second ecclesiastical excursion in Birmingham that day, and he was somewhat sated. Earlier in the day his 'Habit and bare feet created some astonishment in the choir at S. Alban's – but on the whole I made great friends with the clergy & cc – One of the Priests gave me his blessing in the sacristy after service in a very kind manner.'[14] It is easy to see why his friends found Dolben exhausting.

Hopkins's reaction to Dolben's adventure indicates that he was becoming slightly more detached in his view of the young enthusiast: 'I do not know whether it is more funny or affecting to think of.'[15] Newman knew from much experience that young men might burn with anxiety to become Catholics and later regret having done so; the advice he wrote to Dolben was clearly calculated to calm him down. Dolben was worried whether he would be justified in going against his father's wishes by being received, and Newman told him sensibly to 'wait till he was of age, or till his father consented'. His letter concluded with the soothing assurance that 'In the meanwhile I look on you as one of us.'[16]

Hopkins's stay with Bridges was what they both needed. Bridges and his mother, Mrs Molesworth, were mourning the death earlier that year of Bridges's favourite brother, Edward, with whom he had an understanding 'that we would always live together; and such was our affection that nothing but his early death could have prevented its realization'.[17] That summer something of what Bridges had felt for Edward was deflected on to Hopkins. His quiet affection was certainly more calming for Gerard than the presence of Dolben would have been.

Bridges was happy to fall in with Hopkins's need to work, and together they read away the early autumn days, although their ways with a text were as utterly different as their personalities. When they studied Herodotus, Bridges remembered, 'He was so punctilious about the text, and so enjoyed loitering over the difficulties that I foresaw we should never get through, and broke off from him to go my own way.'[18]

Since they were both ardent walkers it is probable that they covered the countryside, although the only certainty we have about their tracks is that during his stay Hopkins took Communion at Todmorden, some ten miles away. It was to be the last time he took the Sacrament in the Anglican Church. One wonders whether he wanted to avoid receiving it from Bridges's stepfather on this occasion, when he was in the last stages of disengaging himself from Anglicanism. He was in awe of the severity of Dr Molesworth, who was Vicar of Rochdale, and he may have been slightly worried about the opinion of Mrs Molesworth, who had flatly refused to let Edward study under the same tutor as Dolben because of his Catholic tendencies.

Hopkins was as full as ever of Dolben while he was at Rochdale, showing how engrained his feelings for Digby were becoming. On the letter that had come from Dolben saying he would be unable to join them, Bridges made a note in pencil that is nearly illegible, although it appears to say 'GMH came to stay with me at Rochdale, & his letters full of DMD family beg intro.'[19]

What Hopkins did not mention to Bridges until just as he was about to leave Rochdale to go to the Oratory was his immediate intention of becoming a Roman Catholic. In part he wanted to avoid burdening his friend with a secret, in part he respected Bridges's reticence so much he wanted to emulate it. In any case he knew that Bridges by now had a deep repugnance for Roman Catholicism. 'You were surprised and sorry, you said, and possibly hurt,' he wrote after leaving Rochdale, 'that I wd. not tell you of my conversion till my going to Birmingham made it impossible any longer to conceal it. I was never sorry for one minute: it wd. have been culpably dishonourable and ungrateful, as I said before, not to have done one's best to conceal it . . . I can never thank you enough for yr. kindness at that time.'[20] His behaviour in Rochdale, full of good intentions but awkward and hurtful in execution, partially explains his treatment of his family when he had to break the same news to them.

Ever since coming to Oxford, Hopkins had taken Newman as his model, but he had not met him until he at last went to the Oratory on his way home from Rochdale. To his pleasure, he found Newman kind without being over-solicitous, genial, and almost 'unserious'. Nearly everyone who met Newman for the first time was surprised at his casual, even slangy, speech, and Hopkins found that his host laughed easily and was considerably less earnest about theological matters than he was himself. Aside from Hopkins's 'matters at home', Newman could see no reason why he should not be received at once, 'but in no way did he urge me on, rather the other way'.

Newman and Hopkins agreed that he should go over from Oxford to the Oratory for his reception early in the new academic term. Since a retreat was 'advisable' for a convert, Newman asked if he would come at Christmas, which was the earliest opportunity. As one would have expected of Newman, he recommended that Hopkins finish his degree at Oxford, and Hopkins said that 'next term at all events I shall be there, since I shall announce my conversion to my parents by letter at the time of my reception. And now I have even almost ceased to feel anxiety.'[21]

A good deal had changed since he resolved in July in Horsham to tell no one of his plans for three months. Hopkins was never good at keeping secrets. After he came back from Birmingham he told Urquhart, 'You are the only friend whom I have deliberately told of my conversion,' but he had to admit that some six or seven others knew. By now he had spoken to Garrett and Macfarlane almost within hours of his decision to say nothing of the matter; he had admitted his intentions to his brother; Bridges and Newman knew of course, and so did Walford, whom he met at the Oratory, and so perhaps did one or two others. 'But now I shall let one friend after another hear till the time of my reception.'[22] He was so full of turmoil that he could no longer contain it, but his news must have been something less than novel by the time he told each friend.

The chief persons he had no intention of informing before he was actually received into the Church were his family. To be fair, all the time that he was letting Bridges and Urquhart know about his plans, his parents were in France, and it may be that he did not want to break the news to them by foreign post. All the same, it was extremely convenient that they were abroad while he was making his plans, and he seems to have been taking the easy way out in letting them know by letter rather than in person.

It is regrettable that he showed some of the less attractive aspects of his personality during this most important decision in his life, which should have brought out the best. Only if we understand his fears about his place in the world, in the University, and in his family, can we comprehend how such a gentle man could be so unfeeling over something potentially deeply wounding to others. Looking back at the events of 1866 from a century and a quarter later, we can easily see that more than religion was at the heart of the conflict between Hopkins and his family, and that it was as much concerned with independence and revolt, with the age-old struggle between father and son, even with the choice between blood father and spiritual father, as with the choice of a particular Church. Because the true conflict was never stated, the overt terms in which the contest was conducted were far more bitter than the immediate situation warranted.

It is easy to see, when he was on fire to become a Catholic, how difficult it would have been for Hopkins to wait patiently until he had taken his degree. The reason he gave for advancing the time of his reception was certainly to the point, but it seems to ignore his own impetuosity: 'I now see the alternative thrown open, either to live without Church and sacraments or else, in order to avoid the Catholic Church, to have to attend constantly the services of that very Church. This brings the matter to an absurdity and makes me think that any delay, whatever relief it may be to my parents, is impossible.'[23]

From this remove it is also possible to see reasons why it was advantageous for Hopkins to set his reception early in Michaelmas term, when he could go from Oxford to Birmingham without arousing unnecessary curiosity in family or friends, then to let his parents know by post what had happened. Above all, he would not be forced to tell them face to face. Fortunately, Hopkins leaked his slightly stale news to his friend Edward Bond, who was acquainted with the senior Hopkinses and realized how irredeemably it would hurt them to be the last to hear the news of their son's conversion, actually after he had become a Catholic. Bond persuaded Hopkins to tell them that he already regarded himself as a convert and that he intended to be received in the near future. Hopkins himself seems to have been insistent that it be done by letter rather than in person.

What must have been near the surface of Hopkins's consciousness was the knowledge that if he were already at Balliol when he wrote to his parents, he would have Oxford as the battleground, rather than the drawing room in Hampstead with all its psychological advantages for his family. Balliol and New Inn Hall Street were familiar to him but not to his parents, and it is no wonder that he instinctively retreated to a prepared position there before sending his letter.

We shall probably never know exactly what Hopkins's announcement of his intentions was like, or even exactly when he wrote it, since many of the family letters of the period have disappeared. Michaelmas term in 1866 began on the 10th of October, but Hopkins was still in Hampstead that day, and a letter to Bridges in the evening suggests that he had no intention of leaving for Oxford until the 11th or 12th. Probably he was waiting to set out for Oxford until the last possible moment before his parents' arrival home from France, thus avoiding any personal confrontation.

When he was back in New Inn Hall Street he sent off the letter he had dreaded writing: it reached his parents on the evening of the 13th, announcing his conversion and imminent reception into the Roman Church. According to his father, Gerard was 'shewing inexcusable selfwill & obstinacy', since he had voluntarily promised 'not to commit himself finally till after Christmas; yet he speaks of himself as "converted", and as already "a Catholic", – as if he had not been one all his life'.[24] From then on for a fortnight there was a blizzard of letters between London and Oxford, its volume increased by the speed of delivery, often only a few hours after posting. Most of them have since disappeared, probably destroyed because of the intemperance of expression on both sides, but their tone can be inferred from those that remain.

On Monday the 15th Hopkins instinctively turned to Newman for consolation: 'I have been up at Oxford just long enough to have heard fr. my father and mother in return for my letter announcing my conversion. Their answers are terrible: I cannot read them twice.' They had urged him 'with the utmost entreaties' to wait until he had taken his degree. But that was some eight months in the future, an almost unimaginable length of time in his present state, and certainly much beyond his own offer of postponing conclusive action until after Christmas. 'Of course it is impossible, and since it is impossible to wait as long as they wish it seems to me useless to wait at all.'[25]

Throughout the whole period of Hopkins's conversion and reception, Newman kept throwing cool, if not cold, water on Hopkins's excitement. He had, after all, been through the process himself with all England watching his smallest move. Since then nearly every intellectual would-be convert had consulted the best-known Catholic in England, and it is not surprising that he remained calm about still another. In one sympathetic but unimpassioned paragraph he put Hopkins's problems in perspective: 'It is not wonderful that you should not be able to take so great a step without trouble and pain.'[26]

The day after he heard from his father, Hopkins was sufficiently composed to send a reply that still seems notable for its distinct note of willingness to be martyred for his beliefs. The first sentence begins with 'a practical immediate point. The Church strictly forbids all communion in sacred things with non-Catholics.' The immediate effect would be that he could not in good conscience attend chapel in Balliol. 'Today the Master sent for me and said he cd. not grant me leave of absence without an application from you.'

What Hopkins needed most at this point was to be free of what he regarded as meddling in his spiritual affairs, and he took a hard line in defying both father and Master:

> As the College last term passed a resolution admitting Catholics and took a Catholic into residence it has no right to alter its principle in my case. I wish you therefore not to give yourself the pain of making this application, even if you were willing: I am of age moreover and am alone concerned. . . . I want you therefore to write at once, if you will, – not to the Master who has no right to ask what he does, but to me, with a refusal: no harm will follow.

The impression that Gerard was more adamant than the occasion required is confirmed by the letter he received from Newman himself, saying that 'There would be no difficulty in granting you leave to continue for a time attendance at the College Chapel, if the authorities did not at once give you leave to absent yourself.'[27] There is no record that he ever told his father of Newman's advice. He did, however, say that Liddon had written to him asking him to wait, and 'If Dr. Pusey is in Oxford tomorrow I will see him, if it is any satisfaction to you.'

As most fathers might, Mr Hopkins worried about how Gerard's conversion would affect his choice of career once he had left the University. Gerard was firm on the matter:

> I am most anxious that you shd. not think of my future. It is likely that the positions you wd. like to see me in wd. have no attraction for me, and surely the happiness of my prospects depends on the happiness to me and not on intrinsic advantages.[28]

It would be hard to disagree with Mr Hopkins, who called the long document a 'hard & cold' letter, but a sympathetic reading of it makes it clear that Gerard felt he was all but fighting for his life. It was surely his desperation, not hardness of heart, that kept him from even referring directly to his mother in the letter, let alone sending his love to her.

The letter his parents wrote in return has disappeared like the others, but there is a draft of it in the Bodleian Library, prepared jointly by his mother and father. Its burden is that Gerard had been unfair to Anglicanism in not talking over his conversion with Pusey and Liddon, only with Newman:

> One thing more – Have you not dealt hardly, may I not say unfairly by us in leaving us in absolute ignorance of all till your decision was finally taken? Were you not on the point of being received into the Church of Rome without even warning us? & were you not saved from what would have been a cruel insult to us, not by your own good feeling, but by Edward Bond's entreaties?

Most of the letter was written by his father, but the draft concludes with a sentence obviously wrenched from his mother: 'O Gerard my darling boy are you indeed gone from me?'[29]

When Hopkins did write to Pusey, he received in return a curiously tired and defeated reply. Its cool formality was the result of knowing that reason was seldom any match for the turbulent fervour of the convert. It is also worth remembering that Pusey was not writing to a stranger but to a former penitent whose confessions he had heard and whose soul and complicated personality he had presumably had a chance to examine carefully. He was not interested, he said, in seeing Hopkins 'simply "to satisfy relations". I know too well what that means. It is simply to enable the pervert to say to his relations "I have seen Dr P, and he has failed to satisfy me", whereas they know very well that they meant not to be satisfied, that they came with a fixed purpose not to be satisfied. This is merely to waste my time, and create the impression that I have nothing to say.'[30] Pusey was no doubt accustomed to using 'pervert' as synonymous with 'apostate', but one wonders whether, in his disappointment, he was guiltless of a slight desire to wound.

Hopkins was quite deliberate in not letting Liddon know of his intentions: for some months he had been avoiding confession with him, and his initial admiration of him had cooled considerably. When Hopkins first told his parents, Liddon was in Bristol before coming back for the beginning of term, and he heard from Coles:

> I am sorry that I should have to be the bearer to you of painful news, but I think you will wish to know it as soon as possible. Besides Challis, Addis, Wood of Trinity, and Garrett of Balliol have been received into the Roman Church, and Hopkins is intending to be received in a day or two, as soon as Dr. Newman can come to Oxford for the purpose. He told me he would see you, if you were in Oxford before his reception. . . .[31]

It was a terrible shock for Liddon to find that five of his protégés were going over to Rome within a few days of each other, at one blow more than doubling the number of Catholics in the undergraduate body of the University. 'If you could examine your own thought fully', he wrote to Hopkins, 'you would probably find that love & sympathy for Addis is the strongest motive that is taking you to Rome.'[32]

Mr Hopkins had written to Liddon, asking for whatever help he could give. But there was, of course, nothing he could do. When Hopkins failed to answer his first letter of remonstrance, he sent two more in quick succession. As Hopkins wrote, with a touch of dismissal, 'All the influence therefore that he has on me has been brought to bear.'[33]

In his answer to Liddon, Hopkins allowed something that can fairly be called condescension to creep into his expression of gratitude: 'I wish to thank you for your kindness and even for the trouble you took to prevent my reception, for of course to you it was the right thing to do.' After assuring Liddon that he had not been converted by 'personal illumination which dispenses with the need of thought or knowledge on the points at issue', he told him that nobody 'ever became a Catholic because two and two make four more fully than I have'. In conclusion he made it clear he had no wish to prolong the correspondence: 'Do not trouble yourself to write again: this needs no answer and I know how precious your time is.'

Liddon had signed his letters 'Ever yours affectionately', and in return Hopkins signed himself 'always gratefully and affectionately yours'. But there is little affection, even gratitude, apparent in his letter.[34] It was only three years since he had felt that his most exciting new friendship was that with Liddon.

Hopkins was to put a good deal of emphasis on his sudden realization on a July day in Sussex that he could no longer remain in the Church of England: at one moment he said he was an Anglican, the next he knew in his heart that he was a Catholic. But conversions, however dramatic their flashes of recognition, seldom operate quite so quickly as that except, perhaps, on the road to Damascus. In spite of his insistence to Liddon on the relentless logic that led to his own, there is curiously little in his surviving letters about the doctrinal positions that had preceded his final decision, and we are forced to conclude that his unconscious drives may have been as powerful in changing his mind as any systematic chain of reasoning. Probably the nearest he ever came to a definition of his reasons for conversion was in the letter he had written two years earlier to Ernest Coleridge which has already been quoted. In it he asserted his belief that the source of all Catholic truth was in 'the Real Presence in the Blessed Sacrament of the Altar. Religion without that is sombre, dangerous, illogical . . .'. His belief in the primacy of the deeply personal aspect of the Sacrament had not altered, but in the years between 1864 and 1866 he had gradually changed his mind about the historical legitimacy of the Church of England to consecrate that Sacrament. After that there was no real reason not to become a Roman Catholic. But it was the recognition that came in a flash not the steps leading to it.

On the 20th of October Hopkins wrote to his mother, telling her that nothing had changed in his faith for months: 'You do not seem to realise how irrevocable my determination was from July – the day of my conversion. My mind is not more made up now than it was then.' His reason for not announcing his plans to her in advance, he said, was that he hoped to spare her unnecessary pain. 'I was never going to be received without warning you, though I was going to give you the warning only at the last.' In the final paragraph he told her, 'I am to be received into the church tomorrow at Birmingham by Dr. Newman. It is quite the best that any hopes should be ended quickly, since otherwise they wd. only have made the pain longer.'[35]

His letter was written on Saturday; the next day he went to the Oratory in Birmingham and was received into the Church by Newman, whose diary records simply, 'Oct. 21. Mr. Hopkins came from Oxford and was received.'[36] On Monday, the day following the ceremony, the announcement of his intention to be received reached his mother in Hampstead.

The worst was over and Hopkins had reached his goal. He had become a Roman Catholic, he had asserted his independence, and in the complicated structure of his familial allegiances he had substituted Newman for the father figures of Liddon, Pusey, perhaps Jowett (although that skirmish had probably been won some time before), and Mr Hopkins himself. Hopkins apparently did not see his parents again before he went home for Christmas that year, and when he stayed there for part of the holidays, his victory was already established. There were undoubtedly letters between Hampstead and New Inn Hall Street in the half-year after his

reception, but they have disappeared, and when regular correspondence began again in 1867 it was as bland as if the whole of the
previous year had never happened.

Mr Hopkins was a powerful father, but he was also fair. Mrs
Hopkins was perhaps too intrusive in the life of her son, as he seems
to have thought, but she was also loving, almost to a fault. Much of
the vehemence of emotion at the time of his conversion was on his
side, not theirs, and some of their demands seem to have been his
own invention. 'You are so kind', he wrote formally, 'as not to
forbid me your house, to which I have no claim, on condition, if I
understand, that I promise not to try to convert my brothers and
sisters. Before I can promise this I must get permission, wh. I have
no doubt will be given. Of course this promise will not apply after
they come of age.'[37] There is no indication that forbidding the
family home to Gerard had ever entered his parents' minds. We are
thrown into conjecture by lack of concrete evidence, but it sounds
suspiciously like a defensive reaction to being told that he was of
course always welcome at home, even if his parents did not want
him to try to convert their other children; when there was no
repression, it became necessary to invent it. The legalistic ag-
gressiveness of his letter is reminiscent of his assertions to his
parents about the impossibility of attending chapel in Balliol.

In any case it is improbable that his brothers and sisters were in
much danger of being converted by Gerard. It may even have been a
slight disappointment to him that they were so tolerant of his
decision. Lionel, still only twelve, was quite unable to understand
why his parents were so disturbed at Gerard's course of action and
thought that their subsequent reconciliation 'argued great tolerance, charity, and, above all, great love for Gerard'. When his
brother became a Jesuit, he said in mild wonder that he could not
understand why Gerard could not have become 'an ordinary
Catholic' like other people.[38]

To tell truth, though the worst was over, the excitement was
finished as well, and Hopkins, while feeling true sorrow at having
had to hurt his family, no longer had the surge of purpose and
energy consequent upon feeling himself a rebel. He had leapt (or
perhaps only hauled himself) over an enormous barrier, one as
much concerned with growth and maturation as with religion, and

it would have been surprising if there had been no sense of let-down.

On the 4th of November, a fortnight after he was received at the Oratory, Hopkins was confirmed in a joint ceremony with Addis and Alexander Wood at the church of St Mary of the Angels, Bayswater, by Archbishop Manning. Garrett, to whom Hopkins had been tentatively confessing his own plans in Horsham, had been so convinced by them that he was baptized as a Roman Catholic three weeks before his friend, and with his minimal seniority as a Catholic, he stood godfather to him at his confirmation. One wonders whether Manning repeated the advice he had given Wood in the same church when he was baptized: 'the neophyte was called aside by the bony finger of the Archbishop and given the startling information that as a Catholic now it was plainly his duty not to return to Oxford.'[39]

With the slightly detached good sense he displayed all through Hopkins's reception, Newman told him not to hurry matters, and that the retreat he had suggested to help him 'get into Catholic ways' might well be postponed: 'it does not seem to me that there is any hurry about it – your first duty is to make a good class. Show your friends at home that your becoming a Catholic has not unsettled you in the plain duty that lies before you. And, independently of this, it seems to me a better thing not to hurry decision on your vocation.'[40] The two pieces of conflicting advice by Manning and Newman might stand as an emblem of the intellectual difference between the two churchmen that made them polite opponents for life.

There was no longer a defensible reason for Hopkins to postpone the work he had been skimping all that year, but settling down to hard study in preparation for his examinations the following spring had a distinct flavour of anti-climax. The Master's reports on his work at the end of term had been considerably less impressive than previously. For Lent term 1866 he was judged as 'working hard', during Easter and Trinity terms Scott noted that his work was 'Satisfactory', but the upheaval of his conversion at the beginning of Michaelmas term made his work only 'Fairly satisfactory', much the least commendatory comment he had received.[41] Newman's exhortation was probably needed.

CHAPTER IX

DEATH OF DOLBEN
1867–8

At his conversion Hopkins had completed almost exactly half his life, and rather than beginning to build upon his previous education, he seemed to his family deliberately to have destroyed the foundations of a successful career. To give him an option, in case he was not welcome at home, Newman invited him to the Oratory for Christmas 1866, but Hopkins sensibly decided the time had come for repairing his family ties. 'You are quite right to go home, since they wish you –', wrote Newman when he received Hopkins's answer, 'indeed, it would have been in every way a pity, had you not resolved to do so.' Instead, he suggested that Hopkins come for a week of retreat in January before the beginning of Lent term.[1] Throughout the whole difficult period, Newman's behaviour was exemplary in not exciting Hopkins further in his rebellion.

Hopkins was slowly learning to deal with his parents, trying to make it clear to them without hurting them unnecessarily, that his decision was irrevocable. On Christmas Eve he sat up late with his family, writing letters, then left them to go off to midnight Mass: he could hardly have made his intentions more apparent.

With friends outside the family he was still feeling his way. 'Unless you think they wd. not be pleased, remember me kindly to Dr. and Mrs. Molesworth,' he wrote to Bridges, showing that his stay in Rochdale had not reassured him about their approval. With Bridges himself he was becoming progressively appreciative of a rock-solid friend. For some time he had customarily signed his letters to him as 'always yr. affectionate friend', but now that they were apart it became easier, more natural, to address him as 'Dearest Bridges'. Through their intimacy, they were outgrowing the public school habit of using surnames only: 'You sometimes now address me by my Christian name and I like it but I do not you by yours, for first it wd. not feel natural to me and secondly it wd. be unnecessary, for your surname is the prettier.'[2] Until the end of Hopkins's life they habitually used Bridges and Gerard in their correspondence.

'Do you hear fr. Dolben?' he asked Bridges. Since he seems to have been in at least infrequent correspondence with Dolben, he presumably knew that his own conversion had 'hastened the end' of any residual doubts Dolben had about the Church. The announcement of Dolben's plans to become a Catholic had worsened relations with his father, and once more he was sent back to study in the country with a tutor. He was still hoping to come up to Oxford, and he planned on arriving for matriculation in January 1867, in spite of being ill. 'I cannot make out whether he is really going both to matriculate and reside next term,'[3] wrote Hopkins, who was beginning to realize that it was unwise to rely on Dolben's intentions.

As it turned out, Dolben did not matriculate in January, nor apparently did the state of his health allow him even to take the examinations. In March he wrote to Newman that he had promised his parents 'not to be received until I have seen them again, that is until after Easter – Then I go up for matriculation at Balliol, and (if I pass) I reside at once, so that I suppose I might be received at Oxford.'[4] On the 1st of May he had another go at the Balliol examinations. This time, however, he told neither Hopkins nor Bridges of his presence in Oxford, and rather than stay at Balliol or at Corpus with Bridges, as he had done on his first visit, he quietly took a room at the new Randolph Hotel. His health had not improved, and during the first day of the matriculation examinations he fainted. Finally facing the fact that he would never enter Balliol, he left Oxford as unobtrusively as he had come, telling his friends of neither his visit nor his failure. Reluctantly he agreed with his father that it would be better to go instead to Christ Church, where the entrance standards were not so stiff. He hoped that he might come up in the following Michaelmas term. His reception as a Roman Catholic was now apparently put off still further by his failure to gain admission to Oxford. When Hopkins learned of Dolben's recurrent troubles with his father, he must have felt again the similar pain he had suffered from his own family: it was yet another reminder of how his life and Dolben's had been running on parallel tracks that seemed destined never to meet.

After his retreat at the Oratory, Hopkins returned to Oxford, where he and his fellow convert and godfather, Garrett, settled into new lodgings in Holywell, putting them much nearer to the little Catholic church in St Clement's than Hopkins had been in New Inn Hall Street. Both young men stayed up in Oxford to work during the spring vacation, but for Holy Week Hopkins returned to the Benedictine Priory at Belmont near Hereford. Once Oxford had been a rival to Hampstead as his home, but now a clerical atmosphere was becoming more familiar than either, so that it seemed more natural to be in Belmont for Easter than in Hampstead. 'I think it wd. be better to go to Oxford at once,' he wrote rather lukewarmly to his mother after the retreat, 'but if I do not go home then I shall not see you before the summer.'[5]

The last indication of his academic progress before taking Final Examinations is the laconic entry in the Master's Report Book for the Lent term, 'Satisfactory'. It is better than the 'Fairly satisfactory' of the previous term, but in hindsight it seems like either blindness or a deliberate coolness about Hopkins's progress, for in June he received First Class Honours in Final Schools. Bridges wrote that he 'had not read more than half the nine books when he went in for "Greats"; this did not, however, prevent his success, and my tutor, Professor Wilson, who was one of the examiners, told me that "for form" he was by far the best man in the first class'.[6] With his First in Mods, this gave Hopkins an exemplary 'Double First', a degree so distinguished that, were he still an Anglican, it would almost automatically have fitted him for an academic career, probably with a Fellowship at one of the Oxford colleges. As it was, his future was uncertain at best.

Perhaps his own worry about his future made Hopkins so self-absorbed that he was less than normally tactful with Bridges about his chances of a degree: 'A 2nd is the class I have always imagined you wd. get: mind it is a good one.'[7] True enough, but it did not come well from a man who had just managed a Double First, nor was it made more palatable by the fact that Hopkins's guess was completely accurate. It shows something of Bridges's sweetness of temper that he was apparently completely unbothered by the remark. When Bridges invited him for Christmas in 1867, Hopkins demonstrated both his occasional social gaucheness and the depth of his trust of Bridges:

> I cannot feel at my ease with regard to Dr. and Mrs. Moles-worth, but beyond that too I am very unwilling, I cannot exactly explain why, to come to Rochdale. Instead of the excuses I might have given I have put it in what I am afraid you may call the rudest way. But the very pleasure I had in my stay last year is part of the reason why I do not wish to make another, if you can understand.[8]

Even before receiving his degree, he had been approached to take a position as tutor at an establishment near Aldenham for coaching young Catholics who wanted to go to Oxford or Cambridge, but he disliked the idea of teaching and told Newman that he was not interested in the life of a schoolmaster. Newman had his eye on him as a teacher in the Oratory school in Edgbaston, but he refrained from mentioning the matter until Walford, the former Eton master, decided to leave the school because he needed time to prepare for ordination. In offering the vacant position to Hopkins, Newman said, 'I think you would get on with us, and that we should like you.'[9] Hopkins accepted tentatively, but it was clearly not a prospect that excited him, in spite of the chance to be near Newman.

While waiting to go to Birmingham, he took several small trips. In the second week of July an undergraduate acquaintance, Basil Poutiatine, son of a Russian admiral, went with him to Paris, probably his first sight of that city. Urquhart invited him to Devon, where he was a curate at Bovey Tracy, and Hopkins expected an invitation to visit Pater and take part in a reading party in Sidmouth, but the plans for that fell through.

The Paris trip was a conventional one of sightseeing, paintings at the galleries, High Mass at St Eustache, Notre Dame, or the Madeleine, and being innocently impressed at dinner with Poutiatine's father 'at the Russian *restaurant*, where the waiters leaned over and talked confidentially to the Admiral'. Both Hopkins's insatiable curiosity about the innate forms of nature and a somewhat ingenuous wonder at things foreign come out in his notes about the French landscape: 'The trees were irregular, scarcely expressing form, and the aspens blotty, with several concentric outlines, and as in French pictures.' When he went to the Bois de Boulogne, he 'noticed the thinness of French foliage, weakness of the general type of the tree, and naked shrub-like growth of the oaks'. Even in his perception of nature there was always a streak of guileless chauvinism, which was a major contributory factor in the loneliness of the last few years of his life, spent out of England.

When they had finished their week in Paris, Hopkins accompanied Poutiatine to Bayeux to meet former undergraduate friends, then went home alone on an exhilarating crossing from Dieppe to Newhaven. 'Got soaked with spray and cheeks frosted with brine, but I saw the waves well. In the sunlight they were green-blue, flinty sharp, and rucked in straight lines by the wind.' After a train trip back to London shared 'with a Norman housemaid', he was in Hampstead again. Hopkins's own description of what should have been a pleasant red-cheeked homecoming is a stark little entry in his journal: 'I found a letter from Coles, which had been waiting since the day I started for Paris, to tell me of Dolben's death. See June 28.'[10]

The last brief phrase is about as close as Hopkins came to indicating overtly how deeply Dolben's death had affected him, for it refers back to an entry in a previous volume of his journal, now lost, where he had presumably entered his own activities in Hampstead the day Dolben died, noting the devastating contrast between the events in Rutland and his own ignorance of them. Three weeks had passed since then, and the whole time that Hopkins was enjoying Paris, Dolben was already lying in the family vault beneath the altar of Finedon Church.

After Dolben fainted at Balliol, he had been sent back to the Revd Constantine Prichard at South Luffenham to prepare doggedly for still another set of matriculation examinations, this time at Christ Church. By now he was deeply bored with the whole process, and according to Prichard he did not seem to be 'looking forward with any particular interest to his Oxford life. He said he thought he shd. like Christ Church better than Balliol, but that he had been much annoyed at not getting in at the latter.'[11]

Dolben had not been wholly unhappy, for he was fond of the countryside and the River Welland, in which he could gratify his love of bathing. He liked and respected Prichard more than any of the other clergymen who had undertaken his difficult tuition. According to Bridges, he put up peacefully with Prichard's gentle objections to Roman Catholicism and even admitted that he found them unanswerable.

On the afternoon of the 28th of June Dolben finished his lessons by construing with Prichard the speech of Ajax taking leave of the world before his death, then he went bathing in the Welland with Prichard's ten-year-old son Walter, whom he was teaching to swim. Dolben tied a sash around the boy so that he could hold him above the water, then swam across a deep pool, with young Prichard on his back. On the further bank they stood resting until Dolben said, 'Come on – I will swim back with you.' Something about his attitude made Walter ask, 'Are you tired?', to which Dolben replied, 'No, not tired, but out of breath.' Together they started back across the stream, then Dolben appeared to have a cramp, and Walter noticed that the water was above Dolben's nose. They both sank beneath the surface, and Walter felt Dolben's hand on his shoulder trying to help him. Then Dolben disappeared, with no sign of a struggle. Young Prichard saved himself by floating on his back and shouting until some labourers in a neighbouring field heard his persistent calling. They pulled him out of the water, but it was hours before Dolben's body was found. Forty years later Prichard said simply, 'He died trying to save me.'[12] It was generally accepted that he had lost consciousness as he had done in the Balliol examinations, perhaps from a cerebral haemorrhage, and that it had been a painless death while he was enjoying himself at the only sport he loved.

After his death an unfinished letter to his father was found among Dolben's papers, asking that in case of grave accident or illness Mr Mackworth Dolben release him from his promise not to become a convert immediately.

There has never been total agreement about Dolben's importance to Hopkins any more than there has been a consensus about the nature of Dolben himself. Because Hopkins wrote very little about Dolben's death, it is easy to underestimate what he felt. In many

respects his journals and diaries are singularly unrevealing documents, save for the notes he made for confession; almost none of the
great crises of his life is recorded there and there are few direct
references to his feelings. These are to be inferred only by the turn of
a phrase or occcasionally by a deliberate omission. When his
emotions in the other crises of his life go unrecorded, we can hardly
expect to find him unpacking his heart at the death of Dolben,
although glancing references to him years later show that his
memory was still green for Hopkins all his life. After his entry
about finding the letter from Coles, Hopkins's journal notes for the
next ten days are so terse that one recognizes how carefully he was
controlling himself. Instead of the usual long rhapsodic descriptions
of nature, there are the briefest of notes of the state of the weather,
often with only one word entered for an entire day: 'Fair', 'Rain',
'Dull chiefly', as if he were afraid to commit himself to more.

There was, of course, a flurry of letters back and forth between
Dolben's friends at his death. It is worth noticing that Coles,
Bridges, and Wyatt-Edgell, the three men who understood both
Hopkins and Dolben best, all wrote at once to Hopkins, in sym-
pathetic recognition of how deeply he was involved with the dead
man. Bridges even considerately forwarded a letter Dolben's sister
had written to tell him about the circumstances of Digby's death.
But it is in some ways Edgell, the one of them who was least close to
Hopkins, whose condolences seem most telling here, for he would
have known of the devotion of Hopkins from only one source,
Dolben himself. Sadly enough, the letter Gosselin wrote to Coles
was so cold and impersonal that one wonders whether he had ever
returned any of the affection Dolben lavished on him.

Some trace of the shock and numbness Hopkins was feeling can
easily be seen in his answer to Bridges's letter, written after nearly
two weeks of attempting to deal with his grief:

I have kept the beginning of a letter to you a long time by me
but to no purpose so far as being more ready to write goes.
There is very little I have to say. I looked forward to meeting
Dolben and his being a Catholic more than to anything. At the
same time from not having met him but once I find it difficult
to realise his death or feel as if it were anything to me. You

know there can very seldom have happened the loss of so much beauty (in body and mind and life) and of the promise of still more as there has been in his case – seldom I mean, in the whole world, for the conditions wd. not easily come together.

But he could no longer ignore Dolben's eccentricities, even in death: 'At the same time he had gone on in a way wh. was wholly and unhappily irrational.' He wondered, too, whether the Dolben family, about whom he had been so curious, were thinking of collecting and printing Digby's poetry. 'Some day I hope to see Finedon and the place where he was drowned too. Can you tell me where he was buried? – at Finedon, was it not? If you have letters from him will you let me see them some day?'[13]

'I do not know about Dolben's verses being published,' Bridges answered. 'His father is a sort of literary man. – Dolben was buried at Finedon, in the family vault under the altar of the famous church there. When you go I should be glad to go with you. We might make an arrangement possibly for some time next year, and then you might go all over the house etc.'[14] It was the religious themes, not the eroticism, of the poems that worried Dolben's family, and it was Bridges himself who finally persuaded the family to let them be published. He and Hopkins never did make the trip to Finedon.

Bridges had known Dolben better than Hopkins did, and there is no indication that he had ever had any of the emotions about him that Hopkins felt, so it was harder for him to think of his cousin as a paragon: 'You will understand what I mean without my prolonging this into a schoolgirl's letter – but did not you think that there was an entire absence of strength in Dolben? It always seemed to me so in spite of his great moral courage as people would call it, in carrying out his "views".'[15]

It took Hopkins more than two months in Birmingham to agree with Bridges as he mulled over this assessment of Dolben's personality, in a turmoil of schoolboys: 'It is quite true, as you say, that there was a great want of strength in Dolben – more, of sense.'[16] It is a more judicious view of his friend than he could have countenanced at the time of Dolben's death, but it indicates no lack of concern and no forgetting.

With the slightly quizzical air that had characterized his dealings

in the affairs of Dolben, Newman wrote to Hopkins a letter of
ambiguous tone:

> Yes – we heard all about Dolben. The account was very
> pleasant. He had not given up the idea of being a Catholic – but
> he thought he had lived on excitement, and felt he must give
> himself time before he could know whether he was in earnest
> or not. This does not seem to me a wrong frame of mind. He
> was up to his death careful in his devotional exercises. I never
> saw him.

One would wonder whether he even remembered Dolben, were it
not for a letter he wrote several years later in which he revealed that
he had felt as much doubt about Dolben's conversion as Pusey had
felt about Hopkins's, and that his own letter to Hopkins had been
deliberately vague, to avoid hurting him:

> I heard of him, as coming in a monk's dress with bare feet, and
> had a feeling in consequence that he was one of those enthusi-
> astic youths whom you cannot depend upon. I knew of his
> deep seriousness from others – but there was nothing to show
> in what they said that he would not after a time, without losing
> his seriousness, become satisfied with the Anglican Church.
> . . . I should have been glad to make him a Catholic, but I
> had no wish he should become a Catholic one year, and, as
> some others, relapse into Anglicanism in the next. I thought he
> ought to take time.[17]

The letter that would probably tell us most intimately what
Hopkins was feeling is his answer to Coles, who had been privy to
both Hopkins's emotions and Dolben's. But it has disappeared.
Even so, it is hard to understand how anyone can read the remaining letters and fail to recognize the central place Dolben had
occupied in Hopkins's life.

Dolben's poetry is largely forgotten nowadays, and he persists as
a brief entry in literary reference books. A few years after his death,
his remaining brother died, and only his sister was left of the four
children. After his mother's death in 1892, her daughter lived in
dwindling splendour in Finedon until her death in 1912, when the

house was sold out of the family. The gardens and park are built over today, and most of the outbuildings of the estate have been converted into modern housing for people working in North-ampton. Even Digby's body has been moved from its original resting place. When last heard of, Finedon Hall was being rescued from demolition, but for years the romantically desolate house stood in ruins, its gables missing and great holes gaping in the walls, with only the beautiful yellow stone hinting at its former grandeur.

For a time Digby Dolben was remembered by a handful of friends, and his poems were assembled by Bridges in 1911 and published with a memoir. It is not his own poems, however, for which he will be recalled but for what he represented in the emotional life of one of England's greatest poets.

For the rest of the summer of 1867 Hopkins apparently got on much more easily with his family than he had for a year. He called on his grandparents and on his aunts and uncles, and he spent more time with his brothers than usual. His telegraphic notes in his journal after Dolben's death gradually grew back into the word studies of nature that had so occupied him before.

On the 23rd of August, after his parents had left for their annual trip to France, he went into a chapel in Notting Hill to pray for help in deciding his future: 'I made my resolution "if it is better".' But his intentions were less fixed than he hoped, for twelve days later he appended a jotting that 'now, Sept. 4, nothing is decided'.[18] It was not until May of the following year that he could say resolutely 'it is better' to his solution of the problem he so teasingly leaves unidentified here.

It is typical of Hopkins's self-contained manner that one of the most important decisions of his life should be phrased so obscurely; it is of a piece with the opaque privacy that kept him from confiding, even to his own journal, all that he had felt about Dolben. We are lucky to have Humphry House's neat detective work in putting together scattered clues to show conclusively that what Hopkins had in mind in the chapel of the Poor Clares was giving up the composition of poetry and destroying what he had already written.

There are a number of reasons why he should have considered the destruction of his poems at this time. Obviously, although he was still heeding Newman's counsel not to rush his fences, he was already considering ordination. His very indecision about taking on a mastership at the Oratory school shows that he had no intention of remaining there long, although being there meant that he would have the invaluable advice of Newman about his clerical future. From there the logical step was ordination. We know from what he wrote when he was finally ordained that he thought the dedications of priest and poet were too much alike to exist easily in one person, since they derived from the same sources. And, like Savonarola, he was aware that art, even when it was guiltless in itself, could be highly distracting. A vocation to the priesthood implied the renunciation of worldly pursuits, and since poetry was surely dearest of those to him, it was the logical activity to be given up.

Hopkins, as he had demonstrated over and over, had a natural bent to asceticism and sacrifice; even the destruction of his journal in June 1866 had shown that. Beyond all this, however, we should recognize that his decision was made only a month after he heard of Dolben's death and that before this he had dimly associated Dolben's absence with the renunciation of poetry. As we have already seen, on 6 November 1865, when he had not heard for some time from Dolben, he wrote in his diary, 'On this day by God's grace I resolved to give up all beauty until I had His leave for it; – also Dolben's letter came for which Glory to God.' The forced conjunction of the two parts of the sentence suggests that, at least unconsciously, renunciation seemed the exacted price for the arrival of the long-awaited letter.

It is a psychological commonplace that anyone who has been bereaved may have dim feelings of guilt at the loss of the beloved, particularly when there has been anything questionable about the relationship in life, and may try to rid himself of that guilt by some form of propitiation. Something of the sort was happening to Hopkins at this time, and the particular form of sacrifice he was considering was made even more appropriate because it was an emulation of Dolben's own action in destroying his poetry while he was at Eton. It can hardly be expected that such a supposition would be supported by much documentary evidence, but it does explain why Hopkins made his decision at this particular time.

Hopkins had always been inclined to carp at Urquhart, but they remained close enough to make it natural for Hopkins to stay with him in Devon. Hopkins's conversion apparently made no difference to their friendship, which is an oblique tribute to Urquhart's equanimity, for Hopkins tried hard to convert him and, when he failed, became more than a touch imperious, as an insider dealing with the recalcitrant heathen. When Urquhart indicated that he had difficulty swallowing the idea of Papal Infallibility, Hopkins counselled him, 'Purge yourselves therefore of every other heresy but yet you will never be received to intercommunion until you approach the Church on terms . . . implying that *the Church of Rome has been right all along in its attitude to the Greeks and yourselves and is the only Catholic Church.*'

Months later he was still scolding Urquhart: 'I am glad you go to confession although there is nothing of a Sacrament in the ordinance as you use it,' he wrote, perhaps forgetting his own difficulties on the same subject, 'but still it has its value *ex opere operantis* and in some cases the shadow of Peter may cure where the touch of Peter is not to be had.' It is the understandable but snubbing zeal of the convert; luckily, Urquhart was good-natured about it.

On another occasion Hopkins was prevented from sending a poem to him because 'there are quotations or quasi-quotations fr. the Bible in it and I must check them by the Douay before I can reproduce the verses'.[19] In time, as he relaxed into self-confidence about being a Catholic, Hopkins became somewhat less rigid in asserting his beliefs.

Throughout his life Hopkins had a considerable liking for stories of miracles and supernatural interventions into physical and human order. Aside from being consonant with his new religion, they were part of his natural tendency to spiritualize nature, but for many of his friends (perhaps most noticeably Bridges) this bordered on credulity and was the hardest part of his conversion to put up with.

Just before leaving Devon, where he had a splendid time walking with Urquhart, Hopkins went by himself to Newton Abbot for Mass and had breakfast afterward with Fr Kenelm Vaughan, who was well known for his 'unworldliness and exuberant habits of prayer'. Fr Vaughan entertained Hopkins with holy gossip and regaled him with barely credible happenings to the faithful:

But this he told me about himself: – he was in consumption, dying: the sisters had a *novena* for him and he was drinking water from St. Winifred's well: one Sunday he had crept down to say mass, when, there being no rain, before the consecration a quantity of water fell on him and the altar so that he sent to ask the Canon whether he should consecrate or not: he was told to do so and Mass went on: after Mass he was perfectly well.[20]

Hopkins had to leave Devon in a hurry to be back in Birmingham before the beginning of term. While he was with Urquhart he had written a fence-mending letter to Liddon, apologizing for not having seen him before leaving Oxford after Finals. He explained that he had left it too late and that Liddon had already gone, but he promised that he would come to call the next time he was in Oxford. The day before the boys returned to the Oratory school, he made a flying trip to Oxford to retrieve the belongings he had left there over the summer. Although he was there for only a day, in Oxford he had time to be entertained by another old friend but, noticeably, not enough to call on Liddon, and there is no indication that even when he came to live in Oxford he sought out his old confessor.

Newman had helped found the Oratory School in a desire to combine Catholic teaching and the intellectual advantages of traditional English public schools, as part of his life-long ambition of Anglicizing Catholicism (and, of course, *vice versa*). It was intended for the education of sons of the Catholic gentry, and he wanted to avoid excessive clericalism by not educating priests in the same institution, as was done in the Catholic colleges like Stonyhurst. 'The only point of *principle* on which we should differ from the Colleges', he said, 'is that we should aim at doing everything above-board – and abjure espionage, listening at doors &c.' It was a noble aim for the betterment of the boys, but it could be taxing for their teachers.

Evelyn Waugh's *Decline and Fall* was written some sixty years after Hopkins went to teach at the Oratory school, but his comic account of the misery of masters and boys at Llanabba Castle shows how little had changed in the small world of boys' schools in that time. Like Paul Pennyfeather in the novel, Hopkins must have thought to himself, 'I wonder whether I'm going to enjoy being a schoolmaster,' and his answer was surely the same. He had a week to get himself accustomed to the atmosphere of the place, living in the Oratory, then moving to one of the boys' houses, where he was so busy that he hardly ever saw anything of Newman and did not often have time to hear him preach. The school had a reputation for working the boys very hard, but that in turn meant that the masters had to work even harder, and there were never enough of them. The Oratory was always short of money, and some of the staff and their families thought of themselves as having a 'shabby-genteel lot amongst dubious papists'.[21]

> Fancy me getting up at a quarter past six; it is however done with a melancholy punctuality nearly every morning. The boys' mass is at seven; then what they call Preparation fr. 7.45 to 8.30; then breakfast in Hall, so to speak. . . . With reading the class books and looking over exercises (which takes a long time) I find all my time occupied. Today however is Sunday and the boys are playing fives like good ones: I wish they wd. play all the other numbers on the clock all the other days of the week.[22]

He taught the fifth form of only five boys during the day, then took two advanced private pupils after supper every day but Saturday. In any time left over he was in charge of their games, first hockey, then football. When the change in games took place, he wrote that he was 'very fond of my "spiritual children", which fondness the fattest and biggest has repaid by laming me at football' with a kick on the ankle.

Hopkins was always fond of the young, even sentimental about them: and he came to 'feel as if they were all my children, a notion encouraged by their innocence and backwardness'. Their teachers were another matter, however, and though they were 'nice souls', he said that the 'masters' table appears to be the dregs of Great Britain; indeed one of us is a Dutchman'. Waugh's Captain Grimes might have felt at home in the Common Room.

In Edgbaston his most intimate companion was Henry Challis,

who had been part of Hopkins's High Church set at Oxford, 'a great swell' according to Hopkins. His conversion had come only a short time before Hopkins's, and, like Hopkins, he was marking time by teaching until he found his feet once more. Although there were several other former Anglicans at the Oratory, Hopkins had that special sense of being an outsider that many converts felt among hereditary Catholics. With Challis he could exchange news of their friends in common at Oxford (only the previous year, although it already seemed 'before the Flood') and speculate about who would be the next convert. It was a great sadness to Hopkins five years later when Challis joined the other friends who had 'apostacized' by leaving the Church again.

There were some pleasures, however, such as chamber music by the quartet made up of the music master, two of Hopkins's pupils, and Newman himself playing the violin. It was probably in emulation of him that Hopkins began taking lessons on the violin. He found the surrounding countryside startlingly pretty in spite of being so near Birmingham, so that he liked to walk when he had time, and there were occasional unexpected treats like that at the beginning of December, when there was a sharp frost 'and the boys flooded the ball-court and slid and skated on it'.

On the whole he was so overworked that he had no time to write letters except on a rare holiday, and his journal notes were jotted down elsewhere to wait for time to make a careful entry. Newman's dear friend Fr Ambrose St John, who was in charge of the school, took pity on him and said that he was 'going to make an arrangement by which I shall get some time for private reading'. But it is improbable that Hopkins ever had much change from his duties, and it is easy to sympathize with his anguished plaint to Urquhart: 'I wonder if there is anything I cd. do, though the income were less wh. wd. give me more time, for I feel the want of that most of all.'

A week before Christmas Hopkins went home for a much-longed-for holiday of more than a month. He knew by now that life at the Oratory, and certainly teaching there, was impossible for him. When he heard that Bridges was going abroad with Muirhead, he wrote a farewell note confessing the disenchantment he could hardly tell anyone else.

The year [actually, six months] you will be away I have no doubt will make a great difference in my position though I cannot know exactly what. But the uncertainty I am in about the future is so very unpleasant and so breaks my power of applying to anything that I am resolved to end it, which I shall do by going into a retreat at Easter at the latest and deciding whether I have a vocation to the priesthood.[23]

He had already determined not to return to the school after Easter, and he had given Newman warning that the matter was on his mind, although he apparently could not screw up his courage to tell him in person; instead he waited until he was at home to let him know by letter. With the patience that characterized all his dealings with Hopkins, Newman replied, 'It seems to me you had better go into retreat at Easter, & bring the matter before the Priest who gives it to our boys. If you think that this is waiting too long, I must think of some other plan.'[24]

In Hampstead his family life went on as before, but once more he was odd man out, not quite able to join in the customary festivities, and certainly unable to talk to his parents of the matter that most occupied him. It is possible that this was one of the loneliest periods of his solitary life. His journal, usually an unconscious but very sensitive barometer of his moods, had been neglected during his last weeks at school, and he took the occasion of a little leisure to fill in the entries that he had previously missed. But when he came to the present, in Hampstead, he was once more unable to think of much except the weather to record, and he was again reduced to monosyllabic entries. Repeatedly he noted the weather as 'Dull', but one suspects that it applied as much to his life as to the skies above London.

To add to his gloom he heard that Alexander Wood, who had become a Catholic on hearing of Hopkins's conversion and who was confirmed with him, was already slipping away: 'His lapse is a most dreadful thing but I have nothing new to say about it: he suffered terrible pain before he finally gave up his belief.'[25] The rumour apparently turned out to be mistaken, but at the time the pain was as great as if it had been accurate. Actual defections among his fellow converts were to become more frequent, increasing his poignant awareness of the roughness of the path he had chosen.

CHAPTER X

SLAUGHTER OF THE INNOCENTS
1868

Although he hated to see them finish, Hopkins's school holidays had been as unsuccessful at raising his spirits as his duties during term. He had been back at the school hardly a fortnight when he was writing wearily to Baillie:

> I must say that I am very anxious to get away from this place. I have become very weak in health and do not seem to recover myself here or likely to do so. Teaching is very burdensome, especially when you have much of it: I have. I have not much time and almost no energy – for I am always tired – to do anything on my own account. I put aside that one sees and hears nothing and nobody here.

For two years or more, real depression had been hovering behind him like thunder in the air, but the frenetic activity of his conversion, of working so hard for his degree, perhaps even the effort of learning to go on after Dolben's death, had helped to push it out of thought. For three and a half months he had tried teaching, and though that kept him busy, it was far from keeping him happy.

During the rest of his life Hopkins was to establish a pattern of recurrent lethargy and hyperactivity, the cyclical ends of his own mental fragility. The activity was often an attempt to demonstrate his talents in a new direction, and usually it came to an inconclusive end. When he ran into such a block in his life, he often fell ill as a result. He was frail, in spite of his determination, and it is no surprise that his body gave way before his will. Then, when he thought he was recovered, he would leap into another burst of activity so intense that it would bring on a physical relapse accompanied by profound depression. The sickening lunge between extremes had probably always been a latent part of his personality, but his gloom on his return to the Oratory school at the beginning of 1868 seems to have been the onset of what was to be only too plain until his death.

Schoolmastering clearly would not suit him, and he was far from sure of his talent as an artist:

> I am expecting to take orders and soon, but I wish it to be secret till it comes about. Besides that it is the happiest and best way it practically is the only one. You know I once wanted to be a painter. But even if I could I wd. not I think, now, for the fact is that the higher and more attractive parts of the art put a strain upon the passions which I shd. think it unsafe to encounter. I want to write still and as a priest I very likely can do that too, not so freely as I shd. have liked, e.g. nothing or little in the verse way, but no doubt what wd. best serve the cause of my religion.

Hopkins was too devout to mistake depression for a spiritual vocation, but the pain of the former perhaps sharpened his search for the latter. Or, to put it as he might have, his mental anguish may have been God's way of directing him to the priesthood. In any case, what strikes a modern reader is how often his spiritual inclinations fitted his psychological needs, and in this case how they also answered his simple need of a way of earning his living.

What worried him most, he told Baillie, was that 'if I am a priest it will cause my mother, or she says it will, great grief and this preys on my mind very much and makes the near prospect quite black.' The result of being 'uncertain as I am whether in a few months I may not be shut up in a cloister' was that he was 'perfectly reckless about things that I shd. otherwise care about. . . . Do you happen to know of any tutorship I cd. take for a few months after Easter? as I am anxious to leave this place then and also not to leave it without having secured something to live upon till, as seems likely, I take minor orders.'[1]

But what Hopkins had in mind was ordination to the priesthood not to minor orders, and it is improbable that all his mother's grief would have kept him from it. The anticipation sustained him through the spring term at the Oratory school, although little else seems to have interested him. His journal that spring is curt and colourless, almost as if nothing had happened that could draw any response, and for the 21st of March he made a simple entry that might stand for the whole period: 'I forget.' He was marking time until Palm Sunday, the 5th of April, when the retreat Newman had mentioned began at the school.

The visiting preacher for the five days of the retreat was Fr Henry Coleridge, a Jesuit, and, like so many of the priests who came to the Oratory, a convert. Presumably Hopkins spoke with him about his own problems, as Newman had suggested he do. It has been surmised that this meeting was in part responsible for Hopkins's decision to become a Jesuit, which seems reasonable though probably overstated. Coleridge's own brother wrote of his choice of orders, 'The more I see and hear of the Jesuits, the more I am struck with their general superiority and freedom from nonsense. I always did rejoice that if my brother must be a R.C., and must be in an order, he chose the Jesuit order rather than any more modern one.'[2] If Fr Coleridge had any reservations about Hopkins's vocation, he must not have communicated them to either Newman or Hopkins himself.

The retreat ended on Maundy Thursday with a High Mass. Hopkins stayed on at the Oratory for Easter, then left three days later, severing his connections there. Unfortunately for him, he also lost the opportunity to see Newman frequently.

A fortnight later he was back in retreat, this time for two weeks of private meditation at the Jesuit novitiate in Manresa House, Roehampton, overlooking Richmond Park. Once more his journal mirrors his mood. With a lessening of his tension the weather seemed to improve immeasurably into a soft English spring saturated with birdsong, and his eye sharpened for the tender leaves of the wych-elms and oaks: 'Note the elm here on one side of beautiful build [sic] with one great limb overhanging the sunk fence into the Park.'[3] The combination of external beauty and internal peace was ideal for making three of the most important choices of his life. Typically, in each case he picked the most difficult of the alternatives.

The first problem to be decided was not necessarily the easiest, a fact reflected in the length of time it took him to make up his mind. The previous August, in the chapel of the Poor Clares, he had determined to destroy his poetry 'if it is better', but he had remained unsure that it was better, and he had taken no action. Five days after he went to Manresa he wrote in his journal, 'This day, I think, I resolved.' The inclusion of 'I think' seems to point to pious hope as much as certainty, but on the 11th of May, after he was back in Hampstead, he noted simply, 'Slaughter of the innocents'.[4] His deliberately elliptical phrase reflects a highly complex reaction. It suggests the pain of the destruction of what he had so far written, but it also invokes wry overtones of the death of the Holy Innocents, ironically comparing their martyrdom to the comparatively trivial burning of the poems, his own children. 'Innocents' probably indicates, too, something of his own dilemma about the morality of poetry, which he believed to be guiltless enough intrinsically, even when he knew it tended to distract him from higher concerns. Three months later, when Bridges asked him for a copy of a poem, he said that it was 'burnt with my other verses: I saw they wd. interfere with my state and vocation'.[5] By this time poetry had become considerably more important to Bridges than vocation; one would like to have seen his answer.

Thereafter Hopkins wrote only 'two or three little presentation pieces' until December 1875, when he broke his long near-silence with 'The Wreck of the Deutschland'. In spite of his formal renunciation of them, however, he did know that Bridges had copies of most of the poems he had already written and that other friends like Baillie and Coles had some as well, so that the slaughter of the innocents turned out to be more decimation than extermination.

The second matter he had to decide at Manresa was more important spiritually but less difficult to arrive at. Only three days after he had determined to burn his verses he wrote in his journal, 'Resolved to be a religious'. By this time his decision can hardly have been a surprise to anyone else, for, whatever he might say, he had known for a long time that he intended to be ordained, although this is the first indication that he intended to become a member of a religious order. Any intention of taking minor orders rather than being a priest had been forgotten by now.

Two days later he finished his retreat: 'Home, after having decided to be a priest and religious but still doubtful between St. Benedict and St. Ignatius.' In hindsight it seems to us as if each of his decisions could have been predicted from the time of his arrival in Oxford for his first year. A self-willed young Oxford man as pious as he could hardly have helped becoming progressively High Church in inclination. Having moved in that direction, he had a sense of compulsion to go as far as possible, so that he finally became a convert. Once he was a Roman Catholic, there was, as his parents foresaw clearly enough, no chance of his not being ordained. And ordination almost inevitably meant that he would not be a simple parish priest or even a member of one of the easier orders. In his quiet way Hopkins was a very headstrong man, determined on extremes. One important ingredient that had been left out of his nature was moderation. Once begun, a course of moral action, particularly a difficult one, had to run its full length before he could let it go in peace. Give his usual preference for the harder of his alternatives, his choice of order seems almost inevitable, since in all obvious ways the Jesuits would be the most difficult for him, as well as for his family and friends.

Occasionally Hopkins seems to have expected more reaction to his choices than he received, perhaps overestimating the importance to others of his decisions. Two years before, he had insisted on answering objections to his conversion that his father had never made but which he had expected. When he decided to become a Jesuit, he seems to have felt in the same way that Newman needed placating because he had not chosen the Oratorians, even when the older man had given no indication of expecting him to. Within a day or two of burning his poems, while the need of independence was still strong upon him, he wrote to Edgbaston to announce his choice. 'I am both surprised and glad at your news,' Newman answered. 'I think it is the very thing for you. You are quite out, in thinking that when I offered you a "home" here, I dreamed of your having a vocation for us. This I clearly saw you had *not*, from the moment you came to us. Don't call "the Jesuit discipline hard", it will bring you to heaven. The Benedictines would not have suited you.'[6] Breathing through the cool kindness of Newman's brief letter is something that sounds remarkably like a sigh of relief, for he can hardly have wanted Hopkins to take up permanent residence in the Oratory after he had been so unhappy there. Nor should Hopkins have expected him to do so, if he had thought the matter through.

Newman's view of the great orders was that 'St. Benedict has had the training of the ancient intellect, St. Dominic of the medieval, and St. Ignatius of the modern.'[7] Wisely, he saw that life as a Benedictine scholar would not make Hopkins happy, although to friends who knew less of his inner life that might have seemed the obvious choice. He had been content at Belmont with his first real exposure to clerical life in the Roman Church, but he needed constantly to assert to himself, and probably to others, that he was cut out for heroic conflict, not the calm pleasures of a library.

Hopkins greatly admired men of action, and in particular soldiers and sailors. His fervent patriotism contained a trace of something very like jingoism, which comes as a shock to readers who think of him only as a gentle, scholarly priest. 'What shall I do for the land that bred me?' he asks in the poem that begins with that line, and his answer is one that makes Kipling seem faint-hearted:

> Where is the field I must play the man on?
> O welcome there their steel or cannon.
> Immortal beauty is death with duty,
> If under her banner I fall for her honour.
> CH. Under her banner we fall for her honour.

It can hardly be accidental that the religious order Hopkins chose for himself should be known as the Soldiers of Christ. His slight body, a few inches more than five feet tall, his oddly feminine walk, his quiet manner, were all unsuited to a military man, but as a Soldier of Christ he was a member of a strictly organized band who took vows of unquestioning obedience, who had a strong sense of being an élite organization outside the normal life of Victorian England, who as outsiders in England or as missionaries in heathen lands ran psychological and physical risks as great as those facing soldiers. The order would seem to have been perfect for Hopkins. Perfect, that is, if his physique, his mental resilience and his ability to live a solitary life had been up to the stern requirements he set himself. One consequence of belonging to either the Benedictines or the Jesuits that he seems not to have considered was that in both orders there was a strong probability he would spend most of his time teaching, which he had so disliked at the Oratory: not the obvious pathway to heroism.

Although Hopkins was telling others (presumably not his parents) of his decision to become a Jesuit, the truth was that he was not yet formally accepted by the Society. However, he would surely not have talked about the matter unless he had at least received encouragement during his retreat at Manresa House. On 20th May, a fortnight after the retreat, he went to Hill Street, Berkeley Square, to see Fr Alfred Weld, the English Provincial of the Society of Jesus, to request admission as a novice. Besides his interview with Fr Weld, who was to judge his background, personality, and motives, he had to appear before a committee of four experienced priests who had to determine whether he met the formal requirements of Canon Law as a candidate for Holy Orders. He could not, for example, be illegitimate, of weak intellect or subject to insanity, an apostate, and could never have belonged to or, according to tradition, so much as tried on the habit of another order. Eleven days later, on his return home from a trip to Oxford, he found a letter from Fr Weld giving him permission to become a novice early in the autumn.

The reason for his trip to Oxford had been to take his BA, almost a year after he had passed his examinations with such distinction. He was prevented by his Catholicism from proceeding to the degree of MA three years later, as he would otherwise have done; when the ban on Catholics taking the degree was lifted, he had presumably lost interest in doing so.

On Degree Day Hopkins wrote that he 'Saw Swinburne. Met Mr. Solomon.'[8] The use of 'Mr' for Solomon suggests that they were meeting for the first time, and 'Saw' rather than 'Met' may indicate that he was not unfamiliar with Swinburne. There had probably been plenty of occasions while he was at Balliol to be introduced to the flamboyant poet, 'the Red Dwarf of Balliol', who often came to Oxford to see his old tutor, Jowett.

Solomon, a talented and outrageously attractive young man, was a protégé of Swinburne and a friend of Pater. When Hopkins met him, he was enjoying a brief period of great success as a painter; five years later, in 1873, he was in prison for homosexual offences, then rapidly went even further downhill when he came out. Presumably Solomon suggested that they meet again, for two weeks later Hopkins went to see his studio in London after he had been at a luncheon given by Pater. The friendship progressed no further, however, and Hopkins still referred to him in his journal as 'Mr. Solomon'. There is no reason to think that Hopkins was in any way involved in the world in which the others moved, and certainly not when he was actually waiting for word about his acceptance by the Jesuits, but the combination of Swinburne, Pater and Solomon suggests that he was still attracted by a distinctly 'Bohemian' circle, one whose sexual overtones he was too intelligent not to recognize. If he ever met Swinburne again, the record of the meeting has disappeared.

While he was in Oxford he failed once more to get in touch with Liddon, but he announced his coming novitiate to him: 'I regret very much that I failed to see you . . . for I am afraid we may never meet again. I came a good many times but your oak was always up. If I had sent you a note in time I shd. have managed better perhaps.'[9] This was almost certainly the last communication that ever passed between the two men, its tepid tone a fit memorial to a withered friendship.

Hopkins was obviously clearing decks, ridding himself of old encumbrances and acquaintances. On the same day that he wrote to Liddon he wrote to Henry Wall, Bursar of Balliol, reminding him that his name was to be removed from the College books, and asking that his final battels be forwarded to be paid off.[10] The letter was intended to settle with Balliol emotionally as well as financially. Its one odd note is that Hopkins indicated his father would settle his account, which must have been galling to him, although there was clearly no alternative.

In June 1868 Hopkins told Urquhart that he would be going into the novitiate in early September: 'Since I made up my mind to this I have enjoyed the first complete peace of mind I have ever had. I am quite surprised . . . at the kind and contented way my parents have come to take the prospect.' The actual accomplishment of what he had longed for and his parents had dreaded seems to have cleared the air remarkably with his family, for there was not much left over which they could differ. Beneath the apparently calm surface, of course, was always the possibility of eruption, and both sides seem to have worked hard at maintaining peace.

His own spiritual contentment and total conviction, however, made him a scratchy friend for Urquhart, whom he was constantly urging to heed the message his conscience was giving him: the necessity of becoming a convert. 'Will it comfort you at death not to have despaired of the English Church if by not despairing of it you are out of the Catholic Church? . . . Will God thank you for yr. allegiance and will He excuse you for it?'[11]

According to Urquhart's daughter, 'To the very end he spoke of the charm of Gerard Hopkins', but this appears to have been the last letter he ever received from him or at any rate the last he kept. Probably Hopkins's inability to write regularly during his novitiate put the finish to an intimacy that had always been slightly difficult because of his own habit of teasing and ridiculing Urquhart while he was an undergraduate, and lecturing him once he had become a convert. The contraction of his old circle was painful, but it did clear the way for a new life.

Before becoming a Jesuit, he had a final holiday in Switzerland for almost the whole of July. On his return, there would be just over a month to spend in Hampstead before going to Manresa. He had not found the tutoring job he hoped for, and it was easier to stay on good terms with his parents if they were not in each other's pockets the whole summer. It was also pointed out to him that Jesuits were forbidden to visit Switzerland, and that this would be his last chance to see the country.

It must have entered his mind that the previous summer, when he returned from a similar trip abroad, he had found the news of the death of Dolben. Now, as he was preparing to go to Switzerland, he called on his Aunt Kate on the 28th of June, the anniversary of Dolben's death, only to be told that she had just seen Ellen Dolben, Digby's sister. No explanation has survived of how they came across each other or, even more mysteriously, how his aunt knew that the meeting had any particular significance for him. Hopkins's journal gives us no clue to his feelings, but the queer little coincidence must have been disturbing to him, particularly when three days later he heard from Digby's close Eton friend Wyatt-Edgell, saying that he had been received into the Church the previous day.

Hopkins's companion on the Swiss trip was his old friend Edward Bond, who was acquainted with the whole Hopkins family. 'I know you must know who Edward Bond is,' Hopkins told Bridges, 'I have so often spoken of him. He is a scholar of St. John's whom I have known ever since I have been at Oxford and rather longer, and intimately, for he lives at Hampstead. He is handsome and very tall and his mother is extremely nice.'[12] Curiously, few records have survived of the friendship. It was Bond who, two years earlier, had been insistent that Gerard tell his parents of his intention of becoming a convert. Hopkins delighted in talking to him about literary matters because both his blame and his praise were so open-hearted and vociferous.

His new-found happiness, of which he had written to Urquhart, as well as the prospect of a new life on his return to England, made Hopkins enter into the trip with pleasure, leaving his depression behind him in Hampstead. His journal bubbles and fizzes with excitement, so that once more he seems the effervescent boy who first went up to Oxford rather than the care-worn young man who was constantly worried and suspicious at Hampstead and Edgbaston. He was no longer writing poetry, but it hardly seems a loss in the face of the exuberance of his journal.

Hopkins and Bond went by Dover and Ostend to Brussels, then Cologne and Basel. In Switzerland they walked miles every day, enough to make the reader's legs ache vicariously, but there is not the slightest protest in Hopkins's journal, nor indication of more than a day's illness to detract from the rudest health, of the kind that had seemed outside his understanding in Edgbaston. He wore a 'pagharee' against the sun, a silk scarf hanging down under his hat and protecting the back of his head. It was not always effective but kept him from burning his neck seriously.

One remarkable aspect of his journal kept on this trip is his constant observation of the persons they saw, a trait not seen frequently before. Repeatedly he tried to define what was typical in the modest faces of Italian women or what was characteristic of 'that repulsive type of French face'. In Basel they met a 'young Englishman who had been to see Charlotte Brontë's school in Brussels'. That night under a full moon they walked about the city, and had the teasingly unspecified 'adventure of the little Englishwoman with her hat off' and saw a woman come 'to a window with a candle and some mess she was making, and then that was gone and there was no light anywhere but the moon. We heard music indoors about.'[13] The painterly little vignettes show a curiosity about other persons with few parallels in his journals.

Walking to Lauterbrunnen they had as companion 'a Frenchman, a man of cultivation and a great mountaineer'; 'Two boys came down the mountain yodelling'; their attention was caught by 'that strange party of Americans'; for a time they were accompanied by 'young Mr. Pease of Darlington'; and they saw 'In the valley a girl with spindle and distaff tending cows.' His attention in all these instances remains visual and external, but it also shows how his curiosity about others was piqued when he was happy.

When they crossed into Italy, they met John Tyndall, mountaineer and natural scientist, who was preparing for his third, and successful, assault on the Matterhorn. Bond had fallen ill, and Tyndall prescribed medicine for him. One of Tyndall's guides refused to climb on a Sunday unless he had gone first to Mass, so Hopkins assisted at 'mass said in a little chapel for the guides going up with Tyndal at two o'clock in the morning and so I got up for this, my burnt face in a dreadful state and running. We went down with lanterns. It was an odd scene; two of the guides or porters served; the noise of a torrent outside accompanied the priest. Then to bed again.'

The journal has, of course, the fine writing that is to be expected of Victorian travellers seeing the Alps for the first (or the tenth) time, for Hopkins would not have been himself if his pen had not leapt unbidden into his hand after the spiritual uplift of a day at the Jungfrau or the Reichenbach falls. 'The Monte Rosa range are dragged over with snow like cream', he noted. 'As we looked at them the sky behind them became dead purple, the effect unique; and then the snow according to its lie and its faces differenced itself, the upward-looking faces taking shade, the vertical light, like lovely damask. Above the Breithorn Antares sparkled like a bright crab-apple tingling in the wind.' But his exuberant mood could easily be ruined by insensitive companions or 'the cold feet, the spectacles, the talk, and the lunching . . . Even with one companion ecstasy is almost banished: you want to be alone and to feel that, and leisure – all pressure taken off.'[14]

There is a great deal more as well in the journal of this trip, including dry humour wrung from the conventional expectations of Alpine travellers. 'Yes,' he wrote at Cologne as if to confound the reader, 'the cathedral is very meagre.'

In *The Way of All Flesh* Samuel Butler indicates the common sense of Ernest Pontifex by comparing his notebook entry at the Hospice of St Bernard with that of his grandfather, who wrote Latin verses to record his dutiful awe and was kept awake by the thought of being 'in the highest inhabited spot in the old world and in a place celebrated in every part of it'. By contrast, Ernest writes simply, 'I went up to the Great St. Bernard and saw the dogs.' Some five years before Butler began writing his novel, Hopkins recorded his own down-to-earth reactions to the same place: 'We saw the dogs and the *morgue*.'

Although Hopkins was not writing poetry, he was busy storing up impressions and images, many of which were to surface years later when he had taken to verse again. For example, he noted that the ends of a glacier were like 'the skin of a white tiger or the deep fell of some other animal'; the difficulty of distinguishing between a mountainous moor and rough animal skin, both referred to as 'fell', is a striking image in one of the late 'Terrible Sonnets', 'I wake and feel the fell of dark, not day', probably not written until 1885. At Grindelwald he observed that water and ice have cross-hatches like the folds of a wimple; in 'The Windhover' he remarks the same phenomenon on the feathers of a hawk's wing. His fascination with vertiginous heights, half fear and half attraction, may also owe something to this trip. After taking a steamer to Geneva, Bond and Hopkins went 'Through Paris to Dieppe and by Newhaven home' on the last day of July 1868. It had been a splendid trip, perhaps the most joyous month Hopkins had known for a long time.

The pleasure he had found in Switzerland was continued in London. He spent several days with Baillie, visiting exhibitions at the National Gallery and walking to St Albans to inspect the restoration of the Abbey. He burnished his friendships with Garrett and Addis, and saw Bridges, probably for the first time since the latter had returned from a six-month trip abroad. When Bridges went to Hampstead, Hopkins noted with a twinkle, 'Bridges came up and Rover bit him.'[15] With Wyatt-Edgell he spent a fine August afternoon talking in Regent's Park, presumably about conversion and about Dolben, who was the most important link in their acquaintance. He was also introduced to Moncrieff Smith, a recently ordained convert, and wrote in his journal that 'they call him F. Dominic', which had obvious resonances for him of Br Dominic, as Dolben had liked to be called.

The first week in September was tiresomely dim, hot, and fine, and Hopkins spent most of it taking leave of his relatives and friends. On the evening of the 7th of September he made his farewells at home and walked to the train by himself. When he reached Finchley Road station, he found that there would not be another train for three quarters of an hour. Rather than go back up the hill, interrupt the family at dinner, and spend a few more anti-climactic minutes with them before saying goodbye again, he went to his grandmother's house in Victoria Road. His Aunt Annie walked back with him to the station to see him off: 'Then to the Novitiate, Roehampton.'[16]

The new life he was starting would last until death unless something cataclysmic went wrong. Because he was a university graduate, he would be forgiven some of the study years that other aspiring Jesuits had to expect; even so, he was only twenty-four, which meant that he could look forward to another nine years of training, since Jesuits were customarily not ordained until thirty-three, the age at which Christ had finished His ministry.

CHAPTER XI

MANRESA
1868–70

In 1868 Roehampton was still a pretty country village some five miles from Hyde Park Corner. Nowhere was its comparative seclusion more evident that at Manresa, cut off both physically and spiritually from its surroundings. The novitiate of the Society had been there since 1861, when it moved from Beaumont Lodge, Windsor, the scene of Dolben's unfortunate visit resulting in his expulsion from Eton. In taking over the estate, the Jesuits changed its name from Roehampton Park* to the more appropriate one of the 'place where St. Ignatius lived for a year doing penance in a cave'. To continue the lustration, they set about the familiar process of guaranteeing sanctity by the systematic destruction of beauty.

The removal had been a gesture indicating that the Jesuits intended to take a more active part in English life. At Windsor they had deliberately kept themselves secret and mysterious from fear of their neighbours, but their new house, so much nearer London, was chosen so 'that we may be accustomed to seeing and being seen, in walks, in catechising, etc.'.[1] Only 42 of the original 110 acres in the park had been purchased with the mansion, which was in run-down condition but still sufficiently impressive to make the rumour credible that the Queen was buying it for the Prince of Wales. The Jesuits did nothing to dispel the rumour, for they were afraid that if the identity of the new purchasers was revealed before the sale, it would be called off.

Hopkins's arrival on his first night was presumably after the

---

*It had originally been called Parkste[a]d, but it was also known as Bessborough House when it was the scene of the Whig intrigues of the Bessboroughs and the Devonshires, as well as the retreat of Lady Caroline Lamb after Byron had dropped her.

communal 7.30 supper had taken place, and he missed the first half of the 'recreation' hour, during which only Latin was spoken. 'Whether I was last in that night I cannot quite make out', he told his mother.[2] There were six other new men in the novitiate arriving at the same time, and they were kept away from the rest of the community until they had undergone a period of contemplation of ten days during which they had an easy chance to repudiate the course of training they were undertaking. Two men who had been novices the previous year were assigned as their 'guardian angels' to answer questions and shepherd them. Curiously, there was another Hopkins in the group of newcomers, this one named Frederick, who became known at Manresa as 'the genteel Hop', while Gerard was called 'the gentle Hop'.

As Hopkins reported, he had a bedroom to himself initially, but as soon as he had finished his probation, he had to move into a dormitory, in which each man had a tiny cubicle ('like stalls in a well-kept stable') cut off from the main room by a red curtain, behind which were a narrow iron bedstead, 'a washstand with a pitcher and basin, and a "Charley", or chamber pot, shoved modestly away underneath'.[3] Outside each cubicle stood a small desk. In the winter there was no heat in the dormitory, and the nearest approach to luxury was a strip of faded carpet beside the bed.

The new men, who were not yet called novices, spent most of their time learning the rules of the Society and the difficulties they might expect to encounter. After a few days they formally began the Long Retreat of thirty days, during which they kept almost total silence. While in retreat they could neither write nor receive letters, and Hopkins had to give up his daily journal entries, although he did squeeze in one glowing entry on the day after the retreat began: 'Chestnuts as bright as coals or spots of vermilion', an observation which surfaced again in both 'Pied Beauty' and 'The Windhover'.

The month-long retreat was clearly gruelling, and it has been suggested that this was the original of the religious experience of the first part of 'The Wreck of the Deutschland'. This seems inherently improbable, since those stanzas tell of an almost unbearable anguish, of which there is no trace in the early autumn of 1868. In any case there would have been other vigils, other retreats on the memories of which he could draw, and it seems limiting to believe that the immediacy of the poem comes from a single occasion.

Only when the retreat was finished were they received as novices, permitted to talk to their seniors, and given Jesuit clothing to wear. This last proved for some men an awkward moment, since each was issued with hat and ancient sleeveless, knee-length gown, with scant regard for fit. They were so patched, so stained and worn and green with age, that many of their wearers remembered their distaste until the end of their days. It must have been particularly repugnant to Hopkins, who was normally fastidious in his dress and grooming, and who was so small that it was hard to find clothes of his size. All the same, it signified his acceptance by the Society, to be confirmed two years later when he took his first vows. Beneath the gown he wore the black suit, shirt, jersey, socks and under-clothing he had brought with him; his puzzled letters home indicate that he was not adept at taking care of them. His hair, which he had worn long, was cut off with a fine disdain for looks worthy of the saints he emulated. Hopkins probably did the shearing himself, as we know he did in later years, when all the familiar photographs show him with closely cropped head.

The timetable of the community sounds monotonous to an outsider, but to Hopkins it had all the charm of the unfamiliar, as well as the spiritual nourishment that he wanted so much. It was probably not a great deal more unvarying than the routine of many other occupations, and for him it was certainly pleasanter than the schedule he had followed as a schoolmaster at the Oratory. They were called at 5.30 to wash, shave, dress, and make a short visit to the chapel for prayer at 6, then meditate for another hour before Mass at 7. Breakfast, usually of porridge, milk, and bread, although occasionally consisting of toast and what was described as delicious coffee, was at 7.45, eaten in silence. After half an hour of pious reading, they began the indoor duties for which they were all responsible: washing up after breakfast, laying places for the mid-day dinner, dusting, sweeping, or acting as scullery helpers to the lay brother who did the cooking; 'we have to keep our rooms tidy to an extraordinary degree',[4] reported Hopkins in slight dismay. At a time when there were plenty of servants, it is improbable that many of the novices had any experience at housekeeping, but most of them came to enjoy it, perhaps because it was a change from the unremitting mental occupations that took up so much of the day.

After another session of learning the rules of the Society, 'they have some free time, during which they can walk in the grounds, pray in the chapel, or read some Life of the saints or other spiritual book'.[5] At 11.30 they assembled for an hour of what many of them found the pleasantest part of the day, when they worked in the grounds, cutting up wood for fuel, sweeping leaves, weeding flowerbeds, or helping on the little farm within the park that grew most of their food.

There were still beautiful shrubs and great trees surrounding the house: 'All bears the traces of former wealth which neglect has however allowed to fall somewhat in decay,' as the Jesuit magazine said.[6] A temple in the grounds had been converted into a shrine, and most of the avenues were given suitably religious designations, so that two were renamed 'Sacred Heart Walk' and 'St Aloysius's Walk'. A few hundred yards from the severely elegant classical front of the house was a ha-ha separating the grounds from the vast extent of Richmond Park, in which rutting stags kept the novices uneasily awake during mating season. The only other building then visible from Manresa was the royal residence, White Lodge, and that was quickly disappearing behind the hedge that had been planted to block out the Jesuits from sight.

Even its institutional use could not wholly ruin the beauty of the exterior of the house, but a certain ingenuity had gone into the conversion of the interior. The first Rector, Fr Weld, had been suspicious of his surroundings and remarked that 'the new house with its beautiful rooms its richly adorned ceilings and splendid park was too smart a place for poor Religious.'[7] He soon took care of all that. Disraeli, who had known it as a private house and had set part of *Lothair* in it, would hardly have recognized Manresa when Hopkins arrived. The great hall had become a recreation room, and on the first floor the state rooms were divided and subdivided: drawing room, dining room and principal bedroom were all turned into dormitories. Dismantled fireplaces and empty niches attested to the former luxurious fittings of the house, some of which had been sold as the Bessboroughs fell further and further into debt. Baroque plasterwork on the walls was covered by plain pine boards, leaving only the delicately moulded ceilings to suggest former splendour, and those were disfigured where the brackets for crystal chandeliers had been taken out without adequate camouflage of the damage. Almost miraculously, the graceful double staircase had survived the change and stood as emblem of a vanished life.

In part the desecration of the fine old house was conscious, for the Society was anxious to accustom its novices to being without luxuries, even visual ones. It was often said that the primary purpose of the long years of Jesuit training was to teach young men to obey unquestioningly, with 'blind obedience', as if they were literally in the army on which the Society modelled itself. The novices were taught to accept without qualification any instruction by their superiors; only in cases where they might be asked to act in ways contrary to their conscience were they free to question orders or even to have mental reservations. Part of the regimen was the suppression of aesthetic pleasure, undertaken as deliberately as their bodies were made accustomed to the uncomfortable beds and the plain, occasionally unpalatable food.

Henry Kerr, who was at Manresa with Hopkins, although he was a few years older, used to declare that 'the only endurable alternative' to Jesuit life 'was the life in the British navy, the same obedience, the same manly contempt of bodily comforts, the same indifference to place or surroundings, being found in both'.[8]

The reputation of the Jesuits was of engrained philistinism, and probably even that was attractive to Hopkins, who so often showed how much he distrusted beauty for its own sake. Pater had done more, in a perverse way, to shape his thinking than he knew. It was in the spirit of what Hopkins thought the Society stood for that he had burned his poems, carrying out the 'Slaughter of the innocents'. As the editor of the Jesuit magazine, *The Month*, was to write more than a century later, in a fair and considered assessment of whether Hopkins had his poetic genius crushed by the Society:

There is no convincing evidence that the Society was an enemy to his genius. His fellow-Jesuits were also fellow-Victorians neither more nor less perceptive than other men of their period and class. They neither helped nor hindered him much. The dark side of his own temperament was a greater enemy. The real trouble was duller but, in a sense, worse. It was the low valuation set on Art by the Society after its restoration, and by no means consistent with its own more ancient and grander tradition. It had become, at least in England and more generally elsewhere, philistine, puritanical. Art, except in banal, popular forms, was regarded as irrelevant, a distraction from the main business of preaching the Gospel. And its preaching see-sawed between the coldly rational and the sickly sentimental.[9]

Yet it is possible for a man to be crushed by a duty he has freely embraced.

Both before and after dinner novices went to pray in the chapel. The meal was substantial, and they were enjoined to eat well, for their health was a matter for careful concern. During the meal silence was general except for the edifying book that one of them read aloud. Three afternoons a week they took a walk of two hours, in a crocodile composed of twos and threes; no one was allowed to choose his companions but had to take them by chance or as the master of novices arranged. 'All special friendships – all preference for one "brother" more than for another – were strictly proscribed.'[10] The walks were indicative of the hope of the Society of becoming more integrated into ordinary English life, but in this case they were fairly ineffective, since there were no other Catholics in Roehampton, and local boys sat on the walls of the drive to watch the unaccustomed sight, frequently to jeer at the novices paired off so demurely.

On other days there were cricket and football in the afternoon, but we know that Hopkins disliked games because of his size. Being kicked on the football field by his pupils at Edgbaston hardly made him more anxious to play at Manresa. From the distinct lack of choice given to novices in other matters we may guess that he was made to play, whatever his inclinations.

Throughout the year there were feast days, processions, half-holidays, long walks to Catholic churches around London to serve at the altar or help teach in parish schools, visits to other churches to augment the choir on important festivals: they all helped to keep tedium at bay. Perhaps the most popular recreation was the June hay-making, when the novices turned out in their scruffiest clothes to dry and cart the hay all through the long sunny afternoons. At teatime they would assemble in the summerhouse built by Lord Bessborough. 'Tired and hot, with our shoes and trouser legs yellow with buttercup pollen, we sat and listened to a novice reading a religious book. This took the place of our spiritual reading.'[11]

Mulberrying was another favourite task, and at the end of his first summer at Manresa, Hopkins, who had a good head for climbing, confided his exhilaration to his journal: 'When you climbed to the top of the tree and came out the sky looked as if you could touch it and it was as if you were in a world made up of these three colours, the green of the leaves lit through by the sun, the blue of the sky, and the grey blaze of their upper sides against it.'

He was always abnormally sensitive to the felling of trees, and it was a shock shortly after when the mulberry was snapped off at ground level in an equinoctial storm, a fine Spanish oak was wrecked, and half a great cedar was hurled into the rye field. Hopkins shook off his fear to run through the storm and see the damage: 'Long unending races of leaves came leaping and raging along the meadow. It frightened one to go among the trees.'[12]

Hopkins's perception of beauty was certainly not conventional, nor did he divide experience into the beautiful and the ugly. Once, during a cold snap, when part of his duty was to clean the outdoor water closets, he wrote in his journal, 'The slate slabs of the urinals even are frosted in graceful sprays.'[13] Such a slight remark indicates how unconsciously he inhabited a world quite different from that of his fellows, one that could seem almost comic in its distance from their reactions.

It all sounds Arcadian, and no doubt it often was, but there were long stretches when the unvarying rhythm was difficult to bear. Naturally, the novices were forbidden to get into quarrels, but the close quarters inevitably bred antipathy to a few of their number. Most of those who left the novitiate did so for what would sound trivial reasons, although in sum they certainly added up to a lack of vocation. Even those who stuck the course had a difficult time of it.

At twenty-four Hopkins was several years older than most of the other novices, and it is not to be wondered at if they sometimes behaved like schoolboys. When they were on edge they were inclined to burst into uncontrollable hilarity at anything unexpected. Joseph Thorp, who went to Manresa some twenty years after Hopkins, said that the strictness of the first retreat of the novices had been moderated in his own day because it too frequently occasioned nervous breakdowns. The atmosphere was so tense that the whole group of forty of his fellow novices would have fits of hysterical giggling. Thorp, who later left the Order, nonetheless insisted that their life was happy.[14]

In this atmosphere tears came as unexpectedly as laughter. Hopkins himself, who was far from imperturbable, told in his diary of his second Christmas at Manresa, when he was on retreat, having his dinner in silence and listening to the lector for the day; it indicates how near breaking his stretched nerves were. One of his fellow novices was reading 'Sister Emmerich's account of the Agony in the Garden' when suddenly Hopkins

> began to cry and sob and could not stop. I put it down for this reason, that if I had been asked a minute beforehand I should have said that nothing of the sort was going to happen and even when it did I stood in a manner wondering at myself not seeing in my reason the traces of an adequate cause for such strong emotion – the traces of it I say because of course the cause in itself is adequate for the sorrow of a lifetime. I remember much the same thing on Maundy Thursday when the presanctified Host was carried to the sacristy.[15]

It is probably relevant that the nun whose account was being read was a German visionary and stigmatic, in religious exile like the tall nun in 'The Wreck of the Deutschland', and that she believed she had inexplicably relived Christ's agony. Hopkins seems always to have been moved by the religiously dispossessed and particularly by women who were so treated. 'To be persecuted in a tolerant age is a high distinction,' he wrote.[16] In the case of Sister Emmerich, although he predictably said that Christ's agony was the primary cause of his near-breakdown, he obviously recognized that the seeds of it were already there in his own character.

Hopkins's perceptions of his motivations are frequently startling, combining as they do an initial attribution to religious reasons, then a subsequent shrewd awareness that they also spring out of the predispositions of his own personality. The two views of the matter are not in conflict, simply phenomena discussed in differing vocabulary but with similar patterns. Had he not been religious, he might well have been a first-rate psychologist investigating the promptings of the unconscious. He was particularly interested in the unexpressed matter of dreams. 'It seems true', he wrote, '. . . that you can trace your dreams to something or other in your waking life, especially of things that have been lately . . . But the connection may be capricious, almost punning.'[17] This is a kind of self-awareness comparatively rare in pre-Freudian writing.

Perhaps Hopkins had not realized how strict his regimen would be. A possibly apocryphal story is told that he was taken aback by being advised that Swinburne's poems would not be appropriate reading for him to take to Manresa. And certainly he underestimated the difficulty of writing to his friends. He could not promise to correspond, he had told Bridges, 'for in that way the novices are restricted, but I have no doubt that now and then I shd. be able to send you a letter'.[18] But from his two years in the novitiate only two letters to Bridges have survived, and it is unlikely that Bridges destroyed others, since many years later he said he had kept them all. Immediately after arriving at Manresa Hopkins told his mother, 'The retreat begins I believe on Monday but will be broken twice or more and this may perhaps give me the chance of writing.' As it turned out, he was unable to write during the retreat, and after he became a full novice he was normally allowed to write only one letter weekly.

Since his parents naturally expected to hear from him frequently, this left him with only a small budget for Bridges and other friends. On at least a few occasions he kept an unfinished letter in a drawer until he could add to it before posting it, thus effectively allowing himself more correspondence. At Manresa and in his subsequent posts both incoming and outgoing letters were read by his superiors, and we know from later correspondence that this nettled Bridges, who had become increasingly anti-Jesuit in his prejudices and could admit no reason why anyone else should see what he had written. Years later he was even certain that the Society was responsible for Hopkins's early death.

Hopkins was afraid that his friendship with Bridges would suffer from his new life, and he was in part right. Since there were no rules against having guests during free time, he hoped to see him: 'perhaps sometime when you are in town you might come and see me: it is quite near, and easy of access by Putney or Barnes.'[19] In practice, however, his time was so limited that when Bridges did come for his first visit without warning, he was turned away because Hopkins was in retreat. In spite of their religious differences, Hopkins maintained his old affection for Bridges, and wrote to his mother of a subsequent visit, 'he is now in town reading medicine . . . and if you thought he wd. like it and you liked it yourself you might, I think, ask him to Hampstead some time – he was a great friend of mine and very kind to me and is very nice in himself, as I believe you know.'[20]

Probably the invitation Hopkins asked his mother to extend was intended to repair the damage from something that had gone wrong when Bridges was at Manresa. There is no clue as to what it was, although it may be fair to guess that it was concerned with religion, for Bridges was constantly on the offensive about the Roman Church, and some of Hopkins's remarks, however innocently meant, sounded patronizing to his Protestantism. Two years later, in asking Bridges to write again, Hopkins said, 'I am sure I must have behaved unkindly when you came to Roehampton.'[21]

A letter to Baillie indicates how difficult Manresa was for visitors: 'Any day will do for me excepting as a general rule Tuesday and Friday mornings and Sundays. . . . Wednesdays are the best days generally speaking but not later than 10 A.M. or 3 P.M. or I should have gone out, it being our recreation day.'[22]

Baillie braved the regulations and brought with him Edward Bond, who had been Hopkins's companion in Switzerland. Some Hopkins cousins also called, but he was away when they arrived. Scott Holland and R.L. Nettleship, a contemporary of Hopkins who became a Fellow of Balliol in 1869, were early callers; T.H. Green responded to Scott Holland's account of the visit with his own view of Hopkins, which was typical of that of a good many of his friends:

I am glad that you and Nettleship saw Hopkins. A step such as he has taken, tho' I can't quite admit it to be heroic, must needs be painful, and its pain should not be aggravated – as it is pretty sure to be – by separation from old friends. . . . I imagine him – perhaps uncharitably – to be one of those, like his ideal J.H. Newman, who instead of simply opening themselves to the revelation of God in the reasonable world, are fain to put themselves into an attitude – saintly, it is true, but still an attitude. True citizenship 'as unto the Lord' (which includes all morality) I reckon higher than 'saintliness' in the technical sense. The 'superior young man' of these days, however, does not seem to understand it, but hugs his own 'refined pleasures' or (which is but a higher form of the same) his personal sanctity. Whence, and not from heterodoxy, ruin threatens Christian society.[23]

Green's dislike (and misunderstanding) of everything Hopkins had chosen was not far from that of several other friends, who were moved to contempt for what they considered unmanly and quite as unthinkable as if he had repudiated his family and nationality. William Anson, who had been at Balliol with Hopkins and was now a Fellow of All Souls, wrote with disdain as ill-disguised as Hopkins's name, 'H. has become a Jesuit and is going as a governess in a Protestant family.'[24]

Informed public opinion about the Society was becoming slightly more tolerant, but middle-class England still distrusted it; when hard fact was unavailable, its place could be taken by prejudice and actual falsehood. There were many scurrilous books about the Order, of which one typical example was called *Plan of the Jesuits for the Seduction of Religious Women*, and Jesuits were stock villainous characters in such novels as Kingsley's *Westward Ho!* or the less well-known story by Catherine Sinclair, *Beatrice: or The Unknown Relatives*, a 'moral tale, purporting to show the joys of Protestantism contrasted with the miseries of Popery' that 'features a vile Jesuit with the usual "bland smile", "insinuating voice", "diplomatic skill", "noiseless velvet step" (Jesuits always "glide" through Victorian novels), and habit of "emptying people's purses with a face of brass and dividing their families with a heart of steel"'.[25]

Naturally, much of the scandal imputed to the Jesuits was sexual in nature, even though some of the members were almost unbelievably *naïf* in their knowledge of such matters. Those novices who had attended Jesuit public school at Stonyhurst were accustomed to the 'nude gods, heroes, heroines, and goddesses' in their classical dictionaries having 'all the more regrettable parts of their bodies covered with neat bathing drawers'. At Manresa one young man of nineteen in the novitiate, to the embarrassment of the Novice Master, had to be told 'the bare facts of sex . . . how babies were begotten'. In their concern to keep the young men pure in both mind and body the senior members of the community set up strenuous programmes of walking, games, and heavy work in the garden, sensibly recognizing that novices had enough trouble with celibacy without being denied regular outlets for animal spirits. They were all given 'modesty powder' for their baths to make the water opaque, but since they were limited to one bath a month, its effects would seem minimal. When all precautions had been taken, however, the clamour of the stags in the Park across the ha-ha must still have aroused disturbing echoes in the hearts of young men whose average age was probably only nineteen or twenty.

When he was Novice Master Fr George Tyrrell sensibly advised Joseph Thorp that for maintaining chastity 'Cold baths and interesting work are of more help than disciplines and chains.'[26] The remark seems to indicate his disapproval of the latter, but they were in standard use at Manresa.

Not surprisingly, little is said of them in Jesuit writing, and Hopkins mentions them only fleetingly, but we know that their use was standard both before and after his time at Manresa, so it seems reasonable to assume that he employed them as well, particularly as he appears to have used them while he was still an Anglican. Disciplines were scourges made of knotted cords for flogging oneself, usually on the back; the knots could be waxed if the novice was particularly zealous. 'They were not constantly used, but only at stated times, such as during Lent; but at any time with permission. During Lent we used them twice a week.'[27] On nights of mortification the novices sat in their cubicles before lights-out and, at the ringing of the bell by the porter, gave themselves precisely twelve strokes. For healthy young men it was neither dangerous nor particularly painful.

'The chain was a neat contraption of wire, horse-shoe links with points turning inwards, which you strapped around your thigh next your skin.'[28] The pain, which was dulled at rest, became intense when the leg was flexed or accidentally brushed against the seat of a chair. It was a point of honour not to limp when wearing it, but few new novices could manage such nonchalance.

In general, corporal mortification, disciplines, chains and hair shirts were left to the individual judgment of the novice, with the advice of his spiritual adviser, but it was important that they should not interfere with his normal duties, so no serious excesses were allowed.

Dispensation from physical rigours was given freely for anyone who was ill or weak, but it was of course a matter of pride not to ask for it, particularly if one were a convert ('vert' in the language of Manresa). Hopkins was unusually assiduous at penance and mortification but unfortunately not very strong. His superiors were watchful about his health and especially careful to excuse him from anything that might endanger it; all during his religious studies his letters are full of complaint when he has been told that he must forgo penance. He was forbidden to fast during his first Lent at Manresa, a fact that is perhaps connected with his falling asleep while the Rector was giving points for meditation.[29] Usually, however, he seems to have been adept at concealing his weakness, and possibly his reluctance to ask for dispensation lay at the heart of his poor health during the rest of his life.

When his superiors put an embargo on other penances, he would undertake 'custody of the eyes' instead, as he did from January to July of 1869. The person undertaking this penance kept his eyes cast down, looking at neither persons nor objects around him. It had been one of the practices that Pusey urged on the Brotherhood of the Holy Trinity, and Hopkins himself seems to have used it while still an Anglican. In truth it was probably a greater penance for him than fasting or fustigation, since it meant that he had to curb his natural tendency to look hard at everything he came across, so that neither his walks nor his perambulations in the grounds of Manresa had their usual delight for him. During that period his journal suffered, and there is almost nothing visual in his notes, although he paid careful attention to the call of the cuckoo, changing daily, and he listened with delight to the Lancashire and Yorkshire speech of two elderly lay brothers, Br Coupe and Br Wells. The latter called a grindstone a 'grindlestone' and called white bryony ' "Dead Creepers", because it kills what it entwines'. 'Br. Coupe calls a basket a *whisket*. – One day when we were gathering stones and potsherds from the meadow Br. Wells said we were not to do it at random but "in braids".'[30] Nonetheless, because of his custody of the eyes, he was prevented from 'seeing much that half-year'.

Hopkins's experience of men from social walks far from his own was being enlarged, and he was also fascinated by the frequent foreign priests who turned up at Manresa for varying periods of time. Many of them were religious refugees from Italy and France, and from them he learned something of the heartbreak of the dispossessed, like that of Sister Emmerich, over whose fate he wept, and like that of the five Franciscan nuns whose exile is at the centre of 'The Wreck of the Deutschland'.

The two-year novitiate at Manresa was devoted less to formal study of theology and philosophy than to letting the young men become acclimatized to the religious life. Part of their training was giving an occasional sermon to their fellows, and Hopkins seems to have been conspicuously successful with a 'brilliant and beautiful' panegyric of St Stanislaus. Most of the novices went to other Catholic churches to help with catechizing the children of the parishes. The usual practice was to have an early dinner, then to walk miles to the church, although a train might be taken if it proved otherwise impossible to arrive in time for the class. Before he left Manresa 'Br Hopkins' had catechized in Isleworth, Brentford, Fulham, and Marylebone.

Between December 1869 and February 1870 he acted as porter, or chief novice, with duties not unlike those of a prefect of a public school, which in many ways Manresa resembled. He kept a porter's journal of the events of the house: readings, retreats, rotation of personnel, occasionally the defection of a man who found he had no vocation for the Society, changes in the daily routine, the times when beds were made, illnesses, even when the chapel was swept. One imagines that Hopkins felt somewhat relieved when he wrote his last entry, 'Br. Macmullin appointed Porter', on 9 February 1870.

At the end of the August that year he went into retreat, and on the 8th of September he and the three other novices who were left of the original seven went individually into a tiny chapel on the second floor of the house, knelt before the Novice Master, and took their first vows as Jesuits. There were no witnesses, 'because of the Penal Clause in the Emancipation Act forbidding the presence of Jesuits in England'. Br Hopkins was now Mr Hopkins. For the first time each man received a brand-new gown, a three-pointed biretta, and a Roman collar. Fr Gallwey, the Novice Master, gave Hopkins a crucifix and some other small gifts; the terms in which Hopkins reported them suggest that only he received anything. Gallwey had been particularly kind to Hopkins and was to continue with special attention in his next post, but it was nonetheless remarkable that he should have singled him out with gifts. At dinner after the ceremony there was wine to celebrate the occasion. Hopkins wrote in his journal simply, 'I took my vows.' He and his three fellows 'took leave of the novices in the evening & joined the Scholasticate'.[31]

CHAPTER XII

STONYHURST
1870–3

One form of obedience Hopkins had learned as a novice at Manresa was the ability to stop immediately what he was doing when another task was assigned. And 'immediately' was the operative word. If one novice was talking to another during a recreation period, at the first vibration of the bell signalling its end, he would cease talking, in the middle of a word or sentence if that is where he found himself, smile, and silently take up whatever task followed. It was a rehearsal in small for welcoming new assignments. To be given an unexpected posting one evening and leave for it early the next morning was normal; occasionally, there would be no more than an hour or two of warning before departure. For the rest of his life Hopkins had to be ready to move whenever he was told to do so, and that was often.

Of the four new scholastics at Manresa who had come there two years before, he was the only one to set off for the Seminary in St Mary's Hall, Stonyhurst, near Blackburn. However, three others who had been at Manresa longer went with him, and there were several men at Stonyhurst whom he had met before, as Jesuits were likely to do, crossing and criss-crossing paths all during their lifetime. Nonetheless, he badly missed Manresa and his fellows there when he found himself in the wilds of Lancashire: 'I feel the strangeness of the place and the noviceship after two years seems like a second home: it made me sad to look at the crucifix and things Fr. Gallwey gave me when I was going.'[1] He had broken his trip from London at Manchester and gone to see the Church of the Holy Name, the vast new Jesuit church then being built. From there he took a train to Whalley and then drove over the Lancashire hills through yellow moonlight to Stonyhurst, where the warm welcome and the excitement of the night kept him awake until almost dawn, looking out of the window of his room to 'a beautiful range of moors dappled with light and shade'. He added in words that were proved true over and over again, 'It has rained many times already and I know it will go on so to the end of the chapter.'[2]

Curiously for one who so loved nature, this was the first time Hopkins had ever lived out of the city, or at least the suburbs, but he might be described as having a retroactive umbilical cord, for he could adjust so quickly to a place he found attractive that it took him only a short time to be at home and feel as if he had never been elsewhere. Only in the last few years of his life was this ability to fail him completely.

From the roofs of the Seminary there was a 'noble view of this Lancashire landscape, Pendle Hill, Ribblesdale, the fells, and all round'. The moors were often bare and bleak, but the three rivers near at hand, the Ribble, the peat-stained Hodder, and the Calder, soon exercised the usual magic of water on him. The scholastics were on holiday for nearly a month more, giving him a chance to investigate his surroundings. The countryside was splendid for walking, and in the River Hodder there was a pool 'all between waterfalls and beneath a green meadow and down by the green-wood side O. If you stop swimming to look round you see fairyland pictures up and down the stream.'

St Mary's Hall was, of course, far less well known than Stony-hurst College, the famous Jesuit public school occupying the central buildings, which liked to think of itself as the Catholic Eton. Besides the main Tudor mansion of the school, there were, as Hopkins wrote several years later:

> a garden with a bowling green, walled in by massive yew hedges, a bowered yew-walk, two real Queen Ann summer-houses, observatories under government, orchards, vineries, greenhouses, workshops, a plungebath, fivescourts, a mill, a farm, a fine cricketfield besides a huge playground . . . ponds, towers, quadrangles, fine cielings [sic], chapels, a church, a fine library, museums. . . .

Hidden away by a row of trees, behind all the grandeur of the school, was the Seminary, a modern building of yellow stone, described by one man who studied there as 'a big rectangular barrack of three floors and the attic. The rooms were all alike', with some thirty Seminarians housed in them.[3] It was not uncomfortable, although it suffered from the draughts endemic to ecclesiastical buildings, and the quality of the life may be inferred from the fact that they were still allowed baths only once a month. The relative geographical positions of the College and St Mary's Hall were fitting enough, since the Seminarians played second fiddle to the public school boys, both in popular regard and in the attention of the Society.

Another building not easily noticed immediately was the associated preparatory school, Hodder, about a mile from the main school. When Hopkins went to St Mary's Hall, another newcomer, who had just made the move from Hodder to the older school, was a homesick boy who described himself as tall and 'pretty stout'. Stolidly he endured an excessive amount of punishment, usually beatings on the hand with a slipper-shaped paddle called a 'tolly', and between punishments he politely resisted suggestions that he might have a vocation to the Society. On the whole he found it best simply to follow his mother's advice about getting along in a Catholic school: 'Wear flannel next your skin, my dear boy, and *never* believe in eternal punishment.' His name was Arthur Conan Doyle.

Hopkins's philosophical studies exercised his intellect and left him feeling 'fagged', but they were much nearer what he had been accustomed to at Oxford than the largely explanatory and disciplinary reading at Manresa, so that he had more time to himself than he was used to. There was no prescribed domestic service of the sort that took so much time in Roehampton, and though the periods reserved for recreation were no more frequent in Stonyhurst, he had more opportunities to be in surroundings that stimulated his creative imagination. All around him lay the 'sublimity' of the moors and fells, and just a few steps from the Seminary he was in wild landscape. Perhaps because of this propinquity, perhaps simply because he had more time for them, Hopkins's journals began in Lancashire to take on the full richness of observation that characterizes his mature writing, both prose and poetry.

The concentration that might have gone into poetry was instead brought to bear on his surroundings. The first entry after arriving at Stonyhurst records a new sight:

> First saw the Northern Lights. My eye was caught by beams of light and dark very like the crown of horny rays the sun makes behind a cloud. At first I thought of silvery cloud until I saw that these were more luminous and did not dim the clearness of the stars in the Bear . . . This busy working of nature wholly independent of the earth and seeming to go on in a strain of time not reckoned by our reckoning of days and years . . . was like a new witness to God and filled me with delightful fear.[4]

In the hard Northern winter, he turned his observation to the forms made by freezing:

> For instance the crystals in mud. – Hailstones are shaped like the cut of diamonds called brilliants. – I found one morning the ground in one corner of the garden full of small pieces of potsherd from which there rose up (and not dropped off) long icicles . . .[5]

The Jesuits had the civilized habit of betraying little curiosity about the eccentricities of others, but Hopkins could hardly help attracting some attention when he hung over a frozen pond to observe the pattern of trapped bubbles or, instead of drinking the chocolate provided as mild refreshment from the austerities of the Lenten diet, put his face down to the cup to study the 'grey and grained look' of the film on its surface. Some thirty years after his death one old lay brother remembered how he would sprint out of the Seminary building after a shower to stoop down on a garden path and study the glitter of crushed quartz before the water could evaporate. 'Ay, a strange yoong man,' said the brother, 'crouching down that gate to stare at some wet sand. A fair natural 'e seemed to us, that Mr. 'Opkins.'[6] Disregard of conventional behaviour, like disregard of traditional rhythm, diction, syntax, and ways of perception, lay at the heart of the originality of Hopkins's poetry, which was all of a piece with his daily life.

The tactile, physical intimacy of his observation of nature is reminiscent of the unconventional way in which the short-sighted Tennyson used to throw himself prostrate on the ground to observe the organization and colouring of a flower before using it in a poem. For Hopkins, to study anything in nature was to bring his full attention to it, breaking down all possible physical, mental or emotional barriers of understanding, so that he seemed to merge with what he was studying. This attention is the source of his striking statement, made at Stonyhurst, of the two-way flow of perception between observer and observed: 'What you look hard at seems to look hard at you.'[7] In that remark is encapsulated all the openness, receptivity, even generosity, he brought to the observation of what he loved, both for its own sake and for its reflection of Divinity.

The empathy he felt with whatever he was considering surely explains a curious syntactical habit that began appearing in the journals at about this time. So far as I have observed, it occurs almost nowhere else, and in the journals it is used only in those passages where he is attempting to penetrate to the nature of what he is looking at. The practice is one that we have all been taught to avoid scrupulously, the 'dangling participle' that is insecurely anchored and so seems to be undecided which of two nouns or nominal conceptions it modifies. For example, he wrote of coming home from confession one night, 'In returning the sky in the west was in a great wide winged or shelved rack of rice-white fine pelleted fretting.'[8] Clearly, the first two words refer to himself, not to the sky, which strictly conventional usage would suggest, but equally clearly, he was far too meticulous about language to have made a simple, ignorant mistake here; instead, he achieves a kind of obliteration of distinction between self and sky.

'Laus Deo – the river today and yesterday', he wrote on another occasion:

Yesterday it was a sallow glassy gold at Hodder Roughs and *by watching hard the banks began to sail upstream*, the scaping unfolded, the river was all in tumult but not running, only the lateral motions were perceived, and the curls of froth where the waves overlap shaped and turned easily and idly.[9]

By his unconventional syntax, he enables the passage to move from the external look of the river into what might be called the viewpoint of the water, back into the observer's mind with 'were perceived', then to 'easily and idly', words that are gloriously ambiguous as to whether they describe the perceptions of Hopkins or the sensations of the water itself. Many other examples might be given of his use of the detached modifier in such a way as to blur the distinction between the human observer and the surrounding physical world. It is difficult, perhaps presumptuous, to say how conscious the process was for Hopkins, but it does demonstrate the fluid quirkiness of his writing when he was dealing with his recurrent theme, the unity of man and nature as parts of Divine creation.

Many of the initial literal difficulties of his poetry come about for the reader because, as here, he is fusing two different modes of perception in one word, meaning both rather than choosing between them. He is capable of a fine disregard of conventional structure when it interferes with his statement of an ambivalent conception. Since he is constantly more concerned with putting across his perceptions than with fulfilling customary expectations of grammar, the recurrent problem of critics today is whether language that so habitually breaks the rules is capable of communicating the intent of the poet. It is a question without a definite answer, but most persistent readers of his poems learn to abandon their usual demands of convention in language, in order to enjoy a fuller poetic process than would otherwise be possible.

Although there is no real evidence that, during his long poetic silence, Hopkins had the conscious intention of returning to the composition of poetry, he could no more have stopped thinking of its language and rhythms and metaphoric content than he could deliberately have ceased breathing. His journals bulge with phrases that were to crop up years later in poems, he is constantly considering his own language and the practice of others, there is a recurring assessment of the symbolic nature of what he saw with his own eyes, and he attempts to forge a critical vocabulary for his own use. Just as it is inevitable to mourn what Schubert or Keats or Mozart might have written had they lived longer, so we can hardly help regretting the seven years during which Hopkins wrote almost no poems (if he actually composed them in his head, there is no written record of them). In truth, however, his mind was so occupied with poetry during that period that when he began writing again, the poems were as mature as if he had been composing all the time. His stay at Stonyhurst was a period not of fallowness but of gestation, for it was there that many of his most important theories were developed.

One of the words closely linked with his aesthetic theory derives from his close attention to the individuality of everything that came under his scrutiny. 'Inscape' is the most famous of the words he contributed to our language, but it resists easy definition. It began appearing in his journals two years before he came to Stonyhurst, so that it was still in the process of development when he arrived. There have been literally volumes of elucidation of the term and the ideas behind it, but Hopkins himself used it somewhat inconsistently. His mind was in constant change and growth, so it is improbable that he would have been interested in a fossilized meaning, even if absolute codification were possible, but it may be fair to attempt a brief explanation of the central core of the idea.

When he said that what you look hard at seems to look hard at you, he was expressing his belief that when one understands a person, an object, or even an idea, through close study, that which is studied radiates back a meaning, one that is necessarily unique because each manifestation of the world is somehow different from any other, so that no two meanings can be precisely the same. Inscape is that meaning, the inner coherence of the individual, distinguishing it from any other example. It is perceived only through close examination or empathy, but it is not dependent upon being recognized; rather, it is inherent in everything in the world, even when we fail to notice it. Although inscape or inner meaning impresses itself on external form and the two things must be consonant, they are distinct. As one scholar has written, 'inscape is not a superficial appearance; rather it is the expression of the inner core of individuality, perceived in moments of insight by an onlooker who is in full harmony with the being he is observing.'[10] For Hopkins the experience of beauty was largely a perception of the uniqueness of what he saw.

Originally Hopkins used inscape as a noun not a verb, and it was chiefly valuable to him as a shorthand word indicating the essence of the specific, arrived at by love and assiduity. To grasp or perceive inscape was to know what was essential and individual in whatever one contemplated. It was a form of identification.

The religious difficulty for Hopkins in such a position was that if one believes that individuation is achieved through the world of matter, of the senses, it becomes a morally dangerous activity to concentrate on the specific because it draws one away from the spiritual to the material. To put the matter at its simplest, Hopkins still felt the potentiality of sin in his love of external nature and in his love of individual human beings. To put too much love into the perception of one flower or into the feeling for one friend was to neglect man's primary duty of love of God; his love of the specific would probably be antagonistic to his devotion to the generic, which was ultimately nearest to the Divine.

To anyone who knows his poetry, it is evident that this was a problem that bedevilled him all his life, and it is equally evident as an eternal dilemma for any Christian caught in the conflict between the phenomenal world and the realm of spirit. It would have been no news to Hopkins to be told that he needed to love both and that they were not mutually exclusive; what he needed was not reminder but a philosophical framework that would act as justification of his innate disposition. He found that framework in July or early August of 1872, when he was browsing in the theological section of the Seminary library. It was a sixteenth-century edition of *Scriptum Oxoniense super Sententiis* by Joannes Duns Scotus, the great medieval Franciscan theologian, and it had come to the Seminary only four years earlier, as part of the benefaction of Edward Badeley, a convert ecclesiastical lawyer. 'At this time', Hopkins wrote, 'I had first begun to get hold of the copy of Scotus on the Sentences in the Baddely [sic] library and was flush with a new stroke of enthusiasm. It may come to nothing or it may be a mercy from God.' So excited was he that 'when I took in any inscape of the sky or sea I thought of Scotus'.[11]

Part of the reason Hopkins had been so devoted to Newman was that he felt a shared identity with him because they had passed through many of the same crises. Probably some of what he came to feel for Duns Scotus on first reading his works stemmed from a similar sense of identity, spanning the centuries, in which he recognized himself in another. In spite of his name, Duns Scotus was generally thought to be English by birth; he had been trained at Oxford before going to France, and, like Hopkins, he felt an overwhelming devotion to the Virgin and to the doctrine of her Immaculate Conception. Much of his life he had been an outsider in the Church, just as Hopkins often felt himself. If Hopkins in part recognized Newman as his clerical father, he surely felt that in Duns Scotus he had found his theological progenitor, and in an odd way he regarded him as a personal friend filling the gap left by his friends at Oxford.

One of the teachings that set Scotus apart from the main current of Schoolmen was his view that the Incarnation would have occurred even had there been no Fall or subsequent Redemption, since it was necessary somehow to make God available to the human senses. This in turn postulated that the material world was a symbol of God, not divorced from Him, a view to which Hopkins wholeheartedly subscribed emotionally, even if he needed the authority of Scotus in order to feel easy with it. Once he had come on Scotism, for Hopkins 'Æsthetic and religious experience became one in the sacramental apprehension of beauty. His sacramentalism, moulded by Scotus and the Spiritual Exercises, gave him warrant for the use of the senses.'[12] Both personally and theologically there were many reasons for Hopkins to identify with Scotus.

It was not quite so easy as that sounds, but during his Stonyhurst stay Hopkins did come to some peace about his love of the phenomenal world, in part because the Society was permissive about Scotism, in spite of considering it mistaken. It has been suggested that Hopkins was marked down as an outsider because of his espousal of Scotus, but there is no evidence that this was so. What was far nearer the truth was that he held himself aloof out of a feeling of being different from his fellow Seminarians.

When he returned to Oxford as a priest some eight years later, Hopkins wrote a loving poem of thanks in 'Duns Scotus's Oxford'; it is bred of the sense of awe that he should be treading the stones where the philosopher had walked five centuries before him, that the very atmosphere of what seemed a 'graceless' city should have been breathed literally by his great predecessor:

Yet ah! this air I gather and release
He lived on; these weeds and waters, these walls are what
He haunted who of all men most sways my spirit to peace . . .

His devotion to Scotus lasted the rest of his life, and as late as 1880 he carried on a correspondence about him with Bishop Mandell Creighton, trying to get every available shred of information about the philosopher.

An even more explicit statement of the liberation he felt to love the phenomenal world because of its ultimate identity as part of God comes in the sonnet 'As kingfishers catch fire', probably written in 1877, in which the inscape of each earthly object and creature cries out its uniqueness and selfhood, just as man's nature is a constant reminder of both his own uniqueness and his origin in Christ:

As kingfishers catch fire, dragonflies draw flame;
    As tumbled over rim in roundy wells
    Stones ring; like each tucked string tells, each hung bell's
Bow swung finds tongue to fling out broad its name;
Each mortal thing does one thing and the same:
    Deals out that being indoors each one dwells;
    Selves – goes itself; *myself* it speaks and spells,
Crying *What I do is me: for that I came.*

I say more: the just man justices;
    Keeps grace: that keeps all his goings graces;
Acts in God's eye what in God's eye he is –
    Christ. For Christ plays in ten thousand places,
Lovely in limbs, and lovely in eyes not his
    To the Father through the features of men's faces.

While he was 'flush with a new stroke of enthusiasm', Hopkins constantly tried his hand at lyrical prose descriptions of the world of Stonyhurst, ranging from recurrent attempts to capture the sensation of being half drowned in bluebells in the woods nearby, to mesmerizing a duck, observing the bounding of young lambs ('They toss and toss: it is as if it were the earth that flung them, not

Manley Hopkins, father.

Catherine Hopkins, mother.

'Mamma': drawing.
MH avoided
drawing faces,
which is one reason
for believing this
may be his work. It
could equally well
be by one of his
talented brothers or
sisters.

Hopkins, 1859.
Watercolours by his aunt
Ann Eleanor Hopkins.

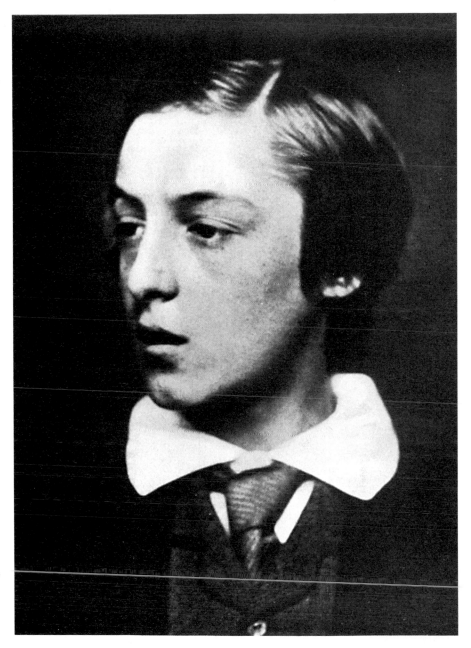

Hopkins, *c.* 1856. Photograph by George Giberne.

Above: Balliol College, *c.* 1857; much of the rebuilding of the College took place during Hopkins's time there.

Benjamin Jowett, Master of Balliol. Photograph by Julia Margaret Cameron.

'Man in punt'. Drawing by Hopkins. An apparent early version exists, in which the man holds a book on his chest; the face has been crossed out, presumably in dissatisfaction. Curiously, in the present sketch there are several ghostly faces suggested in the hatching (e.g., in the left knee of the trousers), as if to make up for the hidden face behind book.

'Gerard Hopkins, reflected in a lake. Aug. 14.' Drawing in 1864 journal.

Balliol group, 1863. Compare his apparent integration here with his isolation in photograph of Catholic Club in 1879. *Standing from left to right*: L.T. Rendell, Earl of Kerry, W. Hulton, M.W. Ridley, W.A. Brown, G.M. Hopkins, R. Entwistle, F.A. Reiss, G.M. Argles, T.L. Papillon, A. Anderson, R. Doyle, [W.A.] Harris. *Seated from left to right*: E.J. Myers, R.A. Hull, C.M.B. Clive, J.F.L[angford], S.J. Fremantle, A. Barratt, A.E. Hardy, E.M. Sneyd-Kynnersley.

Hopkins: detail from same photograph.

Robert Bridges

R.W. Dixon

Henry Parry Liddon

Digby Dolben

'Shanklin, Isle of Wight, 1866'. Drawing by Hopkins.

'Manor Farm, Shanklin, 1863'. Drawing by Hopkins.

A.W. Garrett, W.A. Comyn Macfarlane and Hopkins, 27 July 1866, Horsham.

John Henry Newman, 1865. He is said to have been reading *Ecce Homo* at the time.

Chapel of St Ignatius, St Clement's, Oxford, *c.* 1840. Now an office building.

Manresa House, Roehampton.

Wreck of the *Deutschland*, 6–7 December 1875. *Illustrated London News.*

St Winefred's Well, *c.* 1830.

Catholic Club, Oxford, 1878.
Standing: G.M. Hopkins, A.C. Dunlop, B. Flanagan, H. de la G. Grissell,
B. Harvey, H. Bellamy, B.F. Costelloe, H. Stanton, H. Marten, J. Shiel. *Seated*: C. Dix,
Fr T.B. Parkinson, O. Vassall Phillips, B. Westermann, F. Beckerstaffe Drew.

Church of St Aloysius, Oxford, in left background, tower of St Barnabas's.

University College, Dublin, 86 St Stephen's Green, *c.* 1900.

Hopkins, Oxford, 1879.

Hopkins, [Dublin?] , 1888.

'Bathers', Frederick Walker, 1867.

(detail)

themselves'), the feathers of a gold-crested wren dazzled by the gaslight in his room, and one of the most magically diaphanous of all his descriptions, the movement and pattern of the air on a July day:

> Very hot, though the wind, which was south, dappled very sweetly on one's face and when I came out I seemed to put it on like a gown as a man puts on the shadow he walks into and hoods or hats himself with the shelter of a roof, a penthouse, or a copse of trees, I mean it rippled and fluttered like light linen, one could feel the folds and braids of it – and indeed a floating flag is like wind visible and what weeds are in a current; it gives it thew and fires it and bloods it in.[13]

At Manresa the only holidays Hopkins had were feast days or weekly days of recreation, with almost no time for Christmas and no summer expeditions. At Stonyhurst he stayed at the Seminary for his first Christmas vacation, which lasted from Christmas Eve until the 2nd of January. There were 'talking' suppers at which conversation was allowed, elaborate decorations in the chapel for the Masses, vespers, and benedictions, amateur dramatics, the first skating of the year on the Infirmary Pond, 'which had been illuminated by Tar Barrels and Chinese Lanterns, at the expense of the Philosophers', and fireworks on the 29th of December until 'about a quarter to ten'.[14] There were 'Blandykes'* or monthly free days throughout the year, hockey (both ice and field forms), and plenty of walking. His life at Stonyhurst, he told Baillie, 'though it is hard is God's will for me as I most intimately know, which is more than violets knee-deep'.[15]

In August of 1871, the summer after he went to Stonyhurst, he had his first long holiday since coming into the Society. The first fortnight was spent at the College, where the Seminarians were moved to make room for a retreat of outside priests; their quarters were more commodious than in St Mary's Hall, and they were free

---

* The name probably derives from Blendeques, a village near St Omer, where the English Jesuits had a College founded in the sixteenth century; the boys went to Blendeques for their holidays.

for recreation almost all the time. The second half of the month they took their 'Villa', or annual holiday, in Argyllshire, where at Inellan they had taken three houses with a good view of the Firth of Clyde. As indication of their freedom from the usual rules, they were not required to wear top hats and were given the choice between their regular Roman collars and the turndown version; not very surprisingly, most of them wore the latter.[16]

The party sailed from Liverpool, which they reached by a through carriage on the old Lancashire and Yorkshire railway, and, according to Hopkins, 'We landed at Greenock in the morning and went by a Clyde steamer to Inellan.' There were a number of excursions from Inellan: they took a steamer to Arran, walked in the mountains, paddled barefoot on the sand and swam in the sea, and visited Glasgow and Edinburgh. One group went to Inverary for the 'Homecoming of the Marquis of Lorne and Princess Louise after their honeymoon', but Hopkins had not the energy to join them. On their return journey from Edinburgh 'the rain, which I took for hail, cut one's ears and somebody said was like pebble-stones.'[17]

When they arrived back at Stonyhurst, according to custom they went immediately into retreat for slightly over a week, and then Hopkins had a further three weeks of holiday with his family. It was his first stay with them since he had become a Jesuit, and he found it easier to get along with them than at any time since his conversion, perhaps because he spent only two or three days with his father in Hampstead before joining the rest of the family in Hampshire, near Southampton.

The Society was wise in giving the Seminarians a holiday of nearly seven weeks, for it was their first complete relaxation in three years, a long time even for such young men. Probably all of them needed it badly, but it was a particular necessity for Hopkins, who was beginning to slide back into the trough of his cyclical depression after having been on the crest during his first year at Stonyhurst. Lectures and studies began again at the beginning of October. With only trivial changes the second year repeated the first. For more than twenty years Hopkins had been studying or teaching, and at twenty-seven it was probable that there would be at least another six or seven years before he was ordained. It was the unending vista of repetitive years that must occasionally assault all who undertake an academic career.

There were changes in the routine of Stonyhurst, of course, but they were very small ripples. At Christmas the boys of the College presented *Macbeth* in a version in which Lady Macbeth became Uncle Donald, since women's parts were not permitted at Stonyhurst. As Hopkins said, 'the effect is not so disastrous as you might think it must be'. The following summer the Villa was to the Isle of Man rather than Scotland, and Hopkins was particularly moved by the sight of Peel Castle, with 'the great seas under a rather heavy swell breaking under the strong rocks below the outer side of the castle', just as Wordsworth had written about it in his great 'Elegiac Stanzas'. One wonders whether Hopkins, too, took it as an emblem of 'welcome fortitude, and patient cheer'. On their return to Stonyhurst, 'Fr. Rector came over to wait on us at supper, which touched me.'[18] His emotions were never far from the surface.

The records at Stonyhurst indicate that Hopkins's first practice sermons were more successful than many he delivered after his ordination. Three times a week he spent an hour in one of the major practical preparations for the priesthood, 'circles', an exercise in which one student had 'to give a synopsis of the last two lectures of the professor'. Two others then gave any objection to it that they could 'find in books or invent for themselves', all advanced in syllogistic form. It was intended as preparation in 'sifting out truth from falsehood', and it provided 'those who pass through it with a complete defence against difficulties which otherwise are likely to puzzle the Catholic controversialist'.[19]

Hopkins's old hilarity occasionally swam into view, often when he was making light of difficulties, as in his letter to his fifteen-year-old sister Kate about a very painful vaccination:

> We were all vaccinated the other day. The next day a young Portug[u]ese came up to me and said 'Oh misther 'Opkins, do *you* feel the cows in *yewer* arm?' I told him I felt the horns coming through. I do I am sure. I cannot remember now whether one ought to say the calf of the arm or the calf of the leg. My shoulder is like a shoulder of beef. I dare not speak

above a whisper for fear of bellowing – there now, I was going to say I am obliged to speak low for fear of lowing.[20]

In 1873 he arranged an entertainment, consisting of music and comic or 'half comic' pieces; 'It was mainly got up by Mr G. Hopkins, and was a decided success,' indicating that he could forget his sadness, at least for a time.[21]

But Hopkins's hypochondria (and real illness as well) that had begun manifesting itself at Edgbaston resurfaced at Stonyhurst. Typically, the first few months were exhilarating, and in the spring following his arrival he told his mother that his 'health is in the main robustious, more so than it has some time been'.[22] Equally predictably, after he had been some time at Stonyhurst, his emotions became increasingly chaotic and uncontained. One evening in March 1872 he wrote of his reaction in the refectory at the account of the conversion of the Abbé de Rancé as he heard the monks of La Trappe singing 'the office of our Blessed Lady':

> After a time of trial and especially a morning in which I did not know which way to turn as the account of De Rancé's final conversion was being read at dinner the verse *Qui confidunt in Domino sicut mons Sion* which satisfied him and resolved him to enter his abbey of La Trappe by the mercy of God came strongly home to me too, so that I was choked for a little while and could not keep in my tears.[23]

The rush of his emotional response was out of keeping with the importance of what had caused it, but he was deeply touched because of the application to his own life.

The same kind of emotional flood was released by the cutting down of trees, which had always been painful to him. When an ash tree was felled in the garden, he 'heard the sound and looking out and seeing it maimed there came at that moment a great pang and I wished to die and not to see the inscapes of the world destroyed any more'.[24]

More than most, the Jesuits were accustomed to the presence of death in the midst of their lives. Their old and ill members were not put into separate quarters but brought home to one of the Society's houses when their life could not long be supported elsewhere. Young men, even boys in their teens, became used to living among the aged and tending the dying. On arising in the morning, they might find that the old priest in the next room, to whom they had said goodnight the previous evening, lay in waxen state on his bed, surrounded by candles, the door open to all who came to make their farewells. In theory it made for a tranquillity about death that other men, even religious ones, seldom felt, but some particularly sensitive men never achieved such calm detachment.

Hopkins seems to have had at least his share of death, probably more, and he found it nearly insupportable because of his unresolved attitude towards it. Throughout his stay at Stonyhurst he noted in his journals the almost continuous deaths of friends, relatives, and fellow clerics. Basil Poutiatine, with whom he had gone to Paris, after being refused by the family of the Greek girl he wanted to marry, was found dead in a pool beside a French railway line. Hopkins's friends who told him of the matter 'convinced themselves it was not suicide'. At Stonyhurst 'one of the cleverest boys they had at the College died by hanging. . . . His body was naked except that his shoes were on.' Several pupils from the Oratory died while still in their teens or early twenties. Mr Scriven, apparently a fellow Seminarian, whom Hopkins had visited as he was dying of consumption,

> died at halfpast ten in the morning. In the night he had a great struggle in which he started up in bed and caught hold of the Rector with both hands. Afterwards he was calm. He offered up his life for the Society. It was thought providential that he died on the eve of St. Ignatius.[25]

A Balliol contemporary who had gone to Minnesota was frozen to death in a snowstorm after telling his young wife that it was the last day of his life. These deaths and many more were recorded in Hopkins's journals, and cumulatively they tell us a good bit about what fears most haunted him. In the event he was nearly forty-five when he died; however young it seems, it was almost exactly average for the Society. In 1868 a survey in the Jesuit private journal, *Letters and Notices*, indicated that the life expectancy of a man becoming a novice at twenty-one was twenty-three more years rather than the forty years of males of the same age in the general population.[26]

Hopkins was unduly, even neurotically, obsessed with death, but his fear of it was founded on considerable observation. But he also felt an almost equal attraction to death, something he could not admit openly to himself when he was at the bottom of his horrible cycles of depression. His unnamed longing was even more terrifying than his revulsion. In the late sonnet 'No worst, there is none', he considers the longing for oblivion, to which almost no one is wholly immune:

> O the mind, mind has mountains; cliffs of fall
> Frightful, sheer, no-man-fathomed. Hold them cheap
> May who ne'er hung there. Nor does long our small
> Durance deal with that steep or deep.

Some of the terror of his late sonnets derives from our awareness that he has personally suffered every fear of which he writes.

His obsession with dying, and probably his fear of becoming prey to thoughts of suicide, seems apparent in the care with which he copied into his journals in 1870 and 1872 accounts of two different young women who refused food until their death. One took only a drop of moisture once a fortnight, the other subsisted for years on nothing but weekly Communion.[27] It is noticeable that both were regarded as martyrs, not suicides, and it is impossible not to remember Hopkins's own reported ordeal of three weeks without water when he was a schoolboy, which surely seemed to him of the same order of experience, however much less severe.

These journal entries are further examples of how his fascination with death became part of a remarkable pattern of identification with female saints and martyrs, from the Virgin, through St Margaret, St Frideswide, St Winefred, and holy women like Sister Emmerich. The most important poetical manifestation of this empathy was with the five nuns of the *Deutschland* and his particular identification with the death of the tall nun. Both his own works and what he read elsewhere acted as stages on which his feelings could be played out.

His own health no doubt brought the consideration of death closer to home than it would otherwise have been, for in spite of his assurances to his mother of his 'robustious' well-being, he was often ill, so much so that once more he was forbidden to fast. Most of his troubles seem to have stemmed from general weakness brought on by chronic diarrhoea and bleeding from haemorrhoids. In October 1872 he was confined to his bed:

> That fever came from a chill I caught one Blandyke and the chill from weakness brought about by my old complaint, which before and much more after the fever was worse than usual. Indeed then I lost so much blood that I hardly saw how I was to recover. Nevertheless it stopped suddenly, almost at the worst. This was why I came up to town at Christmas.[28]

Because of his complaint, he went to Hampstead two days before Christmas and had the holiday with his family, instead of remaining at Stonyhurst. Five days later he had an operation at home 'by Mr. Gay and Mr. Prance. It lasted half an hour and yet it seemed to me about ten minutes.'[29] His sister was amazed at his fortitude and cheerfulness when he was in pain. He remained in bed a fortnight, then spent another week recuperating at home, making a trip on his last day to the exhibition of Old Masters at Burlington House. From there he went for another fortnight to Manresa, where he could be examined by the Jesuits' own doctor before his return to Stonyhurst. His superiors were rightly worried about him and kindly did all they could in the next year or two to make life easy for him. In spite of the operation, he continued to have some of the symptoms, and he apparently suffered from diarrhoea for the rest of his life, as well as a bewildering galaxy of small ills. After his operation he was wisely told to give up fasting again for the following Lent.

During his stay at home, there is no mention of his father in Hopkins's journals, although he must have been there. Their relations had been uneasy ever since his conversion, but they had patched up any outward hostility. It is unsafe to argue from absence, but there are no extant letters between father and son from 1866 to 1871, and even if some have been lost, there were surely never many. At Christmas 1871, the year before his operation, Hopkins wrote home in response to his mother's holiday greeting, but he sent the letter to his father, probably in an attempt to re-establish some closeness. It was a failure in its intent, for it is an awkward little note, reduced, for lack of matter and intimacy, to commenting on the engraving of Stonyhurst on his writing paper, and betraying at the end of the message the strained temper of their relations by his correction of his father's spelling. As an overture of friendliness, it was maladroit, and it is no wonder that another three years seem to have elapsed before they wrote to each other again.[30] The stay at home for his operation was another opportunity for better relations to be established, but there is no evidence that it was successful.

Not that Hopkins was an easy correspondent at best. At Stonyhurst he wrote to Baillie at least three times, then allowed a period of five years to intervene before resuming their correspondence. Even Bridges, firmest of friends and most understanding of confidants, resignedly gave up writing to Hopkins, as we have seen, just when he was in greatest need of love and friendship. The probability is that Bridges was more generous about forgiveness and apologies than Hopkins. However, by this time Bridges was a badly overworked doctor and furthermore one who suffered from rude health, so that he could never quite sympathize with what seemed to him the hypochondriacal complaints of Hopkins. It was only because there was a great deal of buried love on both sides that ther friendship survived.

His estrangement from both his father and Bridges contributed to Hopkins's loneliness at Stonyhurst. Although he made friends with other scholastics, his superiors were always on the watch to warn against special friendships between the Seminarians, as they had been at Manresa, and of course none of his contemporary novices had come from Manresa with him.

In his solitude Hopkins became almost pathetically grateful for a kind gesture from others. When he was returning to Stonyhurst after his summer holiday in Hampshire, he noted in his journal, 'I met with much kindness that day – at Bursledon, in the train, and here.' On another occasion he told of the consideration of a fellow Jesuit: 'As I passed the stables later and stayed to look at the peacocks John Myerscough came out to shew me a brood of little peafowl (though it could not be found at that time) and the kindness touched my heart.' And of Fr Gallwey's affection during his illness he recorded that 'Before night litanies he came to my room as I lay on the bed making my examen, for I had some fever, and sitting by the bedside took my hand within his and said some affectionate and most encouraging words.'[31] All these acts would normally be the small change of courtesy and fellowship, but in his frame of mind they ballooned into enormous significance.

It was at this low period in his life that he wrote to Bridges after having heard from him for the first time in two years. Instead of treating Bridges tactfully, as one would expect in the situation, he began the letter by teasing him for his conservatism, under the pretence of believing him to be a communist, then he professed that he was precisely what he accused Bridges of being:

I am afraid some great revolution is not far off. Horrible to say, in a manner I am a Communist. Their ideal bating some things is nobler than that professed by any secular statesman I know of (I must own I live in bat-light and shoot at a venture). Besides it is just – I do not mean the means of getting to it are. But it is a dreadful thing for the greatest and most necessary part of a very rich nation to live a hard life without dignity, knowledge, comforts, delight, or hopes in the midst of plenty – which plenty they make. They profess that they do not care what they wreck and burn, the old civilisation and order must be destroyed. This is a dreadful look out but what has the old civilisation done for them? As it at present stands in England it is itself in great measure founded on wrecking. But they got none of the spoils, they came in for nothing but harm from it then and thereafter. England has grown hugely wealthy but this wealth has not reached the working classes; I expect it has made their condition worse. Besides this iniquitous order the old civilisation embodies another order mostly old and what is new in direct entail from the old, the old religion, learning, law, art, etc and all the history that is preserved in standing monuments. But as the working classes have not been edu- cated they know next to nothing of all this and cannot be expected to care if they destroy it. The more I look the more black and deservedly black the future looks, so I will write no more.[32]

It is an extraordinary mixture of ill-judged teasing and heartfelt sadness at the condition of the country, but it more accurately reflects his own emotional confusion at the time than it does either his feelings for Bridges or his long-term considered political beliefs. Hopkins referred to this as his 'Red' letter, but it would be more to the point to call it 'Black', since it grew so inexorably out of his own emotional darkness, even if it was prompted by the degradation of the English working classes in 1871. He never lost his sympathy with the poor, particularly those of the cities; ten years after this he said his work as a parish priest in the intervening years had only deepened it:

My Liverpool and Glasgow experience laid upon my mind a conviction, a truly crushing conviction, of the misery of town life to the poor and more than to the poor, of the misery of the poor in general, of the degradation even of our race, of the hollowness of this century's civilisation: it made even life a burden to me to have daily thrust upon me the things I saw.[33]

There was little of the communist or socialist in Hopkins's makeup, and he never wanted to overthrow the contemporary English political system, however genuinely he felt its injustices. His attitudes as a priest living among the poor are a more accurate reflection of his deepest feelings, and those vacillated between a kind of sentimental belief in the nobility of poverty when he was living in Bedford Leigh, and a dislike, amounting almost to contempt, for the drunken, lawless lower classes of Liverpool. Like any moderately decent person, he felt sympathy with the oppressed and indignation at the abuse of privilege, but those hardly add up to a committed belief in communism, and the real measure of his feelings is his use of such phrases as 'Horrible to say' in order to describe the possibility of his being a communist – 'in a manner'. One Hopkins scholar has called him a Tory radical.[34] In spite of his generous indignation at the state of the poor, there is little evidence that he ever strayed far from a conventional Victorian acceptance of the inevitability of difference between classes.

If the modern meaning of snobbery is undue deference to social position, to the exclusion of more important values, then no one could have been less snobbish than Hopkins, but he was no leveller. In all his correspondence and journals there is no hint of love of a lord, but equally there is a good bit of exasperation at and incomprehension of the uneducated.

Given the makeup of the Society of Jesus in England in his day, it would indeed be surprising if there had been no feelings of mild snobbery in it. The 'old' Catholics among the Jesuits were largely either drawn from the descendants of the Recusant aristocracy or recruited from the members of traditionally Catholic families in the working classes, and the two did not always mix well. The majority of the middle-class Jesuits were converts, like Hopkins, many of whom were graduates of Oxford or Cambridge. Denis Meadows, who entered the Society some two decades after Hopkins, wrote of the ingrown but innocent way in which priests at Manresa had subtly different attitudes to the novices who came from different backgrounds.[35] At Stonyhurst, because it had been connected with the aristocracy for generations, the feelings were perhaps even stronger for being denied open expression. Fr Martindale, biographer of the famous preacher Fr Bernard Vaughan, who taught at the College in Hopkins's day, remarks that it 'was full of boys who were some sort of cousin to one another – Maxwells, Vavasours, Welds, Weld-Blundells, Cliffords, Tempests, Vaughans, Stourtons, de Traffords, and on Sundays, it was the custom for relatives to walk together', forming a great clan that made it clear who counted and who did not.[36]

In 1872 one of the boys at the College was a young German nobleman who had been sent to England to study philosophy, with the idea of eventually becoming a Jesuit novice. The autobiography of Count Paul von Hönsbröch indicates that his stay nearly stopped his clerical intentions. He and his fellows were given a choice between 'a philosophy course delivered in English, and the Latin course given by Jesuit scholastics in the neighbouring seminary'. He chose to go to St Mary's Hall, but he said he 'learnt next to nothing. For I was soon infected by the idleness which raged with devastating fury among my co-philosophers. The majority of these, sons of well-to-do or even wealthy families, cared only for a life of Epicurean comfort, and took no interest in work or study.' Since von Hönsbröch was far from democratic in his own inclinations, the differences in rank had to be striking to draw his indignation. How much more they must have offended a man as sensitive as Hopkins.

To the young German much of what was wrong with the school was because 'Father Eyre, brother of the Archbishop of Edinburgh' pursued a policy of letting things alone. If we are to trust von Hönsbröch's lurid memories,

> It was an open secret that not a few 'philosophers' made use of the easily granted leave of absence to visit brothels in Liverpool, Manchester and London; some of them even kept their mistresses in little villages in the neighbourhood of the college. In March, 1873, five of us hired a coach and drove to the Grand National Steeplechase, and it was the intention of my companions to finish the evening at some Liverpool brothel.

According to von Hönsbröch, 'A sharp contrast to the general laxity of morals was afforded in characteristic Jesuit fashion, by the strictness of the discipline in regard to outward pious observances.'[37]

Later he was to become a novice, then eventually he left the Society in considerable bitterness, so that his impressions are not necessarily trustworthy, but it is probable that he is accurate at least in conveying the feelings of an outsider suddenly plunged into this alien institution. If only a part of what he says is true, one can see why Hopkins was feeling at the end of 1871 that privilege and rank were corrupt, and that their taint spread so pervasively that even the Society was not untouched.

At this distance it is impossible to be sure which of his feelings most inspired the tone of his 'Red' letter, but it seems highly probable that part of what he was feeling was that desire to lash out at those they love which occasionally infects persons who believe they are misunderstood by their intimates. Somewhere beneath the profession of his own beliefs in the letter a desire to shock Bridges seems to be seeking expression. If so, the move was more effective than he could have wished, for he heard nothing from Bridges for three further years. Once more he broke the silence himself, as if ashamed that he had caused it, and once more his sense of having behaved badly made him edgy and ungracious:

> My last letter to you was from Stonyhurst. It was not answered, so that perhaps it did not reach you. If it did I suppose then and do not know what else to suppose now that you were disgusted with the *red* opinions it expressed, being a conservative. I have little reason to be red . . . So far as I know I said nothing that might not fairly be said. If this was your reason for not answering it seems to shew a greater keenness about politics than is common. . . . I think, my dear Bridges, to be so much offended about that red letter was excessive.

If Bridges took offence, it was probably not at the political opinions expressed in the letter but at the underlying unfriendliness to himself.

The excuse Hopkins had found for writing again indicated in itself how little he really knew of Bridges, for he said he had the previous week come across a review of a volume of poems by Bridges and he had apparently not even realized that he wrote poetry, 'Did I ever before see anything of yours? say in Coles' book? I cannot remember.'[38] If accurate, this tells us a great deal about their friendship. Bridges's own attractive memory of the whole matter a quarter of a century later was that 'When Gerard first saw my first book of poems, – it was in my house in London – he took it up with some curiosity. You can imagine his quiet deliberate examination of it. When he had dipped into it in several places, he looked up and said "I say, what fun, Bridges, if you were to be a classic!" '[39] And this, too, Bridges's memory as well as Hopkins's remark, tells us a good bit about them.

It is not quite true, as is often said, that Hopkins wrote no poetry when he was at Stonyhurst, for he produced a handful of small poems during that time, probably four in Latin, three in English. They are so unlike both his best early poems and the great ones written in 1875 and after that it is fair to say they would not hold us had they been written by anyone else. Since their composition is uncertain, it is difficult to know whether they are so surprisingly conventional because they were needed for a conventional occasion or whether – and this seems more probable – Hopkins was still so new a Catholic that he had not yet shaken off the tired language of the convert and was still using the debased vocabulary that haunts the least successful poetry of any religion. 'Rosa Mystica' is perhaps the most interesting of the lot, and it nearly succeeds because it shows us what his poetry would be in the improbable case of his trying to sound like Swinburne. Once he was writing to please himself rather than his superiors, he reverted to the original, experimental diction we expect of him.

On the Isle of Man, where the community returned for another summer holiday, Hopkins noted that they had 'Mackerel fishing but not much sport. Besides I was in pain and could not look at things much.' He was still suffering from the aftermath of his operation for piles, and his weakness was apparent to others. On one occasion after a long walk, 'We got home in heavy wet and Mr. Sidgreaves covered me under his plaid.' At the end of the holiday he continued unwell, and his physical condition badly affected his emotions. When they returned to Stonyhurst they had to live in the College temporarily. There was almost no gas, and they had to rely on candles: 'things not ready, darkness and despair. In fact being unwell I was quite downcast: nature in all her parcels and faculties gaped and fell apart, fatiscebat, like a clod heaving and holding only by strings of root.'[40] It was an excessive reaction that must have been apparent to the other men.

He had been sent to the College in July to teach for six days while one of the masters was away; the assignment was perhaps intended to prepare him for further teaching that autumn. In August he told his mother, 'Next year, I mean from September, I am to teach one of the higher classes in one of our schools, I do not know which; perhaps it will be Stonyhurst. After that I am to go to my theology, which is a four year's business. The year's teaching was given as a rest.'[41]

On 27 August 1873 he walked to the station at Whalley to say goodbye to some visiting German priests. When he came back, he discussed Scotism with a friend. Then, with the lack of preparation he had come to expect, 'In the evening I received orders to go to Roehampton to teach rhetoric and started next morning early . . . At Manresa I caught the Provincial [Gallwey] who spoke most kindly and encouragingly.'[42]

In sending him back to Manresa as 'Professor of Rhetoric', the Society was putting him in a place he already knew and liked, probably well aware that it would be a comfort to see his family more frequently. At the time the Order was undermanned, and the Provincial was particularly kind in giving him a position in which he might recover his health, rather than putting him to teaching in one of their schools, where he was badly needed. It is easy to underestimate the care the Society took of him.

Critics and biographers have sometimes followed the lead of Bridges in saying that the Jesuits and the severity of their discipline were his ruin. It is true that he was unhappy during most of his time with the Society, but there is nothing to indicate that he would not have been more so elsewhere. The Order was strict, but it was also solid, and Hopkins needed a firm structure of belief and behaviour within which to move: Newman had known what he was talking about when he said that it was the right spot for him. Even if the Jesuits, like almost everyone else who knew him, failed to recognize his rare quality, they were very kind to him and constantly put up with his awkward but lovable personality. One might ask where he would have been happier.

CHAPTER XIII

HALF WELSH
1873–4

Although his posting there had been as abrupt as most of his assignments, his letters indicate Hopkins believed in September 1873 that he would remain at Manresa at least two years. There must have been some wishful thinking involved in his belief.

His reassignment began with the customary retreat a day or two after he arrived. His journal is blank for the ten days of the retreat, since all that he was permitted to write were a few spiritual notes, which have since disappeared. It is surely significant that immediately he could make entries again, the one name that surfaces in his journal had obviously floated through his meditations during the retreat: Digby Dolben. 'I received as I think a great mercy about Dolben',[1] he wrote, apparently in confirmation of his prayers for the eternal rest of his friend. Inevitably the wording of the remark recalls his cryptic notes in 1865 when he was so much taken up with Dolben (see p. 98).

Besides being evidence of the persistence of his emotions about Dolben, his convictions about him during the Manresa retreat indicate a side of Hopkins's belief that had been growing since his conversion. He clearly felt a deep need for direct signs of supernatural approval of his own actions and aspirations, a need that was to make itself felt in a growing preoccupation with miracles, visions, ghosts and heavenly intervention in human affairs. From one point of view it showed his awareness of the deep spiritual significance that manifested itself in nature, of the very immediate presence of God in the human world. From another viewpoint it seemed like the literal belief in the supernatural that Bridges would unhesitatingly have called superstition. What separates them is a fine line that is often difficult to perceive.

Four years after receiving the great mercy about Dolben, Hopkins wrote his mother an extraordinary letter about the death of her father. Although it is out of sequence here, it deserves quotation at some length because it seems to refer directly to his experience during the 1873 retreat and because it demonstrates so clearly his frank belief in the literal convergence of the temporal and the spiritual in what might be loosely called the miraculous:

I am glad that my dear grandfather's end was peaceful and that all his children could be present to witness the last moments of an affectionate and generous father. But there is one circumstance about it which gives me the deepest consolation: I shall communicate it to you, think of it what you like. I had for years been accustomed every day to recommend him very earnestly to the Blessed Virgin's protection; so that I could say, if such a thing can ever be said without presumption, if I am disappointed who can hope? As his end drew near I had asked some people to pray for him and said to someone in a letter that I should take it as a happy token if he died on Sunday the Feast of the Holy Rosary. It is a day signalised by our Lady's overruling aid asked for and given at the victory of Lepanto. This year the anniversary is better marked than usual, for Lepanto was fought on the 7th of October but the feast is kept on the first Sunday in the month whatever the day: this time they coincide. I receive it without questioning as a mark that my prayers have been heard and that the queen of heaven has saved a Christian soul from enemies more terrible than a fleet of infidels. Do not make light of this, for it is perhaps the seventh time that I think I have had some token from heaven in connection with the death of people in whom I am interested.[2]

Hopkins did not believe that everyone had the power to receive such tokens, for there had been in all history, he told R. W. Dixon, only 'a few, a very few men, whom common repute . . . has treated as having had something happen to them that does not happen to other men, as having *seen something*, whatever that really was'.[3] The star seen by the Magi, he said, 'was nothing to ordinary observers, perhaps not visible at all to them'.[4]

In notes made at a retreat in 1883 he wrote that he had in his meditations 'earnestly asked our Lord to watch over my compositions, not to preserve them from being lost or coming to nothing, for that I am very willing they should be, but they might not do me harm through the enmity or imprudence of any man or my own; that he should have them as his own and employ or not employ them as he should see fit. And this I believe is heard.'[5] The last words indicate the same trust in direct heavenly communication that is shown in his remarks about Dolben.

Hopkins believed that he had special access to God, but it was not arrogance on his part, only acceptance as uncomplicated and unintellectual as that of a child. It is part of the attitude that made him believe in fairies and in the efficacy of medals worn against malign influence. Hopkins never confused intellect and faith, but the distinction is always disturbing to persons who think of faith as a generalized state wholly unconcerned with particulars. Because of his deep, literal belief in a personal God he often addressed Him in such disconcertingly familiar terms as 'O thou my friend' or 'Sir', or referred to Him as colloquially as in 'let joy size / At God knows when to God knows what'. It is not presumption on his part, only familiarity in its literal sense. Simplicity is probably the hardest of qualities to appreciate.

This is the attitude that lies behind his perception of nature, in which he was quite willing to accept and even to welcome scientific speculation at the very time he regarded it as essentially metaphor. As he put it, 'all nature is mechanical, but then is it not seen that mechanics contain that which is beyond mechanics.'[6] The direct intervention of Divinity was not to be controverted by physical laws.

The fearful corollary to believing in the close connection between the supernatural and the physical was that it could be manifested in terror as well as exaltation, since evil was as real as grace and often a good bit more tangible. A fortnight after his reassurance over Dolben, he recorded a frightening nightmare: 'I thought something or someone leapt onto me and held me quite fast: this I think woke me, so that after this I shall have had the use of reason.' He felt 'a loss of muscular control reaching more or less deep; this one to the chest and not further, so that I could speak, whispering at first, then

226

louder'. He lay for a time thinking that if he could move a finger, then he could move his arm and so the whole body. 'The feeling is terrible: the body no longer swayed as a piece' and the 'nervous and muscular instress seems to fall in and hang like a dead weight on the chest. I cried on the holy name and by degrees recovered myself as I thought to do.'

The whole terrifying nightmare reads like a medieval description of the visitation of a succubus (or, for that matter, an incubus), with its vaguely sexual suggestion of sweat and terror as the invading presence leaps on to his supine body, initially inhibiting his ability to cry out for help, then disappearing at the invocation of God's name. 'It made me think that this was how the souls in hell would be imprisoned in their bodies as in prisons and of what St. Theresa says of the "little press in the wall" where she felt herself to be in her vision.'[7] It sounds like a censored version of rape, and the reader cannot help noticing that evil is nearly synonymous with physicality. His belief in the threat of evil was orthodox enough, but the face that he put upon it was bred out of his own fears. Years before he wrote of it in his late sonnets he had known the terrifying obliteration of the line between waking and nightmare. What seems in the poems a startling ability to objectify fears is often a literal transcription of the horror he had felt in his own life.

As he had foreseen, his duties at Manresa were the lightest since he had become a Jesuit, and the new time to himself should have helped in recuperating both mind and body. Although he had the resounding title of Professor of Rhetoric, his duties were chiefly to teach Greek and Latin to 'Rhetoricians', or 'Juniors', the young men who had completed their novitiate but needed further academic grounding before they proceeded to the Philosophate, as Hopkins had done. After his own novitiate he had been excused the Juniorate because of his university training and his demonstrated mastery of the classics. On his return to Manresa he had to teach English as well as ancient languages, but he was so well trained by Balliol that preparation for teaching classics surely needed little but a hasty riffle through the undergraduate notes he had prudently kept with him in his various moves. For at least part of the year he acted as assistant prefect of studies. All in all, as Fr Alfred Thomas wrote in breezy summation, for a Jesuit it was a 'cushy berth'.

For the first time he had free days on which he could count, so that he could see his friends in London. 'Sundays and Thursdays are my free days, the afternoons best', he told Edward Bond exuberantly. 'Tuesday afternoon is also free. Walk in the park? Certainly even to Ham common, and so on by Berkshire to Caerleon, Lyoness, Avilion, and the great Atalantis.'[8]

One friend he did not see was Bridges. They were too bound by old ties to drop their friendship, and the long association also made it impossible for them to be out of communication without worry. A year after he left Manresa, Hopkins had to tell Bridges he was no longer in London and so could not call on him. 'But if you had sent me such an invitation last year, when I really was at Roehampton, what a pleasure it would have been and what a break in the routine of rhetoric.'[9]

That the address on the letter was out of date is not surprising, since their correspondence had been sporadic for several years, on occasion so nearly moribund that either of them might have assumed it was finished forever. Without Bridges's letters, it is impossible to be sure who was responsible for the breach, but the air of hurt on Hopkins's side indicates that he blamed Bridges, in particular for the silence of three years he claimed had ensued after his 'Red' letter to his friend. It is obvious that both men were unhappy over the matter, but it was not easy to re-establish their old relations. From what we know of them both, it seems probable that Hopkins was quite as awkward about it all as he said Bridges was. Although several letters passed between them, it was not until 1877, six years after the Red letter, that the correspondence was almost back on its old footing. No matter whose the fault, there had been a double case of stiff neck that deprived them both of the old mutual affection and warmth for too long.

With more leisure, Hopkins tore around London like a tripper on a day-return ticket. He went back to one of his favourite churches, All Saints, Margaret Street, to be sure that he had not overestimated the work of Butterfield, and had to admit the architect's genius in spite of his 'want of rhetoric'. There were visits to the House of Commons with some of the Juniors. 'Gladstone was preparing to speak and writing fast but we could not stay to hear him.' Robert Lowe, sitting next to Gladstone, was an albino, and Hopkins hit

him off neatly as 'looking something like an apple in the snow'.
They also went to the House of Lords, taking a picnic lunch with
them. Another day he heard Lord Chief Justice Cockburn summing
up in the case of the Tichbourne Claimant, in which Hopkins and
most Jesuits were particularly interested because the Claimant's
counsel indicated that the education he pretended to have had at
Stonyhurst had been by men of immoral character; he ridiculously
attempted to support the insinuation by a reference to the production of *Macbeth* that Hopkins had attended at the College, in which
Lady Macbeth was replaced by Uncle Donald.

It was a particular pleasure to visit the galleries with his brother
Arthur, who brought a draughtsman's eye to the pictures they saw,
while Gerard tended to look behind the paint to the inscape of the
works. Only a few days after getting to Roehampton he went for
the first of several visits to 'the Kensington Museum', and soon
thereafter to the Soane Museum. A trip to the Academy produced
pages of jottings in his journals, trying to identify what was
important about the paintings he had seen. Occasionally he found
when transcribing them that he had been inaccurate: 'When I wrote
these notes my memory was a little duller.'*

All during the year that he taught at Manresa Hopkins kept his
eyes peeled constantly, repeatedly jotting down subjects that might
work in poetry, although he still believed – or at least tried to
believe – he would never again write poems. For example, when he
went on holiday in Devon in the summer of 1874, he was invited to
Ugbrooke Park, the home of Lord Clifford, a Catholic peer: 'As we
drove home the stars came out thick: I leant back to look at them
and my heart opening more than usual praised our Lord to and in
whom all that beauty comes home.'[10] Three years later, when he
wrote 'The Starlight Night' in Wales, the experience was surely still
in his mind, either in his conscious memory or fished up from his
journals, which he always took with him:

---

* The uncertainty of his memory was as worrying to him as if he had been a much
older man. Once he was trying to be specific about identifying the unusual colours
he had seen in Richmond Park, and afterwards he admitted in frustration, 'I
marked this down on a slip of paper at the time, because the eye for colour, rather
the zest in the mind, seems to weaken with years, but now the paper is mislaid'. He
was not quite thirty at the time.

Look at the stars! look, look up at the skies!
O look at all the fire-folk sitting in the air!
The bright boroughs, the circle-citadels there!
Down in dim woods the diamond delves! the elves'-eyes!

Hopkins's interests were always so eclectic as to be unpredictable, and the uses to which he put them even more so. Truly, as he reported Fr Gallwey had said of him at Stonyhurst, 'No one knows . . . where I may break out next.'[11] Nor could anyone have known how long an experience might lie sleeping in his memory before it surfaced in a poem. Occasionally it took far longer in gestation than 'The Starlight Night'.

One mark of his magpie curiosity was his fascination with the language of trades and occupations of which he knew nothing. On the very day he came out of retreat in his first weeks at Roehampton, he had talked to one of the lay brothers, Br Duffy, who was ploughing on the little farm at Manresa: 'he told me the names of the cross, side-plate, muzzle, regulator, and short chain. He talked of something *spraying* out, meaning splaying out and of *combing* the ground.'[12] His interest in ploughing and its out-of-the-way terminology sank into Hopkins's unconscious, almost as if forgotten, and did not reappear for some time.

That Christmas he stayed with his family in Hampstead and 'went with Arthur to the winter exhibition of the Water Colours'. One of the pictures that caught his eye that day was painted by Frederick Walker, whose work he had particularly noticed in 1868, when he had gone to the Academy, possibly in company with Pater and Solomon. On that earlier occasion, although there were works exhibited by Leighton, Millais, Watts, and other famous artists of the day, Hopkins had found that the most interesting paintings of the whole show were by Walker and his pupil George Mason.

The work by Walker that compelled his attention in 1874 was 'The Harbour of Refuge', a watercolour reproduction of an oil that Hopkins may already have seen in the Academy show of 1872, when he was staying at home from Stonyhurst. He greatly admired Walker's strength and energy: 'The young man mowing was a great stroke, a figure quite made up of dew and grace and strong fire: the sweep of the scythe and swing and sway of the whole body even to the rising of the one foot on tiptoe while the other was flung forward was as if such a thing had never been painted before, so fresh and so very strong. . . . There was also a pretty medieval ploughing-scene by Pinwell.'[13] No one, even the artist himself, can ever identify all the experiences that lie behind a complex piece of art, but in this case we can begin to see a few of those that gradually coalesced over the years into the inspiration of one of his most famous poems. Apparently the contiguity of the two pictures made the grace and sureness of Walker's mower begin to merge with Pinwell's ploughing scene almost as Hopkins looked at them, so that afterwards they seemed closely related.

If we can judge by his poems, ploughing and its vocabulary as he heard it from Br Duffy were still near the conscious level of his mind three years later during the remarkable efflorescence of his poetic powers in Wales. In 'Pied Beauty', his celebration of the diverse, he praises 'fold, fallow, and plough / And áll trádes, their gear and tackle and trim'.*

In June 1886, three years before his death, Hopkins wrote to R.W. Dixon of having gone to the Academy, where 'There was one thing, not a picture, which I much preferred to everything else there – Hamo Thornycroft's statue of the *Sower*, a truly noble work and to me a new light. It was like Frederick Walker's pictures put into stone and indeed was no doubt partly due to his influence.' The mention of Walker leads him into an extended affirmation of the 'genius of that man'. In this letter Hopkins's association of ploughing with Walker becomes overt as he then praises a reproduction of Walker's 'divine work' 'The Plough', which shows a landscape in which a well-built man leans hard on a plough drawn

---

* An even more interesting piece of evidence about his preoccupation with the subject is the ghost of a ploughman who haunts the last lines of 'The Windhover', his trudge down the sillion making his plough gleam in 'spraying' the soil. Another indication from the same poem of how the memory of what he saw in the year he taught at Manresa persisted into his poems at St Beuno's is the breath takingly familiar image in the description of a bird transfixed in sunlight that he saw in Devon:

The distance, especially westward over Dartmoor, was dim and dark, some rain had fallen and there were fragments of a rainbow but a wedge of sunlight streamed down through a break in the clouds upon the valley: a hawk also was hanging on the hover.

by two horses and led by a boy. Hopkins may have seen the original of the picture when it was first exhibited in 1870.

What probably brought all these discrete elements from his memory into single focus for Hopkins was the experience he had in Westmeath of watching an Irish ploughman, and of being so fascinated by the repetition of what he had seen at Manresa that he finally asked if he might handle the plough himself and was allowed to plough a drill.[14] The resulting fusion of experience in Hopkins's imagination the following autumn was one of his most famous poems, 'Harry Ploughman', a celebration of the kinetic strength and grace of the labouring man. It is a companion piece to 'Tom's Garland', which is 'upon the Unemployed' of the cities. Contrasted to Tom, product of the depressed urban classes, Harry is the lyrical embodiment of the harmony of beautiful countryman and the earth of which he is part:

> He leans to it, Harry bends, look. Back, elbow, and
>   liquid waist
> In him, all quail to the wallowing o' the plough.

One critic has said of it that '"Harry Ploughman" therefore joins W.H. Auden's "Musée des Beaux Arts" and William Carlos Williams' "The Dance" as another fine lyric inspired by a fine painting.'[15] This is true, but Walker's 'The Plough' is only a part of the inspiration of this poem, in which we can see coming together in a remarkable way Hopkins's memories of Manresa, Br Duffy, his brother Arthur and their expeditions, his years of going to art exhibitions, Pinwell, Thornycroft, the Irish labourer, his own admiration of handsome men and their bodies, and probably many more strands of which we have not the slightest trace. What is sure is that for Hopkins, even more than for many other artists, poems were the result of a great coalescence of experience over the years, not of one moment only.

Only too clearly he was full to bursting with poetic inspiration, but he still felt bound to his vow not to write, since it would interfere with his vocation. The truth is that he would probably have been able to devote himself more thoroughly to his clerical life if he had not constantly had the distracting urge to get on to paper his reactions to what he saw around him. Not to look at nature became a deeply painful form of self-discipline. One night coming back from a visit to the Jesuit school at Beaumont, he was hoping to see on the return journey the beautiful landscape he had absorbed while going there: 'All this I would have looked at again in returning but during dinner I talked too freely and unkindly and had to do penance going home.'[16] Probably neither the scourge nor the chain held a tithe of the pain for him that was always threatening in the self-imposed discipline of the eyes.

The year passed quietly. When he worked too hard, his superiors would send him for an excursion in London; he spent a week at Christmas in Hampstead, but without recording anything of how he got along with his family; he continued his attempts to teach himself to play the piano that he had begun at Stonyhurst ('alas! not for execution's sake but to be independent of others and learn something about music'); he watched a 'Sham fight on the Common, 7000 men, chiefly volunteers' and outside the gates of Manresa saw the 'unsheathing of swords by some cavalry, which is a stirring naked-steel lightning bit of business'; he seems to have been deputed to entertain visiting Jesuits, and in the spring 'Took Br. Tournade to Combe Wood to see and gather bluebells, which we did, but fell in bluehanded with a gamekeeper, which is a humbling thing to do.'[17]

It all sounds ideally recuperative, but in Lent he told his mother that once more he had been forbidden to fast. He was always in two minds about mentioning the subject to her, since if he did fast, she worried that it might undermine his health, and if he did not, she worried that it had already done so. On this occasion he told her that all those who were engaged in teaching did not fast, which may have stilled her natural concern.

As he almost always did at the close of the academic year, Hopkins felt weak and depressed. At the end of July his teaching finished 'with two days of examination. . . . I was very tired and seemed deeply cast down till I had some kind words from the Provincial [Fr Gallwey]. Altogether perhaps my heart has never been so burdened and cast down as this year. The tax on my strength has been greater than I have felt before . . . I feel myself weak and can do little. But in all this our Lord goes His own way.'[18]

To Bridges he lamented, 'I taught so badly and so painfully!' The truth seems, however, to have been that less was demanded of him than usual.

When he left on his 'Villa' in Devon he recovered his spirits partially, and once more he filled pages of his journal with notes on the Gothic architecture he saw, as he had done when an undergraduate. On his return to London he went by way of Bristol and predictably admired St Mary Redcliffe, although a good bit of it was not visible because of restoration work. From the suspension bridge he amused himself by drawing little foreshortened figures of the people he saw walking beneath him. In the few days before he had to return to Roehampton he went to Windsor and walked by Virginia Water: 'Went to stroll on Runnymede and bathed at their osier-grown and willowy bathingplace.'

The approach of September was always an uneasy time for young Jesuits not yet sure of their future: 'the changes in the Province *are* like Puss in the Corner and the September ones are sometimes called General Post,' he wrote to his mother. 'Much change is inevitable, for every year so many people must begin and so many more must have ended their studies . . . Add deaths, sicknesses, leavings, foreign missions, and what not and you will see that ours can never be an abiding city nor any one of us know what a day may bring forth; and it is our pride to be ready for instant despatch.'[19]

Hopkins had told his father he expected to teach a second year at Manresa, but on the 26th of August he wrote in his journal, 'Heard definitively that I was to go to St. Beuno's to make my theology.' Two days later he rose early to the light of a 'full moon of brassyish colour and beautifully dappled' and caught a train for Wales. Another stage was passed in the long journey to accomplish what he had begun six years earlier.

Although it had been intended as a rest for him, Hopkins's return to Manresa, as we have seen, had finally resulted in near-breakdown. In going to St Beuno's and the theologate, he was reverting to the status of pupil rather than teacher, and at thirty years of age, he might have been expected to fret at the change. Most of what he had taught at Manresa had been a watering down of his own undergraduate studies at Oxford, so that he was not over-taxed by preparation. At St Beuno's, however, he would have to work much harder, in part because, as he indicated himself, he had no particular ability at theology. Yet, in spite of the additional work, St Beuno's was to be one of the best periods of his clerical life.

Part of his general contentment there was his feeling that he was now a real Jesuit. Shortly after his arrival he received the tonsure and the four minor orders; they were 'those of Doorkeepers, Readers, Exorcists, and Acolytes', he told his bewildered mother, whom he took some quiet pleasure in overwhelming with portentous-sounding details of his clerical advancement. Alas, as he had to admit to her, 'their use is almost obsolete'. Nonetheless, receiving them made it ever clearer to his family that his choice of vocation was irrevocable. The tonsure itself 'consisted of five little snips but the bishop must have found even that a hard job, for I had cut my hair almost to the scalp'. Besides those receiving minor orders, sixteen priests were ordained: 'I was by God's mercy deeply touched.'[20]

His sense of being at home had begun on his arrival at the station in St Asaph, so markedly different from his tardy and awkward entry to the novitiate at Manresa. Henry Kerr, one of the men he had liked best at Stonyhurst, was there to greet him affectionately, with another theologian who would share his studies. 'Mr. Bacon put scarlet geraniums in my room, and everyone was very kind and hospitable.' He had been in the Order long enough to meet old friends everywhere he moved, and now he counted on being with many of them for another four years.

During the rest of his life he was to become only too familiar with the architecture of Joseph Hansom, then much in favour for the design of the Catholic churches and schools and rectories that were going up all over Great Britain, but St Beuno's was his first prolonged exposure to his work. Although this was one of Hansom's most successful efforts, built in 1849, it was not surprising to find that his chief claim to fame was the design of the cab that bore his name. The house 'is built of limestone,' Hopkins told his father, 'decent outside, skimpin within, Gothic, like Lancing College done worse. The staircases, galleries, and bopeeps are inexpressible: it takes a fortnight to learn them.' But, as Hopkins might have pointed out, even Hansom could not diminish the work of the Almighty surrounding the house.

Today, in part perhaps because of an inevitable mellowing by the sea winds of the intervening years, it is a most attractive spot, high on the side of a steep hillside commanding 'the long-drawn valley of the Clwyd to the sea'. In 1874, as today, the garden was 'all heights, terraces, Excelsiors, misty mountain tops, seats up trees called Crows' Nests, flights of steps seemingly up to heaven lined with burning aspiration upon aspiration of scarlet geraniums' to match those in his room. It 'gives you the impression that if you took a step farther you would find yourself somewhere on Plenlimmon, Conway Castle, or Salisbury Craig'.[21] In heavy weather, when the building looked as if it were burrowing into the hillside for protection, the shrubbery and smaller trees seemed to have been blown on for centuries, so that they leaned away from the prevailing winds like dogs with hair streaming back from their faces.

Hopkins's first room was apparently in the new buildings that were added only shortly before he arrived, although their plumbing appeared to have survived from another age: 'Pipes of affliction convey lukewarm water of affliction to some of the rooms, others more fortunate have fires.' He was probably among the 'fortunate', for the new rooms would otherwise have been uninhabitable, but the fires were not allowed until mid-October and were stopped again in April. The uninterrupted wide stone-flagged corridors succeeded only in funnelling the numbing draughts, and the doors banged incessantly with the wind. One bathroom had been provided by Hansom for the approximately forty men in the building, which at least economized on modesty powder; the bedrooms were featureless and dark. It should have been thoroughly depressing, but Hopkins loved it, and it is easy to see why, for spread out below is some of the most beautiful country in the British Isles.

Hopkins had arrived a fortnight before the retreat to mark the beginning of term. Since arrangements were still on an informal basis, he was allowed to choose his own walking companions, as he would not be later in the year. For his first few days he explored the locality with the two Kerr brothers, Henry and William, a pleasantly eccentric pair of Scotsmen who had come late to clerical life. While still in their teens, they had both been converted with their parents, Lord and Lady Henry Kerr, when the Gorham case made their father give up his living as an Anglican parson. William had been in the Civil Service in India until ill health forced his retirement; Henry had been in the Navy and was still given to criticizing the Society for being less than shipshape. In 1867, the year before Hopkins went there, the brothers became novices together at Manresa, where Hopkins first got to know and like them.

With his friends he walked over a good many of the hills near St Beuno's; when one considers his slight frame and frequent illnesses, his stamina was startling. Within a week he was so at home in the countryside that he referred casually to Maenefa, the flat-topped hill that rose directly behind the house, as 'ours'. From there or from the great tower on the front of the house he could see the sunlit shore at Rhyl, glittering against the clouds above the hills that built up to Snowdon miles away to the west. St Asaph, Denbigh and the junction of the Clwyd with the narrower valley of the Elwy were all easily visible on a good day, and nearer at hand in the stone-walled fields there were handfuls of slow-moving sheep, looking like a proliferation of puffballs from a distance. It was a 'Landscape plotted and pieced – fold, fallow, and plough'. And everywhere was the sense of space without limit, the air almost audible in its intense clarity, looking he said like a blue bloom in a basin of hills. The infinite expanse of sky made the dappled play of light particularly spectacular, and Hopkins recorded on one almost edible evening a 'lovely sunset of rosy juices and creams and combs'.

The retreat to open the year began on the evening of the 10th of September, with the first part of the day set aside as a 'Blandyke'. With another new man Hopkins set out for the winding, enclosed valley of the Elwy and the little holy well beside a ruined chapel on its banks: 'We said a prayer and drank the water.' The emanation of spirit that he felt from the very earth made him fall in love with the place as he had probably not done since his early days as an undergraduate in Oxford.

It was the first time he had been with a Celtic population in the country, not the city, and for the first time he felt their attraction, so different from what he had thought of the poor urban Irish. 'I have got a yearning for the Welsh people and could find it in my heart to work for their conversion,' he told his mother. The mystery he sensed in the land was in key with its inhabitants. 'The Welsh round are very civil and respectful but do not much come to us'; he added

237

ruefully that 'those who are converted are for the most part not very stanch . . . They are said to have a turn for religion, especially what excites outward fervour, and more refinement and pious feeling than the English peasantry but less steadfastness and sincerity. I have always looked on myself as half Welsh and so I warm to them.' All this, although 'the Welsh have the reputation also of being covetous and immoral: I add this to forestall your saying it, for, as I say, I warm to them – and in different degrees to all the Celts.'[22] He was later to find it difficult to maintain his enthusiasm when he had to work with Irish immigrants; in Dublin, surrounded by Celts, he usually forgot that he thought of himself as anything but completely English.

In his first glow of happiness with St Beuno's he 'began to learn Welsh too but not with very pure intentions perhaps'. When he consulted the Rector, who had probably seen a good many short-lived enthusiasms of the sort, Fr Jones 'discouraged it unless it were purely for the sake of labouring among the Welsh. Now it was not and so I saw I must give it up.'[23]

It was an early manifestation of the inability to decide what he wanted to do that characterized the later years of his life, when one unfulfilled project followed another. After writing in his journal about his disappointment over Welsh, he added that it had been taken up in the first place because 'my music seemed to come to an end'. Why he had to give up the piano he had begun at Manresa and, presumably, the violin he had taken up in emulation of Newman at Edgbaston, Hopkins never made clear, although he admitted that practising at St Beuno's 'was a burden . . . with a grunting harmonium that lived in the sacristy'.[24]

With neither music (which he had not mentioned for months) nor Welsh (which he had not considered for longer than a day or two) all the charm he had felt so strongly in his new assignment seemed to dissolve:

I had no sooner given up these two things (which disappointed me and took an interest away – and at that time I was very bitterly feeling the weariness of life and shed many tears, perhaps not wholly into the breast of God but with some unmanliness in them too, and sighed and panted to Him), I had no sooner given up the Welsh than my desire seemed to be for the conversion of Wales and I had it in mind to give up everything else for that; nevertheless weighing this by St. Ignatius' rules of election I decided not to do so.[25]

Fr Jones may have spotted that one of the things Hopkins missed most was poetry, and tucked the incident away in his memory to act upon a year later.

When Hopkins had to decide against converting the Welsh and felt that he lacked justification for studying their language, he turned to Br Magri, who had come from Malta and who had received his minor orders with him. Br Magri had 'an interesting history. It is said he was to be married, when he broke off the match, gave his property over to his brother, and fled to our noviceship.'[26] With him Hopkins speculated about the Maltese language and was humiliated to find that his ear did not easily grasp the gutturals. His brief preoccupation with Maltese sounds like a substitute for Welsh, which in turn sounds like a substitute for the poetry that he was still not writing.

There is no indication of why he decided that in fact he was justified in studying Welsh, but by the beginning of the next year he had changed his mind once more and was taking lessons in the language from a Miss Jones and made rapid progress. He learned to love its sound and, with more assiduity than spontaneity, to write poetry in it. His English poems were deeply affected by his studies, particularly in their rhythmic and alliterative quality, but it is questionable whether he would ever have studied the language (he seems to have been the only Theologian in St Beuno's who had any knowledge of it) if he had actually been writing poetry in English at the time.

'Who was St. Beuno?' he wrote to Bridges, trying to forestall any jokes. 'Is he dead? Yes, he did that much 1200 years ago, if I mistake not. He was St. Winefred's uncle and raised her to life when she died in defence of her chastity and at the same time he called out her famous spring, which fills me with devotion every time I see it.'[27] St Winefred's well, a few miles from St Beuno's at Holywell, became a regular place of pilgrimage for Hopkins, who felt a special devotion to the saint. Holywell was just beginning to attract crowds to the beautiful sixteenth-century buildings surrounding the well; a hospice had been opened four years earlier to house pilgrims seeking a miracle in the clear waters. Bathing was segregated by sex, and changing was in fretted wooden cubicles beside the well, put up to shield the pilgrims from the sight of the Protestant youths who gathered to jeer on the footpath outside the surrounding fence.

The well belonged to the Council of Holywell and was leased to local Catholics, but the Church took no official position on the miraculous qualities of the waters or the precise nature of the healing that took place there. Hopkins's love of water, of female martyrs, of antiquity, and of the direct demonstration of Divine grace through miracles, all joined in Holywell. Shortly after he arrived in Wales he recorded in his diary that he had gone there to bathe with another Philosopher and 'returned very joyously'. The visit provided him with a striking image in 'The Wreck of the Deutschland' of the water of grace running down the sides of a voel (Welsh for mountain) to fill a well, always steady on the surface, always being fed from beneath:

> The sight of the water in the well as clear as glass, greenish like beryl or aquamarine, trembling at the surface with the force of the springs, and shaping out the five foils of the well quite drew and held my eyes to it. Within a month or six weeks from this . . . a young man from Liverpool . . . was cured of rupture in the water. The strong unfailing flow of the water and the chain of cures from year to year all these centuries took hold of my mind with wonder at the bounty of God in one of His saints . . . even now the stress and buoyancy and abundance of the water is before my eyes.[28]

In a letter that has not survived, Hopkins also told his parents about the cure of the young man from Liverpool, which was obviously too much for his father, who asked for some proof of the healing. Both his request and Gerard's response show how difficult it was for father and son to see eye to eye on such matters, even when they tried to maintain peace. It is noticeable that Hopkins's reply was sent to his mother not his father, since she had 'not such an altogether unfavourable opinion of the Society' and other Catholic matters as her husband:

> I promised, if I remember, that I wd. let my father know the result of my enquiries about the alleged cure of a case of rupture at St. Winefred's well. I wrote to the young man enclosing a set of searching questions I had framed. He answered the letters and promised answers to the questions in a week or so when he should have been able to tell more certainly the permanence of the cure. Those answers never came. The case therefore was not satisfactory. I have heard of another cure having just been worked in London by the moss or water and am going to enquire into that.[29]

No more was heard of the London cure. As one might guess, his father's incredulity merely reinforced Hopkins's devotion to the well; he went there as often as possible, even in mid-winter, when the water maintained a bafflingly constant heat.

Further evidence, if we need it, of the deep interest in the supernatural that Hopkins felt in Wales is the last entry in his surviving journals, where he records a conversation with his Welsh teacher, Miss Jones, when he asked for the Welsh word for fairy. At first she had difficulty understanding what he meant until he said they were 'little people "that high"', to which 'she told me quite simply that she had seen them' on the Holywell Road 'at 5 o'clock in the morning, when she saw three little boys of about four years old wearing little frock coats and odd little caps running and dancing before her, taking hands and going round, then going further, still dancing and always coming together, she said'.[30] Such supernatural emanations seemed no stranger to Hopkins nor more demanding of special belief than they did to Miss Jones.

CHAPTER XIV

DEUTSCHLAND,
DOUBLE A DESPERATE NAME
1875

Once the term had officially begun on 1 October 1874 life settled down into a familiar pattern. The Theologians in their first two years were particularly hard worked. According to Hopkins's near-contemporary R.F.Clarke, on three days of the week they attended two lectures each morning and three in the afternoon. 'The morning lectures are on moral and dogmatic theology; and those in the afternoon on canon law or history, dogmatic theology, and Hebrew.' Each afternoon there was a 'circle' but it was much fiercer than Hopkins had experienced at Stonyhurst, for the participants were older and wilier at disputation.[1]

There was entertainment, too, of a rudimentary kind, and most evenings there was 'recreation' after supper, but the round of life was highly repetitive, with little change save in the weather. The countryside remained beautiful, although as winter advanced it was often seen through heavy rain, then the other side of the valley vanished in mist and the ground was waist-deep in drifted snow. Worst of all, the weather would not remain out of doors: at the end of February 1875, 'Three of the newly-built rooms facing the court were pronounced not fit to sleep in in consequence of the snow working its way through the roof.' The 'pipes of affliction' gave up, and it was impossible to warm the new rooms above forty-six degrees Fahrenheit; some of the scholastics had to take refuge in the rooms normally set aside for guests and visiting clerics.

Surprisingly, Hopkins's health, both physical and mental, fared quite well, although his old stomach condition apparently persisted. 'Such a backward spring I cannot remember,' he wrote after eight months at St Beuno's. 'Now things begin to look greener and the cuckoo may be heard but our climate on the hillside is a touch Arctic. I have recovered from a cold I caught lately and am well but for daily indigestion, which makes study much harder and our shadowless glaring walks to my eyes very painful.' His mother sent a bottle of remedy for Gerard, who wryly thanked her for the present, 'which came packed in so much sawdust that it will serve to sweep my room for weeks. . . . It is a queer medicine and is like eating death and cremation.'[2]

The time that in good weather might have been spent tramping the hills was often devoted in winter to newspapers and periodicals. At the end of 1874 Hopkins was greatly concerned with Gladstone's pamphlet *The Vatican Decrees in their Bearings on Civil Allegiance: A Political Expostulation*, which attacked Ultramontanism. Hopkins was as far from being Ultramontane as an English Catholic could be at that date, but he reacted against Gladstone, who had called the Jesuits 'the deadliest foes that mental and moral liberty have ever known'.[3] Until his death he was to be distrustful of the GOM, an attitude that was not lessened when he went to Ireland.

Almost certainly he had read in *Letters and Notices* a three-part series during 1873 and 1874 on 'The Migration of the Canonesses Regular from Liège to England in 1793', which told of the frightful journey of a community of nuns driven out by the French Revolution. They had sailed on the Eve of the Assumption from Holland and landed at Greenwich. It was the kind of story of persecution with which Hopkins was familiar from the contingents of refugee Continental priests who had come to Manresa and Stonyhurst. Since *Letters and Notices* was standard reading for every Jesuit, it is most probable that he saw it and had the account of the French nuns in the forefront of his mind in December 1875, when he began reading, in *The Times* and the *Illustrated London News* among other journals, of the foundering of a German ship, the *Deutschland*, on a sandbank near the mouth of the Thames. It had been bound for New York from Bremen, and among more than a hundred passengers were five Franciscan nuns, refugees from Bismarck's anti-Catholic legislation. All five were drowned, but only four of their bodies were recovered.

There were many personal reasons why the death of the nuns

should have struck Hopkins to the heart, not least the date on which they died, 'drowned between midnight and morning of Dec. 7th, 1875', as the dedicatory note to 'The Wreck of the Deutschland' tells us. The 7th of December was the eve of the feast of the Immaculate Conception, an ancient belief that had been officially defined as 'of faith' only in 1854. The promulgation of the doctrine of the conception without original sin of the Virgin was particularly offensive to many Victorian Protestants like Gladstone, frightened of what seemed to them increasing Roman arrogance. It was far from that for Hopkins, who was intensely devoted to her honour. Not least of the attractions of the doctrine for Hopkins was that in the fourteenth century it had been promoted vigorously by his hero, Duns Scotus, who was, like the nuns, a Franciscan.

We have seen how devoutly Hopkins believed in the spiritual significance of particular dates and anniversaries, such as the date on which his grandfather had died. In the day on which the German nuns were drowned he saw symbolic, possibly miraculous, intention, but he may have stretched its significance slightly, since there was no way of knowing whether the nuns actually died on the 6th or the 7th of the month.

The exact facts of the shipwreck are still a matter for argument, and a good bit of time has been wasted trying to pin down the background of the nuns, the reasons for the ship's running aground, why other ships did not come to its rescue, and other facts that would be of absolute importance in any historical account of the wreck, although they seem almost irrelevant to the poem, which Hopkins wrote without knowing all the particulars. Even the proper identification of the nuns, not to mention their character, which have both been questioned recently, seems extraneous to the composition of the poem, for what is important is what Hopkins knew and believed about the wreck. The general outlines of the catastrophe were clear to him, and the newspapers had such vivid, even lurid, accounts that his imagination would not have been stimulated more had he been in possession of more details. What he knew was adequate for writing about spiritual questions rather than marine or meteorological phenomena.

What readers of the poem need to know about the actual wreck is slight. In both the valley of the Clwyd and the North Sea, December began in 1875 with heavy snow and wind. The captain of the *Deutschland* disastrously got off course into the estuary of the Thames, blinded by the dark and by implacable storm. At about 5 A.M. on the 6th of December the ship ran into the sandbank known as the Kentish Knock, and in trying to reverse, it shattered its propeller and began to roll helplessly before the breakers. The crew fired distress rockets, but some of them were never seen, and the seas were too rough for other ships to come to the rescue. It took thirty hours for help to arrive; by then the ship was broken up and more than sixty passengers and crew had died.

As the lower decks filled with water, many of the passengers retreated higher and higher, until they were clinging to the rigging (the 'shrouds'), from which the freezing waves washed them overboard to their death or dashed them to the deck. *The Times*, in an account on the 11th of December, told how

> Five German nuns, whose bodies are now in the dead-house here, clasped hands and were drowned together, the chief sister, a gaunt woman 6 ft. high, calling out loudly and often 'O Christ, come quickly!' till the end came. The shrieks and sobbing of women and children are described by the survivors as agonising. One brave sailor, who was safe in the rigging, went down to try and save a child or woman who was drowning on deck. He was secured by a rope to the rigging, but a wave dashed him against the bulwarks, and when daylight dawned his headless body, detained by the rope, was swaying to and fro with the waves. In the dreadful excitement of these hours one man hung himself behind the wheelhouse, another hacked at his wrist with a knife, hoping to die a comparatively painless death by bleeding.

Two days later another account in *The Times*, again singling out the nun in charge of the little party, said that one of them 'noted for her extreme tallness, is the lady who, at midnight on Monday, by standing on a table in the saloon, was able to thrust her body through the skylight, and kept exclaiming, in a voice heard by those in the rigging above the roar of the storm, "My God, my God, make haste, make haste."'

One aspect of the wreck that touched Hopkins on the patriotic raw was that the nuns were homeless when they set sail, and, so far as he could tell from the early reports of the wreck, it was in large part the fault of the English, through both inefficiency and outright culpability, that they had lost their lives. England had proved even more inhospitable than Germany, from which the nuns had been driven by their devotion to God. It was generally believed that some fourteen English luggers and smacks manned by 'salvors' had stood by, ignoring the distress signals, waiting for the breakup of the ship so that they could begin their pillage. Early reports said that the bodies of the drowned had been stripped of all valuables.

Hopkins's shame over English behaviour was as deep as if he had been personally implicated in the wreck:

> Loathed for a love men knew in them.
> Banned by the land of their birth.
> Rhine refused them. Thames would ruin them.

To add to his empathy with the nuns was his constant belief that he too had been 'exiled' from family, friends and homeland by prejudice against his religion.

The week after their death the four bodies that had been found were buried in St Patrick's cemetery, Leytonstone, hardly a mile from the street where Hopkins was born. The funeral sermon was given by Cardinal Manning. It is hard to imagine what metaphorical significance even Hopkins, with the most sensitive of noses for such matters, could have found in the physical nearness of his own birthplace and the last resting place of the nuns, but it must have stirred at least a moment of imagined familiarity.

In almost no other way were the nuns familiar, for he had never heard of them before the wreck, he had only incomplete reports of what had happened on the deck and in the saloon of the ship, and so far as can be determined he never went near the cemetery in Leytonstone. Certainly, he had no way save intuition to know what was going on in their minds during the wreck. Yet he was so struck by the reports of the occurrence that he almost immediately identified himself with the tall nun and spent half a year in trying to imagine and to give life to the meaning of her last reported words, called out in German that he might not even have understood had he been there. By the end of that time her suffering had become as personal to him as if he had been on the foundering ship, and the salvation that he believed she had achieved had transfigured the anguish.

When the wreck was discussed at St Beuno's, Hopkins said he 'was affected by the account and happening to say so to my rector he said that he wished someone would write a poem on the subject. On this hint I set to work and, though my hand was out at first, produced one.'

Even though he had written little for the past few years, Hopkins had so clearly been rapt in poetry that it is not surprising he leapt with alacrity at the suggestion. The Rector was a kindly man, and possibly he remembered Hopkins's disappointment when he had discouraged him from studying Welsh and was attempting to make up for it. What seems more probable is that Fr Jones, who had no particular interest in poetry, made a vague suggestion about its being a good occasion for a pious set of verses inculcating a moral lesson from a sad event, and that in his eagerness Hopkins heard a more inclusive invitation than the Rector actually extended. If so, Fr Jones must have been astonished at the result, an ode of 280 lines of tortuous diction and revolutionary rhythm that had become a glittering and resplendent meditation on the place in the world of suffering, not least Hopkins's own.

What Hopkins does not even suggest he received from Fr Jones was a blanket permission to write poetry in the future, but from then on he said he felt himself relieved of a prohibition that had never been imposed: 'After writing this I held myself free to compose, but cannot find it in my conscience to spend time upon it.'[4] It is wryly amusing to see how often he imputed to others commands of which he felt need himself – and how often they quietly dropped out of consideration when they no longer had meaning for him. In this case his own eagerness apparently invented both the interdiction of poetry and the subsequent permission to resume writing it. Some time in the fortnight after the 11th of December Hopkins wrote home asking for clippings from periodicals about the disaster, which 'made a deep impression on me, more than any other wreck or accident I ever read of'. A little of the edginess always ready to creep into correspondence with his family is shown in his letter of thanks, rebuking his mother for sending two copies of one account and omitting another, 'the most interesting piece of all. . . . I am writing something on this wreck, which may perhaps appear but it depends on how I am speeded.'[5] After that he seems not to have mentioned the matter to her again for six months.

During its composition he had read parts of the poem to other Theologians, who found it incomprehensible, but he nonetheless pinned his hopes on Fr Henry Coleridge, then editor of the *Month* (and a cousin of his schoolfriend Ernest Coleridge), to whom he submitted his poem in May or June 1876. Hopkins thought of Fr Coleridge as his oldest friend in the Society, and told him he knew he would probably dislike the poem intensely; jokingly and somewhat tactlessly he asked Coleridge to consider the taste of his readers rather than his own. Perhaps with some amusement at Hopkins's gaucheness, Fr Coleridge 'replied that there was in America a new sort of poetry which did not rhyme or scan or construe; if [Hopkins's poem] rhymed and scanned and construed and did not make nonsense or bad morality he did not see why it shd. not do'. The reference was obviously to the work of Walt Whitman, for whose poetry Hopkins had limited enthusiasm and for whose reported personality he apparently had none, attitudes with which Fr Coleridge was probably familiar.

Hopkins made the mistake of many inexperienced writers in assuming that it augured well for publication when he had not heard from Coleridge for some time. When the editor did reply, he said it had been 'too late for July but will appear in the August number . . . He wants me however to do away with the accents which mark the scanning. I would gladly have done without them if I had thought my readers would scan right unaided but I am afraid they will not, and if the lines are not rightly scanned they are ruined.'

It probably never occurred to him that Coleridge might be as determined (stubborn?) as he was himself, or that he might refuse to publish the poem unless all the scansion marks were removed; in anticipation of its publication, Hopkins cautioned his mother, 'You must never say that the poem is mine.' But a month and a half later it was beginning to look as if there were no secret for her to keep: he wrote that his poem was not 'in the August *Month* and whether it will be in the September number or in any I cannot find out: altogether it has cost me a good deal of trouble'. But it was not in the September issue, and at the end of the month he counselled resignation to his mother, although he was probably in more need of it himself: 'About the *Deutschland* "sigh no more", I am glad now it has not appeared.'[6]

What levels of disappointment lay in those last resigned words it is hard to know, for it meant that more than half a year of work had evaporated and that all his trouble had not resulted in a poem that was publishable, even by an editor well disposed to him.

For all its greatness, 'The Wreck of the Deutschland' is distinctly eccentric even today, and it must have seemed totally incomprehensible in 1876. It is hardly surprising that Coleridge refused to publish a work of which he could make neither head nor tail. Trying hard to be fair to the poem, he gave it to another reader, Fr Sydney Smith, who was clearly discontented by the odd blue pencil marks with which Hopkins had tried to make the rhythm clear. Finally, Fr Smith said, 'the only result was to give me a very bad headache, and to lead me to hand the poem back to Fr. Coleridge with the remark that it was indeed unreadable.'[7] Both readers thought well of him, but they were undoubtedly right in believing the poem was unpublishable, at least in the 1870s. Had it appeared, it would surely have met with such bewilderment, not to say hostility, that Hopkins would have been crushed.

In 1975, on the centenary of the wreck, the *Month* made an engaging apology for Fr Coleridge's decision, saying that 'it has to be admitted, as we bite on the bullet, that one unwise blunder has gained for *The Month* more notoriety than all the distinguished articles it has wisely published.' The writer is almost too conscientious in assuming that the journal made a mistake in rejecting the poem. All a bit late for Hopkins, but one could not ask for a more generous recantation.

Hopkins made his first start at the poem with a description of the sailing of the ship from Bremen, then he must have realized that in spite of his sense of identification with the tall nun, he knew too little of her to make her personal emotions the centre of the work. However much he was touched by pity for her, his deepest feelings were really stirred because the literal circumstances of her death paralleled the metaphorical ones of his own life: expulsion from family and friends, suffering for Christ, ultimate reunion with Him. At least, he assumed the nun was reunited with Christ and he hoped that he would be. The pattern was that of the journey of man through the world to eternity, and – even more important emotionally – it was cast in terms of the virgin-martyrs with whom he had frequently identified himself. The nun is less the real subject of the poem than a surrogate for himself and a human metaphor for suffering and salvation. The key to the poem is that the long ode is about his own personal condition.

In rewriting, Hopkins shifted the initial attention of the reader away from the suffering of the nun to the poet's spiritual desolation, which is analogous to her physical and mental pain, as both find their incarnate archetype in Christ's Passion. The first stanza concludes with a striking recollection of Michelangelo's great mural of the creation of Adam, which parallels the poet's own figurative creation in being forced to contemplate the meaning of the shipwreck:

> Thou mastering me
> God! giver of breath and bread;
> World's strand, sway of the sea;
> Lord of living and dead;
> Thou hast bound bones and veins in me, fastened me flesh,
> And after it almost unmade, what with dread,
> Thy doing: and dost thou touch me afresh?
> Over again I feel thy finger and find thee.

Hopkins is brought face to face with one of the central mysteries of Christianity, the reason for the existence of suffering in a world created by a beneficent God. And to the eternal question he gives a standard answer: through suffering man arrives at knowledge and final bliss. Like Milton, he was justifying God's ways to man.

'O Deutschland, double a desperate name!' he wrote of the ship, which was both hearse for her passengers and setting for the salvation of the nuns; the phrase applies to much of the rest of the poem, which is, among other things, a study in double significance.

'Double-naturèd name' he says of Christ. God and His ways are mysterious to us, since man's natural tendency is to look for a simple meaning, whereas experience is complex; God is both 'lightning and love . . . winter and warm'. Nature is the source of both 'lovely-asunder/Starlight' and the 'Wiry and white-fiery and whirlwind-swivellèd snow' that beat the ship into the sandbank. Little, if anything, has a single meaning, and few causes have predictable effects.

The significance of the nun is constantly changing as Hopkins considers her, so that as the levels of meaning accumulate, she becomes both more important symbolically and less so personally. She stands for Hopkins, but also in her own person she is a celebration of the Immaculate Conception, commemorated the day after the wreck of the ship. And in her role as Virgin she is mother of Christ, set out in graphic imagery of parturition, as well as His lover.

Some indication of Hopkins's personal involvement in this poem is the sexual imagery with which it is drenched, nearly always a clue to his writing from feelings so deep that he is ignoring associations in his language that he would otherwise probably have censored. For example, in indicating that the Crucifixion is implicit in the Incarnation ('Warm-laid grave of a womb-life grey'), the intensity of his imagery makes it difficult to see at once whether he is referring directly to Christ's birth or His death, since both events evoke emotions so primal that the distinction between them is blurred:

> The dense and the driven Passion, and frightful sweat;
> Thence the discharge of it, there its swelling to be . . .

Passion (naturally enough, always a deeply emotive word for him), sweat, swelling, discharge: for most readers the association of this grouping of words is as close to tumescence and relief as to either parturition or crucifixion.

There is a long Christian tradition of the association between eroticism and religion, and it was never far beneath the surface in Hopkins's poetry, as we have seen elsewhere. In this poem, probably the central one of all his works, he uses erotic imagery with such startling effect that the reader frequently wonders how consciously he is evoking its meaning. The nun, for instance, in longing for her final union with Christ, calls out in her urgency in language taken from *Revelation*: 'O Christ, Christ, come quickly'. It is almost impossible to believe that Hopkins would intentionally have evoked the sexual ambiguity of her call to Christ, and elsewhere it would be natural to put it down to traditional usage, but it is difficult to ignore the erotic overtone in the context of his asking the meaning of her cry: 'Is it love in her of the being as her lover had been?' The simplest answer to this problem is that Hopkins had strong sexual feelings that he was prevented by principle from 'acting out', and that they naturally seeped into his imagery with unconscious strength. That they should have been evoked by the thought of Christ as lover is an idea that would have seemed familiar enough to generations of poets – and to Dolben in particular. One may even ponder the fact that the poem treats a love-death as sensuously inspired as the *Liebestod* of Isolde, written only a decade before this.

As a figure of speech the awareness of double meaning has the name of metaphor, involving as it necessarily does more than one aspect of perception, linked by a common denominator that looks in two directions at the same time. Or, to put it another away, metaphor is the recognition that experience is not without significance. Rhetorically, the same impulse is manifested in paradox. These are, of course, all the very stuff of poetry, and the reader quickly realizes that among the other strands of experience Hopkins is testing are the nature and function of poetic language.

In stanza 28 both poet and nun discover the limitations of language as they (both of them seem implied here, although the 'I' of the stanza refers only to the poet) attempt to formulate her vision of Christ as she is united with him:

> But how shall I . . . make me room there:
> Reach me a . . . Fancy, come faster –
> Strike you the sight of it? look at it loom there,
> Thing that she . . . There then! the Master,
> *Ipse*, the only one, Christ, King, Head:
> He was to cure the extremity where he had cast her;

> Do, deal, lord it with living and dead;
> Let him ride, her pride, in his triumph, despatch and have done
>   with his doom there.

It is not easy to describe adequately the effect of the gasping, disconnected, inchoate urgency of speech here, followed in the next stanza by a lapse into relaxed simplicity of syntax that is almost childlike, but it seems nearly orgastic. Hopkins is not recreating sexual experience, rather he is drawing on the subliminal power of its expression. This is not to be prurient, only to point out with what completeness of personality he wrote when he was at full stretch, uniting the spiritual and the physical in the pattern that is central to the poem. It is probably this whole-heartedness of response that makes his poetry so attractive to readers.

This is a highly autobiographical poem, and Hopkins once attempted to justify it to Bridges, who did not like it, with that feeblest of critical statements, that it had actually happened to him: 'I may add for your greater interest and edification that what refers to myself in the poem is all strictly and literally true and did all occur; nothing is added for poetical padding.'[8]

But Hopkins was far too subtle to be suggesting that every physical action in the poem was his own, for he was referring to mental and spiritual attitudes. We have seen how often bits of his experience were picked up and used as imagery in the poem, such as his observation of the steady level of the water in St Winefred's well, which struck him as a fitting metaphor for the constancy of grace given by Christ. In the poem, however, he uses the memory of his feeling without trying to recreate the physical scene in Holywell:

> I steady as a water in a well, to a poise, to a pane,
>   But roped with, always, all the way down from the tall
>   Fells or flanks of the voel, a vein
> Of the gospel proffer. . . .

The spiritual likeness is there, but Holywell has disappeared. It is the failure to distinguish between the two orders of memory that often misleads critics into trying to identify exactly in his daily life what is the 'original' of parts of his poems. Fr Devlin, the brilliant editor of his sermons, for example, settled firmly for the long retreat that began Hopkins's novitiate as the model for the vigil that begins this poem, when almost certainly it was born of the sum of Hopkins's experience of vigils. Of such models there is no certainty, although we may reasonably postulate that attitudes that occur and recur in his writings were important to him and hence may have found their way into the poetry.

In 'The Wreck of the Deutschland' Hopkins first liberally employed his characteristic adjectival style, in which words have so many meanings that the poem constantly seems on the verge of punning. In the opening stanza, for example, God is addressed as 'World's strand', suggesting that He is the spiritual warder of the world and sets its borders, but as the poem progresses, the word in repetition gradually takes on the added meaning of that sea margin on which the ship is stranded. Or he hyphenates to show double qualities in one term, as in 'fall-gold mercies', indicating both the mode of their coming to man and the preciousness of their reception. Even within a single word he is concerned to show the principle of duality. It is this dense lushness and irregularity of plenitude that has so often made critics describe the poem as baroque. The word seems especially appropriate, since its general usage is derived from the architectural 'excesses' of the Jesuit church in Rome, and is often applied to the close bond between sex and death in religious ecstasy that characterized much of the art of the Counter-Reformation. For this poem is literally counter-, or perhaps anti-, Reformation, even in its passing reference to Luther as 'beast of the waste wood', a characterization that would have seemed less strange to a Victorian Catholic than it does in our own more ecumenical days. Perhaps slightly more disquieting is the final stanza of the ode, with its invocation of the prayers of the dead nun for the return of England to the true Church. The disquiet, however, is brought out less by the nature of Hopkins's religious opinion than by a feeling that there is something a bit inappropriate about hanging the conversion of Great Britain upon the martyrdom of a German nun who had never intended to be there in the first place. To voice such a niggling doubt seems trivial, but the matter does end the poem on a note that is vaguely but disturbingly out of key.

In describing to Dixon how he came to write the poem, Hopkins said that he was persuaded to do so because 'I had long had haunting my ear the echo of a new rhythm which now I realised on paper.' This was Sprung Rhythm, to use his own name for the metrical system of the poem and of many thereafter. 'System' is probably not quite the word, for it was in part a reaction against regularization of poetic rhythm in favour of a nearer approximation to common speech. 'To speak shortly, it consists in scanning by accents or stresses alone, without any account of the number of syllables, so that a foot may be one strong syllable or it may be many light and one strong.'[9] In other words, a metrical foot is defined by its force and its temporal duration rather than by a strict counting of syllables.

It is a truism that poetic rhythm is an adjustment between a yearning for repetition and regularity, and a need to work variations upon them. Without the regularity there is no basis on which to improvise, or, as Robert Frost once said, it is like playing tennis without a net. What Hopkins was trying to do with Sprung Rhythm was to make the variations more flexible without losing the feel of the basic rhythm, and this attempt he said was wholly traditional. He found it in Shakespeare, in nursery rhymes, in Milton's choruses in *Samson Agonistes*. And, above all, he was familiar with its practice in the liturgy, where unimportant or unstressed words and syllables in sung offices may be either hurried over or prolonged to fit them into an already determined accompaniment.

'Why do I employ sprung rhythm at all?' he wrote in reply to a question by Bridges:

Because it is the nearest to the rhythm of prose, that is the native and natural rhythm of speech, the least forced, the most rhetorical and emphatic of all possible rhythms, combining. as it seems to me, opposite and, one wd. have thought, incompatible excellences, markedness of rhythm – that is rhythm's self – and naturalness of expression . . .[10]

The rhythm is, to that extent, as baroque as his diction, for it is once more the accommodation of the regular and the irregular, or of form and unruly content. Like many of his theories, Hopkins's ideas on Sprung Rhythm were more rationalizations after the fact, to accommodate what he was already doing intuitively, than pondered formulations that he intended to follow thereafter.

It would be difficult to exaggerate the revolutionary quality of Sprung Rhythm, but it is equally hard to be sure how much effect it has had on successive generations of poetry in English, since it was not generally known until after the First World War, when regularity in poetic rhythms was already in the process of dissolution. Certainly, the publication of Hopkins's works came as a revelation to young poets in need of new gods, but in general it has been the spirit of experiment and informality behind his versification that has been most emulated, rather than the specifics of his prosody. If, as has been suggested, modern poetry is frequently derivative in manner from the conversation poems of Coleridge, Hopkins has often provided the example of directness and colloquialism of rhythm and language to accompany that manner. He has been one of the great liberating forces of twentieth-century poetry, certainly an inspiration but seldom a direct model. It would, in any case, be poetic suicide to ape a style as idiosyncratic as his.

'The Wreck of the Deutschland' is a deeply complicated poem whose complexity and grandeur of scale he was never to repeat. Probably not all of it works, and it often offends against a nice sense of precision and order. It can seem tasteless when it is judged by conventional standards, but it is too splendid and expansive to be amenable to 'good' or 'bad' taste. It is possible, too, that its forward movement is occasionally impeded by the sheer ornateness of language. But its success or failure should be judged today within its own terms rather than by the doctrinal considerations that in part marred it for Bridges.

It is not surprising that it is such a mixture of the successful and the occasionally mawkish, since it is the product of at least seven years of silent pondering without the relief of trying anything out on paper. When it was finally composed by Hopkins, it came forth with an urgency that seems almost sexual.

As if the return to writing poetry had fanned his need of greater warmth in Bridges's friendship, in 1877 Hopkins wrote to him from 'St. Beuno's (and not Bruno's) College, St. Asaph (nor yet Asaph's)', asking for a long letter. In a postscript, he asked, 'Usen't you to call me by my christian name? I believe you did. Well if you did I like it better.'[11] Thereafter he often wrote to 'My dearest Bridges', but he never used his friend's Christian name.

It has been calculated that in the last twelve years of Hopkins's life he and Bridges saw each other an average of once a year, and that each time they met something went wrong to spoil the meeting. Even in their correspondence they misunderstood each other frequently. But there had always been a deep tenderness for Bridges hidden beneath the occasionally brusque tone that Hopkins adopted in his letters, and it came out more frequently as the correspondence settled in after its re-establishment. Sometimes it showed itself in affectionate teasing, as when he wrote about some sonnets Bridges had sent. They were, he said, 'truly beautiful, breathing a grave and feeling genius, and make me proud of you (which by the by is not the same as for you to be proud of yourself: I say it because you always were and I see you still are given to conceit . . .)'.[12]

Bridges hated having his letters to Hopkins opened by others and had to be reassured that they were given only a cursory examination with the envelope torn half open and the contents seldom removed. But soon their letters were going back and forth as unreservedly as if they had just left Oxford. Their correspondence was chiefly concerned with poetry, full of Milton, Wordsworth's sonnets (as Hopkins said, 'beautiful as those are they have an odious goodiness and neckcloth about them which half throttles their beauty'),[13] and Bridges's own poetry, to which Hopkins gave meticulous attention. Apparently, however, he did not send Bridges a copy of 'The Wreck of the Deutschland' until two years after it had been rejected by the *Month*, probably because he could not face another adverse opinion.

In response Bridges sent a parody of the poem, to which Hopkins bravely said, 'Your parody reassures me about your understanding the metre.' But he followed up those words with a wealth of explanation, indicating clearly enough that he did not believe that Bridges had understood it in the least. Bridges's letter was the only one we know about in which he seems less than wholly gentle, and he may have been trying to respond in kind to Hopkins's bantering tone. He suggested it might be right to call the poem 'presumptious jugglery', but Hopkins only teased him mildly about his misspelling without taking offence. 'I cannot think of altering anything. Why shd. I? I do not write for the public. You are my public and I hope to convert you. You say you wd. not for any money read my poem again. Nevertheless I beg you will. Besides money, you know, there is love.' Because he thought Bridges had not given the poem a fair reading, he said that his 'criticism is of no use, being only a protest memorialising me against my whole policy and proceedings'.[14]

In their correspondence, which was almost continuous for the rest of Hopkins's life, Bridges often indicated what he disliked about his friend's poetry; he tried manfully, but he never could appreciate this particular poem, even while he recognized that it was probably the central one in Hopkins's works. Rhythm, diction and above all the religious content repelled him. When he came to edit the poem in 1918, he described it in words that have become almost as familiar as the text of the poem itself:

> The labour spent on this great metrical experiment must have served to establish the poet's prosody and perhaps his diction: therefore the poem stands logically as well as chronologically in the front of his book, like a great dragon folded in the gate to forbid all entrance, and confident in his strength from past success.

He was almost certainly wrong in this case, but it was not an unsympathetic reaction, nor does it in any way deserve the reproach that subsequent critics have heaped upon Bridges's head.

Bridges's opinion of the poem was shared by the Hopkins family. Nearly half a century after it was written, he indicated to Hopkins's sister Kate what he thought of it: 'That terrible "Deutschland" looks and reads much better in type – you will be glad to hear. But I wish those nuns had stayed at home.'[15]

CHAPTER XV

GINGER-BREAD PERMANENCE
1876–8

There is a slight puzzle about the poetry that Hopkins wrote at St
Beuno's, for the usual assumption has been that he quite literally
wrote none before 'The Wreck of the Deutschland'. However, one
present-day Jesuit priest who has spent many years at St Beuno's is
certain that there was always a tradition of informal verse during the
Theologate, written either as recreation or as the practice in language that is an inevitable part of the training of a Jesuit, and that
Hopkins would certainly have written verse in this way. Even so,
there would be no misrepresentation in saying that 'The Wreck'
was his first real poem since he had entered the Order, for recrea-
tional or assigned verses usually demand little but formal rhythm
and rhyme, which would have been a long way from his idea of
serious poetry. Certainly, a poet as self-contained as Hopkins
would not have been inclined to open his heart on demand, even as
part of his religious training.

Perhaps because his assigned verses had been obviously more
distinguished than those of his contemporaries, or perhaps because
word had gone around the College about the parts of 'The Wreck'
that his fellow Theologians had read, he was asked in the summer of
1876 to produce some verses celebrating the silver jubilee of the
episcopate of the local Catholic bishop, Dr James Brown: '. . . we
presented him with an album containing a prose address and
compositions, chiefly verse, in many languages, among which
were Chinese and Manchoo, all by our people, those who had been
or were to be ordained by his lordship'. A learned German wrote
the Oriental languages, and 'For the Welsh they had to come to me,
for, sad to say, no one else in the house knows anything about it; I
also wrote in Latin and English.'[1]

259

As usual, Hopkins saw some significance in the date, which celebrated both a quarter of a century of the diocese and the twenty-five years since the re-establishment of the Catholic hierarchy in England. All this, as well as the fact that the day for the ceremony was but two days after his own birthday. It was only several years later that he ruefully admitted that he had miscalculated the date of the re-establishment of the hierarchy, which had in fact been twenty-six years before. All the same, as Fr Jones had no doubt foreseen in suggesting that Hopkins write on the *Deutschland* disaster, he was a useful member of the community when he could write in at least three languages.

'The Silver Jubilee', unfortunately, might have been written by a thousand other cultivated versifiers in Great Britain capable of the tame joke in the penultimate stanza:

> Not today we need lament
> Your wealth of life is some way spent:
>   Toil has shed round your head
> Silver but for Jubilee.

Hopkins's attention seems far away, and no wonder, for at precisely this time he was hoping against fading hope that the *Month* was going to publish 'The Wreck of the Deutschland'. If serious poetry had so little chance, there was perhaps no reason to involve himself very profoundly in a celebratory jingle. Nor is there a great deal more to hold us in the occasional poem he wrote for the visitors' book of the George Hotel in Barmouth during the Theologians' annual 'Villa' in August 1876, inviting those 'who pine for peace or pleasure' to 'taste the treats of Penmaen Pool'.

But a month or two before these verses, in which Hopkins seems to be twiddling his thumbs, he had also written 'Moonrise June 19 1876', an arresting fragment conceived in the half-light of midsummer when he saw the moon above 'our' mountain, Maenefa, behind the College. Suddenly one realizes that the poet who had produced the wonderful jet of poetry about the *Deutschland* is still in full spate:

I awoke in the Midsummer not-to-call night, ⎮ in the white and
    the walk of the morning:
The moon, dwindled and thinned to the fringe ⎮ of a fingernail
    held to the candle.
Or paring of paradisaïcal fruit, ⎮ lovely in waning but lustreless,
Stepped from the stool, drew back from the barrow, ⎮ of dark
    Maenefa the mountain;
A cusp still clasped him, a fluke yet fanged him, ⎮ entangled
    him, not quit utterly.
This was the prized, the desirable sight, ⎮ unsought, presented
    so easily,
Parted me leaf and leaf, divided me, ⎮ eyelid and eyelid of
    slumber.

One wonders what the Bishop of Shrewsbury might have made of
verses of this kind had they been composed for his anniversary.

During 1875 and 1876 Hopkins's health continued to be good,
except for an intermittent complaint about 'indigestion', which is
not to be wondered at when one considers that the fare was so often
meat and potatoes and that the vegetables grown on the College
farm were never sufficient. In the spring of 1876 a whole party of
Theologians set out for Moel Fammau, a high hill 'distant as the
crow flies about nine miles'. Hopkins was one of only four men
who reached the destination, and he gave no indication of being
unduly tired by the eighteen miles. On the return walk he 'caught a
lovely sight – a flock of seagulls wheeling and sailing high up in the
air, sparkles of white as bright as snowballs in the vivid blue'.[2]
Reading his note, one is suddenly aware of how often his physical
sight at St Beuno's is literally directed upward; it is like a reflection
of his unusual happiness there, and both the looking up and the
happiness are reflected in his poetry written in Wales. 'The Wreck of
the Deutschland' released a flood of pent-up poetry, and before he
left St Beuno's nearly two years later he had written approximately
one third of all his mature poetry.

If we did not have the poems that Hopkins wrote in the first nine
months of 1877, not only the achievement of his own poetry but the
canon of the great works of the nineteenth century would look
considerably different. After not having written sonnets for years,

he turned towards them again and produced nine brilliant ones, of which at least two or three are undisputed masterpieces. Most readers would agree that the most important of the St Beuno's sonnets are 'God's Grandeur', 'The Starlight Night', 'As king-fishers catch fire',[3] 'Spring', 'In the Valley of the Elwy', 'The Windhover', 'The Caged Skylark', 'Hurrahing in Harvest', and what is perhaps his best-loved poem, 'Pied Beauty', which is a 'curtal sonnet' (an abbreviated version in which Hopkins tried to compress the form without changing the mathematical relationship of the octave and the sestet; in this case it produced a beautiful poem without convincingly demonstrating the necessity for such a form).

As is surely to be expected, many of the themes and ideas of these sonnets are already familiar to anyone coming fresh from 'The Wreck of the Deutschland'. 'Pied Beauty', for example, is a far simpler celebration in dappled things of the glory of the 'double-naturèd' aspect of the phenomenal world that had occupied Hopkins in the great ode. 'The Windhover' considers the same sense of transformation that illuminates 'The Wreck' but without the deep cost of pain and unbearable anguish. Almost more than at any other time in his career, he seems totally at home with the connection of God and nature, content to accept and praise it without, as Keats almost said, any irritable reaching after fact and reason. To put it in Hopkins's own terms, he seems never to have been so happily engulfed in unquestioning faith.

One of his most charming poems sprang out of his absorption in the natural beauty of the valley of the Clwyd, a sonnet called with good reason 'Spring'. It is alive with lambs and pear blossoms, the innocent sexuality of juice and joy, the blue of thrushes' eggs, and if there is an awareness that the Fall inevitably succeeded a previous Eden, or that innocent childhood is succeeded by a peccant maturity, such possibilities are considerably muted:

> Nothing is so beautiful as Spring –
>   When weeds, in wheels, shoot long and lovely and lush;
>   Thrush's eggs look little low heavens, and thrush
> Through the echoing timber does so rinse and wring
> The ear, it strikes like lightnings to hear him sing;
>   The glassy peartree leaves and blooms, they brush

The descending blue; that blue is all in a rush
With richness; the racing lambs too have fair their fling.

What is all this juice and all this joy?
    A strain of the earth's sweet being in the beginning
In Eden garden. – Have, get, before it cloy,

    Before it cloud, Christ, lord, and sour with sinning,
Innocent mind and Mayday in girl and boy,
    Most, O maid's child, thy choice and worthy the winning.

It is tempting to emulate Hopkins's attitude to nature in 1877 and simply to accept with thanks the beauty of the poems without questioning any aspect of them. In some ways, the best form of examination is quietly to read them. But this is perhaps to patronize the sonnets by not taking them seriously enough. Ungratefully, since charm is in short supply in the world, one feels that 'Spring' depends more on stock romantic responses than on intellectual provocation. The matter is important only when the St Beuno's sonnets are put beside 'The Wreck' or, more appropriately, next to the 'Terrible Sonnets' written at the end of Hopkins's life. As a man he was torn apart when he was in doubt, but it was precisely when he was impelled, perhaps neurotically, to examine all aspects of a problem, including its unattractive side, that his poetry came most fully alive. Poetically, he probably thrived more on uncertainty than on unadulterated happiness, and to that extent he is a good example of the unpalatable dictum that some poets must be destroyed personally in order to be whole artistically. So far as this sonnet is concerned, the problem is that neither the employment of the form nor the theme is conducive to complex thinking. It seems churlish not to yield to such innocent ecstasy, but 'Spring' finally impresses the reader as an enactment of Hopkins's perceptions rather than as an intellectual process bent on discovery, and to that extent is disappointing in a poet whose mind is so often explosively curious and investigative.

    The same objection might fairly be made to 'The Starlight Night' and 'God's Grandeur', but it hardly applies to 'The Caged Skylark'. Even less is it relevant to 'The Windhover', which he called 'the best thing I ever wrote'; in this case the poet was the best judge of his own works. The poem has been written about so exhaustively (and so contentiously) that further criticism would be otiose, but my own reading of it agrees with that group of critics who see in it transformation accomplished by reduction or destruction, precisely as Christ's glory was accomplished by His physical death. As the glorious bird is reduced to a heap of feathers, or physical grace crumples, or the chevalier and his steed are compacted to the ploughman and his plodding workhorse, so the beauty of Christ was destroyed physically. Yet from His death came the splendour of the gold and vermilion Crucifixion, and from the end of temporal beauty comes eternal beauty. The point here is not to quarrel over the 'meaning' of the poem but to indicate that the turning away from the physically celebratory to the spiritual is accomplished within the poem itself, so that the reader has full exposure to two kinds of perception, contradictory but equally valid views of life.

No one could expect even a sonnet as good as this to consider the question of transformation with the richness of a long ode like 'The Wreck of the Deutschland', but perhaps it has even more of the surprising revelation that is surely one of the pleasures of poetry and of the sonnet in particular. To read the two poems together is to become aware of the varying effects of leisurely contemplation and of revelation at a flash.

One brilliant critic of Hopkins's works takes another view of the sonnets, recognizing in them a contraction of the 'stylistic extravagance' displayed in 'The Wreck'. He chooses to 'characterize these poems with an image from the title of one of their number – the caged skylark. Unlike Shelley's "blithe spirit", Hopkins's symbol of the poet suggests limitation, entrapment, a kind of stifling imprisonment of the spirit.'[4] Without agreeing wholly with this view, one can see that it is a possible attitude to the change in Hopkins's works at St Beuno's. After this both the man and his poetry after seem cramped by doubt or fear but never threatened by sheer exuberance. After St Beuno's we are seldom aware of his eyes constantly being lifted in unclouded praise.

The one aspect of many men's lives that never comes near surfacing in Hopkins's letters or poems or journals at St Beuno's is having too little to do. While he was writing these sonnets he was preparing for his examinations in March in moral theology 'to see whether I am fit to hear confessions'. After that would come his final examinations in theology, to determine whether or not he went on for a further year of study in Wales, and at the end of the summer he would be ordained. Enough, it would seem, to occupy him when he was also writing poetry, but he continued with his Welsh, probably with the idea that he could use it the following year. 'I can read easy prose and can speak stumblingly', he told Baillie, but he had trouble with writing Welsh poetry, in spite of having tried his hand at it for Bishop Brown. He continued studying Hebrew, although he claimed it was only for practical reasons, and he flirted with the idea of learning Egyptian. Only too obviously, he was beginning to dither between interests, as he did when he was worried.

At the beginning of March he passed his examinations in moral theology, which left him very tired, as he told Bridges, scarce able to 'go or creep'. Perhaps because of his exhaustion he had a humiliating failure a week later, when he had to give a Sunday evening sermon in the dining hall of the College. How good his sermons had been before this we do not know, but at Manresa he had been very successful speaking of St Stanislaus, and he was probably expected to do well on this occasion.

He chose to talk on the miracle of the loaves and fishes and took as his text John vi, 10, 'Then Jesus said: Make the men sit down.' With admirable fidelity to the Composition of Place he had learned in the Ignatian Spiritual Exercises, he set the scene, beside the Sea of Galilee, and to make it easily imaginable, he likened it to the Clwyd Valley. It was, he said, 'shaped something like a bean or something like a man's left ear; the Jordan enters at the top of the upper rim, it runs out at the end of the lobe or drop of the ear'. The other Theologians were as tired as Hopkins, and their fatigue had no doubt brought on the disposition to hilarity that lurks so near the surface in young men. Hopkins was standing in the wall pulpit in the hall, above the seat of the Rector and the staff, and he was dismayed to hear laughter. Exactly where it started, he does not tell us, but it is easy to imagine that it began as he continued his geographical journey around the ear, the hair, the brow, the cheek, and 'the tongue of flesh that stands out from the cheek into the hollow of the ear'.

Hopkins was never one to stint learning, and bit by bit he continued setting the scene and explaining. Because Christ asked Philip where to buy bread, Hopkins made an excursion into His motives in asking the question:

> He said it to try him. Why to try St Philip. Here, brethren, remark a mystery. Philip is a Greek, not a Jewish, name; it has a noble air; it suits noblemen, like Guy or Marmaduke or Perceval – with us. It means fond of horses, proud of his stud; not fond as a groom is of the horse he grooms or a ploughman or a coachman of his team but as a wealthy man is of his stud, his show of cost and wealth and pride.

With all the detailed curiosity at his command, Hopkins examined each minute aspect of the story of the miracle, until the modern reader (and presumably the Theologians in his audience) becomes unclear about the point of the sermon. Yet the curious mixture of the learned and the homely in this discourse is closely related to the unexpected combination of orders of experience that makes his best poetry witty.

What else may have contributed to the mirth of the Theologians is not clear, but his intensity must have seemed amusing to them, presumably because it was very much what they already knew of Hopkins. At last, in one paragraph he said five times the words of Christ, 'Make the men sit down.' It was too much for his auditors. As Hopkins himself wrote, 'People laughed at it prodigiously, I saw some of them roll on their chairs with laughter. This made me lose the thread, so that I did not deliver the last two paragraphs right but mixed things up. The last paragraph, in which *Make the men sit down* is often repeated, far from having a good effect, made them roll more than ever.' A blue pencil mark on the sermon indicates the spot at which he had to stop speaking.[5] It must have been a humiliating experience for him, and it indicates that curious lack of proportion which he occasionally displayed in the pulpit when he wandered over the line of the witty into the ludicrous or inappropriate.

At the end of July Hopkins stood his final examination in dogmatic theology, an hour of questions conducted in Latin. In spite of his deep fatigue, he seems not to have anticipated any particular difficulty about it; probably he had done so well up to this point that he was justified in his confidence.

Each summer the Theologians were examined on their work of the past year in order to determine whether they should go on for another year of theology, the 'Long Course'. Hopkins had expected when he came to St Beuno's to stay for a full four years, and at the beginning of 1877 he had told Baillie that he expected to be ordained in September and then to stay on for his fourth and final year.

According to one Jesuit scholar who has carefully studied the records, one of the four examiners indicated that he had surpassed the average, one that he had barely surpassed average, one that he did not surpass average, and one that he was average. It was a sufficiently creditable performance for him to be judged as having passed the examination, but it was not good enough for him to continue his studies for a fourth year.[6]

There has been considerable guesswork about whether Hopkins's Scotism contributed to his poor showing in the examination, since the general tenor of the Order was anti-Scotist. But it seems improbable that his examiners would have allowed their feelings on the subject to influence their judgement of Hopkins. Probably his habitual inability to perform at his best in public was even more against him, and he was certainly not helped by that curious lack of empathy with an audience that had ruined his sermon on the Miracle of the Loaves and Fishes.

Technically, it was not a failure, but Hopkins can hardly have felt that way about it. All through Highgate and Oxford, and in his nine years as a Jesuit, he had done well in his academic work and had taken a Double First at Oxford, which was probably considerably more than any of his examiners had achieved, but none of that changed the fact that he had been found wanting. So far as he had known at the time, becoming a Roman Catholic had knocked out any chance of a post at Oxford, but now there seemed little chance that he would be given the best teaching positions in the best Jesuit schools or that he would be asked to return to St Beuno's or Stonyhurst to teach in the Seminary. Other circumstances were occasionally taken into account in keeping a man on for a fourth year in the Theologate, but none was sufficiently in his favour to mitigate his performance in the examination. There is no proof of it, but one cannot help wondering whether his complete *débâcle* in the pulpit played any part in the decision to demote him to the three-year course in theology and end his stay at St Beuno's.

It appears from his letters that when he left St Beuno's for his summer holidays on the day after the examination Hopkins still did not know the results. He was in London for nearly three weeks, most of it spent with his 'parentage' in Hampstead; his uneasiness with them is indicated by the casual phrase he used in telling Bridges they would 'put me up', a peculiarly impersonal way of referring to a stay with one's family. Before he returned to St Beuno's he had heard that he would be moving on that autumn: 'Much against my inclination I shall have to leave Wales,' he told Bridges.[7] While still in London he had an appointment with the Provincial, when he may have learned his destination on leaving St Beuno's after ordination.

The previous September he had been able to write entertainingly about its being the time of 'General Post', when new appointments were announced, but in 1877 there can have been little amusement for Hopkins in knowing that later in the autumn he was going to Mt St Mary's College, the Jesuit school near Chesterfield. When he came back from London to St Beuno's he wrote sadly, 'No sooner were we among the Welsh hills than I saw the hawks flying and other pleasant sights soon to be seen no more.'[8] Now he was leaving the place that had been more like a home than any since he had been a Jesuit. In his remaining time in Wales he walked, fished, and wrote poetry, then in the middle of September began the week of retreat preceding his ordination. On three successive days he and fifteen others received the major orders of subdeacon, deacon, and priest, the last conferred on Sunday morning. There was a grand luncheon in celebration, with 'Roast Mutton, Soup, ham & fowls', and a concert, followed by a Solemn Te Deum and Benediction. None of the Hopkins family was among the guests at the ceremony which capped his nine years as a Jesuit.

Six days after his ordination Hopkins was confined to his bed with illness, then on the 4th of October a surgeon from Denbigh visited the College 'and performed successfully on Mr. G. Hopkins circumcision'.[9]* His condition was presumably the reason for his being run-down the previous spring and for his being unable to fast more than one day a week in Lent.

His recovery was rapid, and a fortnight after his operation he left for Derbyshire. What he had heard about the place waiting for him at Mt St Mary's was not exhilarating: 'The work is nondescript – examining, teaching, probably with occasional mission work and preaching or giving retreats attached.'[10] There was only a small community in charge of the school, but it was said to be like a family. Although he had heard that 'the country round' was not very interesting, 'at a little distance is fine country, Sheffield is the nearest town. The people call the place Spink Hill, Eckington is the station.' His description sounds as if he were being sent into exile in an unknown land. Probably part of his distaste for what he had heard of the place was caused by his disappointment over his

---

* Recently several persons interested in Hopkins have suggested to me that his circumcision was for psychological rather than physiological reasons. In considering someone as ridden by sexual anxiety as he, it is probably natural to wonder whether Puritanical impulses connected with cleanliness or even with confused reparation for past sins (a symbolic castration?) may have had an unconscious part in his decision to have the operation. The suspicion is perhaps strengthened by his several mentions of circumcision in his correspondence and by what seems an unusual interest in the operation recorded in his undergraduate lecture notes. Furthermore, we know, from his preoccupation with the discipline of the eyes from undergraduate days until his death, how he neurotically connected what he regarded as sin with the corresponding physical organ; near the end of his life his obsession had so increased that he thought he was losing his sight by an incurable disease, although the oculist assured him that his eyes were perfectly healthy. It is a mental process that may well have psychological parallels with a wish to be circumcised.

Such speculation is not beside the point, but the truth of Hopkins's circumcision is probably a good bit simpler, since the usual reason for the procedure in adult men is the occurrence of phimosis, occasionally followed by balanitis, which may in turn cause ulceration: this would explain his being bed-ridden with his illness, an otherwise improbable result. Phimosis and the accompanying pain were probably at the base of his ill health in the spring of 1877, when he told his mother, 'I am thinner, I think, than ever I was before now.' In light of the primitive state of anaesthetics in 1877 and the risks involved in any operation, it is improbable that Dr Tournour would have performed the circumcision unless he thought it was necessary physically. It is perhaps less certain that Hopkins, ascetic as he was, would have shrunk from having the operation, even after the rigours he had undergone during his haemorrhoidectomy.

theology examination, which would have disposed him to be unhappy at almost any assignment that took him away from St Beuno's.

There was real cause for dissatisfaction among both clergy and pupils at Mt St Mary's. Particularly in the teaching of science, there was considerable pressure to bring up the standards of the place in a hurry. None of the Jesuit schools in England specialized in science, and it was hoped that there would be an influx of both Catholic and Protestant pupils if the old emphasis on classics were changed; the Society was willing to take in a good many non-Catholics if they could bring up the enrolment to three hundred, which was twice the number of boys when Hopkins was there.

So far the recruitment had not been very successful, and part of the reason for its failure was the generally bleak and inhospitable countryside in which the College was located. Another problem was that there was an inadequate supply of water because a nearby mine had taken away half the flow from the brook that filled the tanks. As a result, 'the boys used often to go without second washing for want of water – not a nice thing to be said of a College', as one priest remarked after the experience of 150 boys on a winter day. A great deal of money was needed for rebuilding the dilapidated property, and since it was not forthcoming, there was a general air of discouragement about the school, which seemed depressingly ready to accept its inferior status.

A set of new buildings was being put up, but they were done on the cheap and looked 'bald and stark'. The lawn 'between the Church and the garden front had been transformed into a howling wilderness of builders' materials, and the drive churned into ruts and quagmire by the wagon loads of brick and stone'. In the winter the snow was streaked with soot that must have made Hopkins look back with regret to the untouched view of Snowdon from St Beuno's.

What records we have of both Mt St Mary's and Stonyhurst indicate that there was far more change of teaching staff during the term than would be expected. Hopkins arrived several weeks after the beginning of the term at 'the Mount', but it was apparently not a matter for comment. He was given the title of 'subminister', indicating that he was in charge of the kitchens and refectory, rather like the steward of an Oxford college, but Fr Francis Keegan has concluded from the school records that he probably never actually performed those duties, since the need was much greater in the schoolroom, where the recent attempts to recruit in science studies meant that 'there was no one with any pretensions to classical scholarship'. There were strict rules governing the numbers of masters, and the 'appointment of a subminister may have been a device for securing extra staff without contravening regulations'.[11] None of this made him feel more at home in the College, nor did the assignment of teaching religion to the two senior classes without a compensating relief from the duties he was already carrying out.

It sounds like a replay of his experience at the Oratory (except that mercifully he was not being kicked on the football field, as he had been in Edgbaston). In Spinkhill he found, too, that the best part of his duty was his affection for his pupils. By the time he had been there a few months, he was writing home to his mother about them, 'I have become very fond of the boys I have had to do with as pupils, penitents, or in other ways. I think they lead a very happy life with us, though the discipline is strict.'

Chief among the boys Hopkins had in mind was one who sounds the sort of pupil any schoolmaster would like to teach. Pictures make Herbert Berkeley look a stumpy little tough, but his appearance belied him, according to Hopkins, for he was 'clever and hardworking and I had not much to do with the result'.

That year Berkeley ran off with three first prizes in competition with the other Jesuit schools: one for classics, one for religious knowledge, and the third for verse, although the records do not indicate whether for Latin or English poetry, both of which he would have been taught by Hopkins. A fellow schoolboy remembered him as 'one of the most gifted boys I ever knew. An excellent writer of English, witty and amusing of speech, a good classical scholar, actor and elocutionist and a pretty cricketer.' With all those attainments, however, 'he lacked in a marked degree the mathematical mind. He had no idea of value in goods or money, direction, distance.' Even so, it is not surprising that Hopkins was delighted with him.

Berkeley was presumably writing his entry for the poetry prize in April 1878 under the guidance of Hopkins, who would have been responsible for setting the topic for the competition, which that year was the loss of the training frigate *Eurydice*. She had been wrecked on the 24th of March by a sudden squall off the Isle of Wight with a loss of some three hundred seamen. There is no record of what the schoolboys made of the event, although it is improbable that they used the catastrophe as a way of considering the loss to England of the Roman Church at the time of the Reformation, as Hopkins did himself. He took the same subject and title for his own poem 'The Loss of the Eurydice', which he began writing at Mt St Mary's in April 1878. It would be revealing to know the reason for the coincidence: was his own poem a byproduct of the boys' competition, or did he assign the topic because of his own interest in disasters of the kind that had inspired 'The Wreck of the Deutschland', or did he want to work more closely with Berkeley? If the last, it seems to have been the only time that he even cooperated in writing a poem except with Dolben in his undergraduate days.

During the Christmas holidays at the end of 1877 the boys did not go home, but at school they presented 'plays and concerts every night', including two charity performances of the play whose mutilation at Stonyhurst had so amused Hopkins, when Lady Macbeth had been turned into Uncle Donald. 'Berkeley my particular pupil is a born actor,' Hopkins wrote to his mother, 'a very amusing low comedian and still better in tragedy; his Lady Macbeth, in spite of being turned into "Fergus" Macbeth's younger brother, was quite a "creation".' Hopkins himself wrote a prologue to the play, obviously with Berkeley in mind. It 'consisted in the speaker seeming to forget all the points, but Berkeley did it so naturally that he overshot the mark and most part of the audience thought he had forgotten in earnest and that his strange behaviour was due to "refreshments" behind the scenes'.

When he was preparing to leave the school, Hopkins wrote wistfully to his mother of Berkeley, 'I shall not easily have so good a pupil again.' It is tempting to wonder whether Hopkins was more impressed with the mind or the flattering personality of the boy, who was obviously an affectionate lad: 'He is eager to take down everything I say and repeats it with minute accuracy long afterwards.' Hopkins deeply needed affection, however rigid his exterior, and he may have been on the verge of wanting too much in this case.

Hopkins's general disposition to be moved by the young is nowhere more apparent than in 'Brothers', a poem written apparently after he had seen the loving mixture of pride and embarrassment of one of his pupils who sat waiting for the first appearance on stage of his younger brother in one of the plays given at the school for Shrovetide: 'with what heart's stress / He hung on the imp's success'. When at last the smaller boy makes his entrance, his brother is unable to watch him:

> . . . in his hands he has flung
> His tear-tricked cheeks of flame
> For fond love and for shame.

The sight of the boy's emotion is the occasion for the poet to recognize that love and empathy are as much a part of our natural heritage as evil:

> Nature, bad, base, and blind,
> Dearly thou canst be kind . . .

Probably true, but many readers feel that the emotions dealt with are too easy, ultimately inadequate as stimuli to provoke the conclusion. In short, it is a deeply sentimental poem about emotions that are a bit sloppy in adult readers, however moving they may be in children. Hopkins himself realized how slight the armature was on which to build the poem, and he tinkered with it for several years, trying to make it more Wordsworthian, but he never quite got it right. His innate kindness to children, which made him a sympathetic teacher, also predisposed him to find deeper meaning in the simple emotional reactions of young boys than most readers can summon up.[12]

Hopkins's tendency to spoil the young did not always make for either strong discipline in the classroom or even a natural caution about the antics of his pupils. One of the boys at the Mount recalled half a century later the advent of 'Fr. Gerard Hopkins, young and newly ordained, with a well deserved reputation for scholarship'. One day he assigned that tired Byronic chestnut 'The Assyrian came down' to be translated into Latin verse. To the boys' ill-concealed delight it was a poem which they had already 'turned into flawless elegiacs'. W.F. Lee had kept two or three verses of the earlier translation, which he slipped in among his own work. Hopkins was censorious about the latter, but alongside the crib he wrote, 'Extraordinarily good'. According to Lee, he 'had found the wheat amongst the tares, but was too trustful to have suspected me of borrowing, and I feel ashamed to have deceived him'. The good temper and affection of the boys at the Mount kept them from taking too much advantage of him, but when he went to University College in Dublin, the atmosphere was, if possible, less adult than that in Mt St Mary's, and his pupils, older and more cynical, treated him shamelessly with an unkindness that seems to have hurt him more than almost anything else in those unhappy years. There can never have been many men with more rigid control of themselves than Hopkins, but he had little of others.

Although he suffered from diarrhoea during the winter, Hopkins was in better physical shape, and for the first time in several years he said he had 'kept the strict Lent. It has left me no worse, but thinner than I ever saw myself in the face, with my cheeks like two harp-frames.' He took several pupils on trips to local beauty spots, the Norman ruin of Steetly chapel, the Duke of Newcastle's seat at Clumber Park, and Cresswell Crags, but his plans to accompany them to Chatsworth and Haddon Hall and Hardwick Hall were thwarted in late April when he received an unexpected summons to come to London that summer as an assistant priest at the Mayfair church of the Immaculate Conception in Farm Street. In the three intervening months he was to go to Stonyhurst once more, this time to coach the boys for their London University examinations. It was probably flattering, but Hopkins had begun to be more cautious about the possibility of permanency anywhere.

He regretted that his departure was just when the mining country around the school was being transformed into its 'gayest and prettiest, as vermilion tiles and orchard blossoms make it', but he was not sorry to turn his back on Spinkhill, where life had been 'dank as ditch-water'.

We have few records of his stay at Stonyhurst that year, but it seems that he was not overworked, for he began rewriting and adding to both 'Brothers' and 'The Loss of the Eurydice'. The latter, although it derives of course from the same interest in shipwreck that first drew him to 'The Wreck of the Deutschland', is a much simpler and more straightforward poem, a fact that recommended it to Bridges.

It is generally accepted that the nucleus around which the poem was formed was the description of an unidentified sailor, whose male beauty stands for the pricelessness of all that was lost in the wreck. Hopkins took infinite pains over the original lines, reworking them until he achieved the final version:

> They say who saw one sea-corpse cold
> He was all of lovely manly mould,
>   Every inch a tar,
> Of the best we boast our sailors are.
>
> Look, foot to forelock, how all things suit! he
> Is strung by duty, is strained to beauty,
>   And brown-as-dawning-skinned
> With brine and shine and whirling wind.
>
> O his nimble finger, his gnarled grip!
> Leagues, leagues of seamanship
>   Slumber in these forsaken
> Bones, this sinew, and will not waken.

Although he gives the real-life names of the captain and his mate, the wreck and the lost crew are actually as anonymous as the lone drowned sailor, and there is no single character in the poem to absorb our attention, like the nun in 'The Wreck of the Deutschland' or, for that matter, the poet himself in that poem. As Hopkins says of the drowned sailor, 'He was but one like thousands more.' If, as most readers feel, 'The Wreck' seems finally to be about Hopkins himself, 'The Eurydice' is decidedly impersonal, concerned with the fate of England rather than of any of its individual inhabitants, and to that extent becomes less immediate for the reader. There is far less of the reckless virtuosity of language, too, compared to 'The Wreck of the Deutschland'. Whatever Bridges thought of it, it has never had for most readers the appeal of the earlier work.

During his spell at Stonyhurst Hopkins resumed frequent correspondence with Bridges, sending him both ship poems, begging that he read 'The Eurydice' more than the one time he had tried the other. With the badly mixed feelings of most writers who ask for criticism, he was very thin-skinned about adverse comments by Bridges at the same time that he pooh-poohed his praise. Perhaps the best comment on his feelings is his own elaborately casual remark to Bridges: 'What you have got of mine you may do as you like with about shewing to friends.'[13] He still felt scarified by the experience of being turned down by the *Month*, but whatever he might say at other times, he had not wholly given up the idea of publication.

We are lucky that Bridges recognized the intention behind the words, for it is to him we owe the careful preservation of Hopkins's manuscripts. The more one reads of the one-sided remains of the correspondence between the two men, the more Bridges's character shines out as imperturbably patient and understanding with his friend, ready to put up with small snubs because he has the loving insight to see that Hopkins never felt anything but affection for him. If there is a touch of the stolid about Bridges that gets reflected in his poetry, it is also the source of the strength on which Hopkins counted so much. Without that strength Hopkins's mercurial intelligence and immense talent might have been hopelessly diffused, and he knew it. It is painful to read modern critics who are patronizing to Bridges, for Hopkins, who knew his real worth, was occasionally betrayed into slight condescension to Bridges, but behind his manner he never mistook him for less than he was.

While he was at Stonyhurst, not wholly occupied with his tutoring, Hopkins not only consolidated his intimacy with Bridges but began – or, rather, renewed – his acquaintance with the other poet to whom he was closest for the rest of his life. Richard Watson Dixon, as we have seen, had been an assistant master at Highgate School for some months in 1861, while Hopkins was a pupil. Since then he had been Second Master of Carlisle High School, and for the past two or three years had held a living in Hayton, a few miles from

Carlisle, where he lived as a widower with two stepdaughters, a pony, a clutch of cats, and a black retriever to which he fed port wine. He was tall, stooped, grey, with a straggly beard that gave him a frequently remarked and unfortunate resemblance to a scholarly goat.

From his schooldays Hopkins remembered him as the man 'who would talk Keats by the hour'. In 1864 he had run into him again at a large literary party at the Gurneys' house in London, but they seem not to have spoken to each other, and though Hopkins noticed the other man, he was apparently too shy to introduce himself. Nonetheless, he had continued reading Dixon's poetry and when he became a Jesuit and knew that he could not keep books of his own and was unlikely to come across Dixon's works in a seminary library, he had copied out several poems that he had kept with him ever since.

At Stonyhurst Hopkins felt the time had come to get in touch with Dixon once more, and he wrote to him, 'I take a liberty as a stranger in addressing you, nevertheless I did once have some slight acquaintance with you. You will not remember me but you will remember taking a mastership for some months at Highgate School, the Cholmondeley School, where I then was.' On leaving the school, Dixon had given a volume of his poems to another master, through whom Hopkins had come to know them. From there he went on to read the other volumes and to introduce them to his friends; 'if they did not share my own enthusiasm, [I] made them at all events admire'.

With a glowing goodwill that took the edge from his words, Hopkins pointed out that Dixon's work had almost disappeared from view. 'I do not know of course whether your books are going to have a revival, it seems not likely, but not for want of deserving.' Then, in a few sentences he recalled how moved he had been by Dixon's Pre-Raphaelite richness and 'medieval colouring'.[14]

At the time Hopkins was thirty-three and Dixon was twelve years older. He had settled into a quiet acceptance of the fact that his years of promise were over, that he was never going to light the sky with either his churchmanship or his poetry, and he had resignedly begun a six-volume work on the history of the Church of England that could be counted on to occupy him for the rest of an uneventful life. Hopkins's letter was the most exciting, the most unsettling thing that had happened to him for years.

For two days Dixon was unable to respond to the letter 'chiefly through the many and various emotions which it has awakened within me'. He was 'deeply moved, nay shaken to the very centre, by such a letter' which now was valued 'among my best possessions'. Breathing through his words is the not-quite-spoken feeling that in middle age, when he expected nothing, he had been stirred into life once more. His friend Burne-Jones the painter had said to him, 'One only works in reality for the one man who may rise to understand one, it may be ages hence.' To which he could now say to Hopkins with a full heart, 'I am happy in being understood in my lifetime.'

The warmth of his reply was the measure of the man, and it must have meant a great deal to Hopkins, particularly when he wrote:

> I think that I remember you in the Highgate School. At least I remember a pale young boy, very light and active, with a very meditative & intellectual face, whose name, if I am not vastly mistaken, was yours. If I am not deceived by memory, that boy got a prize for English poetry. I may be deceived in this identification: but, if you have time to write again, I should like to know. I little thought that my gift to Mr. Lobb, which I had quite forgotten, would bear such fruit.

With hardly more than a tremor he agreed with what he thought Hopkins had said about the advantages of having missed fame, which 'leads a man to try to excell himself, or strike out something new incessantly, or at least not to work so naturally and easily as if he did not know that the world was watching to see what he will do next'.[15] The tangle of rhetoric and double negatives is a clue to how little he really despised fame but was nonetheless anxious to agree with Hopkins.

In his second letter, written scarcely more than a week after the first, Hopkins answered ruefully that the want of fame may do as much to harm men as an excess, for it is 'a spur very hard to find a substitute for or to do without'. His conclusion, although perfectly orthodox in conception, sounds a bit off-centre here: 'The only just judge, the only just literary critic, is Christ, who prizes, is proud of, and admires, more than any man, more than the receiver himself can, the gifts of his own making.'[16] The words are neither hypocritical nor canting, but it is nonetheless easy to see how much Hopkins wanted both heavenly and earthly recognition, and who is to blame him?

For the rest of his life Hopkins was to maintain his correspondence with Dixon, judiciously praising what he liked about his poetry, gravely accepting Dixon's enthusiastic judgement of his own work. But Dixon's appreciation was not merely polite, and one frequently senses that he really liked Hopkins's poetry considerably more than Bridges did.

Improbable though it was that it should spring up between a rural parson and a Jesuit priest, this was the beginning of one of the most rewarding of Hopkins's friendships. The two men met only once in middle life, but what they lacked in shared experience of the outer world, they made up for by their common love of poetry. Often they seemed to understand each other without explanation, for they were both more at ease in letters than in person.

Occasionally, we feel that Hopkins was slightly rough on Bridges, but he was always gentle to Dixon, treating him unfailingly with an exquisite politeness, deferring to him even when he knew that he was right and Dixon wrong about an aesthetic matter. His consideration was quite unlike his brusqueness with his own family, since he felt no threat from Dixon. It is difficult to say how much Hopkins really thought of Dixon's poetry, for he clearly admired it but seems equally not to have felt in it the flash of genius. As the editor of the letters of Hopkins and Dixon wrote, 'Dixon's poems are far from incompetent, but some virtue that appealed with particular force to a former generation is less obvious now.'[17] Perhaps the very fact that Dixon was an Anglican was an improbable bond, since Hopkins often seemed to be making infinite allowances for a man who could be so admirable about other matters when he was so wrong in his religious belief.

According to Hopkins he had been for some time requested at Farm Street by the Rector, Fr Peter Gallwey, who was to become perhaps the best-known Jesuit of the day in England, and surely one of the best loved. In all the inevitable criss-crossing with other members of the Order, Gallwey had been the older priest who was most like a father to Hopkins, first as Novice Master at Manresa, then as Superior of St Beuno's and as Provincial of the Order. Clearly he felt a particular affection for the younger man, and he had given him a crucifix and other small gifts on Hopkins's leaving Roehampton; when Hopkins was ill at Stonyhurst, Gallwey sat patiently on the side of his bed, affectionately holding his feverish hand.

His generous heart and voluble affection made Fr Gallwey much beloved by those who knew him, either as fellow Jesuit or as spiritual guide, and made them forget his furious temper, which would turn his pale Italianate face blue with rage, so that his admiring pupils at Stonyhurst had been accustomed to refer to him as Blue Peter. He loved telling old chestnuts, with so much enthusiasm that no one ever had the heart to say how often they had been heard before. In church, however, he brought such thought and reverence to saying Mass and to his famous sermons that the services in Farm Street were startlingly popular with even those Protestants who had no thought of going over to Rome. He was a cultivated man who wrote poetry and loved music with a passion that seemed to be denied by the weak, tuneless voice with which he insisted on joining the choir. Hopkins felt great affection for him, and he would have been a most unusual man if he had not done so.

The previous year, after serving a term as Provincial, Fr Gallwey had returned as Rector to the Jesuit church in Farm Street, easily the most conspicuous of churches in the English Province (he was to remain there for three decades until his death in 1906), and he was building up a group of clergy suited for the centre of Catholic activity in the city.

Farm Street was one of the very few Catholic churches that could be said to be smart; it ministered to many fashionable worshippers, with congregations and penitents from far beyond the parish bounds in Mayfair. Four not untypical members of the congregation who looked to Fr Gallwey for spiritual guidance in the sixties were the Ladies Lothian, Buchan, Londonderry, and Herbert. It was where most well-born converts came to be received, and as a result it had a partially unfair reputation for keeping an eye out for parishioners more conspicuous for wealth and social position than for humble piety. For nearly two decades there were more than a hundred converts a year.

What no one could dispute was that the services were liturgically impeccable. The building, which was only a quarter of a century old, was one of the finest examples of 'the decorated English style of architecture' in the nineteenth century. It was dark and suitably mysterious in the nave, with a great explosion of light blazing above the high altar in the enormous window representing a Jesse tree (it has since been replaced by a smaller window). The preaching was by some of the best speakers in the Church, the vestments were opulent, and the choir was of a standard that put many English cathedrals to shame, with expansive Cherubini, Mozart and Schubert Masses most Sundays. Hopkins greatly preferred plain chant when he had an opportunity to hear it.

Obviously, Fr Gallwey was giving Hopkins a splendid opportunity, but what Hopkins himself thought of it is doubtful; if we can judge by his remarks a year or two later about smart congregations, it suited him less than perfectly, although he was happy to be in London again. It was, however, the kind of post to soften opposition to his vocation in his family and such doubting friends as Bridges, whom he was able to see frequently while he was there.

Even Hopkins had to admit that he was not overworked in Farm Street, and all during July he seems to have done little except to help hear confessions and say Mass, but he was nervously preparing a trio of sermons to be given the first three Sunday mornings in August. They have not survived, but we know that after the first he felt he had been inadequately prepared. It may well be that he was also worried about his preaching voice, which a friend in Dublin some years later found 'weak but sweet, rather plaintive'. Bridges was in the congregation, one of the few times he attended services in which Hopkins took part; his support of Hopkins was so wholehearted that he occasionally went to a Roman Catholic service, even when Hopkins had asked him not to do so. Typically, Hopkins was overcome with feelings of failure about the sermon, as he indicated to Bridges in an apologetic letter afterwards: 'I was a very little nervous at the beginning and not at all after. It was pure forgetting and flurry. The delivery was not good, but I hope to get a good one in time. I shall welcome any criticisms which are not controversy. I am glad you did not like the music and sorry you did not like the mass.'[18]

As often happened, Hopkins's account is quite at variance with what others saw. Bridges reported the same sermon to Lionel Muirhead: 'Gerard Hopkins is in town preaching and confessing at Farm St. I went to hear him. He is good. He calls here; and we have sweet laughter, and pleasant chats. He is not at all the worse for being a Jesuit; as far as one can judge without knowing what he would have been otherwise. His poetry is magnificent but "caviare to the general".'[19]

The other sermons went less well, even with considerable care put into them, and one of them was ruined by his inability to see what was appropriate to his congregation, the same lack of understanding that had sent his audience of fellow Theologians into fits of laughter at St Beuno's. In this case, his congregation is said to have been a group of women, presumably Mayfair ladies, to whom he was speaking about the efficacy of the sacraments. The sermon was pithy, allusive, and of course original, which last quality was his undoing. He compared the Church to a cow full of milk, with seven teats, the sacraments, through which grace flowed. Not surprisingly, his superiors were unhappy with his performance and he was presumably astonished that any offence could have been taken.

Since arriving in Farm Street, he had hoped to put down roots there, as he told Bridges, but he hedged his bets by not being optimistic: 'I am, so far as I know, permanently here, but permanence with us is ginger-bread permanence; cobweb, soapsud, and frost-feather permanence.' By November his suspicions were fulfilled. He wrote stiffly to tell Bridges he was returning to Mayfair after a brief trip away for a retreat in Windsor, 'But I am to leave London.'[20]

There was, of course, plenty of reason why the Order needed him elsewhere, since there was a severe shortage of Jesuit manpower at that period, as his work at Mt St Mary's had shown. Nonetheless, Fr Gallwey, as a recent Provincial of the Society, had wielded enough influence to get him to Farm Street in the first place, and it seems reasonable to believe that he might have been able to retain him if he had thought he was the right man for the post. No matter how much Gallwey's affection and admiration inclined him to make extra allowances for the younger priest, Hopkins was clearly not cut out for parish work, at least in Mayfair. From Farm Street he was bundled off to a curacy in Bristol, which was intended as a long-term assignment, but he cannot have been badly needed there, either, since after a week he was moved on again, this time to Oxford, the place one might have guessed for him initially. It would have been madness for him, or any other Jesuit, to expect anything more than ginger-bread permanence so early in his career, but the frequency of his moves must have made him worry about his own competence.[21]

CHAPTER XVI

THE VERY BUTTONS OF
MY BEING
1878–9

Whatever Hopkins's understanding of the matter, Fr Gallwey's request for him at Farm Street may have been intended from the beginning to fill only an interim or probationary position, for it was never easy for the Jesuits to find the right duty for this extraordinary priest. Clearly he was brilliant in spite of his comparative failure in theology, he was almost frighteningly devout and selfless in his spiritual duties, but he was also self-contained to the point of seeming withdrawn. For all his tractability and obedience, his manner sometimes failed to demonstrate absolute submission to his clerical superiors in mental and moral questions, and now and then there was a hint of peremptoriness to those under his care. When he did not work out as expected at Farm Street, it must have seemed an inspired solution to send him back to Oxford, scene of his scholarly successes and conversion, where his heart so clearly lay. In the last week of November 1878 he went to Oxford as curate in St Aloysius's church, which had been consecrated only three years before, and which he had not yet seen.

Hopkins had apparently not been in Oxford 'except once for three quarters of an hour' since taking his degree in 1868.[1] To any man first returning to his university, change is far more evident than continuity. The occasion is usually his initial awareness of the brevity of undergraduate history and of his own relegation to that grey mass of the elderly made up of all those who have passed out of academic life. It is a shock to realize that to a man of twenty, a thirty-four-year-old is scarcely younger than a sexagenarian even if, like Hopkins, he is sympathetic with the young.

When Hopkins's friend and contemporary Henry Scott Holland had been gone from Oxford less than a year, he wrote of his sense of loss, 'I can hardly help crying to think of the old Balliol days that are over; the dear old place that has been meat and bread to me all these years; no more to link her name with mine, no more to be hand and glove in all her life; this is dreadful.'[2] For Hopkins much more time than that had passed since he had last walked out of the gates of Balliol into the Broad, and the poignancy of his feeling of separation was heightened by his knowledge that much of it was due to his own conversion. He was to discover, as he told Bridges, that 'Small as Oxford compared to London is, it is far harder to set the Isis on fire than the Thames.'[3]

St Aloysius's was the culmination of years of trying to get a more suitable and central Catholic church than the little chapel of St Ignatius in St Clement's. Ever since 1861 the local Catholics had been petitioning the Bishop of Birmingham for a new place of worship that would not be a disgrace. As Newman put it, 'A back yard in St. Clements and a barn to say Mass in, are not the proper representatives of the visible Church.'[4] The Bishop of Birmingham referred to the school at St Ignatius's as a 'sort of scullery' attached to the priest's house. It was customary to say of the little church that it looked like a Dissenting chapel; in the midst of the Gothic revival, it was hard to see beauty in its round-headed windows and un-adorned simplicity, although most modern observers would think it considerably more attractive, even in its present debased state, than St Aloysius's, to which it had become a mere adjunct.

The new church was big and graceless, looking more French than English, and usually described as being in the 'Transition' style, which was one way of avoiding more precise definition. It had cost £7000 and was built to the plans of Joseph Aloysius Hansom of Birmingham, with whose architectural efforts Hopkins was already familiar at St Beuno's. When Hopkins first saw it, the yellow brick of which the church was built had not yet been softened by soot and time; the gaunt, high-shouldered bulk stood at the beginning of the Woodstock Road, at the junction between ancient Oxford and the new suburbs of red-brick propriety erupting to the north. These were seats for four hundred and opti-mistic provision for enlargement of the church to seat as many again, since the parish was huge, extending from Binsey on the west to the county border at Thame on the east.

A row of shops formed a screen that hid the church from the street, except for a narrow pathway leading back to the door. As the Jesuit publication *Letters and Notices* admitted candidly a century later, 'There was, at the time of the new church . . . the danger or supposed danger of the building being rushed by a mob, and so the actual church was set back from the street, with a narrow entrance that even now can't take a fire engine.'[5] Hopkins had a sitting room and sleeping alcove in the imposing presbytery looming over the church, which he assured Bridges were 'very comfortable'.

As its builders had feared, there was a great deal of hostility to the new church, so threateningly close to the centre of the city. In a burst of Protestant indignation, the *Oxford and Cambridge Undergraduate's Journal* of 13 June 1878 said that the only reason for the Jesuits' 'being in Oxford is their singular skill in argument, persuasion, and propagandism' and that the 'avowed object of the church is to reclaim students, and to bring them back to the true fold'. The journal was particularly indignant that the presbytery was 'inhabited by a band of brethren, whose sole object is to guide men of money, or weak brains, or both, into the Romish haven of rest and peace'.

In an amusing reversal of their usual demand to be treated as adults and allowed to do their own battles, the undergraduates now accused their elders of leaving them unprotected:

When the Great Western Railway works were likely to invade Oxford, a shout of indignation came from the University authorities. Dirty mechanics would demoralize the tone of undergraduate minds, and an influx of working men would be subversive of all order in the streets. When the scheme of the Cowley Military Centre was propounded, a strenuous opposition was raised by many academic notables, lest the officers of the army should inoculate students with new vices, and the common soldiers spread immorality among the citizens of Oxford. But when rumour said that the Romish Communion was about to build a church, furnished with all accessories of decoration and ritual, a church to be served by a staff of clever controversialists, selected with special reference to the needs of Oxford, there was no bold protest sent forth by the College Dons, to whose care nearly two thousand young men are intrusted, and who are naturally expected by parents to act the part of guardian to their offspring, and to do something more than merely teach their sons how to win intellectual honours.

Somewhat priggishly the newspaper pointed out that after all 'Parents send their sons here to be educated, not to be captured as converts for Rome' by what was described as 'a trained band of Proselytizers'.[6] The journal was in part right to suspect that St Aloysius's had been intended to stimulate the flow of Oxford converts. The consistent appointment of convert priests to serve it indicated the hope that clerical example might inspire another generation of undergraduates to come to Rome. This is presumably why Hopkins had seemed unusually qualified to go there from Farm Street.

The truth was that the Jesuits wanted badly to recruit for the middle ranks of the Roman Church in England; at the top there had always been a residual few of the aristocracy, mostly descended from Recusants, and there had always been the lower classes, many of them deriving from Ireland and Scotland. But there had not been an educated and professional middle class in the Church in England for centuries, and it was that unhealthy gap that both Newman and the Jesuits recognized and sensibly thought to begin filling by conversions from the universities.

A further suggestion that St Aloysius's was intended in part for proselytization was the fact, surely more than coincidental, that it had been built on the edge of the land Newman had bought some years before in the expectation of establishing an oratory for the joint use of Roman Catholic undergraduates and townspeople, hoping that it might in time become a hall in the University and at last a full college. Newman had been soundly defeated on that issue by the combined opposition of the prelates Manning, Wiseman and Vaughan, who were worried that the attraction of Newman's presence might make Oxford too alluring to Roman Catholic youth. But even without Newman in the vicinity, St Aloysius's might still fulfil some of the functions intended for an oratory, and it was in an air of conciliation that Cardinal Manning had been invited to preach at the consecration of the church. Unfortunately, he took the opportunity to deliver a scorching denunciation of both tone and teaching of the University.

The priest in charge of the church in 1878 was Fr Thomas Brown Parkinson, whom Hopkins had known at Stonyhurst. He was formerly a Church of England clergyman, and he never quite lost the air of his first ordination. According to his obituary, 'Father Parkinson's manner through life still retained much resemblance to that of an Anglican parson, and was particularly suave, serious almost to demureness, and impressive by reason of the judicial gravity and air of conviction with which he in measured terms pronounced his opinion.'[7] As one undergraduate in Hopkins's time remembered him, 'Both in appearance and character he was the most typically English, John Bullish person I have ever known. He used sometimes to stretch himself slightly with much deliberation (he was already sufficiently large) and to say slowly with great distinctness of utterance – as unlike an Italian as anyone possibly could be: "And they say that *I* am a Roman."'[8]

Some of his fellow Jesuits pretended to believe that Parkinson's initials stood for 'Truly Benevolent', and in time this slid over into the less flattering undergraduate name for him, 'Extreme Unction'. He was known, both within the Church and without, as being unusually receptive to conversions. One near-convert who slipped through his plump fingers was Oscar Wilde, who regularly came to breakfast. He daydreamed 'of a visit to Newman, of the holy sacrament in a new Church, and of a quiet and peace afterwards in my soul', until at last he was sure he was 'caught in the fowler's snare, in the wiles of the Scarlet Woman' – and made his escape.[9]

On the numerous occasions after Sunday evening service when he entertained undergraduates in the presbytery Fr Parkinson carefully cultivated his donnish airs and loudly professed fidelity to his own Cambridge. Once he went so far in his loyalty as to refuse to drink in celebration of an Oxford victory over Cambridge on the playing fields.

Hopkins usually managed to hide his exasperation from Parkinson, but occasionally his sense of humour overcame him when writing to Bridges. Once he reported on his superior's reading of Bridges's poems:

> The hymn to Nature is fine and has much impressed the mind of my chief, Fr. Parkinson, the Parkinsonian mind, I shd. prefer to say; who read it murmuringly out over tea, with comments and butter. But as he read it I was struck with a certain failure in the blank verse.[10]

Good manners normally defeated irritation, but when they slipped, one can see why his clerical superiors were less than pleased with Hopkins.

Hopkins was so different in temperament from his expansive 'chief' that he never got on easily with him. Parkinson was thought by some to be 'distant, close-handed, and perhaps a little selfish'.[11] Hopkins might have added that he also expected a great deal of work from a curate, since he was asked to do everything that had been taken care of earlier by two priests. It should be added in favour of Parkinson that he had got on well with the Irish members of his parish in Glasgow, and it was perhaps in recognition of that skill that he had been brought to Oxford, with Hopkins added as his assistant to lend intellectual weight to the presbytery.

With some reason the clergy of St Aloysius's felt that the University authorities totally ignored them except when trying to keep undergraduates from attending their services, and that they were habitually regarded from afar with the innate distrust most Englishmen felt for Jesuits. Their fellow Roman Catholics distrusted converts from the Oxford Movement as much as Anglicans did. They had a reputation for being troublesome because they were not agreeable to starting their religious lives from the beginning again, either as laymen or as priests, but asked to be accepted immediately into the Church of Rome. Convert priests were always distrusted, and some ignorant parishioners refused to be baptized or confessed by them, or to receive Communion at their hands, in the belief that ordination, even within the Church, could not be valid for such men.[12] It could hardly have been a more trying position for Hopkins, returning to the city he loved and finding that he was now an outsider from both Anglicans and Roman Catholics. To be a convert was bad enough, to be a Jesuit was to be doubly suspect.

Unfortunately, the flood of University-trained deserters from the Church of England had dwindled in Oxford to little more than a trickle. In 1879 there were thirty-nine converts in the parish of St Aloysius's, but few of them were of the middle classes. In the University the real growth in religious fervour was in High Church Anglicanism, and as its popularity waxed, the Roman conversions waned. Across Walton Street, only a few hundred yards from St Aloysius's, lay the new High Church parish of St Barnabas, where the church had been consecrated the year after Hopkins took his degree. At the other end of Oxford, not far from the chapel in St Clement's, were the Anglican Cowley Fathers and their mission, from which they were to be seen emerging daily, striding around the city, conspicuous in their habits. St Thomas's, which for years had been a lonely bastion of Ritualism near the railway station, was now only one, and not the most important, of the Oxford churches where incense, confession and reservation of the Sacrament were to be found. It was to these churches that the fickle youth of the University were going. O.R. Vassall-Phillips wrote that a year or so before, 'When I first knew Oxford, Catholicism was hardly in the picture at all.'[13] Between St Barnabas's in Jericho, and Cowley at the eastern extreme of the city, all Oxford seemed in possession of High Church, including the enclave of Pusey, Edward King, William Bright, and Liddon at Christ Church.

Once the natural Oxford drift had been from Ritualistic Anglicanism to Romanism at St Aloysius's, a progression indicated in a much later rhyme attributed to Ronald Knox:

> The rather-rathers
> Go to the Cowley Fathers;
> But the whole-hoggers
> Go to Allowoggers.

By 1878, however, it had begun to seem that Ritualism, in offering so much that had previously been the sole province of Rome, was actually stopping conversions. By now there were enough chasubles in Anglican churches to have satisfied even Dolben, although some of them were fairly exotic, usually because their wearers were

unfamiliar with more traditional vestments.* Gladstone noted that
the new wealth flooding England was often allied with ritual, and
that new churches, vestments, altar frontals and the like were
evidence of a kind of conspicuous consumption of goods showing
off the donors' wealth in a fashion so socially acceptable that it
nearly sanctified ostentation.

In Oxford St Barnabas's had been established in Jericho, the mean
quarter lying between Walton Street and the canal. It was intended
for the spiritual welfare of the residents who worked in the University Press and the small factories nearby, but it had become
unexpectedly fashionable, drawing precisely those members of the
University that St Aloysius's wanted to attract. Even Walter Pater
was to be seen there occasionally. As a Fellow of one college said,
'When I want a spiritual fling I go to St Barnabas.' On Sundays the
narrow streets of Jericho were choked with carriages, and undergraduates poured in to fill all twelve hundred seats for the 11 a.m.
High Celebration ('High Mass' was still not in common usage
among Ritualists). The music was superbly performed, with Mer-
becke eventually giving way to Gounod and Mozart. The vicar and
his two curates were all Christ Church men and celebrated in full
vestments before tall candles scarcely visible through the haze of
incense in the sanctuary. It was all considerably more ritualistic than
St Aloysius's, and one bewildered convert, who had been a
parishioner at St Barnabas's, complained sadly that worship at St
Aloysius's seemed extremely bare, even Spartan, in comparison.[14]

It was noticeable elsewhere that many of the most militantly
Ritualistic churches were in unfashionable areas, as were both St
Barnabas's and the Cowley Fathers. Even in London the leading
churches in the movement were such parishes as St Alban's,
Holborn; St-George's-in-the-East; and St Barnabas's, Pimlico, all
of them in working-class districts or slums. And it was undeniable
that their very location gave worshippers the pleasant thrill of

* The more outré devotees loved inventing their own dress. One perhaps extreme
example was Robert Stephen Hawker, Rector of Morwenstow, Cornwall, the
excesses of whose liturgical garments may be guessed from his usual attire for
walking around his parish: a purple cassock and brimless hat, which he claimed
was like those worn by the Greek clergy, hessian boots and a blue fisherman's
jersey in the side of which was knitted a red cross at the spot where the centurion's
spear had pierced Christ's side.

ecclesiastical adventure, even of something illicit, that attendance at a Roman Catholic church had once done. In its bid for respectability in Oxford, St Aloysius's had succeeded only in achieving a dull middle-class sobriety in a building of considerable banality. The tall Italianate campanile that Blomfield had designed to soar above the stark walls of St Barnabas's was plainly visible from St Aloysius's and seemed to dwarf it both architecturally and in spiritual attraction.

To the east of St Aloysius's, even closer than St Barnabas's on the west, stood the brand-new chapel of Keble, the High Church college built in memory of the founder of the Oxford Movement. Rising boldly above the entrance to the University Parks, the blindingly red and white building seemed an emblem of the triumph of Tractarianism in Oxford. Perhaps most telling for Hopkins was the fact that it had been designed by the one modern architect he admired almost unreservedly, William Butterfield, whose buildings he had travelled around the country to see, and whose work at Merton and Balliol had inspired him while he was still an undergraduate. Bracketed by two of the triumphs of Victorian architecture, St Barnabas's and Keble, both of them Anglican, St Aloysius's dwindled into visual unimportance in the city Hopkins loved best.

St Aloysius's must have seemed doubly austere to Hopkins after the vestments, the Cherubini and the dim religious light of Farm Street, which was so conspicuous an exception to the starkness of most Catholic churches in the country. It was, of course, no surprise to him that his feelings for beauty were less well served by the Roman Church than they would have been had he remained an Anglican; he had realized this much at the time of his conversion, when he wrote to his father, 'I am surprised you shd. say fancy and aesthetic tastes have led me to my present state of mind: these wd. be better satisfied in the Church of England, for bad taste is always meeting one in the accessories of Catholicism.'[15]

'Bad taste' in the Church was a real hurdle for many would-be converts and even acted as one well into our own century. Evelyn Waugh, for instance, believed that it was a peculiarly English phenomenon: 'The medieval cathedrals and churches, the rich ceremonies that surround the monarchy, the historic titles of

Canterbury and York, the social organization of the country parishes, the traditional culture of Oxford and Cambridge, the liturgy composed in the heyday of English prose style – all these are the property of the Church of England, while Catholics meet in modern buildings, often of deplorable design, and are usually served by simple Irish missionaries.'[16]

Although St Aloysius's had succeeded St Ignatius's as the centre of Oxford Catholicism, it had not wholly replaced it, for many members of the University and of the old county Catholic families still preferred to attend Mass in familiar surroundings. The congregation of St Aloysius's, in contrast, was largely composed of Irish servants from north Oxford, itinerant navvies and bargees from the canal beyond Walton Street, and some of the shopkeepers and lodging house keepers who were beginning to be received into the Church. It was a dramatic contrast to Hopkins's undergraduate life and his friends of a decade before, who had chiefly been sons of the squirearchy and aristocracy.

Hopkins not infrequently spoke of how much he liked simple parishioners with no social skills, but the truth was that he seldom found it easy to be at home with a class much different from his own. A letter he wrote to his family shows how awkward he felt with the Oxford congregation:

On Monday evening we had a small parochial concert . . . Neither voices nor choice of music was very good, still the effect is humanising, as they say. There was some recitation also. It was given by our Young Men's Association: they are shopkeepers and so on, a fine wellmannered set of young men, but their peculiarity and all our congregation's (excepting the University men and some of the gentry) is that they have a stiff respectful stand-off air which we can scarcely make our way through nor explain, but we believe it to be a growth of a University, where Gown holds itself above and aloof from Town and Town is partly cowed by, partly stands on its dignity against Gown. These young men rally to us, frequent and take parts in our ceremonies, meet a good deal in the parishroom, and so on, but seem as if a joke from us would put them to deep and lasting pain.[17]

The clue to his attitude to social distinctions is surely in the one word 'humanising'. Here, as in several other parishes he served, Hopkins was regarded with respect, even a guarded affection, but apparently never with familiarity. It would have taken someone more self-confident than he to be completely at ease in an unfamiliar background. Unfortunately, it was probably difficult to warm to the slight, somewhat vehement young priest with an effeminate manner and the disconcerting habit of waving a large red pocket handkerchief to punctuate his conversation. Those who per-severed, however, found him lovable.[18]

Hopkins was not the kind of priest to be unduly interested in making conversions: certainly, he felt the duty to save souls that was basic to his faith, but he was not keen on rivalry with the Anglican Church, nor did he feel the competitive urge to count up the numbers of converts that animated many of those who left Canterbury for Rome at the same time that he did. Nonetheless, when he went to St Aloysius's he could hardly help being affected by the waning popularity of conversion.

The most striking relic of his stay in Oxford is a photograph of the University Catholic Club, taken in the portico of St Aloysius's With Hopkins are Fr Parkinson, largely and comfortably planted in his chair in the front row, among thirteen undergraduates, their beards, moustaches and bowlers making them look a good bit older than the clean-shaven Hopkins, who was a decade senior to most of them. But he is removed by a good deal more than age. He stands to one side of the group, his back against a buttress, his eyes turned sideways to the camera, the whole tense angle of his body suggest-ing his detachment from the others, as if his attention were far away. As usual his expression is reserved, hoodedly enigmatic, and the light that falls prismatically on the planes of his cheeks is a totally exterior illumination, giving nothing away. It is difficult to believe that he felt much in common with the men around him.* There

*See plate 13a. In the original photograph the man with folded arms standing two places away from Hopkins is actually a cut-out figure pasted into a convenient gap in the back row. In the copy of this picture reproduced in *All My Eyes See*, p. 7, the effect of Hopkins's isolation within the group is lost because the full-length figure of this same man (identified as both 'B. Flanagan' and 'Terence Wolfe Flanagan', p. 6) has been added to the left of Hopkins; a careful scrutiny shows that Flanagan's figure is slightly out of proportion to the others in the photograph. Apparently he could hardly be a more telling contrast to the group picture taken when he was an undergraduate himself, surrounded by friends at Balliol (see plate 6a).

The Catholic Club was the precursor of the Catholic chaplaincy, which was not established until twenty years later. Although they may not have represented all the Catholics then in the University, the handful of young men on the steps of St Aloysius's indicates how slow conversion in the University was in 1879. Probably three or four were converts, but the Irish names of others suggest that they were already Catholics when they arrived in Oxford.*

The official position of Congregation in Rome and the hierarchy in England, which Newman had been unable to budge, was that it was dangerous to their faith and morals for Catholics to attend a heretical university, and their parents were supposed to ask leave in the confessional before sending their sons to Oxford. Cardinal Barnabó, Prefect of Propaganda, had said that it was next to impossible to imagine circumstances in which Catholics could, without sin, attend non-Catholic universities. Converts were expected to leave the University when they became Roman Catholics, but in practice few of them did so, and some clerics even defended their right to remain. It was debatable whether the Jesuits themselves were not at least skirting the prohibitions of the hierarchy by encouraging the Catholic Club, but they were in a slightly anomalous position outside immediate jurisdiction of the diocese, with direct allegiance to the Pope through their Provincial, and hence perhaps less vulnerable to control.

*According to Shane Leslie, in 1872 there had been only eight Catholic undergraduates in Oxford, and a decade later there were only four Englishmen among the ten Catholics in the University. The rules and constitution of the Catholic Club list sixteen members, including Hopkins, but this seems to include graduates as well as undergraduates in residence.

was absent when the original picture was taken, and the photographer inserted his figure before making a final copy of the group.

One suspects there may have been more fakery involved in the photograph, since the two figures just to the right of the central column (B.F.C. Costelloe standing, O.R. Vassall-Phillips seated) resemble each other so startlingly as to look like identical twins; the curiously huddled quality of the head of Vassall-Phillips suggests that a photo of the head of Costelloe may have been substituted for his own.

Newman, who had twice been defeated in his plans for a Catholic college in Oxford, continued to suggest that it was to the advantage of both Church and University for young Catholic intellectuals to study at Oxford, and he reasonably pointed out that they were in no more danger from mixed education there than they would be if they were to attend Sandhurst or Greenwich, which were not forbidden to them. 'Catholics did not make us Catholics,' he wrote. 'Oxford made us Catholics.'[19]

In spite of the abolition of the religious tests for the University, undergraduates were still required to attend chapel in their colleges, where the services were of course Anglican, although they could be excused from attendance by their own colleges, as Hopkins had been. Occasionally the University proctors would stand at the door of St Aloysius's, taking the names of undergraduates who went in for Mass. They were considerably more lax, however, about patrolling the little chapel of St Ignatius in St Clement's, where Hopkins himself had been apprehended in 1866. Some undergraduates who came to Mass were still Anglicans while tottering on the edge of conversion, but attendance there did not seem so much like a public announcement of their intentions as an appearance at St Aloysius's. The Jesuits had turned the chapel over to the diocese in 1859, but in 1872 they resumed its care, providing celebrants and preachers, so that it acted as an outpost of their own mission. (It continued in use until 1911.) Something of the hostility that the chapel instilled in its neighbours in St Clement's is indicated by the fact that the Sacrament there had to be locked into an iron safe to keep it from sacrilege.

Much of Hopkins's time in Oxford was spent in St Ignatius's, an atmosphere far more congenial to him than St Aloysius's, and there he saw more of undergraduates than he did with Fr Parkinson. He watched over the running of the little school at St Ignatius's, since there was not yet one at St Aloysius's, and acted as chaplain to the infirmary at Nazareth House, which took care of small children and the aged. He was also expected to minister to prisoners in the gaol.

Another important part of his duty was as chaplain to the 52nd Light Infantry in the Cowley Barracks ('over the hill/There'). It is somehow hard to imagine Hopkins among soldiers, but he left one important legacy of that period in 'The Bugler's First

Communion', in which he writes tenderly of a young Irish boy who received the Eucharist from Hopkins's hands for the first time, and of his own emotions on that occasion:

Here he knelt then ín regimental red.
Forth Christ from cupboard fetched, how fain I of feet
    To his youngster take his treat!
Low-latched in leaf-light housel his too huge godhead.

There! and your sweetest sendings, ah divine,
By it, heavens, befall him! as a heart Christ's darling, dauntless;
    Tongue true, vaunt- and tauntless;
Breathing bloom of a chastity in mansex fine.

Frowning and forefending angel-warder
Squander the hell-rook ranks sally to molest him;
    March, kind comrade, abreast him;
Dress his days to a dexterous and starlight order.

How it dóes my heart good, visiting at that bleak hill,
When limber liquid youth, that to all I teach
    Yields tender as a pushed peach,
Hies headstrong to its wellbeing of a self-wise self-will!

Hopkins was always moved by innocence in the young, particularly when it showed itself in religious observance. It is a subject that must be treated carefully to avoid mawkishness. In this poem his concern that the boy might grow up into less than his promise is so strong that it seems overwrought. Because of its insistence on the bugler boy's 'limber liquid youth' and his 'mansex fine', the poem is occasionally cited as proof of Hopkins's homosexuality, but it is more convincing as a demonstration of his wince of pain at the prospect of the inevitable corruption of innocence. And it is hardly surprising that in the Victorian Army corruption should have been sexual in nature. There are overtones of strong sexual awareness in the poem, but they are subservient to the theme of the transience of purity. Within two months of the events recorded the bugler went overseas to the Punjab. It says something of Hopkins's fastidiousness about sexual corruption that when he sent the poem to Bridges he wrote with it, 'I am half inclined to hope the Hero of it may be killed in Afghanistan,'[20] presumably so that his innocence might be preserved.

Like many men leading lives primarily of the mind, Hopkins felt an exaggerated admiration for men of action or those who were much at home in their bodies; it colours such poems as 'The Loss of the Eurydice', 'Felix Randal', and 'Harry Ploughman', as well as 'The Bugler's First Communion'. In these works the virility that is an implied theme helps ward off the sickliness of sentiment that overwhelms the sonnet 'The Handsome Heart', which also grew out of Hopkins's parochial experience in Oxford. He told Bridges that 'two boys of our congregation gave me much help in the sacristy in Holy Week. I offered them money for their services, which the elder refused, but being pressed consented to take it laid out in a book. The younger followed suit; then when some days after I asked him what I shd. buy answered as in the sonnet.'[21] According to the poem the boy 'with the sweetest air' replied, 'Father, what you buy me I like best.' The sonnet slips over the edge into the sentimentality that always threatens Hopkins's poetic treatment of children. The same excess is noticeable in the language of his subsequent note about the smaller of the boys: 'The little hero of the Handsome Heart has gone to school at Boulogne to be bred for a priest and he is bent on being a Jesuit.'[22]

His need of the help of the two boys, Hopkins explained, was 'that my chief Rev. T.B.P. has thought well to break his collarbone and be laid up in a charming country house commanding the White Horse Vale, throwing the whole of the work at the hardest time of the year on his underling'. Another time he described Fr Parkinson as having 'sprung a leak (exema) in his leg and been laid up and I in consequence laid on all the harder'.[23] Lenten services would in any case have occupied the time of two priests, but he was suddenly left to himself, with the additional duties of St Ignatius's, the Barracks and the Infirmary to fill.

Even with heavy parochial duties he was occasionally lonely in Oxford. With the loyalty Hopkins had come to expect, Bridges made the trip down from London to see him, and a few old friends looked him up; Lionel Muirhead, for example, came into Oxford from his country house, Haseley Court, to see him, and seems to have invited him to stay there. However, his prickly fear of being patronized as a Jesuit probably made him feel less welcome than he actually was. As an old member of Balliol, he would surely have been welcome, even as a Jesuit, but he seldom went there, if ever. He saw something of Jowett, but the years had not increased their intimacy. One of his friends had earlier written to warn him that Jowett was becoming an exaggerated version of his younger self, refining the essence of his self-regard:

> Jowler preached yesterday in Chapel amidst intense excitement, 110 people in Chapel. He looked so fatherly and beautiful and brought out the best bell-like silvern voice with quite rich tones that he had hitherto hidden in the depth of his stomach, and preached the most lovely little practical sermon in a quite perfect style with the most wonderful grace. I have only said all this laud in anticipation of having to confess that though I felt how beautiful it was in its way, it was most unsatisfying to me. It was just Platonism flavoured with a little Christian charity: Christianity is gutted by him . . . He is perfectly self-sufficient; self-dependent, without any consciousness of anything beyond a certain human weakness in carrying out his ideal; there is not an atom of the feeling of prayer, of communication with God, of reliance on any one but self.[24]

Hopkins seems to have been willing to overlook the foibles of his old tutor, who had by now fulfilled his long ambition to be Master of Balliol: he commented merely, 'Jowett has been preaching curiously.' Nonetheless, they saw little of each other.

Another of the Fellows he saw infrequently was T.H. Green, whom Hopkins as an undergraduate had found rather offensively heterodox. Now, however, he saw that he was 'upright in mind and life', and he called on him at least once. 'I wish I had made more of the opportunities I had of seeing him in my 10 months at Oxford,' he wrote regretfully some years later, 'for he lived close by.'[25] It was a relationship doomed by both ideas and personality, for Green found it hard to convey personal affection when he so disliked everything that Hopkins's Church stood for:

It vexes me to the heart to think of a fine nature being victimised by a system which in my 'historic conscience' I hold to be subversive of the Family and the State, and which puts the service of an exceptional institution, or the saving of the individual soul, in opposition to loyal service to society.[26]

Perhaps the only one of his old friends who became much closer to him during Hopkins's time as a priest in Oxford, and who appealed to him considerably more than either Jowett or Green, was Francis de Paravicini, who had been an undergraduate acquaintance and was now a Fellow of Balliol. The fact that he seems usually to have been entertained at the home of the Paravicinis rather than at Balliol may suggest that he was unsure of his welcome in his old college. It may also indicate how far out of the intellectual mainstream of Oxford his host was, for a contemporary wrote that 'Paravicini was a fine scholar, interested neither in politics, metaphysics nor religion; and he led a somewhat solitary and . . . a very careless life.'[27] Since Paravicini's wife was also a Catholic convert, Hopkins had no need to feel awkward in their house at being a priest, as he did elsewhere. After he left Oxford he confessed to them that he had been unhappy, 'but there were many consolations and none pleasanter than what came from you and your house',[28] a pretty building very near St Aloysius's.

Hopkins had never totally lost touch with Walter Pater, and he had been pleased to hear, only a year before he returned to Oxford, that Pater remembered him vividly and continued an interest in him. In the decade intervening since Hopkins was an undergraduate, Pater had become something of an Oxford star because of his *Studies in the History of the Renaissance* with its famous – or scandalous, according to one's view – conclusion, invoking the authority of aesthetic experience as a guide to life and exhorting the reader to burn with a hard gem-like flame. During the same period he had also become sexually involved with a Balliol undergraduate, and as a result had become estranged from his old tutor, Jowett; the matter had been hushed up, and there is no reason to think that Hopkins knew of it, but his continued friendship with Pater may have contributed to the awkwardness with Jowett.[29]

Pater was one of the first of former friends whom he met on his return. 'More of my acquaintances are up than I thought would be', he wrote to Bridges. 'I have seen Pater.'[30] It was heartening to find that one of the best-known men in Oxford greeted him with pleasure. At least two or three dinners together followed for the two men, and possibly a few of the long peripatetic conversations they had engaged in when Hopkins was an undergraduate. In February 1879 he had dinner with Pater and his sisters in the overstuffed comfort of their north Oxford house.[31] There was obviously no time for him to see much more of his old tutor, and his statement after he left Oxford that 'Pater was one of the men I saw most of'[32] did not necessarily mean that they had often been together. The irony of their being friends is underlined by Bridges's saying of Hopkins that when last heard of, 'he was *converting Pater at Oxford*. Whether he is actually sent to undermine undergraduates steadily or not I cannot say.'[33] Sadly enough, there is no indication that during his stay in Oxford Hopkins either saw or got in touch with Liddon, who maintained his rooms in Christ Church for occasional stays after moving to London when he became a canon of St Paul's Cathedral; in any case it is improbable that they would have had much in common after their split over Hopkins's conversion.

To Hopkins's pleasure, his aunt, Mrs Marsland Hopkins, widow of his father's brother, took a house that year in Holywell Street, near the rooms where he had lived as an undergraduate, and he seems to have been in her house frequently. In the spring of 1879 his sister Kate came to Oxford to stay with her and to see Gerard. He also went to occasional concerts, and he continued his long walks around the city.

When he was helping with pastoral work in Chesterfield, Hopkins had seen a little of the day-to-day slog of a parish priest, but his chief allegiance had been to Mt St Mary's. There had been a few parish duties connected with Farm Street, too, but life in Mayfair was scarcely the usual experience of a Jesuit priest, in spite of having to say Mass, preach, hear confessions, and probably help instruct the converts who came there from all over England. In Oxford for the first time he lived the life of the majority of the members of the Society of Jesus, hearing the confessions of the illiterate, visiting the sick, sitting for long hours at the bedsides of the dying, helping to teach in the school at St Ignatius's, organizing the clubs and guilds and sodalities connected with the Church, walking several miles a day back and forth across Magdalen Bridge between St Aloysius's and St Ignatius's or on to the Barracks or the Infirmary. It is the aspect of nineteenth-century Catholic priesthood that evokes the smell of waxed linoleum and oil lamps, straight wooden chairs with slippery leather seats, impermeable sofas in tightly closed sitting rooms, and corridors adorned with mass-produced oleographs of the Holy Family. Like most of us, Hopkins tended to subscribe to the romantic notion that the life of his poor parishioners was mysteriously more 'real' than that of the Fellows of the colleges in Oxford, and the knowledge that Balliol lay only a short distance away, across St Giles, made him guiltily aware of how much his life had changed, how much grace had gone from it in the acceptance of Grace.

It is small wonder that he sometimes became vehement in asserting his preference for the life of the poor, but his protestations smack of self-preservation rather than hypocrisy. His hurt at feeling excluded also makes understandable some notes for a sermon in St Ignatius's that would otherwise seem intolerably complacent:

> *This is the house of God*, this is the gate of heaven. None but you and the congregation at St. Aloysius' can say this. See the old churches, temples of God turned to dens of thieves. Pious according to their lights but are children of those who stoned the prophets, i.e., of those who persecuted the people of God.[34]

On the whole, Hopkins seems to have been fairly unsuccessful as a parish priest. According to a fellow Jesuit who has studied his pastoral career, 'Hopkins, it seems, was a man who in his shyness felt enormously awkward when he had to perform any public task. His mind and his hand seem to freeze; he begins to worry and fuss, and nervousness seems to consume him before even the most routine public utterance.'[35] It is moving to see the manuscripts of some of his poems from 1878–9, jotted down on the backs of appeals for the needleworkers of St Aloysius, who did their sewing at St Joseph's Convent in Wellington Square under the supervision of Mrs de Paravicini. Of necessity poetry fitted itself into the cracks of his day and sprouted in his moments of reflection.

The sad truth was that Hopkins was largely cut off from his roots, a stranger to those with whom he had more in common in background than he had with his own Order and Church. Oxford, which he had once claimed in a burst of undergraduate exuberance as 'my park, my pleasaunce', had become a private garden in which he feared to trespass. He was often in a black mood, he told the de Paravicinis, one in which his chief consolation was 'not only the literal sun but nature and the many things which make Oxford attractive'.[36]

He was, of course, in the habit of turning to nature for consolation. At St Beuno's, with the magnificent valley of the Elwy at his feet, it had been easy enough to believe in the constant Divine renewal that kept nature from being touched at its core by man's depredations, so that the worst ravages, moral and physical, were wiped out in a daily reassertion of the sanctity of the external world. That assertion also became for Hopkins an avowal of the holiness of man's nature. In Wales he had written one of his most exultant sonnets, 'God's Grandeur', celebrating the immutability of nature, in a kind of Maker's guarantee by the third Person of the Trinity:

> The world is charged with the grandeur of God.
>   It will flame out, like shining from shook foil;
>   It gathers to a greatness, like the ooze of oil
> Crushed. Why do men then now not reck his rod?
> Generations have trod, have trod, have trod;
>   And all is seared with trade; bleared, smeared with toil;
>   And wears man's smudge and shares man's smell: the soil
> Is bare now, nor can foot feel, being shod.
>
> And for all this, nature is never spent;
>   There lives the dearest freshness deep down things;
> And though the last lights off the black West went
>   Oh, morning, at the brown brink eastward, springs –
> Because the Holy Ghost over the bent
>   World broods with warm breast and with ah! bright wings.

When Hopkins returned to Oxford, it had become difficult to be confident that man could not ruin the world, and his hesitancy may have owed something to his stay in Derbyshire, its beauty disfigured by mining, then to the pressure in London of the great Victorian slums crushing in on every side, deforming both inhabitants and townscapes. Oxford itself seemed bleared with toil and trade as it began the change from small, somewhat rural university town to rail hub and business centre, poised on the brink of becoming a manufacturing city. Even the University was expanding cancerously, and the north Oxford houses of angry red brick were obliterating the pale Cotswold stone of the medieval town. Nature, which once had been so exquisitely attuned to the town, was now portioned into the gardens of the new villas and the domesticated walks of the University Parks. The spiritual ambience of Oxford retained little but an attenuated whisper of the Middle Ages, almost unheard in the roar of the nineteenth century.

In 'Duns Scotus's Oxford', his magnificent tribute to the philosopher 'who of all men most sways my spirits to peace', Hopkins wrote of the souring decay of grey beauty of the

> Towery city and branchy between towers;
> Cuckoo-echoing, bell-swarmèd, lark-charmèd, rook-racked,
>   river-rounded . . .

It was hard to keep in mind that the 'base and brickish skirt' of the nineteenth century had not wholly cancelled the memory of Duns Scotus himself, who in this poem takes on something of the shy and fugitive symbolic meaning that the Scholar-Gipsy had once had for Arnold.

Some of Hopkins's scrupulous attention to physical transience can be seen in 'Binsey Poplars', to which he added a subscript, 'felled 1879'. At the beginning of February that year he wrote to his mother of the violently changeable weather that had plagued him. 'The long frost, severer, it is said, at Oxford than elsewhere, has given place to great rains and those to fine weather. The floods are high: they were high before the frost too, so that the great expanse of Port Meadow was covered over and the room for skaters above and below Oxford was perhaps as much as you could get anywhere.'[37]

Hopkins could not be pent up indoors by rough weather nor kept by it from walking the wind-swept Port Meadow to his beloved Binsey, visible across the river behind the great double row of aspens hanging over the towpath, where the bells of the city and the hoot of the railway receded into imperceptibility. A fortnight after he wrote to his mother, Hopkins began a letter to R.W. Dixon telling him that he had come back to Oxford and had been walking in the wintry river landscape that had inspired Dixon to some of his own poems, to which Hopkins tactfully refers:

> You will see that I have again changed my abode and am returned to my Alma Mater and need not go far to have before my eyes 'the little-headed willows two and two' and that landscape the charm of Oxford, green shouldering grey, which is already abridged and soured and perhaps will soon be put out altogether, the Wytham and Godstow landscape. . . . We have passed here a bitter winter, which indeed still holds out, and Oxford is but its own skeleton in wintertime.

Hopkins was lured away from the opening of the letter into a discussion of Sprung Rhythm, in one of the digressions that were becoming more common in letters to intimates now that he had so few comrades with whom to talk in person. The byways of rhythm detained him, and he did not sign the letter until two weeks later, on the 12th of March. Once more he was dilatory about sending off the letter, and the following day he added a bleak postscript reflecting his shock: 'I have been up to Godstow this afternoon. I am sorry to say that the aspens that lined the river are everyone felled.'[38]

At best aspens are short-lived, and it is impossible to guess how many generations of trees have been there before the row of saplings that line the banks today, but in his momentary desolation the destruction seemed to Hopkins irremediable, an emblem of the loss that man inflicts on the planet. The trees that he had known and loved since he was a brand-new freshman were gone, and with them had gone his youth. Since childhood the felling of trees had been intolerable to him, causing an anguish that was probably neurotic and finally inexplicable, but which clearly had something to do with his sense of the impossibility of ever making amends for destruction or of replacing any object or created thing, since the inscape of each made it literally irrecoverable.

His feelings were perhaps in part familial, for his father in January 1879 published verses in a local Hampstead paper lamenting the proposal to fell some trees in Well Walk, where Keats had lived. Mr Hopkins sent the lines to his son in Oxford, whose sensibilities on the subject may have been sharpened by reading them almost exactly a month before the stumps at Binsey were to shock him so profoundly. The day he came upon the ruined riverscape he wrote 'Binsey Poplars':

> My aspens dear, whose airy cages quelled,
> Quelled or quenched in leaves the leaping sun,
> All felled, felled, are all felled;
>   Of a fresh and following folded rank
>   Not spared, not one
>   That dandled a sandalled
>   Shadow that swam or sank
> On meadow and river and wind-wandering
>   weed-winding bank.
>
>   O if we but knew what we do
>   When we delve or hew –
>   Hack and rack the growing green!
>   Since country is so tender
>   To touch, her being só slender,
>   That, like this sleek and seeing ball
>   But a prick will make no eye at all,
>
>   Where we, even where we mean
>   To mend her we end her,
>   When we hew or delve:
> After-comers cannot guess the beauty been.
>   Ten or twelve, only ten or twelve
>   Strokes of havoc únselve
>   The sweet especial scene,
>   Rural scene, a rural scene,
>   Sweet especial rural scene.

In itself the loss of the aspens was poignant enough, but by one of those grim little ironies that seem so common in Hopkins's life, it was made even more significant because the trees had been cut down for use as brake blocks, or 'shoes', for the locomotives of the Great Western Railway, the company that had always seemed to Hopkins the arch-enemy of the beauty of the Thames valley landscape.[39] Hopkins, who loved the names of the 'gear and tackle and trim' of all occupations, clearly had been fascinated by the railway term, which came tumbling out of his memory as he wrote the poem, accounting for the curious word 'sandalled' to indicate the negligent elegance of the trees before their felling, contrasting with their mundane use as shoes, the raw material of commerce. The poem is a good example of how Hopkins constantly brought together in his poetry so many discrete aspects of his sensibility: the irrecoverable loss of time, the integrity of nature and his love of it, the thoughtlessness of man, the gradual loss of the England he loved by industrial depredation, even the roots of the alienation he felt in Oxford.

By April 1879 he had become convinced that he would not be kept on at St Aloysius's: 'I do not much expect to be long at Oxford. I shd. like however to see the Spring out.'[40] There is no indication of why he thought he would soon be moved again, although he could hardly have helped knowing that his parochial work had not been exemplary. The usual time for changing posts was in the early autumn, and Hopkins might reasonably have expected at least another six months in Oxford. Moves were made at the disposition of the Provincial, but Hopkins probably believed Fr Parkinson did not regard him sympathetically and had no intention of making any special plea to keep him on as curate. 'In all Hopkins' comments on reassignment the only unusual aspect', according to Fr Feeney, 'lies in how frequently he expected a change even when none proved forthcoming.' Some ten or twelve times he demonstrated his penchant for 'groundlessly foreseeing some new assignment'.[41] In nearly every case he felt he had somehow been inadequate, and it was perhaps easier to believe that a new assignment had been given without reason than to admit to himself that it was in part his own doing.

At Oxford there seem to have been further grounds for his

defensive fears, somehow connected with his undergraduate career. It is a teasing business, with tantalizingly little evidence about its nature, although it obviously had some connection with his feelings of alienation during his time at St Aloysius's. 'I hardly know what you allude to at Oxford, it is better that I should not,' he wrote to Bridges after he had left St Aloysius's. 'I used indeed to fear when I went up about this time last year that people wd. repeat against me what they remembered to my disadvantage. But if they did I never heard of it.'[42] It sounds as if he had a particular incident in mind, rather than any general feelings about him; the easiest explanation would be that he feared the rediscovery of something discreditable he had done as an undergraduate, but if so all record of it has disappeared. It seems more probable that the ruction over his conversion a decade earlier had ballooned in his memory into a full-blown scandal, one that had never existed. What is most interesting in his hunted reaction is that he should have believed others would recall anything of so little general significance.

Because practically all of his letters to Hopkins were destroyed, there is no evidence of what Bridges had written, but months later Hopkins was apparently still worrying at the matter to Baillie: 'I could have wished, and yet I could not, that there had been no one that had known me there. As a fact there were many and those friendly, some cordially so, but with others I cd. not feel at home.'[43] It is a small matter, about which we shall probably never know more, but it does indicate how often Hopkins was beset by monsters of his own begetting.

When he worried about his inadequacies Hopkins consoled himself by reflecting, perhaps ungenerously, that whatever had gone wrong was as much Oxford's fault as his own and that any failure in human relations was the doing of others. To blame his surroundings for his unhappiness was as much a part of his personality as celebrating them when he was buoyant. Six months after leaving, he explained to Baillie why he still felt bitter about his stay in Oxford:

You say it is something of an affectation for me to run up the Lancashire people and run down 'Oxonians' – unpleasant word, let us say the Oxford ones. I do not remember quite what I said; are you sure it was, as you assume, of Gown, not Town I was speaking? Now I do like both. Not to love my University would be to undo the very buttons of my being and as for the Oxford townspeople I found them in my 10 months' stay among them very deserving of affection – though somewhat stiff, stand-off, and depressed. And in that stay I saw very little of the University. But I could not but feel how alien it was, how chilling, and deeply to be distrusted.[44]

To Bridges he was even more frank about his disappointment in his Oxford parishioners:

I saw little of University men. . . . My work lay in St. Clement's, at the Barracks, and so on. However it is perhaps well I am gone; I did not quite hit it off with Fr. Parkinson and was not happy. I was fond of my people, but they had not as a body the charming and cheering heartiness of these Lancashire Catholics, which is so deeply comforting; they were far from having it. And I believe they criticised what went on in our church a great deal too freely, which is d—d impertinence of the sheep towards the shepherd, and if it had come markedly before me I shd. have given them my mind.[45]

He had been wrong in guessing the length of his stay in Oxford, but he was right in thinking that he would not be kept there. Early in October he was sent to Bedford Leigh near Manchester to help in St Joseph's parish for three months, before moving to Liverpool.

CHAPTER XVII

LEIGH AND LIVERPOOL
1879–81

A change of parish assignment from the gardens and pale stone of Oxford to the 'smoke-sodden' little brick town of Bedford Leigh between Manchester and Liverpool would not be the first choice of most clergymen, but Hopkins declared that he was very glad to make the move, although there is little to substantiate such a claim except his profound feelings of disappointment at his Oxford year. Leigh was 'a darksome place, with pits and mills and foundries', but he said he felt at home almost at once. 'Oxford was not to me a congenial field, fond as I am of it', he told Baillie; 'I am far more at home with the Lancashire people.'[1]

'Leigh is a town smaller and with less dignity than Rochdale and in a flat' he wrote to Bridges, whose home had been in Rochdale after his widowed mother's remarriage; 'the houses red, mean, and two storied; there are a dozen mills or so, and coalpits also; the air is charged with smoke as well as damp; but the people are hearty. Now at Oxford every prospect pleases and only man is vile, I mean unsatisfactory to a Catholic missioner.' Nearby was St Helen's, 'probably the most repulsive place in Lancashire'.[2] But in Leigh approximately a quarter of the inhabitants were Catholic, filling the twelve hundred seats in St Joseph's church (another unhandsome building by the architect of St Aloysius's), and the eight hundred pupils in the school 'being nearly all neatly dressed, present a smart and attractive appearance'. The only great drawback was that the workers were 'too fond of frequenting the public-houses', a habit that Hopkins, who never learned to skirt a problem, determined to meet head-on in the pulpit.

At this distance it is not difficult to see that what Hopkins loved in Leigh was that his flock was welcoming and respectful, with no 'd—d impertinence of the sheep towards the shepherd'. And in Leigh there was no group so hyper-critical as the University community in Oxford, which had robbed him of his fragile self-confidence. Possibly he was also helped in Leigh by not having to prove himself, for he knew that whether he performed his parish duties well or ill, he was to be there only three months, until the arrival of the exiled German Jesuit who was to replace him. His congregations would not be so critical of his sermons as they had been in Farm Street, and it would be hard to imagine the down-to-earth labourers being shocked by a reference to the likeness of the sacraments to the seven teats of a cow.

They appear to have been equally unperturbed by Hopkins's saying how much he looked forward to seeing the transcendent physical beauty of Christ, describing Him in terms that sound saccharine to us, though presumably they did to neither Hopkins nor his congregation: 'moderately tall, well built and tender in frame, his features straight and beautiful, his hair inclining to auburn, parted in the midst, curling and clustering about the ears and neck as the leaves of a filbert, so they speak, upon the nut'. His awareness that his words were accepted uncritically by his congregations almost magically made him know how to speak to them, and his sermons at Bedford Leigh are among the best he ever delivered, colloquial and direct. In preaching on the evils of bad company, he spoke of the way it leads inexorably to drunkenness,

> which is shameful, it makes the man a beast; it drowns noble reason, their eyes swim, they hiccup in their talk, they gabble and blur their words, they stagger and fall and deal themselves dishonourable wounds, their faces grow blotched and bloated, scorpions are in their mind, they see devils and frightful sights.[3]

There is no indication of what his sermons did to the attendance in pubs, but at least his parishioners knew unequivocally what he thought. 'I dearly like calling a spade a spade', he said of preaching, but before coming to Leigh his frankness had not worked well.

His new ease in the pulpit speaks of his happiness in the rest of his life at Leigh. Whether his rough parish liked him as much as he liked them is debatable, for he must still have had some of the difficulties of getting close to them which he suffered with his Oxford parishioners. What is more important is that he believed they were very fond of him. 'And then it is sweet to be a little flattered and I can truly say that except in the most transparently cringing way I seldom am.'[4]

It is not surprising that his contentment as a priest made him more sensitive to the feelings of his friends, more aware of when he had spoken woundingly. To Bridges he wrote a letter of apology for having criticized his poetry severely enough to damage his self-esteem; it is so gentle and affectionate that it seems almost worthwhile for him to have offended in the first place:

> One thing you say in your last is enough to make me quite sad and I see that I shall have to write at some length in order to deal with it. You ask whether I really think there is any good in your going on writing poetry. The reason of this question I suppose to be that I seemed little satisfied with what you then sent and suggested many amendments . . . You seem to want to be told over again that you have genius and are a poet and your verses beautiful.

The last sentence is an echo of his usual teasing, but with a tenderness that had not been habitual in their correspondence. Patiently he outlines his admiration of the quality of Bridges's mind and soul, even his appearance: 'If I were not your friend I shd. wish to be the friend of the man that wrote your poems. They shew the eye for pure beauty and they shew, my dearest, besides, the character which is much more rare and precious.'[5] It says much for the maturity of affection in both men, but particularly in Hopkins, that he could write in this way in the calm assurance that Bridges would not be made uncomfortable. It also suggests that his ease at Leigh had rubbed off on to his relationships with old friends.

Since his first exchange of letters with Dixon, they had been corresponding regularly. While Hopkins was still at Oxford Dixon had asked to see 'The Wreck of the Deutschland' and 'The Loss of the Eurydice'. Hopkins had sent them to Bridges, but when they were returned, he was pleased to let Dixon have them (he had but one copy, for it was such labour to write them out, so that they were in constant danger of being lost forever). Dixon read them with 'delight, astonishment, & admiration. They are among the most extraordinary I ever read & amazingly original.' With whole-hearted but flat-footed admiration he suggested that they should be published: 'Can I do anything?' He had just finished his next volume of Church history, in which he had mentioned the Society of Jesus, and he proposed to insert 'an abrupt footnote' about Hopkins's poems. 'You may think it odd for me to propose to introduce you into the year 1540, but I know how to do it. My object would be to awaken public interest & expectation in your as yet unpublished poems.'[6]

Thereupon ensued a comic minuet of misunderstanding between the two. From the very first letter he had received from Hopkins, Dixon misunderstood his position about publication and fame. Hopkins, who had actually been sympathizing with Dixon for not having gained attention, tried to make him understand that, no, he wasn't totally averse himself to becoming famous . . . But Dixon was one of those generous correspondents who makes up his mind at once what his friends mean and continues trying to help them articulate their wishes, even when he has completely misunderstood. In this case he thought Hopkins was so shy that he could not bear to come before the public, and that all he needed was a firm hand from a friend.

To Dixon's offer of putting a notice about his poems in the forthcoming volume Hopkins said that 'it would not at all suit me', for he expected the offer to 'come from one of our own people', and that to publish would be 'a sort of insubordination to or double-dealing with my superiors. . . . The life I lead is liable to many mortifications but the want of fame as a poet is the least of them. I could wish, I allow, that my pieces could at some time become known but in some spontaneous way, so to speak, and without my forcing.'

What he did not mention was that he had his sights set a good bit higher than a note in a book of Church history, for he was hoping that 'The Loss of the Eurydice' would be published by the *Month*, even if its predecessor had been refused by the editors. His polite refusal of Dixon's help seems clear enough, but it was misunderstood, for Dixon thought he was too shy to accept the push he needed. He then proposed to send the poem, or at least a part of it, off to the local Carlisle newspaper. His ambiguous style did not make it clear whether he merely intended to or had already done so.

With admirable forbearance Hopkins refrained from saying that publication of a section was not what he had in mind and least of all in a provincial newspaper, but he begged Dixon not to send it if it had not already been dispatched: 'If it is too late to recall them the matter can not be helped.' In any case, 'no great harm will have been done, since Carlisle papers are not likely to have more than a local circulation'.

It is not easy to see how Dixon could have misunderstood that, but he was so intent on being helpful that he was quite unable to take in the clear message from Hopkins. Less than a week later Hopkins was writing somewhat hysterically, 'Pray do not send the piece to the paper; I cannot consent to, I forbid its publication. You must see that to publish my manuscript against my expressed wish is a breach of trust. . . . You say truly that our Society fosters literary excellence. Why then it may be left to look to its own interests.' Besides, he asked, how could a clergyman of the Church of England 'stand godfather' to some of the verses mourning the loss of Catholic England to the Anglican Church? Dixon's reply to Hopkins's impassioned plea has not survived, but he seems not to have been offended at his declining his offers of help; indeed, he seems scarcely to have noticed. 'You are very welcome to shew my poems to anyone you like,' Hopkins wrote, 'so long as nothing gets into print.'[7]

In the event, the *Month* decided not to publish the poem. It was not quite the end of Hopkins's hopes of publication, but it indicated clearly that it would be difficult for him to find a place to publish that would be suitable for a Jesuit.

It is hard to be precise about what Hopkins thought of the possibility of fame for his poetry, although some writers have seen no difficulty in the task.[8] For example, Fr Devlin, editor of his *Sermons*, begins that fine edition with the uncompromising statement that 'Gerard Hopkins set small store by poetic fame.'*

---

* In fairness it should be added that he obviously had some second thoughts on the matter before finishing the introduction to the edition.

Hopkins's blanket permission to Dixon (and to Bridges) to show his poems to any interested reader hardly indicates a desire for anonymity, nor do his instructions to Bridges about the disposition of his works after his death:

> When I say that I do not mean to publish I speak the truth. I have taken and mean to take no step to do so beyond the attempt I made to print my two wrecks in the *Month*. If some one in authority knew of my having some poems printable and suggested my doing it I shd. not refuse, I should be partly, though not altogether, glad. But that is very unlikely. All therefore that I think of doing is to keep my verses together in one place – at present I have not even correct copies – that if anyone shd. like, they might be published after my death. And that again is unlikely, as well as remote.[9]

It would be hard to find a more patent example of desire to publish struggling through conventional modesty. So Bridges took it, for he felt this was justification for his publication of his friend's poems many years after his death.

In 1886 Hopkins made an even more overt statement of his position:

> . . . before God, I would have you and Canon Dixon and all true poets remember that fame, the being known, though in itself one of the most dangerous things to man, is nevertheless the true and appointed air, element, and setting of genius and its works. . . . To produce then is of little use unless what we produce is known, if known widely known, the wider known the better, for it is by being known it works, it influences, it does its duty, it does good.[10]

It is noticeable that both these strong statements were made to Bridges, who understood him perfectly. To Dixon, however, he seemed constantly to hedge his deep wish for his poems to be famous, giving as objections his own doubts about their quality, his fears that he could not get permission from his religious superiors to come before the public, the fact that St Ignatius looked on individual fame 'as the most dangerous and dazzling of all attractions'. As he said of his own Order, 'Brilliancy does not suit us.'[11]

But Dixon was no fool, and his understanding of Hopkins's motivation was as often shrewd as obtuse; anyone with his deep empathy with his friend's poetry could not be wholly wrong about the poet himself. Certainly his offer to help him publish recognized what Hopkins deeply desired, even if Dixon's solution to the problem was the wrong one. In 1881 Hopkins said his priestly calling was the reason he wrote so little and sought no fame: 'my vocation puts before me a standard so high that a higher can be found nowhere else'. Dixon, who knew as much about religious duties as Hopkins did, although he was more reticent about them, answered shortly, 'Surely one vocation cannot destroy another: and such a Society as yours will not remain ignorant that you have such gifts as have seldom been given by God to man.'[12]

Hopkins recognized better than the next man how difficult his poetry was for the general reader, and he naturally feared exposing his desire for publication, when the difficulties made that seem so improbable: 'No doubt my poetry errs on the side of oddness . . . Now it is the virtue of design, pattern, or inscape to be distinctive and it is the vice of distinctiveness to become queer. This vice I cannot have escaped.'[13] He must have known, too, that if there had been a chance of his poetry being widely recognized, his superiors would have put no obstacle in the way of its publication, since they were surely as aware as he that there are many ways of serving God.

It would be asking too much to expect Hopkins to admit nakedly his thwarted poetic ambition when there was so little chance of its being fulfilled. As he did so often, he was claiming religious sanctions for necessities imposed upon him by his own personality, but his confusion of the two was far from being hypocritical, since it was completely unconscious. Only with Bridges was he sufficiently at ease for the true causes of his behaviour to swim to the surface of his mind.

In 1883, when he was still mulling over the problem, he decided in retreat to ask 'our Lord to watch over my compositions . . . that he should have them as his own and employ or not employ them as he should see fit'.[14] His resignation was sincere, but it was only part of his attitude to the reputation of the poet, and even in this tossing into the lap of his Creator of the responsibility for his works he displays a splendid assurance that they are in no real danger of extinction, and that the Lord will look after His own.

Leigh had been a blissful idyll in the most unpromising of surroundings, and he was naturally sad to leave it in the last days of 1879. He spent Christmas at St Beuno's, with the valley before it looking more than usually beautiful. On Boxing Day he walked to Holywell and bathed in St Winefred's well, 'which, as it is always at the same temperature, was lukewarm and smoked in the frosty air'.[15] Three days later he went as Select Preacher (a grand title for a junior curate) to St Francis Xavier's church in Liverpool. Probably disillusionment would have set in had he remained in Leigh, but his stay had been enough to confirm in him the belief he had been carefully fostering, that his true vocation lay in ministering to the poor and the uneducated. Liverpool was to lay a great hairy paw in the middle of that romantic illusion.

Ever since he had first heard of the Society, Hopkins had known that its members might be required to go, without qualm or explanation, to any remote part of the world, to wander in the trackless jungles of South America or to simmer slowly in the steamy heat of India or the stewpot of an African cannibal. He had perhaps not foreseen that he might go to the parish of St Francis Xavier, Liverpool. It is not difficult to imagine that many priests would have been very happy in a church so externally successful, for in the three decades since it was built, it had become the largest Catholic parish in Liverpool, which was probably the most solidly Catholic city in England, in which a third of the inhabitants were members of the Church.[16] A young, vigorous, athletic, unquestioningly devout priest with a gift for administration, double-entry bookkeeping, and leadership of the young, who loved to preach to enormous congregations ready to be swayed by his words, could hardly have found a more congenial setting. Hopkins was, unfortunately, none of those things.

The church, of chilly blue limestone, in the manner of 'the early decorated Gothic period', had been opened in December 1848. By the time Hopkins got there, the furnishings were almost complete, in French/English exuberance. The pulpit was installed and the altar had replaced the dresser that had filled in for it initially. 'Later came an elaborate gilded throne with curtains of pearls and gold thread with kneeling angels at each side, with censers in their hands.' On the exterior, work had begun on the immensely high steeple that was not finished until after Hopkins's departure, but the tower itself was so tall that it could be seen for miles, from the docks and the business district, or from across the Mersey.

Thirty-five years before, when building had begun, the church stood in the sparsely populated 'outskirts of the city, with only a few but fashionable houses scattered in the neighbourhood', but its opening had coincided with the potato famine and a tidal wave of the starving into the chief port serving immigrants from Ireland. Many of the hungry had spread out over England and Scotland, but an undue number had remained within a few miles of where they had left the ships. There was little manufacturing in Liverpool, and shipbuilding had already begun the decline that led in our own day to the gaunt and empty docks along the Mersey. The inevitable result was unemployment and poverty of almost unbelievable degradation. In the direction of Everton there were still a few large houses belonging to the 'superior classes', while spilling away from the church down the hill towards the estuary and the city were stinking slums.

The inundation of Irish meant that the parish was swollen to nearly ten thousand, of whom six or seven thousand attended Mass on Sunday. The nextdoor presbytery was nearly as stretched, to accommodate the nine priests who were on the regular strength of the parish. Even with such a large staff of clergy, the best that the church could do was to organize each activity for many times more persons than the priests could decently serve. The consequences of the crowding were the Men's Sodality, the Boys' Guild of St Stanislaus, the Women's Sodality of Our Lady of the Immaculate Conception, which held bazaars to raise money for the church, the Altar Society, the Guild of St Agnes for girls; shortly after his arrival Hopkins took on the duty of chaplain of the Brotherhood of St Vincent de Paul, which went into some of the most noisome slums to help the poor and encourage them to attend Mass. There was scarcely a moment of day or dark when the church buildings were not in use.

The parish ran Ragged Schools for both boys and girls, providing food as well as education for the pupils, in miserable buildings so riddled with holes that on one day just before Hopkins arrived, there were between two and three hundred rats running around a room in the girls' school as a teacher played the piano. Connected vaguely with the church in an extra-parochial relationship was a preparatory school for boys whose families could afford fees.

Almost inevitably, in its desperate attempt to provide wholesome occupation for the thousands of penniless, the church took on some of the functions of a place of entertainment. While the Catholic youths of the Boys' Guild of St Stanislaus were belting the stuffing out of each other in boxing class in the basement of the presbytery, the members of the Guild of St Agnes were practising for corporate Communion, 'in a modest dress of white, with veil, wreath, and blue sash'. The services became increasingly theatrical: in 1866 at the Forty Hours' service, 118 pounds of wax were burned in candles, to the value of £12, and only eight years later the same service had fifteen hundred lights and enormous arrangements of flowers. There were Christmas crèches, a brass band with green rosettes, and for the Easter Grand High Mass an orchestra of sixteen pieces.

Both men and women sang in the choir, which, in those days before the Papal reform of liturgical music, was much given to Mendelssohn, or would leap to its feet for performances of the Halleluljah Chorus if given but half a chance. During Hopkins's time there, the *Liverpool Mercury*, which may have had a Protestant bias, called it 'one of the most indifferent choirs' in the city, picking out for particular notice the leading soprano, 'Miss Canavan, a lady with a full but unfortunately uncultivated voice' and the basso, Mr Hayes, who 'has a fine, robust voice of good quality, but he is rather inclined to shout . . . Until recently Mr Hayes wielded the baton, but has wisely given it up, as he was evidently ignorant of its use.' The plain song he loved must have seemed very remote to Hopkins.

With nine priests and ten thousand parishioners in constant movement, it is no wonder there was too little time left for contemplative spirituality of the kind to which Hopkins had been accustomed, both as Anglican and as Roman Catholic. There were no more quiet vigils before the altar in a chapel, penance came to mean to him hours of confinement in a confessional as interminable lines of penitents waited for weekly absolution, and sermons had to be adjusted to move the hearts of two thousand people at a time. The result at St Francis Xavier's was preaching that in the words of the *Month* of 1975 'see-sawed between the coldly rational and the sickly sentimental', with more of the latter than the former.

Preachers were judged on points not unlike those awarded in the punch-ups of the boys in the presbytery basement, and often the balance was decided by how few of the congregation kept dry eyes throughout the sermon. The Rector, Fr James Clare, was an eloquent speaker himself, relying more on presence and ability to sway his congregation than on intellectual content, and probably he had made the better choice in order to move his uneducated auditors to repentance and to contrite resolutions for the future. He was, in any case, too busy either to prepare more subtle sermons or to encourage his curates to do so; his task as Rector was superhuman, but he did the best he could.

It became fashionable for Protestants as well as Catholics to come from all over the city to hear the sermons, and members of the parish had to be up early if they expected seats. For services that had particularly well-known preachers, tickets were sold. In October 1880 Fr Tom Burke, a Passionist noted for his flamboyant speaking, came to preach at the opening of new rat-free schools in the parish, and the crowds were so great that the parishioners at the ten o'clock Mass were trapped in the church by the press of bodies of those waiting to get into the next Mass to hear Fr Burke, and had to make their way out of the church by way of the sacristy and around the back of the high altar. Before they could escape, the incoming crowd had forced the doors open, and even those without tickets came in waving their money and demanding to pay.

When Fr Burke climbed into the pulpit, he surveyed the crowd occupying every seat and standing place in the church, then threw out his right hand and thundered three times: 'To Hell with the Jesuits.' The congregation was silent as he paused dramatically, then lowered his arm and said quietly, 'Such is the cry of today.' It is easy to see why the Rector had thereafter to keep the doors locked between services, to control the crowds pouring off the overloaded trams and demanding entrance.

It was formidable competition for the new Select Preacher, whose own sermons had not been attracting equal attention; even if his title was something of a formality, it did indicate part of the duties expected of him. His sermons at Leigh had been a success, but his record at Farm Street would certainly not have made him seem the obvious man for the post.

His first sermon was delivered only five days after his arrival in Liverpool, and it was probably a replacement for one scheduled to have been given by another priest, for it is very short by Hopkins's standards and after his record of the text (*'Thy will be done on earth as it is in heaven'*), he wrote, 'taken at random', which was contrary to his normal practice.[17] Apparently it went well enough for Fr Clare to assign him the same hour on Sunday evening for a further three weeks, to make up a short series of four sermons. The second Sunday he spoke on 'Thy Kingdom Come', indicating at the beginning that the theme of the series would be 'On God's Kingdom'. Neither this sermon nor its successor suffered from brevity; the third sermon was actually so long that he had to cut it short before making his point. Hopkins's anxious notes written on his sermons indicate how hard he tried to accommodate himself to his auditors and how little understanding he had of the limited abilities of poorly educated minds to understand difficult sermons. 'What they wanted, no doubt, was the broad, heart-warming message of the Gospel transposed into modern dress.' His sermons read well, but they are far too concerned with verbal discriminations for simple congregations, particularly when one takes into account his lack of force in speaking.

He called the last of the little series 'The Fall of God's First Kingdom' and took for his text 'Every kingdom divided against itself shall be made desolate and every city (commonwealth) or house divided against itself shall not stand.' On the surviving manuscript of the sermon he indicated Fr Clare's attempt to deal with complaints about the earlier sermons: 'I was not allowed to take this title and on the printed bills it was covered by a blank slip pasted over.' His text, too, had to be changed to the previous week's, 'and had to leave out or reword all passages speaking of God's kingdom as falling'. However well meant Fr Clare's prohibition, to keep from misleading the congregation, it must have been disheartening to anyone as easily discouraged as Hopkins.

After this there is no indication that he was asked to preach until the end of April, which would have been further reproach to the sensitive nerves of the Select Preacher. In preparing the sermon he began by making notes, 'for it seems that written sermons do no good'. Apparently, however, his superiors were worried lest he overrun his time limit, and shortly after that, he wrote that 'the Rector wishes me to write'. Fr Clare's instincts were sound, even if they did little to curb Hopkins's too verbal imagination; in the event he ran out of time before he had finished his sermon.

Another month followed before he was asked to preach again, but a week before it was to be delivered, when he had the sermon nearly finished, he wrote at the end of the completed portion, 'This sermon is not to be delivered and therefore will not be finished, as Fr. Kavanagh of West Leigh is coming here to preach for his two new missions instead.' A few weeks later, another partly composed sermon breaks off with the words 'This sermon is not to be preached either.'

Admirably, Hopkins managed to swallow his discomfiture, even to laugh at it occasionally, and at the end of June he wrote that what he had at first taken to be tears in his hearers proved to be sweat they were wiping away in the early summer heat. At the conclusion of the same sermon 'one of my penitents told me, with great simplicity, that I was not to be named in the same week with Fr. Clare. "Well" I said "and I will not be named in the same week. But did you hear it all?" He said he did, only that he was sleeping for parts of it.'

Hopkins, as Fr Parkinson at Oxford had discovered, was not always an easy assistant. At Liverpool he seems to have held himself apart from the other priests of the parish, and Fr Clare is the only one of them mentioned by name in the Hopkins papers that have survived. After he left the parish he remembered with gratitude the kindness of one 'yokemate' (the word tells its own tale) in Liverpool, who 'used to come up to me and say "Gerard, you are a good soul" and that I was a comfort to him in his trouble'.[18]

In Hopkins's notes the Rector, though never quite ridiculed, is made to look, at best, uncertain of his own mind. In October 1880

Hopkins preached on the concern for man manifested by God, Who 'heeds all things at once. He takes more interest in a merchant's business than the merchant, in a vessel's steering than the pilot, in a lover's sweetheart than the lover, in a sick man's pain than the sufferer, in our salvation than we ourselves.' In the surviving copy of the sermon Hopkins wrote, 'In consequence of this word *sweetheart* I was in a manner suspended and at all events was forbidden (it was some time after) to preach without having my sermon revised. However when I was going to take the next sermon I had to give after this regulation came into force to Fr. Clare for revision he poohpoohed the matter and would not look at it.' It was hard to be treated like a child, but it is only fair to say that his reaction did not always take into account Fr Clare's distraction with other matters.

There is no indication that Hopkins ever made much impression as a preacher, as anyone might have predicted from his fiascos in the pulpit at St Beuno's and at Farm Street. Perhaps worst of all was that one of his sermons that had been very successful at Leigh fell completely flat in Liverpool. Understandably, if not fairly, he began to blame the place rather than himself.

As Fr Devlin, the editor of his sermons, wrote of Hopkins's difficulties, 'The trouble, which was becoming more and more apparent to himself, was that he did not like the Liverpool people.'[19] It had not always been so, and initially he had tried to like the inhabitants of the city, even though he had not wanted to come there; it was only after he had become thoroughly disillusioned with his work and his parishioners that he began remembering that his welcome to his parish was cool.

Even his early disappointments in the pulpit had still not soured his outlook when, only five months after his arrival, he wrote to Baillie of the 'Lancastrians' of Leigh and Liverpool, 'I felt as if [I] had been born to deal with them. Religion, you know, enters very deep; in reality it is the deepest impression I have in speaking to people, that they are or that they are not of my religion.' But later in the very day that he wrote those words, he was told that his sermon had been cancelled and that Fr Kavanagh would preach in his stead. On getting the news, he stopped the letter, but he kept it open, rewriting it 'and reading it with my head first on one side, then on the other' for a fortnight, until he decided that it would be best merely to say that he no longer felt he had a permanent place in the parish: 'I do not think I can be long here; I have been long nowhere yet. I am brought face to face with the deepest poverty and misery in my district. On this theme I could write much, but it would do no good.'[20] Being among Catholics obviously meant less when he believed that his feelings for them were not reciprocated. It was a familiar but very understandable pattern in his life.

The parish was divided into districts, each taken care of by one priest. Hopkins's own territory was mapped out in the litany of unlovely names of streets he recited when offering to see one of Bridges's friends: 'I will do all that Jenkinson Street and Gomer Street and Back Queen Ann Street and Torbock Street and Bidder Street and Birchfield Street and Bickerstaffe Street and the rest of my purlieus will spare of me to entertain him.'[21] It was not the most squalid part of the parish but it was not much better, with 'dens of iniquity' to which Hopkins had to minister, crowding around the church itself. In later years he remembered with distaste, 'Alas, brethren, to what filthy places have I not myself carried the Lord of Glory! and worse than filthy places, dens of shame.'[22] Within a few years of his departure, the authorities at last managed to sweep away the brothels, and in this century German incendiary bombs even more efficiently rid the area of the worst slums and damaged the church itself.

Already there was not only hostility to the Irish in the city and even stronger anti-Catholic enmity by the Orangemen who lived on the boundaries of the parish; there was an air of intense menace in the summer as the Orange processions paraded along Shaw Street, a few hundred feet from the church, to the thunderous beat of drums as the flutes played such anti-Papal tunes as 'We'll kick the Pope over Dolly's Brae'.

The personal habits of his spiritual charges were often revolting to someone as fastidious as Hopkins. Years after he had left the place, he remembered with an inward shudder that 'as I went up Brunswick Road (or any street) at Liverpool on a frosty morning it used to disgust me to see the pavement regularly starred with the spit of the workmen going to their work; and they do not turn aside, but spit straight before them as you approach . . .'.[23] His aesthetic reaction in Liverpool to the spittle was very different from his startling pleasure in the frozen sprays of the urinals at Manresa, and the difference was probably due to his feeling for the place.

In Leigh Hopkins had managed to forgive drunkenness, even in the face of constant provocation, but somehow he found it intolerable in Liverpool and began to think of it as a specifically Irish failing (although the drunkards in Leigh had been largely English). The difference again lay in the reception he thought he received in the two places. He found Liverpool, as he told Paravicini succinctly, a hellhole. One priest who was on the parish staff of St Francis Xavier's some forty years ago was told by an elderly colleague that he had once asked a parishioner if she had known Hopkins. She replied, 'Oh yes, I remember *little* Father Hopkins. He was a fine priest, but, my, he had a *bit of a temper!*'[24]

In the spring of 1881 he went to the annual Liverpool parade of horses and was disappointed in the spectacle. The result was a fit of Swiftian disgust at the contrast between man and beast: 'While I admired the handsome horses I remarked for the thousandth time with sorrow and loathing the base and bespotted figures and features of the Liverpool crowd. When I see the fine and manly Norwegians that flock hither to embark for America walk our streets and look about them it fills me with shame and wretchedness.'[25] There was perhaps more than a simple admiration for Houhynhnms in his response to the horses, as his poetry of the time suggests.

As he told Bridges, he felt dried out by cities, spiritually and poetically. One of the few periodic reliefs he had was an occasional duty visit to Rose Hill, Lydiate, a country house a few miles north of the city belonging to the Lightbounds, a Catholic family, where priests from St Francis Xavier's said Mass weekly. It was a short train trip, and he would go overnight, so that he could be there in the morning for Mass; he liked to take the opportunity to read and to write letters, and it was there that one of his few poems of the period was written, 'Spring and Fall'. Unfortunately, even country air was not always enough to put him in a good mood, and on one occasion he talked 'so outrageously' on politics to Mr Musgrove, a family friend of the Lightbounds, that it was some weeks before Musgrove would speak to him again.

With no close friends in the presbytery and cut off from his friends elsewhere by what he thought was a shortage of time for writing,* he was very lonely, a feeling exacerbated by knowing that Bridges and Dixon, his two most constant correspondents, both of whom kept asking to see him, had begun seeing each other. When Bridges suggested he join them both, Hopkins said the proposal *'has nothing but its goodnature to lift it above imbecility'*.[26] Apparently, the only times he saw Bridges during his Liverpool stay were during his summer holidays in Hampstead, but Bridges constantly wrote 'very flattering and endearing' letters to him. His own letters were usually full of apologies for not having written: 'time and spirits were wanting; one is so fagged, so harried and gallied up and down. And the drunkards go on drinking, the filthy, as the scripture says, are filthy still; human nature is so inveterate. Would that I had seen the last of it.'[27]

In the autumn of 1881, near the end of his assignment to Liverpool, he made detailed, almost obsessive, plans for meeting Dixon, but after several letters, written with '"stylographic" or fountain pen' and full of train times, he sent a negligent telegram saying he would be unable to keep their appointment.

One friend who came to see him, and stayed in the presbytery, was Alfred Wyatt-Edgell, whom he had known through Dolben. They had met several times in London, since Edgell lived near the church in Farm Street. He was a convert, whom Bridges found 'stiffish – there is an exclusive pushiveness in his Catholicism'.[28] Recently he had succeeded to the title of Lord Braye, which had done nothing to curb his snobbish tendencies. There is little evidence that Hopkins thought well of him, but they were linked, loosely but inescapably, by their shared memories of Dolben.

The aridity and lack of pattern in his inner life is indicated by the plain fact that during his more than a year and a half in Liverpool he produced only three poems, one of which ('The Brothers') he had largely written while he was still at Mt St Mary's, while another was written at Rose Hill. His letters bristle with references to how

---

* One of his letters was written in the confessional while he was waiting for a penitent in an unusual break in the queue. Another time he tried writing on large paper in the hope it would look as if he had written more.

little conducive to poetry the city was. Writing to Dixon of his wearying work that left him 'nothing but odds and ends of time', he said that 'There is merit in it but little Muse, and indeed 26 lines is the whole I have writ[ten] in more than half a year.' Another time he wrote that 'Liverpool is of all places the most museless.'[29]

On 5 September 1880 Hopkins began a letter to Bridges, then finished it five days later, by which time he was able to write, 'I enclose a little piece composed since I began this letter, not founded on real incident.' It was 'Spring and Fall', which he had composed on the 7th of September while he was at Rose hill; *'to a young child'* is subscribed beneath the title:

> Margaret, are you grieving
> Over Goldengrove unleaving?
> Leaves, like the things of man, you
> With your fresh thoughts care for, can you?
> Ah! as the heart grows older
> It will come to such sights colder
> By and by, nor spare a sigh
> Though worlds of wanwood leafmeal lie;
> And yet you *will* weep and know why.
> Now no matter, child, the name:
> Sorrow's springs are the same.
> Nor mouth had, no nor mind, expressed
> What heárt heárd of, ghóst guéssed:
> It is the blight man was born for,
> It is Margaret you mourn for.

If we take at face value Hopkins's statement that this poem was not founded on real incident, we may be getting at the heart of why it seems so much less sentimental than most of his poetry that concerns children. Since, within the poem, he did not have to try to reproduce a feeling about a person he had known in real life, he felt no compulsion to exaggerate the emotion in order to make it seem as important to the reader as it had to him. The result is nearly as direct as the Wordsworthian tradition it follows. Probably because of its naked straightforwardness about a child's intimations of mortality, it has always been one of the most popular of his poems. To those readers interested in the man behind the poem, it seems clear that it is Hopkins, not Margaret, he mourns for.

The other poem written at Liverpool is certainly founded on real incident and on a real character who was one of Hopkins's parishioners.[30] Among the streets he had named to Bridges as part of his district was Birchfield, and at number 17, on 21 April 1880, a thirty-one-year-old farrier (or smith) named Felix Spencer died of pulmonary consumption after a long illness, in the last stages of which Hopkins had served as his spiritual comforter and had become fond of the 'hardy-handsome man', now contracted to a shell.*

Felix Randal

Felix Randal the farrier, O is he dead then? my duty all
    ended,
Who have watched his mould of man, big-boned and hardy-
    handsome
Pining, pining, till time when reason rambled in it and some
Fatal four disorders, fleshed there, all contended?

Sickness broke him. Impatient, he cursed at first, but mended
Being anointed and all; though a heavenlier heart began some
Months earlier, since I had our sweet reprieve and ransom
Tendered to him. Ah well, God rest him all road ever he
    offended!

This seeing the sick endears them to us, us too it endears.
My tongue had taught thee comfort, touch had quenched thy
    tears,
Thy tears that touched my heart, child, Felix, poor Felix
    Randal;

---

* By a curious coincidence of the sort that Hopkins appreciated more than most, his brother, who reported his death, lived in Gerard Street. It is probably just as well Hopkins made nothing of this.

How far from then forethought of, all thy more boisterous
  years,
When thou at the random grim forge, powerful amidst peers,
Didst fettle for the great grey drayhorse his bright and
  battering sandal!

Probably Hopkins felt even more strongly about the death of Felix
Spencer than he would otherwise have done because of his own
growing sense of loneliness. For all the personal emotion that lay
behind the poem, however, he never allows it to degenerate into
sentimentality, largely because Felix is kept as impersonal as the
poet is personal, and the reader is invited to see the joy behind his
death, an emotion implicit in his name. Throughout the sonnet
Felix becomes increasingly an icon rather than a man, until at the
last his innate nobility is suggested by 'powerful amidst peers' and
in the spacious image of the last line he has the classical majesty of
aspect that Hopkins had so admired in the paintings of Walker,
brought in here by the word 'sandal', which he had used with some
of the same effect in 'Binsey Poplars' and which may have
accounted for the rhyming name he gave Felix when he did not feel
free to use his proper surname.

As Fr Thomas has suggested, Hopkins probably heard in his
inner ear an echo of the great passage in *Ecclesiasticus* describing the
ideal workman: 'The smith at his anvil is absorbed in his handi-
work. The breath of the fire melts his flesh and he wastes away in
the heat of the furnace. He batters his ear with the din of the
hammer . . .'. Both in literal detail and in suggested symbolic
meaning, there is great likeness between the passage and the man.
Whatever more personal feelings Hopkins may have had for the
farrier, and one suspects from the emphasis on strength, good
looks, and achieved spiritual intimacy, that they were many, he sub-
dues them all to the relationship of spiritual father and child, then
to the apotheosis of man and manhood at the conclusion of the
poem, suggesting the natural nobility of the 'workman's part in
the commonweal'. All the same, part of the splendour of the final
line is achieved by the invocation of the drayhorse–Pegasus–
chevalier–Christ association that had run through so much of his

poetry, ever since the days when he confessed that stallions galloped through his dreams. (And which may, for that matter, have accounted for his rather unexpected attendance at the Liverpool horse procession.) His poetry is often strongest when the surface is firmly supported by subterranean emotions, even when he apparently did not recognize them.

In March 1881 came proof that Hopkins was certainly not averse to having his poems published. T.H. Hall Caine, an intimate of Rossetti, was making a collection of sonnets, and at the suggestion of his friend wrote to ask for contributions from Dixon, who with his usual generosity sent him copies of 'The Starlight Night' and 'The Caged Skylark' with his own poems. Remembering how upset Hopkins had been the last time he tried to get the priest's works published, Dixon assured him that they were intended for inspection only, 'not of course for publication without your consent'. Within a week Hopkins had sent Hall Caine three more of his own choice.

After nearly a month had passed, Hopkins told Bridges that Hall Caine 'acknowledged them in a somewhat effusive postcard and promised to write more fully in 2 or 3 days, but did not'. At last he reported that Hall Caine had written: 'He is not going to print me' and had shown his poems to 'a critic of utmost eminence' who agreed that they should not be published. With some justice, Hopkins was annoyed to have Hall Caine indicate that he thought Hopkins a 'young aspirant' when he was in fact nearly a decade Hall Caine's senior. With no apparent justification, Hopkins decided that the critic Hall Caine had consulted was Matthew Arnold.[31] Generously, he directed most of his indignation at what he took to be bad treatment of Bridges by Hall Caine. It was for Hopkins a frustrating outcome of his having been manoeuvred into admitting that he wanted to be published, and it stifled any disposition to expose himself to further disappointment.

One of the saddest aspects of Hopkins's artistic life at the time was not that he failed to write poetry but that he could not be content to lie fallow until he was able to write again. Instead, he spent most of his spare time writing long letters of criticism of the poems of Bridges and Dixon, wonderful help to them but a substitute activity for himself. Betweentimes he talked of the ambitious poems he was going to write, chief of which were probably the tragedy he planned on St Winefred and 'a great ode' on the martyrdom of his Jesuit predecessor, Edmund Campion. Many pieces of the former are scattered through his papers like broken columns on an archaeological site, but his death intervened before he ever developed a sufficiently firm conception of the structure of the drama to erect them; no trace remains of the Campion ode. Every writer knows the desperate feeling of being unable to write and of turning instead to talking about what he is going to produce in the future, then discovering that the energy and inspiration for the project have been dissipated by squandering them in conversation or letters. Of this Hopkins knew only too much. It became almost a certainty that any poem he mentioned in the course of its composition would never be finished. 'One night, as I lay awake in a fevered state,' he told Bridges, 'I had some glowing thoughts and lines, but I did not put them down and I fear they may fade to little or nothing.' He had more than enough imagination for a dozen poets and scarcely the energy for one.

He turned increasingly to writing music, which he assured Bridges was the 'only Muse that does not stifle in this horrible place'. He apparently regarded musical composition as a natural consequence of having learned to pick out notes on the piano and the violin: 'I am sometimes surprised at myself how slow and laborious a thing verse is to me when musical composition comes so easily, for I can make tunes almost at all times and places and could harmonise them as easily if only I could play or could read music at sight.' However, when he asked a competent musician to play over what he had written, he was crestfallen, for 'What had sounded rich seemed thin.'[32] Since he was unable to harmonize his own music, he was constantly being surprised that anyone should find the ability a prerequisite to composition.

Hopkins would have dismissed with contempt an amateur who had set up as a serious poet with as little training and experience as he brought to music. Several musical scholars have said essentially that he was more facile than most non-musicians who pick out tunes on the piano, but that it would be stretching things to treat his compositions seriously; that he did so himself seems an indication that he was really seeking a substitute for poetry. Inevitably his poetic silence in a period when he actually had time to write is reminiscent of that between his novitiate and 'The Wreck of the Deutschland'. It even suggests that during those earlier years he may at some deep level have felt that he had no genius at poetry, and that it was easier to tell himself that it would interfere with his 'state and vocation' than it was to admit that he was going through a period of poetical dryness. To be sure, all during the years between 1868 and 1875 he had thought about and talked about and written about poetry, and had been obsessed by what he would write if only he were free to do so, but those activities were suspiciously like the ones with which he occupied himself in 1880–1, and they may have sprung from a like need to find something that would keep him so busy he would not have to make excuses to himself for not writing poetry.

To listen to Hopkins's music performed today is to be made painfully aware that there is little real connection between 'musical' verse and music itself, and that all the high adventure of his poetry is very unlike the comparatively tame settings of poems he composed. Actually there are a few good tunes among them, such as his setting of a 'war-song' called 'What shall I do for the land that bred me', which can probably be counted a partial success, since it certainly conveys in another medium the four-square thump of the verse that he wrote specifically to be put to music. It is, he said, a 'task of great delicacy and hazard to write a patriotic song that shall breathe true feeling without spoon or brag',[33] and one feels that he did not manage it; he was particularly jingoistic at the time he wrote it, which may account in part for its unsubtlety, but more probably simple lack of musical craft was at fault.

All during his stay at Leigh Hopkins had not complained of bad health, but when he got to Liverpool, he predictably fell ill. Because Bridges was a medical man, Hopkins confided to him practically all his symptoms, so that their correspondence gives an exaggerated idea of how bad his state was, but it was real enough to him. Bridges continued, as he had done for a long time, to consider that he probably was exaggerating his symptoms, a reaction perhaps as characteristic of physicians as hypochondria is of poets. Since Bridges himself had an attack of pneumonia with consequences so prolonged that he decided to give up his medical career,* Hopkins was rather muted to him about his own health, but shortly after he arrived in Liverpool he worked too hard during Easter week and came down with 'a bad cold, which led to earache and deafness'. On another occasion he took up 'a languid pen' to tell Bridges he was 'down with diarrhoea and vomiting, brought on by yesterday's heat and the long hours in the confessional'.[34] It is probably useless to speculate a century later about the exact nature of his illnesses, but there was at least a noticeable correlation between his health and his general happiness with his surroundings and work.

In August 1881 came the release he had been hoping for, when he was sent to Glasgow as assistant in St Joseph's church before going back to Manresa to begin his Tertianship, the third and last year of his noviceship. Liverpool sent him away with a memory he kept for years, of the church organist who got drunk at the organ and was dismissed: 'I have now twice had this experience: it is depressing, alarming, agitating, but above all delicately comic; it brings together the bestial and angelic elements. . . . He was a clever young fellow and thoroughly understood the properties of narrow-necked tubes.'[35] Once he was safely away, he could afford to laugh at what had been a dispiriting experience, but until he finally left the Province in 1884 he was constantly afraid he might have to go back to Liverpool, and he would characterize his experience there as being a time when he had never once been inside the public library.

To Baillie he inadvertently confessed a good part of his reason for disliking the place: 'Though Glasgow is repulsive to live in yet there are alleviations: the streets and buildings are fine and the people lively. The poor Irish, among whom my duties lay, are mostly from the North of Ireland. . . . They are found by all who have to deal with them very attractive; for, though always very drunken

---

* When Hopkins was ill, Bridges had on more than one occasion volunteered to come to him and give treatment. Now it was Hopkins's turn, and he offered to visit Bridges, wishing that he might give him spiritual relief by anointing him, as he had done Felix Spencer ('Randal'). He had already told him of the remarkable recovery from typhus made by one of his parishioners after Hopkins had anointed him. Although Hopkins would very much have liked Bridges to become a convert, he realized his intransigent dislike of the Church and normally said nothing about it; in this case Bridges's illness probably worried Hopkins sufficiently to make him less tactful than usual.

and at present very Fenian, they are warm-hearted and give a far heartier welcome than those of Liverpool. I found myself very much at home with them.'[36]

From Glasgow itself he had written, 'Things are pleasanter here than at Liverpool. Wretched place too Glasgow is, like all our great towns; still I get on better here, though bad is the best of my getting on. But now I feel that I need the noviceship very much and shall be every way better off when I have been made more spiritual minded.'[37]

CHAPTER XVIII

FORTUNE'S FOOTBALL
1881–3

In August 1881 Hopkins had gone to help in St Joseph's, Glasgow, for a fortnight, but he was asked to stay on there until the end of September, so that he was deprived of a real holiday before going to Roehampton at the beginning of October. In niggardly recompense he was promised before he left Scotland 'two days to see something of the Highlands', but even that was little 'more than a glimpse of their skirts. I hurried from Glasgow one day to Loch Lomond. The day was dark and partly hid the lake, yet it did not altogether disfigure it but gave a pensive or solemn beauty which left a deep impression on me.'[1] He landed for a few hours at Inversnaid, where he thought of a tune for a poem by Canon Dixon and walked by the peaty brown burn that tumbled into the lake after a tumultuous journey flinging its foam to either side. The contrast was compelling between the fecund moisture and the desiccated heat of Liverpool and Glasgow; on the 28th of September (presumably the day he had been in the tiny settlement), he wrote the date on the manuscript of 'Inversnaid', of which the last quatrain has become in our own day something of a manifesto for the forces of conservation:

> What would the world be, once bereft
> Of wet and of wildness? Let them be left,
> O let them be left, wildness and wet;
> Long live the weeds and the wilderness yet.

The poem is almost a literal augmentation of his own complaint to Bridges of how cities dried him up spiritually and poetically. Even the ten months ahead at Manresa, of which he had affectionate

335

memories, were to be on the outskirts of London, in an area that was rapidly becoming near-suburbia, quite unlike the banks of Loch Lomond.

'There, I mean at Roehampton,' he told Bridges, 'I am pretty well resolved, I will altogether give over composition for the ten months, that I may *vacare Deo* as in my noviceship proper.' It would be impossible to doubt the sincerity of his renunciation, but it is also noticeable that he was giving up something he had not practised, except for 'Inversnaid', for more than a year. Then, more realistically, he added, 'I therefore want to get some things done first, but fear I never shall.'[2]

The limitation he was imposing on himself was in key with the general aims of the Tertianship, which was intended by the Society to reaffirm the duties of the priests who would be taking their final vows after years of preparation. Although most of them had been acting as parish priests since the end of their time at St Beuno's, they were brought back to the status of novices, to enable them 'to recover that fervour which may have cooled through application to study and contact with the world', and to that end were effectively cut off from the world for the greater part of ten months. They were assigned individual rooms, and a lay brother brought coal and removed the ashes from their fires, which was a great change from their first year, but Hopkins had to carry his own water, clean his room, and empty his slops. Like the novices, he worked in the park and on the farm, as well as acting as kitchen boy. Tertians could not go out of the grounds alone without leave, they could not go to London without special permission, they were forbidden to speak to the Juniors or novices, their correspondence was opened and examined, and they were not allowed to read newspapers or periodicals or any books but spiritual ones during their whole stay at Manresa. On Wednesdays the Tertians were paired off for their community walk by 'Fr Instructor', but on Fridays and Sundays walks were 'ad lib' and they could choose their own companions. Hopkins was a man of thirty-seven reduced to the status of schoolboy, but he seems not to have chafed at the restraints.

In the years since Hopkins was a novice, Manresa had been considerably enlarged, but even so it was bulging at the seams. There were more than a hundred members of the community living

there, including eleven Tertians[3] and fifty novices, which indicated
the thriving state of the Province, since there had been only seven
novices when Hopkins was one thirteen years earlier.

A month after he arrived, the Tertians went into the Long Retreat
of just over a month, with only three 'repose days' to break their
intense concentration. Hopkins kept especially full notes of the
retreats, both of what was said by the priest giving the retreat and
his own reflections; they are not easy for a non-Jesuit to follow, but
he seems to have been aware that he would soon spend much of his
time giving retreats himself and that his notes would prompt his
considerations. It is also possible that he was already collecting
material for a treatise he meant to write on the Spiritual Exercises.
Thirteen times during the retreat the Tertians were aroused at
midnight for meditations in the chapel; what may have struck
others as a physical ordeal was probably more than welcome to
Hopkins as a contrast to the uncontemplative life he had been
leading in Liverpool, when he was so 'gallied up and down' by the
quotidian concerns of the parish.

When he heard that Hopkins was returning to Manresa, Dixon
wrote to him in Anglican puzzlement, 'So you are entering on your
last year of novitiate. I suppose you are determined to go on with it:
but it must be a severe trial – I will say no more.'

'I see you do not understand my position in the Society,' Hopkins
explained. The Tertianship was not a period during which a
candidate was still free to withdraw, since the vows taken at the end
of the first period of the novitiate were perpetually binding,
although they were renewed every six months, 'not *for* every six
months but for life', until the end of the Tertianship.

In the midst of his cut-and-dried explanation, Hopkins suddenly
put down a few sentences that uncover his 'sheer plod' in day-to-
day fulfilment of vows that after so many years had gradually lost
the magnetism which first drew him to his vocation:

As for myself, I have not only made my vows publicly some
two and twenty times but I make them to myself every day, so
that I should be black with perjury if I drew back now. And
beyond that I can say with St. Peter: To whom shall I go? *Tu
verba vitae aeternae habes.* Besides all which, my mind is here

more at peace than it has ever been and I would gladly live all my life, if it were so to be, in as great or a greater seclusion from the world and be busied only with God. But in the midst of outward occupations not only the mind is drawn away from God, which may be at the call of duty and be God's will, but unhappily the will too is entangled, worldly interests freshen, and worldly ambitions revive.[4]

The reminder that he would be 'black with perjury' if he were to withdraw seems more an admonition to himself than an answer to anything Dixon had asked.

Dixon was the kind of correspondent whose sweet temper constantly shamed his friends. As Hopkins wrote, 'I feel in reading him what a gentleman he is and it brings on that feeling that I am a blackguard.'[5] The reference is to his poetry, but it applies equally well to his letters. The affectionately blundering Dixon continued to believe that he could cajole Hopkins into writing even when he did not want to. 'I hope that you are going on with poetry yourself,' he suggested, and Hopkins replied, 'I shall, in my present mind, continue to compose, as occasion shall fairly allow, which I am afraid will be seldom and indeed for some years past has been scarcely ever. . . . In no case am I willing to write anything while in my present condition: the time is precious and will not return again and I know I shall not regret my forbearance.'[6]

Although he was not writing poetry, Hopkins continued advising his friends on their own, and his letters of this year are full of quick, accurate thumbnail sketches of the work of their contemporaries. Of Browning he wrote that 'he has got a great deal of what came in with Kingsley and the Broad Church school, a way of talking (and making his people talk) with the air and spirit of a man bouncing up from table with his mouth full of bread and cheese and saying that he meant to stand no blasted nonsense. There is a whole volume of Kingsley's essays which is all a kind of munch and a not standing of any blasted nonsense from cover to cover.'[7] He had rapidly lost most of the respect he once felt for Browning, and when he wanted to accuse Bridges of being biassed in reading his poetry, he said wryly that Bridges's opinion of his verse was 'like mine towards Browning's; I greatly admire the touches and the details, but the general effect, the whole, offends me, I think it repulsive'.[8]

His letters of the period are full of small beer, not unhappy but usually without a great deal of sparkle: he has trouble with his teeth and gets permission to see the dentist five times during the ten months; improbably, he tests his strength in 'Indian wrestling' with another Tertian, who twists his wrist so hard he is afraid a ligament has been broken; he notices that Fr Morris's first-year novices are somewhat staid and with the air of a man twice his age remembers that 'we used to roar with laughter if anything happened, his never do'.[9] There are storms at Manresa, ravaging the park, which brings out his predictable sadness at the loss of trees. Curiously, he seems to have been more moved by their loss than by the luck of two fellow Tertians who were nearly killed in a storm and for whose narrow escape there was a subsequent public *Te Deum*; it seems an odd little manifestation of his tendency to pay closer attention to nature than to man. He still found Manresa beautiful, though it had suffered from 'decay of nature and more from the hand of man'; it put him in 'a very contented frame of mind',[10] and his health was better that year than it had been for some time.

Like the other Tertians, he occasionally went to say Mass or hear confessions in local parish churches that were short of clergy; when he said Mass for the nuns of the Roehampton Convent, 'he impressed them all so much, they all felt he must be a Saint'.[11] At Christmas many of the other Tertians were sent off for duty elsewhere, but he spent the holiday in the 'topsy-turvy cheerful air' of Manresa, where his brother Lionel came to see him for a pleasant afternoon marred only by the smoking of the chimney in the guest room. Some of the holiday cheer was dissipated by 'hourly expecting orders to return to Liverpool' to take the place of one of the priests who had died suddenly. His position, Hopkins thought, would inevitably be filled from the Tertians at Manresa, and with his too frequent tendency to assume the worst, he wrote on New Year's Day 1881, 'I feel little doubt it will be by me and that this is probably the last night I shall spend at Roehampton.'[12] Finally, however, he was saved from what he obviously regarded as one of the most distasteful things that could happen to him, and he remained his full term.

At the beginning of Lent Hopkins went to Preston to take duty in the parish, then spent the last fortnight in March at Maryport on the Cumberland coast, where he took part in a mission. He had never conducted a mission before and engagingly described it to Bridges as being 'something like a Revival without the hysteria and the heresy'. Presumably he was able to use some of the notes he had made during the Long Retreat. The emotional pitch of the occasion exhilarated him and made him 'speak very plainly and strongly', which he enjoyed thoroughly.[13]

On his return journey he was asked to come back to Preston for the remainder of Lent. He took the opportunity to go by way of Carlisle, stopping for some three hours between trains, which gave him the chance to see Dixon for the first time in many years. The Canon came in from Hayton and gave Hopkins dinner before showing him around the Cathedral. Dixon always seemed abstracted, and he was so ingenuously polite that he would seldom speak until he was sure he was not preventing another from doing so. Perhaps they had waited too long, perhaps they had always been the kind of friends who are more intimate on paper than in person: the result was that Dixon was too reticent for them to get on to 'intimate or even interesting' subjects in their conversation. 'I fancied you were shy and that time would have been needed for this to wear off,' wrote Hopkins. 'I think that for myself I have very little shyness left in me, but I cannot communicate my own feeling to another.'

To Dixon the Highgate schoolboy he had known years before seemed to have changed but little. With deep tenderness and consideration, Dixon confessed that the awkwardness had been of his own making:

I dare say I seemed 'shy': I have an unfortunate manner: & am constantly told that I am too quiet: I have often tried to overcome it: but the effort is always apparent to those with whom I am, & never succeeds. You must therefore forgive it: it is not from want of feeling or affection.[14]

What Dixon had to say of himself applied doubly to Hopkins; he was not truly shy, but he was unable – more probably, afraid – to display great affection, particularly in person, which was why so few of his friends felt they really knew him. Long before, as an undergraduate, he had been spontaneous in his affections, but he had lost the openness in the intervening years, making the last part of his life far more unhappy than it should have been. By his own admission he had recognized Dixon's shyness, but had been unable to do anything to alleviate it. The two men never met again; probably they both knew that their intimacy was preserved best at a distance. Dixon's letter suggests that he believed he had bored Hopkins, and Hopkins seems to have felt that the older man brought so much more affection and intimacy than he had expected that it was easiest to deal with Dixon's emotions by post.

Dixon's attitude to Hopkins is perhaps best shown in a remark he made to Bridges in 1881: 'I heard from Hopkins this morning; sending two of his sweetly terrible poems. There is something in his work which always makes my heart ache.'[15]

A month or two later Bridges brought a small nephew with him to Roehampton to see Hopkins, who wrote to Bridges with the incomprehension of the childless, 'I am afraid he felt dull. He is shy I dare say. . . . It cannot be denied nevertheless that the presence of a third person is a restraint upon confidential talk.'[16] It was his imagination, not his heart, that failed him on these occasions.

Dixon, Bridges, and Baillie: these are the correspondents and friends to whom Hopkins's most revealing letters were written. Many other letters have doubtless disappeared which would have enlarged our knowledge of his circle of friends, but it is improbable that they would have given us more sense of what it was like to be as close to Hopkins as anyone could be, since his emotions are more often found in the implications of his letters than in their direct messages.

Although Hopkins had seen him infrequently after leaving Oxford, Baillie said, 'His rare visits gave me the keenest pleasure. . . . Apart from my own nearest relatives, I never had so strong an affection for any one.'[17] He reads Hopkins's letters with the eye of friendship, but to an outsider they seem fairly impersonal, possibly because they were so infrequent; 'Perhaps occasional letters are the best, as I believe', he told Baillie in apology for his remissness.

The letters to and from Dixon display more gratitude for the friendship on his part than on Hopkins's, but the frequency of his own letters indicates how much Hopkins needed to write to his old teacher. It shows a good bit about his feelings that it was primarily the poems of Bridges and Dixon that he set to music. All three of his close friends were extremely generous men, and, curiously, all three were Protestants.

Hopkins was fully aware of how much he needed Bridges and how fond he was of him, but he occasionally exploded at him, usually on religious matters, not poetry. He found it hard to understand how a friend of such long standing should not agree completely with him on religion, forgetting that since their first meeting at Oxford it was he, not Bridges, who had changed most. But after he had written a hurt or angry letter, he was only too willing to write another to smooth over any difficulties, usually without mentioning whatever had gone wrong, frequently leaning over backwards, in his unformulated remorse, to call Bridges 'my dear heart'. It was a friendship made up of brilliance on one side and frequent forbearance on the other.

While Bridges was at Manresa with his nephew, Hopkins had mentioned that there would be a Corpus Christi procession there on the 8th of June, but when Bridges offered to come, Hopkins tried to dissuade him by saying he would be engaged with the celebration and would not be able to give time to a guest. All the same Bridges showed up, with a pocketful of prejudices and an overwhelming affection for his old friend. There is a Manresa tradition, perhaps apocryphal, of the exact first-floor window overlooking the court-yard in which he stood to watch Hopkins and the rest of the procession.

Hopkins had a deep devotion to the celebration and was on tenterhooks that Bridges might not understand its significance or that he might judge the whole occasion simply by the physical beauty of the ceremony. As he explained, the first Christmas, the first Easter, Holy Thursday, Whitsunday 'and so on were to those who took part in them festivities *de praesenti*', although today they are only anniversaries or commemorations. 'But Corpus Christi is the feast of the Real Presence, therefore it is the most purely joyous of solemnities.'

In another letter he apologized for the inadequacies of the procession, and then launched unexpectedly into what seems an angry attack on Bridges:

> It is long since such things had any significance for you. But what is strange and unpleasant is that you sometimes speak as if they had in reality none for me and you were only waiting with a certain disgust till I too should be disgusted with myself enough to throw off the mask.

With the detailed memory for past injury that proves real hurt, he recalled Bridges's saying 'something of the sort walking on the Cowley Road when we were last at Oxford together – in '79 it must have been. Yet I can hardly think you do not think I am in earnest.'

What is perhaps most remarkable is that this outburst is in the same letter as an exquisitely funny account of his leavetaking of Bridges after the ceremony, making fun of himself:

> . . . another train came up on that train's tail, and indeed it was a dull duncery that overhung us both not to see that its being Ascot day ensured countless more trains and not fewer. There was a lovely and passionate scene (for about the space of the last trump) between me and a tallish gentleman (I daresay he was a cardsharper) in your carriage who was by way of being you; I smiled, I murmured with my lips at him, I waved farewells, but he would not give in, till with burning shame (though the whole thing was, as I say, like the duels of archangels) I saw suddenly what I was doing.[18]

The time of year was approaching when the Jesuit General Post took place, and it was presumably to say farewell to Hopkins, who would soon be leaving for Stonyhurst, that Bridges visited him again at Manresa at the end of July. There is no record of open dissension that day, but Bridges came away saddened, as he told Dixon: 'I saw Gerard last Sunday. Those Jesuits do bully their men dreadfully. He shuns even his Jesuit fellow creatures – perhaps though these more than others.'[19]

Bridges comes out of most of their differences so well that it is easy to neglect what the thin-skinned Hopkins perceived as his abrasiveness. It is a matter that is hard to judge from a one-sided correspondence, but occasionally Bridges seems to have taken a small pleasure in venting his dislike of the Jesuits, and Hopkins naturally responded badly. None of which should blunt our gratitude to Bridges, not only for having saved Hopkins's poems and published them but, perhaps even more, for the care with which he tried to preserve his friend's equanimity and make it possible for him to face the world – and to write his poetry. In the summer of 1882 there was clearly another rupture for a month or two, since at the end of September Hopkins began a letter to Bridges by writing, 'I *must* break this mournful silence. I began a letter yesterday, but am not pleased with it.'[20]

On the feast of the Assumption, 15 August 1882, after fourteen years of training, Hopkins took his final vows in the handsome Italianate chapel the Jesuits had added to Manresa. Eight men took them at the same time, three as Professed Coadjutors, five (including Hopkins) as Spiritual Coadjutors. It was the first public indication since leaving St Beuno's of the change in Hopkins's status that had come about as a result of having done poorly in his examinations there. Unlike the Professed, he could never hold a major office in the Society, nor would he be able to participate in general congregations or take the special vow of obedience to the Pope. Occasionally, if he demonstrated special talents, one of the Spiritual Coadjutors might be raised to the higher rank.[21]

On the 22nd of August Hopkins left Manresa. He was to begin teaching 'Philosophers' in Stonyhurst in September. In the meantime the Provincial had given him leave to go for a holiday to any of the Jesuit houses in the country. Fr Purbrick's generosity in letting him think things out during his wanderings was particularly noticeable because the Provincial was known as a hearty believer in obedience, who discounted introspection as selfish, perhaps because he seldom indulged in it. His level-headed approach to emotional matters is suggested by his remark after receiving his own father into the Church on his deathbed: 'There are sharper sorrows than parting with a father prepared by the sacraments for death.'[22]

There is no indication that Hopkins went home to Hampstead before going to Stonyhurst. One place he certainly did not visit was Yattendon in Berkshire, where Bridges had just moved into the Manor House, to which he hoped Hopkins would come during his brief holiday. In telling Bridges of the Provincial's kindness in letting him travel where he wished, Hopkins reported, 'He said moreover that if I wanted to go elsewhere I was to apply to him. He would not doubt readily have given me leave to visit you and, had there been the possibility of saying mass, I might therefore have seen Yattenden. But it was not to be.'[23] Hopkins's inability to give up his priestly duties even for a day or two is easy to understand, but there is something ungraceful in his insistence on thrusting them into the face of a friend as resolutely anti-Jesuit as Bridges.

There was probably not an assignment available to a recent Tertian that was more enviable than Hopkins's new one, teaching the top level of pupils in the best Jesuit school in the country; it is not surprising if it provoked Hopkins to wonder whether the Provincial had his eye on him as a possible future Professed Coadjutor. Clearly, the Society was not yet sure how to use him, but he had the advantage of having taught at Stonyhurst twice before: his brief period of six days as a teacher in the College in 1873, and his return there in the summer term of 1878, when he had been called away from Mt St Mary's.

Hopkins's new duties were to teach Latin, Greek and some English to the 'Philosophers' in preparation for the BA at the University of London. The Philosophers were a curious breed of young men, spawned by the attitude of the hierarchy to education at Oxford and Cambridge. Since they were in theory not permitted to go to the older universities, Catholics who had completed their school education were tacitly allowed to go to non-denominational colleges in London, and at Stonyhurst they were kept on for an extra year or two of special tuition. It was an expensive process, chiefly confined to the rich, of whom many were interested only in a pleasant and not too demanding holiday after leaving school. They were the idle, often corrupt, youth of whom the young Count von Hönsbröch had complained at the time Hopkins was studying at the Seminary in Stonyhurst; their response to tuition could not help being a disappointment to Hopkins, after teaching boys like Herbert Berkeley at Mt St Mary's.

The ill-defined position of the Philosophers also pointed to a vague hope that Catholic education, which had so far been denied a reasonable English college or university, might make Stonyhurst the nucleus of a new university run by the Church. The *Tablet* had been suggesting such a possibility only the month before Hopkins arrived; it is improbable that he could have accepted this as a suitable proposition, and, if we can judge by his behaviour elsewhere, he would have made it clear, not to the advantage of his assimilation into the community.

That the Society still had high hopes for Hopkins seemed indicated when the Provincial told him of the Stonyhurst position: 'what time was left over I might employ in writing one or other of the books I had named to him. But very little time will be left over and I cd. never make time. Indeed now, with nothing to do but prepare, I cannot get forward with my ode [on Edmund Campion].'

While at Manresa he had completed sixteen pages of rough draft of a commentary on the Spiritual Exercises, presumably one of the books of which he had told Fr Purbrick. As he admitted tepidly to Bridges, it would be of no interest to anyone but a Jesuit, but, he added unenthusiastically, it was 'interesting enough' and 'very professional'.[24]

What he was forced to face directly for the first time was the blunt fact that his failure to write poetry was not the fault of external circumstance but of his own personality. The barrier to his creativity lay far deeper than what is usually meant by the facile term 'writer's block', for it indicated an ability to find the poetic harmony of heavenly and physical that had become the external mark of his faith. Only four months after arriving at Stonyhurst, he told Baillie in an unusually intimate letter that he was near the end of his resources:

> I like my pupils and do not wholly dislike the work, but I fall into or continue in a heavy weary state of body and mind in which my go is gone (the elegance of that phrase! as Thackeray

says, it makes one think what vast sums must have been spent on my education!), I make no way with what I read, and seem but half a man. It is a sad thing to say. I try, and am even meant to try, in my spare time (and if I were fresher or if it were anyone but myself there would be a good deal of spare time taking short and long together) to write some books; but I find myself so tired or so harassed I fear they will never be written.[25]

When he had to acknowledge that he was not short of time, he could hardly claim giving up poetry as a penance, as he had done at least twice before, saying that it detracted from his spiritual duties; particularly was this so when writing seemed actually enjoined on him by the Provincial of his own Society.

The sad truth was that Fr Purbrick was not rewarding Hopkins but seeking desperately for a way to use him profitably. He liked and admired him but found him so eccentric that, as he wrote to a colleague in Dublin, 'I am trying him this year in coaching B.A.s at Stonyhurst, but with fear and trembling.'[26] It is unthinkable that he would say such a thing to Hopkins himself, but his feelings probably percolated through into the community at Stonyhurst, so that Hopkins would be dimly aware of them. Hopkins's sense of his own inadequacy comes through his envious remark that an energetic contemporary 'never lets a minute go idle and after his teaching-work at once returns to his own studies'.[27] To his fellow teachers Hopkins's inability to work seemed to spring from sloth-fulness rather than the bone-deep spiritual weariness in which it was truly rooted. It was an attitude in his fellows to his lassitude that was to follow him from Stonyhurst to Dublin and make him miserable. Worst of all for Hopkins was that he was not always able to distinguish between the causes himself, so that guilt about his torpor became self-infecting and further increased his inability to work.

At Stonyhurst, as at almost every place he had been posted since ordination, Hopkins found the builders in command of an eruption of new physical facilities, in this case to take care of three hundred boys, which had been determined as the ideal community for the College. After all its years of expulsion the Society felt behind architecturally and was hurriedly making good the lost time. While he was at Mt St Mary's Hopkins never saw the buildings without a mask of scaffolding; in Oxford St Aloysius's was a not-yet healed scar in the old city; during his Liverpool exile St Francis Xavier's was building new schools and trying to finish the church; the handsome old mansion at Manresa had been almost lost in a welter of new living quarters and commodious chapel. A spiritual growth parallel to the architectural development was not always immediately evident to him. At Stonyhurst the new College seemed in constant movement with contractors, builders, masons, bricklayers, carpenters, stonecutters and carvers swarming over it; twice a day a traction engine fetched stone from a quarry on the fells; 'engines of all sorts send their gross and foulsmelling smoke all over us; cranes keep swinging . . .', as the old country house and its dependencies were transformed into a busy community the size of a village. No one, least of all Hopkins, would have wanted the Church to withdraw from the nineteenth century, but at times it seemed as if it were in competition for growth with the railways and cotton mills. Hopkins himself found the new buildings imposing in spite of their lack of beauty, and he thought their fittings 'a joy to see', none of which detracted from his sense of unease at what was happening to the countryside.

As he had feared, he wrote little poetry at Stonyhurst. In two years he produced only three poems of consequence, of which one had been largely written two years earlier, and one was a strictly 'occasional' poem for the May celebration of the month of the Blessed Virgin. Both 'Ribblesdale', a sonnet about the squandering of the earth by 'dear and dogged' man, and 'The Leaden Echo and the Golden Echo', intended as a chorus in his drama on St Winefred, are painfully concerned with the death of beauty.

'Ribblesdale' grew out of his return to the austere beauty of the Lancashire countryside and his awareness of the fragility of that prospect. There is no indication that he had in the forefront of his mind the construction of the new College, but it can hardly have helped contribute to his obsession with the rapine of 'Earth, sweet Earth, sweet landscape'. Man is the heedless legatee of 'our rich round world', which he thoughtlessly wastes without 'reck of world after': a phrase in which echo overtones of both the consequent physical wasteland in which his descendants must live, and of his life in the world after this one.

'Ribblesdale' is about man's wanton destruction of natural beauty, 'The Leaden Echo and the Golden Echo' about his wrong-headed sorrow at the loss of youthful, physical beauty, when the beauty that should concern him is the eternal one of the spirit. Not a wholly new subject, one must admit, but it is treated in this experimental poem almost as an exercise in alliteration and assonance. In all his works there is none in which Hopkins was more concerned to advance his argument by sheer sound. The opening immediately sets up the association of k and l with keeping or locking, b with beauty, a with affirmation, then pits them against the consonants associated with death (d), wrinkles (r) and negation (n) and this becomes the tension of the entire poem:

> How to keep – is there ány any, is there none such, nowhere
>   known some, bow or brooch or braid or brace, lace, latch
>   or catch or key to keep
> Back beauty, keep it, beauty, beauty, beauty, . . . from
>   vanishing away?
> Ó is there no frowning of these wrinkles, rankèd wrinkles
>   deep,
> Down?

The sense of despair at the inevitable transience of the purely physical was surely a very personal one for Hopkins at the time, since he was feeling far older than his thirty-eight years, and the immediacy is reflected in the supercharged words he puts rather incongruously in the mouths of the maidens who are meant to speak the chorus:

> . . . O why are we so haggard at the heart, so care-coiled,
> care-killed, so fagged, so fashed, so cogged, so cumbered . . .

Inevitably they bring to mind his lament to Bridges about his time in Liverpool: 'one is so fagged, so harried and gallied up and down

. . . human nature is so inveterate. Would that I had seen the last of it.'

In the dialogue of the poem, the resonance of the leaden echo is much greater than that of the golden, so that a reader probably comes away from the chorus with a stronger sense of the voice of despair than Hopkins presumably intended. Since the drama was never completed, it is impossible for us to see how its placing would have modified the effect.

In its own way 'The Blessed Virgin compared to the Air we Breathe' is as experimental as the chorus from the St Winefred drama, since Hopkins was trying the unfamiliar and constricting form of iambic trimeter, and it demonstrates how much he needed space to expand, even when writing in conventional forms. It was the custom at Stonyhurst to 'hang up polyglot poems in honour of the Blessed Virgin' each May, and this, his contribution as the English offering, was as he suggested, 'partly a compromise with popular taste'. By this last he presumably meant that it was conventional in its praise of Mary, demonstrating more piety than poetic inspiration. Probably because of the subject, or perhaps because of the constricted poetic lines, he did not expect Bridges to like it, but surprisingly enough, Bridges thought it admirable.[28]

When Bridges read 'The Leaden Echo and the Golden Echo', he said he detected the influence of Walt Whitman in the lines, provoking Hopkins to reply that he had read no more than half a dozen of his poems, as well as a number of short extracts in a review by George Saintsbury of *Leaves of Grass*, although even that short exposure was adequate to give him a good idea of the American's idiosyncratic manner, thought and rhythm:

> I always knew in my heart Walt Whitman's mind to be more like my own than any other man's living. As he is a very great scoundrel this is not a pleasant confession. And this also makes me the more desirous to read him and the more determined that I will not.[29]

All the same, he thought that Bridges, on a second reading, would see no real resemblance between Whitman's poetry and his own.

It has often been said that Hopkins felt some secret kinship with

Whitman's homosexual inclinations, and that he was scandalized not by those but by his democratic bellowings. One critic, however, has questioned how widely Whitman's sexual leanings were recognized at the time,[30] to which the simplest answer is that in the review Hopkins read, Saintsbury could scarcely have made the matter clearer, short of bluntly labelling his emotions. It was, Saintsbury wrote, to his democratic beliefs that

> we may fairly trace the prominence in Whitman's writings of the sexual passion, a prominence which has given rise, and probably will yet give rise, to much unphilosophical hubbub. This passion as the poet has no doubt observed, is almost the only one which is peculiar to man as man, the presence of which denotes virility if not humanity, the absence of which is a sign of abnormal temperament. . . . He is never tired of repeating 'I am the poet of comrades' – Socrates himself seems renascent in this apostle of friendship . . . and in this respect [he] fully justifies . . . Mr Symonds' assertion of his essentially Greek character . . .[31]

It is probable that Hopkins was worried that readers might equate freedom in rhythm in both their works with a similar freedom in morals. His real concern is indicated by his later remark to Bridges about 'Harry Ploughman' that if there was 'anything like it in Walt Whitman, as perhaps there may be . . . I should be sorry for that'.[32] Any accidental similarity in their rhythms, he said, was due not to imitation but to a shared inheritance of a venerable tradition in English verse.

It is a curious little exchange; though Hopkins never really explained how his mind and Whitman's were alike (a similarity in their rhythms seems an inadequate basis for such a linking), his patent worry that readers might sense a connection between them is some indication of how conscious he was that his poetry contained more of his interior life than he intended to reveal. He had been rubbed into a more personal statement than he usually made at this period of his life, and it comes as a surprise to us because there are so few other surviving intimate documents to provide the kind of direct evidence about his emotions that his journals had given in earlier years. It is ludicrously improbable, for example, that he was unaware of or unworried about his own sexual nature, but we are forced to turn to his poetry for indications of his buried life. And of poetry there was comparatively little.

The handful of poems he wrote at Stonyhurst was a meagre production to show for a year and a half, and in despair he told Bridges that he was jaded without knowing why, 'and my vein shews no signs of ever flowing again'.[33] He was so desperate at having no inspiration that he even considered writing out his thoughts first in prose, then versifying them, a procedure that could not have been more antithetical to his usual method of composition, in which language itself was a mode of thought.

In July 1883 his old worry about reassignment came up, just as it always did at the time when appointments for the next year were announced:

> It seems likely that I shall be removed; where I have no notion. But I have long been Fortune's football and am blowing up the bladder of resolution big and buxom for another kick of her foot. I shall be sorry to leave Stonyhurst; but go or stay, there is no likelihood of my ever doing anything to last. And I do not know how it is, I have no disease, but I am always tired, always jaded, though work is not heavy, and the impulse to do anything fails me or has in it no continuance.[34]

One of the things that had initially been most attractive to him about the Society was its stability of purpose, but what he had not taken into account was the cost to him of the unpredictability of its assignments. On this occasion, as on several previously, his fears proved unfounded, and he was told he would remain another year at Stonyhurst.

Almost immediately after he heard his assignment he left for Hampstead, to be with his parents for a week; after that he had special leave to accompany them to Holland for a brief stay. So few papers survive from this period that it is difficult to guess the state of his relations with his family, but the trip suggests that their differences had been almost completely patched up. His sister Grace had been engaged to a young Prussian who died suddenly, before they could be married. Shortly after his death, in the summer of 1883, she had gone to Germany to be with his family, and now Hopkins and his parents were to accompany her home from the Continent. It was his first trip out of the British Isles since his novitiate, and it was to be his last.

Neither reconciliation with his family nor the knowledge that he did not have to leave Stonyhurst at once was enough to make him happy, but at least by the end of the summer of 1883 he was looking hard for resignation and acceptance in place of the sting of remorse. In September he went into retreat at Beaumont, where 'an old and terribly afflicting thought and disgust' drove him to consult an old friend, Fr Kingdon. 'He advised me not further to dwell on the thought.' During the retreat he resigned his poetry to God to use as He saw fit; 'And this I believe is heard.' The following day he found further understanding in considering the reasons for his unhappiness: 'In meditating on the Crucifixion I saw how my asking to be raised to a higher degree of grace was asking also to be lifted on a higher cross. Then I took it that our Lord recommended me to our Lady and her to me.'[35]

In the summer of 1883 he met the third of the poets with whom he was to have a long correspondence on aesthetic matters. For Speech Day the College was in the habit of inviting famous Catholics to hand out the prizes. Distinguished Catholic poets were a bit thin on the ground, and their choice fell on Coventry Patmore, a convert of some twenty years, who was invited to shed lustre on the proceedings for three days. Probably a great many more of his fellow teachers knew that Hopkins was a poet than he usually admitted; in any case, he seems to have been sniffed out on this occasion as the proper person to take care of the poetic guest, although no one had bothered to tell Patmore that his host was also a poet, however unknown and however unproductive he was at the time.

Three days under such circumstances can seem a long spell, and the two men naturally talked poetry a great deal, exchanging names of poets they knew personally. Hopkins offered Bridges and Dixon. For his ignorance of Bridges's poetry Patmore gave the threadbare explanation that he had read the reviews but had tried with no success to get the works themselves from booksellers. Hopkins could show him no volumes, since his vow of poverty kept him from owning any, but in his innocence wrote to ask how Patmore might buy them, a request that must have startled Bridges, who knew that booksellers were seldom sold out of his works. The only poems by Dixon that Hopkins had were in manuscript and seem therefore to have been outside the terms of his vows; although Patmore had not heard of the Canon before, Hopkins gave him an armful of his works 'and made an enthusiastic convert of him'.

What was probably more important in winning the favour of Patmore was that Hopkins knew and admired his poetry; Patmore heartily concurred with his admiration, although as the years passed it had become increasingly difficult to find others to agree. Unlike many converts, he had little but disdain for the priesthood in normal circumstances, since respect for it would have been to diminish his opinion of himself, but he was willing to forgive Hopkins his calling, since he was obviously so knowledgeable about good poetry. He told Hopkins that before bringing out a new volume in the autumn he would send it to Stonyhurst for his suggestions. 'I do not know but it was bragging to mention this,' Hopkins wrote to Bridges, 'however now there it is, all blubbering in wet ink.'[36] By the end of the year five months later, some twenty-five letters had been exchanged between the two new friends. Into the flurry of paper Hopkins threw all the energy that he was unable to muster for his own poetry, a response that clearly surprised Patmore.

With a directness which that publication seldom displays, the *Dictionary of National Biography* describes Patmore as 'haughty, imperious, combative, sardonic . . . at the same time sensitive, susceptible, and capable of deep tenderness'. To Hopkins, as to many others, he displayed the latter qualities before revealing the former. Only a month after they met Hopkins was declining an invitation to stay with the Patmores, and shortly thereafter he offered a Mass for Patmore's dead son.

Whatever result Patmore expected from his attendance at Speech Day, he can hardly have anticipated the avalanche of letters Hopkins wrote to him about his work. To a letter of two or three paragraphs Hopkins would reply with one ten times as long. It is a curious correspondence, for it is the only one that has survived in which Hopkins says so little of his own life; instead, the pages are devoted to line-by-line analysis of Patmore's works. Furthermore, his criticism is of a crampingly individual nature; most of his critical letters to others are concerned with general principles of poetry, but the Patmore letters seldom are, and one suspects that it is Patmore whose personality and interests are the cause.

Another odd aspect of the correspondence is that, compared with the letters to Bridges and Dixon, they contain relatively little religious discussion. One wonders whether their common background as Catholic converts was not actually a division rather than a bond. Perhaps their shared experience made it unnecessary to mention such matters, but it may also be that they wanted to avoid subjects on which they were expected to agree, when they were actually so far apart.

Hopkins subjected Patmore's poems to a minute scrutiny for tone, diction, rhythm, often for simple fact: '"Link catching link": only goods trains do this; passenger trains are locked rigidly,' he typically wrote of one line. Even more carefully he examined Patmore's attitude to relations between the sexes. To understate the matter, Hopkins could not be said to share Patmore's interests totally, since he was one of the most flagrantly uxorious men of the century, one who quite simply worshipped women and all they stood for. He was thrice married, each time with the undiminished enthusiasm of a bridegroom of twenty, and his most famous work was *The Angel in the House*, a long celebration of the spiritual and physical delights of courtship and marriage, in which the sexual union is a symbol of Divine love. It is surely pertinent that his library was said to have as many erotic books as religious ones. Hopkins was far from censorious in such matters, and he had admired Patmore's poetry since his undergraduate days. As we have seen over and over, he could not always completely separate his own feelings for God and for other men, but the fact that Patmore was writing about heterosexual love may have caused a slight unease about his poetry.

In criticizing one of Patmore's poems Hopkins was led into a statement that sounds remarkably like Milton:

Adam sinned by love of his wife, that is he sinned for, or through love of his wife; but, formally speaking, the sin was

355

one of disobedience and its act eating the apple. To him no doubt it seemed gracious, *chivalrous*, as we should say, to share Eve's fate; he even thought God would look at it in this light; but to us, the circumstances considered, the act appears grievous, selfish, for it ruined a race for the sake of two. . . .[37]

Patmore, who preferred his praise undiluted, began sliding out of direct answers to adverse criticism. On one occasion he thanked Hopkins for his 'new batch of suggestions, which I see, at a glance, are very important . . . I find it better not to take off the edge of the work of correction by familiarizing myself too much with your suggestions until I come to the actual labour; therefore I abstain from writing about individual points.' Three weeks later he was writing to say that Hopkins's 'careful and subtle fault-finding is the greatest praise my poetry has ever received'.[38] Probably the gratitude was genuine, but 'fault-finding' may hint at a trace of other feelings.

Hopkins was so used to the no-holds-barred exchange of criticism with Bridges that he expected everyone to operate by the same rules. His own letters usually show a sweet-tempered lack of resentment at being taken to task by his old friend, and so far as we can judge without seeing his letters, Bridges took his own knocks with equal good humour. Some six months after he first met Patmore, Hopkins, who was often tactless about the failure of his friends to achieve poetic fame, mentioned to Patmore that he had been reading in the *Spectator* of a selection of the best living English writers in prose and verse. Browning headed the list, and Tennyson, Ruskin, Newman and Arnold all did well: 'I saw your name nowhere. Indeed I believe you were not in the running.' He proceeded casually to suggest that Patmore's lack of recognition came about because he was almost 'too full of meaning'. But the damage had been done. Patmore replied coolly, 'As to what you note of the paragraph in the "Spectator", I shall not consider myself "out of the running" so long as there are a dozen men in England to think or speak of the "Unknown Eros" as you do.' Beside he added dryly, 'the "Angel" obtained for me, at one time, a very sufficient taste of public applause'.[39]

Hopkins had hoped to keep secret from Patmore the fact that he was a poet, but both Bridges and Dixon seem to have let the cat out of the bag, and Patmore wrote to ask if he might see some of the poetry. His memory for imagined slights was infallible, and his exchange with Hopkins over poetic reputation was still clearly in his mind when he received a package of his poems some two months later.

Patmore read the poems several times, his first impressions confirmed with every reading:

> It seems to me that the thought and feeling of these poems, if expressed without any obscuring novelty of mode, are such as often to require the whole attention to apprehend and digest them; and are therefore of a kind to appeal only to the few. But to the already sufficiently arduous character of such poetry you seem to me to have added the difficulty of following *several* entirely novel and simultaneous experiments in versification and construction, together with an altogether unprecedented system of alliteration and compound words; – any one of which novelties would be startling and productive of distraction from the poetic matter to be expressed.

With a concession about the poems that was at best ambiguous, he admitted that 'no one who knows what poetry is can mistake them for anything but poetry'. He said that a few poems like 'The Blessed Virgin compared to the Air we Breathe' were exquisite because they were free of the 'self-imposed shackles':

> I can conceive that, after awhile, they would become additional delights. But I do not think that I could ever become sufficiently accustomed to your favourite Poem, 'The Wreck of the Deutschland' to reconcile me to its strangeness.

It is the one of his poems that we might expect Patmore to have liked best, for its baroque religious eroticism. To Bridges he wrote that Hopkins's poetry 'has the effect of veins of pure gold imbedded in masses of unpracticable quartz'. Later he told Bridges that he was sorry that he had to tell Hopkins of his objections, but he had either to be silent or speak the truth: 'I have seldom felt so much attracted towards any man as I have been towards him, and I shall be more sorry than I can say if my criticisms have hurt him.'[40]

The truth was that Hopkins, who was so vulnerable in other ways, was seldom worried by objections to his poetry, so long as he knew they were well intentioned. We do not know what his reaction to Patmore's strictures was, but two or three weeks later Patmore was writing to sound him out, 'Pray let me have one line some day to say that, however much you may despise me, you are not offended.' Patmore could not imagine that his silence could have been occasioned by anything but his criticism, but one suspects that Hopkins was more offended by the manner than by the matter of what Patmore had said. Some letters are clearly missing from the sequence that has survived, but the next one we have was not written for more than another year, and by that time Hopkins's circumstances had changed so much that he had probably forgotten the whole matter, for its tone is as friendly as ever, even if the air of slight formality has not lessened.

In 1885 Hopkins stayed for a few days in Hastings with Patmore and his family. Patmore was married for the third time, and Hopkins had a typical bachelor's reaction at meeting their two-year-old Epiphanius, an alarming child who treated animals as if they were human and howled if he so much as heard they were hurt. 'I witnessed some cases,' Hopkins said. 'I should not like it in a brother of mine.' During his stay, Patmore showed his guest the manuscript of a prose work he had been writing for some ten years, *Sponsa Dei*, about the connection between Divine and sexual love. However much covert or unconscious sexuality went into his own poetry, Hopkins did not approve of its public expression in the works of others. According to Patmore, he read the little book, then said with a grave and clerical look, 'That's telling secrets'.[41] So strong was his moral authority that Patmore said he felt he must throw the book on the fire, a dramatic statement and a true one so far as we know, but Patmore did not mention that he delayed two years before destroying it, which takes some of the point from what he told Hopkins. The two men never met again, but their correspondence continued until it seems to have died of inanition in the last year before Hopkins's own death.

When he first went to Stonyhurst, Hopkins was sure he would

not be able to squeeze in any music: 'I fear I shall not have time even for necessities, let alone luxuries or rather bywork,'[42] but within a few months he was asking Bridges to send him some of Purcell's music to pick his way through on the piano, since he was finding Bach's fugues too much like 'beginning at the end', and before his first year at Stonyhurst was up, he had sent a composition to Bridges, asking that it be given to Dr (later Sir John) Stainer for his opinion. When he had heard from Bridges, he admitted, 'I think from what you say it had better not go to Stainer.'

The range of his activities was so wide that it would be tempting to think he was not wasting time, were it not that he knew perfectly well where his first allegiance lay. At the end of 1883 he wrote a series of three letters to the magazine *Nature* about 'The Remarkable Sunsets' that had resulted that year from the eruption of the little Pacific island of Krakatoa, sending volcanic dust into the upper air. Insofar as science consists of the accurate observation of phenomena, these letters are perfection, for he had kept close track of the sunsets for months, recording them in his meticulous and poetic prose. The glow from the sunsets was intense, but on the 4th of December, he took a note of it as 'more like inflamed flesh than the lucid reds of ordinary sunsets':

> But it is also lustreless. A bright sunset lines the clouds so that their brims look like gold, brass, bronze, or steel. It fetches out those dazzling flecks and spangles which people call fish-scales. It gives to a mackerel or dappled cloudrack the appearance of quilted crimson silk, or a ploughed field glazed with crimson ice.[43]

It was becoming increasingly clear that nearly everything he was doing was marking time. He was ready for a change, and it came at the end of January 1884 when he was invited to become Professor of Greek at University College, Dublin, as well as Fellow of the Royal University of Ireland.

CHAPTER XIX

TO SEEM THE STRANGER
1884–5

Hopkins's new titles sounded considerably grander than they were in fact, and what lay behind his invitation to Dublin was more complicated than was indicated by his simple announcement to Bridges of his new position, to which he had added a laconic postscript: 'There was an Irish row over my election.' It was a neat understatement of a flaming Hibernian controversy that began in filling a vacant teaching position and quickly spilled over into a familiar series of tribal grievances: nationalism, politics, rivalry between secular priests and Jesuits, fear of England and Protestantism, hatred of the Anglo-Irish, and the whole question of the function of higher education. It is not clear how much Hopkins knew of what had already happened when he wrote to Bridges, but before long he had certainly heard all about it, and it helped to sour his pleasure in his new assignment.

The Royal University of Ireland was a rickety structure, not much more than a name given to an examining body that was responsible for granting degrees to successful candidates from the three endowed Queen's Colleges in Cork, Galway and Belfast, as well as from a handful of unendowed private schools and colleges. The RUI had been set up in 1879 in unstated opposition to the older University of Dublin (Trinity College).

At the time that the new University was established, the main Catholic college in Dublin was the Catholic University College, which had been founded by Newman a quarter of a century earlier and which had never been successful. In 1879, in hope of changing its fortunes, the hierarchy changed its name to University College Dublin, at the same time taking over Newman's old buildings in St Stephen's Green, and arranging that the Fellowships and other appointments of the RUI intended for Catholics should be concentrated there. By 1883 it had already become clear that the new College was no more successful than its predecessor, and Cardinal McCabe wanted badly to be rid of it. Thomas Arnold wrote that 'The poor C.U. is being walked about from one master to another like a White elephant, or like the "tall horse" of the Pickwickians, which they could not let go, but would have given anything to be quit of.'[1] It was a great relief to the hierarchy when the College was taken over by the Jesuits under the ebullient leadership of Fr William Delany. Both the hierarchy and the Jesuits thought they had secretly got the better of the other in the bargain.

As one of Hopkins's new colleagues explained the matter, the first duty of the new College was 'by hook or crook to put our College in front of Belfast . . . to beat Belfast at the exams: so as to show that Cath. Irishmen were capable of doing more in an unendowed College than Belfast in a richly equipped one'. It was hardly a form of competition with which Hopkins could be expected to sympathize deeply, and we can only assume that when he agreed to go to Dublin he had not understood the problem in those terms.

Fr Delany had considerably less than total support from his Irish Provincial, Fr Tuite, so he went over his head to the Fr General in Rome for approval of his plans, a move that naturally did not endear the project to the Provincial. Nor did Tuite like Delany's intention of turning the place into an intellectual, and probably social, rival to Trinity College, gradually getting rid of the moribund remains of Newman's teachers and replacing them with first-rate scholars. To Tuite this smacked of setting scholarship above Irish nationalism and might well involve bringing in English scholars, a renewal of the practice he was convinced had been the cause of Newman's failure. Particularly he disliked the idea of English converts, 'who are sometimes – well let us say – unsuited to this country and its thoroughly Catholic people'.[2]

Almost a year before the Jesuits formally took possession of the College Delany had begun scouting for new talent, with Stephen's Green in mind; his activities fulfilled Tuite's worst suspicions, for he was looking at possible candidates in the English Province, as well as in several other countries. He suggested to Fr

Purbrick, the English Provincial, the names of seven English Jesuits as possibilities for Dublin, and while he was waiting for an answer, he heard from Fr Porter, the English assistant to the Fr General in Rome, saying he was sure Purbrick would not consider releasing most of the men in the Province, although one, Hopkins, was a possibility, if not a good choice: 'He is clever, well-trained, teaches well but has never succeeded well: his mind runs in eccentric ways.' When Purbrick's own answer arrived a few days later, it assured Delany that of the seven he had asked about, six were 'the cream of the province' and could not possibly be spared. Once more an exception was mentioned; he was currently teaching at Stonyhurst, rather against the best instincts of the Provincial: 'Fr. Hopkins is very clever and a good scholar – but I should be doing you no kindness in sending you a man so eccentric.'[3] Not surprisingly, Delany let the matter drop.

By November 1883 the Jesuits had moved into their new quarters in Stephen's Green and had already begun raising enrolment impressively. At the time eight of the University Fellowships were vacant, and Delany assumed that two, in Natural Science and in Classics, would be awarded to University College. Once more he cast a net for new men, and this time his first choice seems to have been Hopkins, 'most qualified of the candidates'. Quite how he had become so well qualified in the interim is not obvious, although this time the College had asked for formal recommendations, and they were presumably so impressed by the testimony of Jowett and R.L. Nettleship about Hopkins's ability that they decided to ignore the tepid quality of Fr Purbrick's earlier assessment. Jowett was reputed, probably erroneously, to have called him 'the Star of Balliol', and Nettleship wrote that he was 'one of the cleverest and most original men at Oxford in his time', particularly in his delicate perception of language.[4] What neither of them knew about, or perhaps cared about, was the quality of his teaching.

When he was asked formally whether Delany might invite Hopkins to be a candidate, Purbrick gave his permission readily, probably with a sigh of relief, indicating his own feeling that intellectuals were not to be judged as other men and that the standards of Dublin was somewhat lower than those of Stonyhurst:

'I fancy also that University work would be more in his line than anything else. Sometimes what we in Community deem oddities are the very qualities which outside are appreciated as original & valuable.'[5]

Early in December 1883 Delany went to Stonyhurst to interview Hopkins and decided he was the best Jesuit classicist he could get, in spite of his peculiarities. What lay largely unspoken behind all the negotiations was the absolute necessity of finding a Jesuit for the vacant Fellowship, as it carried with it £400 per annum, and since Jesuits were prohibited by vow from having money, the sum would revert to the College as part of the much-needed funds for running the establishment. What seems a small amount today was very important when the College had no endowment.

While Fr Delany was proceeding with securing Hopkins, negotiations of a very different sort were going on under the prodding of the Revd Dr William Walsh, President of St Patrick's College, Maynooth. Walsh thought the specifically Catholic Fellowships should be dispersed among all Catholic colleges, not confined to University College, and he proposed to nominate the Headmaster of Blackrock College, Father Reffé, one of the Fathers of the Holy Ghost, rather than the Jesuit Hopkins. Both Delany and Walsh were members of the University Senate, which had already gone on record as favouring dispersion of Catholic teaching, but Delany apparently felt the resolution did not apply in this case. Walsh, who had never been outside Ireland in his training, was democratic in his educational ideas, reminding us of many twentieth-century theorists devoted to spreading higher education as far abroad as possible, no matter how thin the spread becomes. Delany, who had trained at Stonyhurst, had, like many Jesuits, a dilutedly aristocratic view of universities, believing that the best ones should be devoted to training the best minds with a combination of high-minded Christianity and the best of secular thought. In short, very like the ideals of Newman, which in their turn derived from the Oxford ideal. Two such different views were sure to come into conflict in setting up colleges and a university. To Walsh awarding the Fellowships to University College would be a capitulation to the 'Castle Catholics', or 'West Britons', particularly if either Fellowship was given to an Oxford man; to Delany, awarding them elsewhere would be a betrayal of the conditions under which the Jesuits had moved to Stephen's Green.

Both men consulted Cardinal McCabe, and each believed that he had succeeded in stiffening His Eminence's wavering approval of his own candidate. Delany urged on him what seemed a particularly telling qualification, Hopkins's talent at verse, which would be useful 'on account of the competition with Trinity College which prides itself on its verse writers'.[6] After the interview he felt that Hopkins's election was a certainty, even though the Cardinal had said that 'this place has had too much of Englishmen in its past history'.[7] On 29 January 1884 Delany telegraphed the good news to Hopkins that he would be elected on the following day at the meeting of the full Senate. Late that night he heard that the Cardinal had belatedly expressed his preference for Walsh's candidate and said that he wanted Delany to withdraw the name of Hopkins. Even if he had wanted to do so, it was too late for Delany to communicate with Hopkins, and there was nothing to do but let the election go forward the following day.

At the Senate meeting there were twenty-three votes for Hopkins, three for Fr Reffé. Recriminations over the part taken by both sides occupied the newspapers and the talk in common rooms long after the election. Fr Delany had won but only at the cost of the resignation from the Senate of the Cardinal and of Delany's former friend Fr Walsh. Walsh had lost but had managed to muddy the waters completely for the incoming Professor of Classics; a dozen years later, when he was successor to Cardinal McCabe as Archbishop of Dublin, he still publicly lamented losing the struggle. Hopkins was the one person whose feelings were not considered.

In all the years he had been a Jesuit, Hopkins seems never to have been consulted about future assignments; indeed, he had found their uncertainty hard to bear. It is unlikely that Fr Delany would have proceeded with his candidacy if Hopkins had shown any strong reluctance to go to Dublin during their meeting at Stonyhurst, and Fr W.A.M. Peters stresses that he went there by invitation not order: 'The strong tradition is that those in responsible positions of authority explain the situation and give reasons why they think that a Jesuit should take a particular job.'[8] But there are many kinds of explanation, and Fr Purbrick, who was so patently ready to be rid of him, may unwittingly have made it clear, even to Hopkins, that everyone would be best served by his departure. Hopkins told Newman that at first he tried to decline the offer out of a sense of his unfitness, which still kept his spirits from soaring. 'But perhaps the things of most promise with God begin with weakness and fear.'[9] To be sure, he was soul-weary at Stonyhurst, it was flattering to become a Professor of Classics after being a teacher of spotty schoolboys, he would be in one of the most musical cities in the British Isles and one reputedly among the most charming, he would have a great deal of free time in which to pursue the scholarship expected of him, and he would be lifted out of the world he had known for fifteen years, during which he had exhausted its novelty. Probably best of all, he would be following in the tracks of his beloved John Henry Newman, just as he had done ever since he was an undergraduate. Now, as he wrote to his mentor, he hoped to restore to the College the success that had languished since Newman's departure from Dublin.

Not everyone was anxious to go to Stephen's Green. Thomas Arnold the younger, whose original appointment there had been made by Newman, was Professor of English, but his wife was not with him. She had been furious at his conversion in the first place and was not placated when he returned to Anglicanism; when he was converted to Rome a second time, she felt it was too much. '*Once for all, I will not leave England and go to live in Ireland*,' she told him. She was suffering from cancer and announced with her usual vehemence, 'I should loathe it, if things were not as they are, but as things are *I will not do it. You have pleased yourself and* as you have made your bed so must lie on it, but while I live I will never know one of your R.C. friends.'[10]

Near the door of 86 Stephen's Green is the familiar tablet marking buildings connected with famous persons. It brings a catch to the throat to read there the names of the three great writers who so casually went up and down those worn stone steps and passed familiarly through the heavy door: John Henry Newman, Gerard Manley Hopkins, and James Joyce. In part Hopkins had come there in emulation of Newman, but his life in the dishevelled stone house was to be more like something from the greyer pages of Joyce's *Dubliners*.

As we might expect, in his correspondence Hopkins hardly mentioned the 'Irish row' over his election to his Fellowship, but he probably knew about it even before he first arrived in Dublin, which made more poignant his gratitude for the generosity of his reception, when he may have expected resentment at his appointment. 'I have been warmly welcomed and most kindly treated,' he told Bridges. 'But Dublin itself is a joyless place . . . I had fancied it quite different.'[11] That spring the University Senate was asked to restrict its Fellowships to graduates of the University, a sideswipe aimed at the English and in particular at Hopkins's election, which must have made his already awkward position even more uncomfortable.

No man could have come through a conversion from Anglo-Catholicism to Roman Catholicism without being aware of how bitter the acrimony of sect could be for sect; what he was not used to was the infighting within the Church itself, although he was soon to learn all about that. He was following in Newman's footsteps in ways he had not anticipated.

The city to which Hopkins came for the first time was in a deeply dispiriting state of decline. A century before it had been celebrated for its elegance and sparkle, with a provincial brilliance that made it Britain's closest approximation to the dukedoms and grand duchies that lay scattered through Germany, and like them it had provided the glitter of the aristocracy at the cost of those who worked for them. In Dublin most of the upper classes were Protestant, and Anglo-Irish at that. By the time Hopkins arrived, a large number of them had moved out of the city, chiefly to the newer suburbs to the south, which were solidly Protestant. The Catholics, who had always been in a numerical majority, were now beginning to assume control and their mood was punitive as they sought to make their new importance evident.

The establishment of the Royal University in 1879 had been in part a provision for training a new professional class of Catholics to replace the Protestants who still dominated the law, the Army, medicine, and such parts of the academy as Trinity College. In 1881, for example, although eighty per cent of the population was

Catholic, only forty per cent of the doctors and lawyers were Catholic, and most of those were on the lower rungs of the ladder; it was an inequity that clearly had to be changed, although the method was in dispute. As one historian of the city has written, 'The small rising Irish middle class had an extremely utilitarian attitude to education, viewing it as a passport to careers and respectability. . . . Intellectual curiosity in the classics was the preserve of a few.'[12]

In describing Irish education, one could use the labels of Catholic and Protestant, but non-denominational was a term that simply had no meaning. Within the Church the most important division was between those who thought of religion and education as ways of transcending petty nationalism, and those who thought of them as means of perpetuating what was specifically Irish, means which could also be used as sticks to beat the English and the Protestants. Hopkins, as we have seen, was a deeply patriotic Englishman, who came to believe in Home Rule and recognized the injustices to the Irish but did not feel that they warranted jettisoning everything else in which he believed; it was a position that was bound to make him uncomfortable with either side.

Among the Catholic community of Dublin there were a few priests, chiefly English by birth, who shared his dilemma, but most of the clergy were anti-English and somewhat jealous of the advantages they considered the English priests had enjoyed in their education. In turn, many of the Dublin Catholics who were born English considered that the Church in which they believed was responsible for bad Irish education. Thomas Arnold, Hopkins's colleague at University College, was convinced that the earlier difficulties of Newman's foundation had their roots in 'the peculiar character of the Irish priesthood, and in the intellectual and social superiority of the Protestants'. What surer way existed, he asked, of having bad priests

than to make the whole period of a priest's *education* (always a period of many years in the Catholic Church) free of all cost to his parents, and when that education is completed and he is ready to commence his career, to leave him to shift for himself and get a living how he can? Of course the consequence is that

367

the poorest cottier can look forward to making his son a priest, and *thereby to a rise in the social scale for himself and his family*. In the Protestant church it is just the reverse. The education of a clergyman is costly, and therefore only within the reach, speaking generally, of the higher classes. . . . On the whole the result is that the Irish priesthood, taken as a body, are not *gentlemen*, while the Protestant clergy are, and all the political and social consequences that inevitably follow from that one fact, you will instantly perceive. . . . I really do not believe that while the Irish priesthood continues to be of this low class, the Establishment is in any serious danger.[13]

Prejudiced though the letter obviously is, it states squarely the real basis of much of the friction within the Church in Ireland.

Visually, Dublin had begun to take on the air that any visitor senses nowadays, of the shabby remains of a once superbly beautiful city. It was, Hopkins told Bridges, as smoky as London, and it was covered in soot. In Stephen's Green or Merrion Square the windows still sparkled and the steps were immaculately swept, but nearby many of the patrician Georgian town houses had declined into squalid congeries of rooms in each of which lived an entire family. An elderly doctor I once met said that at a time somewhat later than Hopkins's stay there, he had been a medical student at the Rotunda Hospital, from which he went to deliver babies in houses that were exquisitely proportioned on the exterior but so crowded within that a woman might be giving birth on a newspaper-covered bed, surrounded by eight or ten other children intent on their play beneath the swags of an ornately plastered ceiling. It was the kind of contrast that shocked the sensibilies of the tender-hearted Hopkins and provoked him into both sympathy and rage. After his death his sister told Bridges that 'he was made miserable by the untidiness, disorder & dirt of Irish ways, the ugliness of it all'.[14] At least, as Lionel Hopkins said when he heard how dismayed Gerard was by his surroundings, it was 'better for him than drudgery among drunken Liverpool roughs'.

The poverty of the city in 1884 was in part responsible for its appalling death rate, which only five years earlier had been so bad that many country families were afraid to visit there. A stroll along the Liffey quickly made evident the noisome reason for much of the disease, since the river acted as the chief public sewer for the city. Dublin was too poor to put in adequate public drains, and even if they had been installed, disease would still have been spread by the poor sanitation of practically all the houses. Low-lying areas like St Stephen's Green were among the worst parts of Dublin, and those residents who could afford to do so tried to live on higher, better-drained terrain. 'Part of the flight from the city by the prosperous middle classes was motivated by an urge to escape from unhealthy, noxious conditions deemed to exist even in prosperous areas.' St Stephen's Green was still far better than merely respectable, but 'many houses had been turned into schools, others combined residences and professional rooms for city lawyers, doctors, gentlemen, outfitters, house furnishers, auctioneers and other commercial workers'.[15] In the centre of the busy square that the College buildings faced was an unrailed green, an oasis in which were to be found both children cared for by nursemaids and an array of other children begging or selling matches, not to mention the omnipresent tramps and drunks. For Hopkins it served only to invoke longing for the open fells of Lancashire or the green valleys of Wales. Their best substitute was Phoenix Park, which he loved, but it was 'inconveniently far off'.

The buildings (number 86 and the smaller house next it) into which the College had moved had fallen into 'a deep dilapidation' since Newman's day, and when the Jesuits came were 'a sort of wreck or ruin' The heavy and graceless but 'costly last century ornamentation of flutes and festoons and Muses on the walls' was incongruously surrounded by 'dinginess and dismantlement'.[16] The Chippendale and Hepplewhite furniture was all gone, replaced by prickly horsehair chairs, wire blinds on the windows, and indifferent pictures of the saints on the walls.

It was Hopkins's fate to spend much of his clerical career in great houses that had come down in the world socially, like Manresa, Stonyhurst, and University College: the difference between them was that the two earlier stages in his life were both in communities that, like him, were growing and full of hope, the last part in a setting that accurately reflected the melancholy of his own experience. Ironically, the home of the College had been built about 1769 by Richard Chapell Whaley, an eccentric politician and ardent Protestant who had earned the nickname of 'Burn-Chapel' Whaley because he had set fire to so many Catholic churches. Whaley's unattractive intention in building the house had been to make it so grand that Lord Clanwilliam's house at number 85 would look a pigsty by comparison. He may be said to have succeeded in his ambition, since it is an overpowering house, indeed bigger and more grandiose than its neighbour, which was joined to it by the Jesuits in Hopkins's time. Upon Whaley's death the house and £10,000 p.a. had passed to his son, a spendthrift rake whose career made the bucks in eighteenth-century novels look strait-laced by comparison. On one occasion he wagered that he would jump from a drawing room window of his 'palace' into the first barouche that passed, and kiss its occupant – and won the bet.

Even today, when the building has taken on an unmistakably academic look and smell, it is hard to imagine Hopkins in its frayed-at-the-cuff splendour of foaming plasterwork and polished flags. His room was at the back, looking down into a fine big garden. It was high, rather narrow but adequately large, and it served him as combined study and bedroom; today it stores a motley collection of furniture and books dating from the period when he was there, the forerunner of what is expected to become a museum to him. From the window of the room can be seen the apse of the beautiful little Byzantine church that Newman had built when he was Rector, but by the time Hopkins arrived it no longer belonged to the College, which had a makeshift chapel in number 86 where he said Mass. Today the church serves the parish; it is hard anywhere, either in the church or the College of which it once was a part, to find a trace of Newman's glowing spirit that had drawn Hopkins there.

The extreme poverty of the College and its chaotic state made it 'like living at a temporary Junction'. Dry rot was widespread, and even the window from which he looked over the garden could not be opened until he had used 'gentle but continued pressure' on a carpenter to repair it. More ominously, the sanitation was in an appalling state, and since the house was built on such low ground, the basement is said to have been disgusting, full of filth and rats, two of which found their way into the stewpot in the kitchen on one occasion. As Hopkins put the matter fastidiously to his mother, 'the College is poor, all unprovided to a degree that outsiders wd. scarcely believe, and of course – I cannot go into details – it cannot be comfortable.' The matter was of more than aesthetic interest, for the lack of decent sanitation may have contributed to his own death.

Mrs Hopkins, with a natural maternal concern, thought that Gerard's circumspect letter meant that he was cold, so she sent him heavy clothing by return. He wrote to his sister Kate in mock-Irish that 'twas not the inclimunsee of the saysons I was complainin of at all at all. Twas the povertee of books and such like educational convaniences.'[17] The truth was that the most essential part of any college was completely missing, for when UCD was turned over to the Jesuits, the committee that had invited them removed the entire library to the Diocesan Seminary at Clonliffe, where Hopkins said it lay, 'acquiring antiquity and the interest of "worming"'. Fr Delany finally made an appeal to the Bishops, who passed a resolution that it should be restored to St Stephen's Green, even though they did not really believe that any of the books had been removed in the first place. Not surprisingly, nothing was done in response to the resolution, so Thomas Arnold complained to the Cardinal, who responded with a diplomatically phrased archiepiscopal letter, and in his turn did nothing. 'Now the students are petitioning', Hopkins wrote; 'I shall be curious to see what becomes of their petition.'[18]

During Hopkins's time in the College the books remained scattered around the Catholic institutions in the country. Gradually a minimal library was acquired, but by then the places in the College once occupied by books had been taken over for other purposes, so that he complained about having 'more money to buy books than room to put them in'. Even if he had been a better teacher than he was, he would probably have been defeated by such a paucity of necessities. As an Oxford graduate he was allowed the use of the library of Trinity College himself, but that was of no use to his pupils. The central house of his College was, he said, an empty birds' nest.

When he faced for the first time the prospect of conducting six University-wide examinations each year by setting the papers himself, then marking them, he thought that St Stephen's Green, 'the biggest square in Europe', paved with gold, would not pay for his efforts. The previous year there had been 750 candidates for matriculation, normally the largest examination of the year. According to one modern study of the examinations, by 1887 there were two sets of matriculation examinations each year, two sets of first BA, one set of second BA exams, and a smaller number each for the BA degree and the MA degree.[19] All in all, there were 1795 examination scripts for him to mark that year, and for the six years he taught in Dublin the numbers varied between thirteen and eighteen hundred. For the first time he was finding out what it meant to teach in a university where honours and degrees were awarded for rote not investigative intelligence.

In addition to this, he was expected to teach the Arts undergraduates in University College, of whom there were about a hundred the year he arrived, although there were only a handful resident in the College itself. In his first half-year, from January to October 1884, he was not asked to lecture, since another man had already been engaged for the tuition.

It was just after this period that he wrote to his mother of his conviction that the College would weather its initial difficulties, for the simple reason that Fr Delany had 'a buoyant and unshaken trust in God' and worked whole-heartedly for the success of the College: 'He is as generous, cheering, and openhearted a man as I ever lived with.'[20] Delany was generally loved, but his desire for the College's success included some hard-headed planning that Hopkins had not yet learned to recognize. The 'Fathers of the Society of Jesus', who published a history of University College in 1930 had a collective memory of Delany as a Rector who looked for Fellows not for the future, 'but for present value'. He particularly wanted Jesuits because the College would receive the money for their Fellowships, and also because 'they would teach, not one or two hours a day, but the whole day'.[21] He was fond of Hopkins and did his best for him, but he was not the man to sacrifice the College for the comfort of one of his teachers. Before long Hopkins was teaching full time in the College as well as marking for the entire University, and it nearly killed him. Perhaps it did. Nonetheless his labours contributed to the eventual success of the College, which was finally Delany's aim.

The story is often told, with variations, of how Hopkins was so scrupulous in his marking that he would be found in the middle of the night with a wet towel wound round his forehead as he assigned grades, which he calculated precisely down to quarters and halves that he was subsequently quite unable to add up. Probably justifiably, he complained of overwork, and his letters are full of the numbers of examinations loaded on to him; in the autumn of 1884 he had 557 on hand ('let those who have been thro' the like say what that means'); in 1886 '331 accounts of the First Punic War with trimmings' sweated him down to his 'lees and usual alluvial low water mudflats, groans, despair and yearnings'.[22] In each case there were five or six other examinations during the course of the year.

Even when he had finished his marking, Hopkins felt that he was harassed by the incompetence of the clerical bureaucrats who ran the University and by 'having to deal with officials whose behaviour was overbearing and ungentlemanly'. On one occasion he had to witness the humiliating censure of a colleague, 'one of the old school of fine and laborious scholars'. His best hope was that the Royal University would have a speedy demise.[23]

For a man so given to self-questioning, the bitterest times were those when he came to doubt any value in the 'great, very great drudgery' of examining, a question that must occur occasionally to the least sensitive person who indulges promiscuously in the practice. 'I can not of course say it is wholly useless,' he complained to his mother, 'but I believe that most of it is and that I bear a burden which crushes me and does little to help any good end.'[24] Few things could be worse for him than discovering the utter futility of what he was forced to carry out against his will.

Lectures were no better for him, and he longed for holidays: 'As a tooth ceases aching so will my lectures intermit after tomorrow for Shrovetide', he wrote in the last year of his life.[25]

The number of papers Hopkins claimed to have read was very near that recorded in a modern study of the matter, and we have no reason to think that he was in any way consciously exaggerating, but some of his contemporaries believed that he was complaining without cause. Fr Joseph Darlington, also a convert, had been at Oxford and studied with Pater, and now was his colleague in St Stephen's Green. Years later he said that Hopkins had not had to work particularly hard, that he taught Greek three times a week to a class of five or six, for a total of only about three hours in all, and that Greek examinations were held only twice a year, with very few candidates in either: 'The only sufferings of Hopkins in Dublin were physical and spiritual ones.' One may wonder what other kinds of suffering would have been worse for Hopkins.

By all accounts Fr Darlington was a charitable man without malice, but even so it would be natural to take his testimony as veiled envy were it not that a reviewer of Bridges's edition of Hopkins's poetry, who seems to have known Hopkins personally, also said that 'it was absurd of Mr. Bridges to speak of the classical examiner's work as drudgery; it was nothing of the kind: there could hardly have been found for him in all the Irish Province a less exhausting work'. Another Jesuit writer, Fr G.F. Lahey, wrote in the first biography of Hopkins that his work in the Royal University 'itself was interesting and consoling, and his friends congenial and satisfying; then too, the monotony of routine was easily broken by the utmost freedom he had received from his superiors'.*

In 1933 Fr Darlington still felt so strongly about the matter that he told a visitor that Hopkins's true task in Dublin had been 'to give his energies to pushing the University business ahead – *which he did not do*: he did his routine teaching well and was "a very holy fellow, and all that", but wasn't really concerned about university politics'.[26]

It is difficult to adjudicate between such different views of his work in Dublin, but probably all have at least some truth in them. Hopkins was surely accurate in the numbers of examinations he claimed to have set, and he knew better than anyone else how much distress they caused him, but those who saw him daily also knew that he complained a good deal about work that was much like what they were doing themselves routinely. It is not surprising if they resented his attitude so much that they felt he was wrong on most other counts as well. As we have seen earlier, he often twisted the truth slightly without realizing what he was doing. He had come to

---

* Fr Lahey obtained much of his information about Hopkins's College life from Fr Darlington, who seems to have forgotten that Hopkins taught Latin and English as well as Greek. It seems possible that Fr Darlington was the ultimate source of all the testimony as to how little overworked Hopkins was. (See Appendix.)

Dublin with a reputation for being strange, and he was fulfilling it. At the time he was the only Jesuit from the English Province who was assigned to Ireland.[27] He brought with him what seemed to most of the Dublin priests strange habits of manner and thought better suited to England and to Oxford than to a hard-working community in Ireland, and probably they thought he felt superior on that account.[28] There are many stories of how odd his manner was in the College and of how he kept himself to himself in the community, which perversely liked to compare itself, in its *camaraderie*, to what it resented most, the common rooms of Oxford. It is significant that one of the other priests, a Frenchman named Mallac, felt far less an outsider than Hopkins and would say of him, 'I don't like that little Englishman.' More than two decades after Hopkins's death another member of the community said that no one in the group took him seriously and that he 'was thought by most to be more or less crazy'. Part of his awkward manner must have stemmed from his awareness of the suspicion of his fellow priests and their contempt for his tenaciously held loyalties.

It is hard to ignore this barely concealed hostility to Hopkins in the denials by his brother Jesuits of his being overworked, even if it is no longer certain what had caused their resentment. The Jesuit history of the College shifts all the blame to Hopkins's shoulders, saying that he perhaps 'ought never to have been a Jesuit', and that 'though he had many trials to endure, they were mainly due to his highly-wrought temperament.'[29]

As was to be expected, Hopkins was far from successful as a teacher. The official historian of the College wrote of him, 'His career as a teacher had not been successful in the English Jesuit schools, and those who remembered his lectures in Dublin seem to be agreed in their verdict that he was quite unable to impart the knowledge which he had gained at Oxford as a pupil of Nettleship and Jowett.'[30] Probably with another audience he could have communicated the love of learning his mentors had encouraged, but the young men in the College were more interested in facts that they could repeat in examinations than in the play of the intellect. All the luminous idealism Newman had brought to those rooms had long since evaporated, and Irish politics now seemed more important than Greek philosophy or even Christian theology.

Many of Hopkins's colleagues had not the foggiest idea of how his mind worked or what he was attempting to do in the College, and most were not even aware that he wrote poetry. Four years after his death Dixon was in Dublin and went to St Stephen's Green in search of the memory of Hopkins. He spoke to one of the priests who had known him well and who

> had a great opinion of Gerard, without, I think, knowing of his genius. He spoke of him as a most delightful companion, & as excellent in his calling, and so on, intimating at the same time that there was something unusual about him; that he was fond of pursuing niceties to an extent that rather stood in the way of his general usefulness. [And] that he dwelt on the niceties of the language, in his classical lectures, in a way that rather stopped the progress of the classes. Also he was fond of taking up unusual subjects for himself. . . .[31]

Hopkins's lectures and classes were conducted in an uproar. One of the arguments that had been dug up against his appointment in the first place was that it would give students of classics at the College an unfair advantage in examinations, since their teacher would be setting the papers and might therefore coach them on precisely the subjects that he would ask about in the examinations. Hopkins's over-conscientious reaction was predictable, although it would not be in anyone else: he announced he would not lecture on any subject that he included in the examinations. The result, of course, was that his pupils were often deprived of the most elementary instruction, putting them at a great disadvantage, only slightly offset by the knowledge that anything they heard in one of his lectures was not something they needed to remember for the examination. As Humphry House has written, the lectures were 'not of much marketable value' to the undergraduates. Since they felt no compulsion to listen to him with any care, they talked, laughed and created a constant disturbance. Because of his old-fashioned English Conservative views, they constantly ragged him about politics, treatment he unwittingly invited by his unruffled courtesy and 'his strange innocent seriousness'. He is said to have lamented, to the amusement of his auditors, never having seen a naked woman. According to W.H. Braydon, Hopkins, unlike his colleagues, did not silently skip the rape scenes in the classical texts he was discussing, but at their conclusion, he would throw up both hands and exclaim, 'O those poor girls!' It has often been told how a colleague came into one of his lectures and found Professor Hopkins on his back on the floor being dragged by his students around the table by his heels to demonstrate Hector's fate at Troy.* 'I do not object to their being rude to me personally,' he said to Katharine Tynan, 'but I do object to their being rude to their professor and a priest.'[32] There were no tutorials, no conferences of the kind that had been the best part of his teaching at Stonyhurst and Mt St Mary's, so that he had little of the consolation he had received there from close acquaintance with clever boys and young men. Somewhat shamefacedly he admitted to his mother that his best pupil was actually a Scottish Protestant.

The Jesuit community that Hopkins joined in 86 St Stephen's Green had ten members, of whom four were teachers, the rest administrative staff and three resident students. Previously, when he had moved from place to place, he had constantly run into old acquaintances, some from his novitiate, some from Stonyhurst, and so on. The English Province was a loose family, and most of its members knew each other, but in Dublin Hopkins was thrown in with nine men he had never seen before, which naturally contributed to his sense of loneliness. Of that lot one man was to become so close for a time that he might be numbered with others such as Bridges, Dolben, Dixon, Baillie or Addis as the most intimate of the acquaintances of Hopkins's life.

In the first surviving letter from Hopkins to his mother from Ireland he praised Fr Delany and said that the rest of the community gave him almost equal pleasure, 'but in particular Robert Curtis, elected Fellow with me, whom I wish that by some means you could someday see, for he is my comfort beyond what I can say and a kind of godsend I never expected to have'.[33]

Curtis, who had already been a lecturer at the College for several months, was made a Fellow in Natural Science in January 1884 at

---

* Sometimes the story is told that Hopkins was dragging one of his students, but the point is hardly changed about the disorder of his classes.

the meeting of the University Senate that elected Hopkins. In some important ways they were a great deal alike, in spite of Curtis's being eight years junior to Hopkins. They came from the same kind of middle-class background, which always meant more to Hopkins than he liked to admit: Curtis's father was a brilliant barrister who became Crown Prosecutor for the Counties of Kilkenny and Tipperary the same year that his son went to University College. The family was prosperous, Conservative in politics, Anglo-Irish but Roman Catholic, and lived in a handsome house in North Great George's Street, to which Hopkins became a frequent visitor.

Robert Curtis had been an undergraduate at Trinity College, Dublin, where he received as many honours as Hopkins did at Balliol. It has been said that he was tipped for a Fellowship at Trinity, but he preferred becoming a Jesuit. In many ways he was indistinguishable from the sort of young men who had formed Hopkins's circle as an undergraduate, and Hopkins seized upon this new friendship with the same alacrity he had displayed in Balliol. Curtis was unique in Hopkins's life in being probably the only intimate Irish (or at least Anglo-Irish) friend Hopkins ever had.

There was another way, however, in which Curtis was completely unlike Hopkins's other friends. When they met, he was thirty-two, near the age at which most Jesuits were ordained, but he was a permanent scholastic, still hoping to study further for the priesthood but kept from doing so by the epilepsy from which he had suffered since his undergraduate days. He was a naturally energetic man, but he was restricted to three hours of work daily, during which he was tentatively continuing the study of theology as well as teaching mathematics. His illness was scarcely more disabling than the depression that was swiftly growing on Hopkins, and their common ill health seems to have drawn them together without in any way becoming a central or neurotic issue in their friendship. As a mark of their intimacy, Hopkins called his new friend 'Robert', as he might not have done in those days had he been a priest. It seemed a long way from the years at Manresa when Hopkins had not even been able to pick his own companions for walks. Curtis 'had a rich fund of humour and gaiety which made him particularly beloved by his religious brethren'.[34] He and Hopkins apparently laughed together a great deal on the excursions they took in their spare time. In spite of his disability Curtis was as good a walker as Hopkins, with considerably more persistence and stamina, and the two men shared a passion for swimming.

Probably there were subterranean reasons why Hopkins needed a particularly close friend at that juncture. Dixon had married a second time in 1881, ending a long lonely period after the death of his first wife; more to the point emotionally, Bridges married in September 1884, at the age of forty, after declaring for years that he would never do so. Hopkins, in spite of his own celibate state, was a great proponent of marriage for his friends, but when Dixon and Bridges took wives, it naturally emphasized the loneliness of his own life, which should be remembered in considering his joy in the friendship of Curtis: 'to see him (or know him) is to love him', he wrote in a burst of pleasure.

Hopkins probably never needed intimate friendship more than he did in Dublin, especially during his first year there in 1884, when he felt so alien. Certainly, his correspondence was never more despairing, and as always, his emotions were directly reflected in his physical state.

The most complete evidence we have about his health in 1884 is contained in his correspondence with Bridges. In his very first letter from Dublin in March he laments his weakness, and a month later he breaks into unrelated matter to indicate his distraction in capitals: 'AND WHAT DOES ANYTHING AT ALL MATTER?'. The conclusion of the letter discusses the death of Sidney Lanier, the American poet, only two years younger than Hopkins, with whom he felt great empathy for his 'chaotic life and thwarted aspirations'. Hopkins's feeling of identification with Lanier is painfully evident, probably connected with his own fascination with death during these months; what is less certain is whether he was unable to restrain himself from these outbursts in his letters to Bridges or whether he was aware that he was making a covert plea for love, understanding, and sympathy.

There can be no question that he was beginning to lose control of his emotions, but it is not always easy to know in a specific document or at any particular moment how fully his control was gone. Certainly, his deep depression and occasional manic elation were in part cyclical. His next letter to Bridges, exactly a fortnight

379

after his mention of Lanier, is a delightful note of congratulation on Bridges's engagement, beginning with a joke and continuing with affection and good wishes for the approaching marriage. It is only the postscript that spoils the mood, for it seems added as if to ask Bridges not to forget his old friend in the midst of his happiness: 'I am, I believe, recovering from a deep fit of nervous prostration (I suppose I ought to call it): I did not know but I was dying.'[35]

Hopkins was too fundamentally kind to want to spoil the pleasure of an old friend, but in his own desperation he seems to have been driven occasionally to take the bloom from Bridges's happiness. In a less affectionate man, it would appear remarkably like resentment or jealousy. In July he tardily answered in what seems a negligent manner the invitation to be Bridges's best man at his September wedding; he then turned the subject to his own health:

> . . . there is no reason to be disquieted about me, though weakness is a very painful trial in itself. If I could have regular hard exercise it would be better for me.
>
> The reason of course why I like men to marry is that a single life is a difficult, not altogether a natural life; to make it easily manageable special provision, such as we have, is needed, and most people cannot have this.[36]

What he meant by 'special provision' is not specified, but it was apparently not adequate, for it is noticeable, almost unpleasantly so, that he was unable to suppress his own unhappiness in order to contribute to the pleasure of another.

Some awareness of this lies behind the statement of Bridges to Hopkins's mother, a year after his death, about the letters Gerard had written during those dark years: 'I found among them more distinct references to Gerard's state of mind than I remembered. One in particular is very plain. I always considered that he was over nervous about himself, and exaggerated his symptoms – which I think he did. In fact I think his mental condition was of this sort.'[37]

Bridges took some pride in his own considerable down-to-earth rationality, and in reading his letters we often feel that his usual sympathy with Hopkins's illnesses was a triumph of affection over native inclination; perhaps he would have said a triumph over common sense. From London it seemed only sensible to assume that there was less wrong with Hopkins than he believed. If Bridges had not been so removed geographically from Ireland or if he had been less preoccupied with his own busy life in England, he would undoubtedly have seen clearly what he was on the edge of understanding, which was that Hopkins's exaggeration of his own symptoms was not the result of selfish introspection but part of the illness from which he was suffering. The simple literal truth of life was often beyond his comprehension. Exaggeration was itself a symptom.

Hopkins was only too jaggedly aware of the dangers of his own state and tried his best to discover what was leading him to the brink of mental disaster. When he could not understand his own feelings and even someone as close to him emotionally as Bridges failed to see in what a serious condition he was, we probably have little chance a century later of knowing precisely the causes of his depression. All the same, it is obvious that one of his greatest deprivations was of unquestioning affection. The excitement with which he embraced his friendship with Curtis is an indication of how badly he needed a core of identification when all the externals of his life were so alien, but his need was not for only a one-to-one relationship of the sort he had glimpsed with Dolben. He required a whole atmosphere compounded of human warmth. In Oxford he had found it in the excitement of his circles of friends, and in his subsequent stays in English religious communities he had felt part of the aspirations of the men around him. In Dublin he could hardly believe in most of the practical aims of the College, he felt shouldered away by many of his colleagues, and he came to doubt the legitimacy of his own efforts as teacher, as scholar, or even as poet. To an outsider, it seems that his function in Dublin was hardly that of a priest, and that he might equally well have fulfilled his duties had he still been a layman. It would be surprising if the idea did not occur to Hopkins himself. No wonder that he stood on the verge of complete breakdown.

A year after his arrival in Dublin he wrote to Bridges in a vain effort to understand his own case, 'I think that my fits of sadness, though they do not affect my judgment, resemble madness.' It was the intermittent lucidity of his judgement that could fool those around him to believing that all was well with him. In what was perhaps his most open cry for help, he told Bridges, 'I must absolutely have encouragement as much as crops rain.' It was a sign that there was at least a temporary improvement in his state that he could continue, 'I have after long silence written two sonnets, which I am touching: if ever anything was written in blood one of these was.'[38]

This was the first mention of the group of five or six sonnets usually known as the Terrible Sonnets or, more exactly, the Sonnets of Desolation. They are, quite simply, like nothing else in English poetry since the Metaphysical poets of two centuries before. The best of Hopkins's poems had heretofore sprung out of the certainty of his religious belief, but these frightening sonnets are the expression of a doubt so profound that it can often find comfort only in the belief that death may be not eternal salvation but utter and welcome annihilation. To be accurate, they do not reflect doubt of the existence of God but a belief in something far more terrifying, the certainty that He exists and an almost equal certainty that His mercy does not extend to the poet himself or that He is unaware of the individual or careless of his fate. Even such a poem of physical horror as 'The Wreck of the Deutschland' had been conceived as a reconciliation of personal disaster and Providence, but in the Terrible Sonnets, the inspiration comes directly out of terror and does not really transcend it. Religion and creativity are still linked in them, but the terms in which those words are understood are completely altered.

On 1 September 1885 Hopkins wrote to Bridges, 'I shall shortly have some sonnets to send you, five or more. Four of these came like inspirations unbidden and against my will.'[39] There is no direct evidence about which poems he was referring to, but the most likely candidates are 'To seem the stranger', 'I wake and feel', 'No worst, there is none', 'Carrion Comfort', 'Patience, hard thing', and 'My own heart'. The sequence of their composition is equally uncertain, but they were probably all written in the summer of 1885, four months of what must have been hell for him. Yet it must be admitted that without the evidence of the poems themselves, it would be difficult to guess from the bulk of his correspondence during that summer that he was undergoing a breakdown, or even much more than his usual unhappiness. A few flashes of misery to Bridges, and that is all. It is a perfect example of the way that he could exist on two levels, both real enough but apparently incompatible, just as he conducted himself in the College so that sympathetic colleagues could see him daily and never suspect that he was so deeply unhappy in Dublin.

The real evidence about his emotional life must be his poems. If it can be said of any work of art, it is true that these are not poems about misery but the feeling itself. They are not emotion recollected in tranquillity or even in terror, they are experiences so immediate that the reader constantly feels that they wholly possessed Hopkins at the very moment of composition, as indeed they probably did. Some indication of their personal immediacy is that four of the six poems use 'I' and 'me', as if Hopkins were expunging the usual line between the poet as man and as artist.

Perhaps the most remarkable aspect of these poems is the sense of contained anarchy, of inchoate, almost unspeakable emotion given verbal form. And no less remarkable is that Hopkins should have picked the sonnet for the purpose. Whether or not he thought out the matter, the fact is that he chose one of the most disciplined verse forms because it best held his explosive emotions in check. These poems shock doubly because of the contrast between the decorum of the sonnet form and the dark energy pulsing against its restraints. For at least this reader they provide something of the same *frisson* that one feels at the *dies irae* of Verdi's Requiem Mass, a work composed only a decade before the sonnets, in which the terror of the Last Judgement strains against the order of the music.

Our natural reaction is to attempt to fit the sonnets into his life, to show that their existence is due to his profound deracination in Dublin, but the truth is more complex. External circumstances can provide a stimulus for emotional and spiritual life, but they can only work on what already exists in a man's mind or soul. Probably Hopkins was already deeply unbalanced mentally when he came to Dublin; whether that was a result of heredity, chemical imbalance, original sin, or childhood experience, we can hardly judge at this distance, but we must accept it without total understanding, an acceptance that should be no more difficult than accepting that a totally ordered personality may exist even if we do not comprehend its sources.

Hopkins's sonnets are themselves evidence of some success in holding on to sanity, even in the worst of his mental troubles. They seem so not because they employ a demanding form but because it is a singularly sane, ordered one, an indication that he could accommodate the chaos of his unconscious within the stringent bounds of an exigent verse form. It seems part of a recurrent pattern in his life, the necessity to give rigorous shape to what was frightening and dimly understood, just as he had chosen the most demanding of orders when he became a Jesuit. The sonnets did not quell the rebel emotions that disturbed him, any more than his vocation removed temptation; both, however, made the ramping beasts tractable. During a profoundly disturbed year or two in Dublin, when his religion was unable to make him happy, poetry helped to mediate between spiritual aspiration and the realities of daily life.

Hopkins's instinct, like our own, was to locate a specific, identifiable cause for his malaise, and what may have been the first of the Terrible Sonnets was a recognition of the impossibility of understanding emotions by rational explanations. 'To seem the stranger' sets out what at first appear to be perfectly comprehensible causes for his alienation: his removal from his family by their differences in religion; Englishmen's misunderstanding of him as a Catholic; now his sojourn in a foriegn land. In all three instances he receives kindness (from man or from God?). But either heaven or hell prevents him from ever understanding the meaning of his own situation when it is sought on the level of logic, and he is left where he had begun his attempt at comprehension, lonely and puzzled:

> To seem the stranger lies my lot, my life
> Among strangers. Father and mother dear,
> Brothers and sisters are in Christ not near
> And he my peace/my parting, sword and strife.

> England, whose honour O all my heart woos, wife
> To my creating thought, would neither hear
> Me, were I pleading, plead nor do I: I wear –
> y of idle a being but by where wars are rife.

I am in Ireland now; now I am at a thírd
Remove. Not but in all removes I can
Kind love both give and get. Only what word

Wisest my heart breeds dark heaven's baffling ban
Bars or hell's spell thwarts. This to hoard unheard,
Heard unheeded, leaves me a lonely began.

Inevitably, the word 'wife' stands out for the reader, and it becomes clear that this is in part a poem about human relations as well as Divine, and that Hopkins has drawn his metaphors from his deep absorption with his own loneliness when those dearest to him were otherwise engaged.

Although we have no proof of the actual sequence in which he composed the Terrible Sonnets, they can easily be put in a rough progression that seems to parallel his emotions in 1885 as we guess them from other sources, so that they have some of the effect of a sonnet sequence, even if that was probably far from Hopkins's purpose. 'I wake and feel' may have followed 'To seem the stranger', with a realization that in part man has become his own tormentor, and that his pathological introversion is his own worst enemy, producing a bitter pain in the belly and a sour taste in the mouth that are images of eternal punishment, which condemns one to perpetual self-contemplation:

I wake and feel the fell of dark, not day.
What hours, O what black hours we have spent
This night! what sights you, heart, saw; ways you went!
And more must, in yet longer light's delay.

With witness I speak this. But where I say
Hours I mean years, mean life. And my lament
Is cries countless, cries like dead letters sent
To dearest him that lives alas! away.

I am gall, I am heartburn. God's most deep decree
Bitter would have me taste: my taste was me;
Bones built in me, flesh filled, blood brimmed the curse.

Selfyeast of spirit a dull dough sours. I see
The lost are like this, and their scourge to be
As I am mine, their sweating selves; but worse.

It indicates some of the continuity of his affections that for his
images of desolation he should revert to the pain he had felt as
an undergraduate when he wrote constant, unanswered letters to
Dolben.

'No worst, there is none', which repeats some of the imagery
initiated in 'I wake and feel', advances the argument until he has to
acknowledge that only the destruction of the individual can save
him from self-torment, and that the comfort of Jesus and Mary
seems of a world that has no relation to the brute reality of man's
physical surroundings:

O the mind, mind has mountains; cliffs of fall
Frightful, sheer, no-man-fathomed. Hold them cheap
May who ne'er hung there. Nor does long our small
Durance deal with that steep or deep. Here! creep,
Wretch, under a comfort serves in a whirlwind: all
Life death does end and each day dies with sleep.

'Carrion Comfort' deals with the natural progression from the idea
of death as escape to the terrible resistance that is necessary to keep
one from self-destruction. Several writers have believed that
Hopkins actually contemplated suicide during this period; this is
some of the best evidence on the matter:

Not, I'll not, carrion comfort, Despair, not feast on thee;
Not untwist – slack they may be – these last strands of man
In me ór, most weary, cry I can no more. I can;
Can something, hope, wish day come, not choose not to be.

With the clotted determination of that sonnet Hopkins seems both
to touch bottom and to begin swimming upwards once more.
Surely, such deeply felt poems reflect his most intense personal
emotions at the time. 'Patience, hard thing' asks for strength and

resignation to face our failures, and in the asking achieves one of those images that makes it so apparent why Hopkins was a major poet:

> . . . Natural heart's–ivy Patience masks
> Our ruins of wrecked past purpose.

'My own heart' seems the natural culmination of the little 'sequence', with a resigned acceptance of the poet's fallibility and of his inability to be comforted without God, whose radiance comes not at our bidding but at His own chosen moment of revelation:

> My own heart let me more have pity on; let
> Me live to my sad self hereafter kind,
> Charitable; not live this tormented mind
> With this tormented mind tormenting yet.
>
> I cast for comfort I can no more get
> By groping round my comfortless, than blind
> Eyes in their dark can day or thirst can find
> Thirst's all–in–all in all a world of wet.
>
> Soul, self; come, poor Jackself, I do advise
> You, jaded, let be; call off thoughts awhile
> Elsewhere; leave comfort root-room; let joy size
>
> At God knows when to God knows what; whose smile
> 's not wrung, see you; unforeseen times rather – as skies
> Betweenpie mountains – lights a lovely mile.

In this great series of poems Hopkins seems stripped before us, so that no conventions of nationality, period or religion come between poet and reader to obscure the sense of profound emotion they share. 'The Wreck of the Deutschland' is Hopkins's single most important, most experimental poem, but, more than any others, these deeply personal sonnets make us feel that Hopkins is speaking for all of terrified humanity.

There are plenty of other fine poems from the Dublin period of Hopkins's life, so that they form a group quite as impressive as the ones composed at St Beuno's, although few of them light up with the happy radiance of those works. 'Spelt from Sibyl's Leaves' is part of the Terrible Sonnets in spirit, since the insistently recurring image is of the Last Judgement, when man's fate is to torture himself in ways that recall 'I wake and feel' ('recall' is perhaps the wrong word, since the relative dates of composition of the two poems are not certain); eternal damnation becomes 'a rack / Where, selfwrung, selfstrung, sheathe-and-shelterless, thoughts against thoughts in groans grind'. Hopkins himself called it the 'longest sonnet ever made' because of its baroque experimentation in language and overburdened lines, and it probably loses something of the Hopkinsian impetus because of its encrustation of image. It seems to lean backward in time to 'The Wreck of the Deutschland' and would be even more impressive if it were not necessarily compared to the Terrible Sonnets, which seem pressing hard to achieve naked directness.

'Tom's Garland' has attracted more attention in our own day than it did half a century ago, largely, one suspects, because it is concrete evidence of Hopkins's concern with the unemployed whom he saw all about him in Dublin. Most readers of Hopkins have a certain level of difficulty beyond which they say he has lost the thread of communication; understandably, this poem is often their limit. Hopkins himself realized that it was almost impossible for others to make sense of it, and when both Bridges and Dixon confessed themselves baffled, he obligingly provided a crib: 'It is plain I must go no farther on this road; if you and he cannot understand me who will?'[40] The road is hard going, and though the complexity of language can be unpicked, it is such labour that few feel it has been worth it in the end. 'Commonweal / Little I reck ho! lacklevel in, if all had bread' finally conveys something like 'If there were no starving, I should not really mind some inequality of status'; most readers get an impression of wilful, even selfish, playfulness of diction that finally ignores communication with the poet's audience. My own feeling is that it is partly a symptom of Hopkins's disturbed emotions, when he was unable to make a complete connection with other persons. This is not to judge his

This is the beginning of an ode on Everard's marriage.
Fill up the following blanks :— It begins on p 3 at A — supposes some
boys bathing in a brook. goes on (with hiatus) at B a stranger arrives
at the bathing - pool Examination No. B go to C. The stranger undresses
& bathes also — then A begins the application of which there is a hint.
Subject (it is in Gerard's most difficult manner)   R. B.   [Here specify Pass or Honours.]

If there be more than one paper in this subject, specify whether the
answers given in this Book relate to the First or Second Paper.

Write only on the ruled side. Do not write on the margin. No part of this Book is to
be torn off. The rough work and calculations, as well as the final results, should be shewn
in this Book.

First he fears. lovely all is ! no more:
with — down he flings
wool-woven
wear.
Careless these in
tumbled to then with
forward falling, frowning forehead, lip crisp
his fingers, while his
fast his tackled boot
wings; he opens fast and off at last
wings.
And now he walks the world with bare feet
has marked a copper
Of self-quarried guarined rocks
cover into stemmed with silver
and shoots,
and heaven-fallen freshness from the moorland more
Here, there he will the fleet
And flinty, kind cold element let creaks about his limbs,
Turn. There we leave him.

Ms, 'Epithalamion', 1888

poetry by the state of his mind, only to suggest that the latter is to some extent responsible for the knotted difficulty of the former. 'Tom's Garland' finally testifies more to the largeness of his heart than it does to his communicative powers when he was most troubled.

'Harry Ploughman', a companion poem to 'Tom's Garland' written a few months earlier, owes much to the paintings of Frederick Walker (see pp. 230–2). It celebrates the 'barrowy brawn' of the agricultural labourer and his 'Churlsgrace too, child of Amans-strength'. Behind both poems lies Christian idealism, but religion is not on the surface, as it usually is in Hopkins's poetry.

Another poem written in Dublin and owing a great deal to Frederick Walker is the evocation of a happier past in 'Epithala-mion', his attempt at a poetic offering for the marriage of his brother Everard in April 1888. To see the manuscript of this poem is to realize how little we actually know about the physical circum-stances of his writing. Usually we are lucky if we know even the general locality in which he wrote, but what is apparently the first draft of this poem is scribbled on examination paper of the Royal University, suggesting that he was writing in the dead patches of invigilating, his mind far from the dust of the classroom, perhaps in the tumbling brown waters of the bathing place in the river Hodder at Stonyhurst. It is crossed out, difficult to decipher, and bears all the marks of the hard work that finally made the completed section so easy and charming to read.

The setting perhaps seems an odd one until we remember that most elegant of wedding poems by Spenser, his 'Prothalamion', set on the Thames. He was a poet whom Hopkins seldom mentioned, although a casual remark or two suggests that he knew his works well, and that his own poem began as both gift to Everard and tribute to the Elizabethan poet. It is probably relevant that the earliest extant of his poems, 'The Escorial', uses a Spenserian stanza.

'Epithalamion' is a poem drenched with the innocent, probably unknowing, sensuality that seems peculiarly Hopkinsian. The energized landscape hovers delicately on the punning edge of sexu-ality without ever quite going across the border into the explicitly physical, no matter how much it is hinted at in the language. Once more we are teased into wondering how aware Hopkins was of the reverberations of what he wrote:

> . . . lend a thought now, make believe
> We are leaf-whelmed somewhere with the hood
> Of some branchy bunchy bushybowered wood,
> Southern dean or Lancashire clough or Devon cleave,
> That leans along the loins of hills, where a candycoloured,
>   where a gluegold-brown
> Marbled river, boisterously beautiful, between
> Roots and rocks is danced and dandled, all in froth and
>   waterblowballs, down.

The centre of the poem is a bathing scene in a river pool, in which a 'listless stranger' hears the shouts of a group of town boys, watches them leaping naked in and out of the water, picks a pool for himself, hurriedly takes off his own clothes ('off with – down he dings / His bleachèd both and woolwoven wear'), and jumps in:

> Here he will then, here he will the fleet
> Flinty kindcold element let break across his limbs
> Long. Where we leave him, froliclavish, while he looks about
>   him, laughs, swims.

Reading it, one is suddenly aware of how pagan the poem is, as much a product of Greece as of Ireland or Lancashire. It is a pure hymn to physical beauty, to the celebration of bodily exultation, and only when Hopkins attempts to allegorize the episode does he come unstuck in the poem. It is like a paradigm of his whole poetic career, in which the search for figurative meaning could be deeply inhibiting to his verse. Although he is using partly facetious language, there is an underlying seriousness in his attempt to renounce pagan beauty in favour of significance:

> Enough now; since the sacred matter that I mean
> I should be wronging longer leaving it to float
> Upon this only gambolling and echoing-of-earth note
> What is   the delightful dean?
> Wedlock. What the water? Spousal love

But the energy of the poem has depended upon his celebration of the physical, and with the weak attempt to wring allegory from what he has loved for itself, he leaves the poem unfinished. There is a distinct feeling that he left it incomplete because he was unable to imbue the physical world with spiritual meaning.

Although he mentions little except his delight in the bathing vignette, the poem is rich with the love he had felt for water throughout his life. Half-forgotten memories of bathing jostle for place in the poem: Kenwood in his schooldays, the Isle of Wight, Runnymede, Scotland, plunges with Curtis, every opportunity he had in his holidays.*

The poems Hopkins wrote in Dublin seem to us a respectable total of lines, but they came agonizingly to him, and he felt constantly that he should be writing more, as if there were a definite correlation between the poetry he produced and his spiritual state, and almost as if he was aware that he had but a limited time left in which to write. But it was a painful circle, for the more guilty he felt at not writing, the more difficult it became to produce anything. To verbalize his sense of sterility, he dredged up from his memory the literal image for it that he had first used when he was an undergraduate, lamenting the unfruitfulness of his life without Dolben: 'if I could but get on, if I could but produce work I should not mind

---

* The use of such a word as 'Fairyland', describing the bathing place, may connect the poem specifically with Stonyhurst and the Hodder (see p. 200 for his letter about the pool there). What seems more significant is that the scene he describes is very like that in Frederick Walker's painting 'Bathers', which the artist considered one of his most important works, and on which he had worked intermittently almost until his death in 1875. It is a study of some eighteen boys swimming and frolicking, most of them nude (see plate 16). Hopkins had probably seen the painting exhibited in 1868, although he does not mention it specifically in his discussions of Walker's works. Almost twenty years later he was still writing enthusiastically, almost obsessively, about his paintings and about the etchings of them made by R.W. Macbeth, whose studio he visited with his brother Arthur, where it seems probable he saw at least a reproduction of 'The Bathers' [see LII, 134]. This poem is like an improvisation on the theme of Walker's picture.

Interestingly, Philip Dacey, in his poem 'Gerard Manley Hopkins meets Walt Whitman in Heaven', suggests that Whitman's poetry springs from some of the same impulses as those of the painter Thomas Eakins, who painted scenes that are like Walker's in both subject and tone; Whitman was one of Eakins's few admirers at the time. In Dacey's poem Whitman hails Hopkins noisily as a fellow devotee of nude bathing and lover of the male body.

its being buried, silenced, and going no further; but it kills me to be time's eunuch and never to beget'.[41] Increasingly, he resorted to sexual metaphor to describe the barren state of his soul.

CHAPTER XX

MY WINTER WORLD
1886–9

As he had done so often before, Hopkins turned to alternative activity when he could not write poetry: 'For it is widely true, the fine pleasure is not to do a thing but to feel that you could.'[1] In September 1885 he was projecting a work on metre, although he had little hope that anything of his would ever see light again; consideration of the topic lasted at least a year. He hoped, when he had read more, to convert it into a complete philosophy of art, but it inevitably flickered out. Aeschylus and Greek negatives each promised briefly to be the subject of the great work he felt he should write as a professor of classics. He sent a paper on Sophocles to the *Classical Review*, but it was not accepted. Another, on Statistics and Free Will, was sent, he said, by invitation to the *Lyceum*, an Irish publication, and 'it is to appear next month. And yet I bet you it will not: my luck will not allow it.'[2] His guess was correct. In 1886 he was even considering a popular account of Light and Ether. The same year he carried on a spirited and protracted correspondence with Baillie about the possibility of the derivation of Attic culture through the Phoenicians from Egypt. It would require a specialist to say how reasonable his suppositions were, but for one without particularized knowledge the letters seem overheated, as if he were putting all his energy into them rather than into subjects on which he was more expert. After a year or so they shade off into more generalized speculations about English linguistic derivations and about the misdoings of Gladstone.

The fervour with which he threw himself into such correspondence was, he recognized himself,

part of my disease, so to call it. The melancholy I have all my
life been subject to has become of late years not indeed more
intense in its fits but rather more distributed, constant, and
crippling. One, the lightest but a very inconvenient form of it,
is daily anxiety about work to be done, which makes me break
off or never finish all that lies outside that work. It is uscless to
write more on this: when I am at the worst, though my
judgment is never affected, my state is much like madness. I
see no ground for thinking I shall ever get over it or ever
succeed in doing anything that is not forced on me to do of any
consequence.[3]

Baillie, who was an independent scholar, had the leisure to put up
with all that Hopkins wrote, and to answer in his turn; his letters
have disappeared, but from Hopkins's side of the correspondence,
it is clear that they were understanding and, above all, loving,
which is what Hopkins most needed.

And so the projects went; the impression from his letters is that
not even Hopkins really thought they would ever be completed,
and it is occasionally difficult to believe that they had ever existed
apart from the pages of the letters in which they are mentioned. 'All
impulse fails me: I can give myself no sufficient reason for going on.
Nothing comes: I am a eunuch – but it is for the kingdom of
heaven's sake.'[4] Almost as if he were preparing to die, he com-
menced destroying his old letters, which had been accumulating
since his schooldays. It was deeply painful to read them, since they
reminded him that what he might have done well was now only
'ruins and wrecks'.

As he had done before, he became more active in music when he
was poetically impotent. Apparently he had believed that the
atmosphere of Dublin would inspire him to composition, but the
musicians who saw his work were not encouraging, and more and
more his plans for musical activity coincided with those times when
he was denied the use of a piano, so that he could do nothing. Not
surprisingly for one who was protecting his own emotional vulnerability by investigating form rather than emotional content, he was
fascinated by canons and fugues, and in December 1887 he wrote to
Dixon, 'I am at work on a great choral fugue! I can hardly believe

it.'[5] But little more was heard of that enthusiasm. He said he needed but one thing, 'working health, a working strength', in order to accomplish what he undertook, but he needed emotional wholeness far more.

While he was trying to write music he corresponded with and frequently saw Sir Robert Stewart, conductor, composer, and Professor of Music at Trinity College. Stewart was fond enough of Hopkins to address him as 'Darling Padre!' and perhaps demonstrated the depth of his affection even more by looking over and correcting Hopkins's musical compositions. Surprisingly, the friendship survived Stewart's sharp criticism of Hopkins:

> I saw, ere we had conversed ten minutes on our first meeting, that you are one of those special pleaders who never believe yourself wrong in any respect. You always excuse yourself for anything I object to in your writing or music so I think it a pity to disturb you in your happy dreams of perfectability – nearly everything in your music was wrong – but you will not admit that to be the case – What does it matter? It will all be the same 100 Years hence – There's one thing I do admire – your hand-writing![6]

A year after arriving in Dublin Hopkins was beginning to console himself with that most dangerous of comforts, that is better to fail than to win, and for his example he chose Christ, whose unsuccessful earthly career ('he was doomed to succeed by failure') he invoked in writing a consoling letter to Dixon when the Canon did not get the Chair of Poetry at Oxford. Behind his message to Dixon, however, it is easy to perceive that Hopkins was making excuses for himself.

Increasingly, he began living in the past, which was easier to think of than the untidy present. In 1866 he wrote to Bridges on the day that he had been a Catholic for twenty years; the following year he was reminded that 'Tomorrow morning I shall have been three years in Ireland, three hard wearying wasting wasted years'; he noted when it was twenty years since he began his noviceship; he recalled the anniversary of his first vows; above all he was conscious of his advancing age. When Katharine Tynan told him that she had taken him for twenty and a friend had thought him a mere fifteen, he could only say that 'they should see my heart and vitals, all shaggy with the whitest hair.'[7]

Bridges wanted a portrait of Hopkins, but it was hard to pin him down, until he arranged with a friend, the artist Henry Woolridge, to begin a watercolour portrait from photographs, with the idea that he would finish it off when Hopkins was there in person (see front cover). When Bridges asked for information to pass on to the artist, Hopkins replied with a flash of his old humour shining out of his sadness:

> The irises of the present writer's eyes are small and dull, of a greenish brown; hazel I suppose; slightly darker at the outer rims. His hair (see enclosed sample, carriage paid) is lightish brown, but not equable nor the same in all lights; being quite fair near the roots and upon the temples, elsewhere darker . . . and shewing quite fair in the sun and even a little tawny. It has a gloss. On the temples it sometimes appears to me white. I have a few white hairs, but not there.
>
> . . . I am of late become much wrinkled round the eyes and generally haggard-looking, and if my counterfeit presentment is to be I shd. be glad it were of my youth.[8]

Presumably by chance, the two major photographs still in existence of Hopkins in the last decade of his life show him sitting in almost exactly the same position in a photographer's chair, his face in three-quarter profile, his eyes averted from the camera (see plates 15a and 15b). In the first, taken in 1879, which Hopkins said he preferred, he is still young and smooth-faced, although his expression seems to indicate considerable reserve of personality. In 1888, the year before he died, the contours have scarcely changed in his face, his hair has receded but little and shows little grey in the photograph, yet he looks decades older and more disillusioned, preserved rather than young, with a defensive touch of vulnerability. His expression has changed from reserve to something very like suspicion, the bones are prominent in the slightly sunken cheeks, there are pouches beneath his eyes, and the eyes themselves look hunted. From a distance one would presumably have seen remarkably little change, and it is easy to understand why he might still be taken for a lad of fifteen or twenty until seen up close, but the two photographs seem to show how he had been remorselessly ground down by his unhappiness in Liverpool and Dublin.

Bridges continued implacably to blame Hopkins's troubles on the Society to which he belonged. 'That dear Gerard was overworked, unhappy and would never have done anything great seems to give no solace,' he wrote after his death, diminishing both the Jesuits and Hopkins's poetry. 'But how much worse it would have been had his promise or performance been more splendid. He seems to have been entirely lost and destroyed by those Jesuits.'[9] More temperately Hopkins's sister Kate decided that his suffering 'was a good deal from feeling that he could not fully use or develope the gifts he possessed'.[10] The Jesuit judgement of him in his obituary indicates a wholly different but plausible view: 'His mind was of too delicate a texture to grapple with the rougher elements of life.'[11]

In fact, the Society seems to have done all it could to take care of him, short of giving him permanent sick leave, which would obviously have been of little help. It may even be that the failure of his superiors in the Society was in allowing him too much freedom, not too little. All his life he had felt a strong instinctive need for structure and routine, and it had been supplied successively by school, university, novitiate, and the carefully graded stages leading to his ordination. As a man of nearly forty, during his Tertianship at Manresa, he was not even free to choose what companion to have by his side on their Wednesday walks. Novice masters had watched his every step during his training, and when he became a parish priest he was under the constant supervision of his rectors. That aspect of his personality which thrived on nominal submission had been satisfied by such a life.

His chair in Dublin had seemed so inviting from Stonyhurst because it allowed him unimaginable intellectual and artistic freedom, but it failed him because it provided so little direct framework for his existence. The difference between his new life and his old was not that one exacted discipline and the other asked for none: both demanded it, but his Dublin position asked him to supply it himself, and this he was unable to do. He held himself aloof from the common room in University College, which to him seemed hostile, and he had few other friends. It was surely a retreat from social involvement that made him adopt the habit of going to bed every night at ten, just when the other priests in the College felt free to talk in unbuttoned sociability.

The two great forces that had always imposed order on what was for him a chaotic world were religion and poetry, and now neither of them was for the moment able to provide him with happiness. Two decades after he had sought final order in conversion, it seemed to be failing him. The discipline he had instinctively sought on becoming a Jesuit was now less demanding than it had ever been, and without its support his life was falling apart.

With what they intended as generosity, his superiors left him free between terms to go where he liked, but he became conspicuous in the house for not wanting to leave. His first summer in Dublin he took a circular ticket on the train, to see as much of the country as possible, stopping at Jesuit houses on the way, happily breaking his itinerary to fall in with priests he met in his travels; it seems to have been a carefree trip, but soon he was back in St Stephen's Green, unwilling to stay away long.[12]

Even his first Christmas in Dublin, in 1884, he preferred not to go home, although he had permission to do so; he had many good reasons for not going, so many in fact that none of them seems wholly convincing. It would be much better for him not to come home, he told his mother: 'You can easily understand reasons. If I came now I could not again so soon. Travelling long distances in winter is harder, more tiring, and the broken sleeps are a great trial to me.' Besides, his sister Grace was away. 'Then it is so soon after coming to Ireland; it does not look so well. Then the holidays are short and I have an examination at the end of them.' Rather anti-climactically, he added, 'Altogether I do not welcome it.'[13]

The Hopkins family had always made a great deal of Christmas as a family gathering, and his mother could not have been pleased to hear that he accepted an invitation for the holiday from Lord Emly, who was on the verge of becoming Vice Chancellor of the Royal University, and that he went next to stay in the New Year at Clongowes Wood College, hoping to write.

The following year he decided again not to go home for Christmas, and once more outlined carefully to his mother all the reasons it would be impossible; they were just as lengthy as they had been the previous year, and just as unconvincing. It is hard to escape the feeling that he was not anxious to see his parents, or at least that he felt that his mental health deteriorated when he was with them.

The surviving letters to his mother, written at the end of his life, seem extraordinarily stiff, more often dutiful observances of anniversaries or holidays than spontaneous expressions of affection. Few of the infrequent letters he sent to his father during the same period have survived. We know that more were written than were kept, but the very fact that Mr Hopkins did not keep them is probably indicative of the sadly polite estrangement.

In the summers of 1885 and 1886 he visited his family, in the second of those years at Court's Hill Lodge in Haslemere, where they had moved when Mr Hopkins had partially retired and no longer needed to go to London daily. Despite his difficulties with his parents, Gerard remained on affectionate terms with his brothers and sisters, in particular Arthur, Everard, Grace and Kate.

For reasons he never made explicit, he clearly felt little sympathy with Milicent, who had become an Anglican nun and was the only other member of the family who was a religious. He told Baillie that she was 'given to Puseyism: she is what is called an out-sister of the Margaret Street Home, which is a mummery nunnery. Consequently she will be directed by some Ritualist, which are the worst hands she could fall into: these men are imperious, uncommissioned, without common sense, and without knowledge of moral theology. The second, Kate, is a sort of humourist. Grace, the youngest, is devoted to music, for which she has a gift.'[14] Hopkins made conventional protestations about his intention to get in touch with Milicent, but there is no indication that he ever did. With Lionel he shared the family quirky sense of humour, and with Arthur and Everard he corresponded affectionately on artistic matters.

He had spent a fortnight in England in the spring of 1886. He was between examinations, and he could easily be spared from Stephen's Green, but it seems probable that he was being given a tactfully unspecified sick leave by his community, since he had been in such a depressed state. With his brother Arthur he went the round of exhibitions and artists' studios in London, spent a short time in

Oxford at St Aloysius's, visited the Paravicinis, and for the first time went to Yattendon to see Bridges and meet his new wife, whom he found charming, although the best compliment he could summon up was to tell Bridges awkwardly that she 'was not as fancy painted her (indeed fancy painted her very faintly, in watered sepia), but by no means the worse for that'.

Although he had seen a good many people, the trip seemed somewhat aimless, but he said that he came back from the holiday much 'improved', with his anxiety mostly gone, adding characteristically, 'there is more reason than ever for it now, for I am terribly behindhand and cannot make up.'[15] Once he was back in Dublin, he inevitably felt he had to escape, but when he managed to do so, he felt uprooted and homeless.

In Stephen's Green his recurrent emotional see-saw soon began going down again, and by September 1886, when he had completed another set of examinations, his spirits were so low that he had to get away, whatever the consequences. The resulting holiday was perhaps the happiest fortnight of his entire Irish years. His travelling companion was Robert Curtis, so that for almost the entire time he was with an affectionate friend. It was probably part of his happiness that he had the responsibility of keeping a close eye on Curtis's health.

Hopkins was forty-two, Curtis eight years younger; there is something amusingly schoolboyish in men of their age being given £20 by the Rector to spend between them for their holiday. As they left, they were asked to give their Welsh address to the Secretary of the Royal University in case any examinations had to be sent to them, and in reply they sent a blank card. Originally they had wanted to go to Yorkshire to see Fountains Abbey, but they were not sure their money would stretch so far, so instead Hopkins suggested Wales, always 'a mother of Muses' to him. The centre of the fortnight was Snowdon, which they approached by the mountain railway from the north during a week in Caernarfon, then on foot from the south during the following week in Tremadoc. The weather was wet almost continuously, but it did not stop their day-long walks, on some of which they covered twenty or thirty mountainous miles with no apparent ill effects to either of them, however listless they had felt before the beginning of the trip.

In spite of their precaution with their address, Curtis was bombarded with telegrams and letters from St Stephen's Green, twice asking him to reset an examination that a colleague had botched. Hopkins found his lack of resentment instructive: 'I used to do the cursing; he bore all with the greatest meekness.'

Tremadoc was even better than Caernarfon: remote, beautiful, and convenient for a trip by miniature railway to Blaenau-Ffestiniog or by foot to the torrent of notably green water at Pont Aberglaslyn, 'the beauty of which is unsurpassed'. The pretty little village was some distance from the sea, but the weather was completely unsuitable for the bathing that had been part of the reason for their choice of the Welsh coastline. Hopkins's unorthodox sense of beauty, which bubbled up when least expected, made him appreciate the slate quarries: 'nowhere I suppose in Europe is such a subjection of nature to man to be witnessed. The end is that the mountains vanish, but in the process they take a certain beauty midway between wildness and art.' In the street they were pleased at the sight of itinerant Breton vegetable sellers wearing jerseys, earrings, and wooden shoes. As Hopkins put it in his happiness, 'My situation is that Wild Wales breathes poetry on the one hand and that my landlady gives me the heartiest breakfasts on the other': what more could man want?

Before the second week was out, Curtis was recalled to Dublin, and Hopkins stayed on, saying Mass at Pwllheli before he left. Unlike most travellers, he regretted only that they had been so economical, for he returned with £8 of the original £20 they had taken, a piece of 'mismanagement' to which he was reconciled by knowing that it would encourage Fr Delany to trust his parsimony in the future. It had been a rejuvenating holiday, and its effects lasted for several months, but no amount of vacation was going to restore Hopkins completely.[16]

Actually, his superiors allowed him a large number of holidays, certainly far more than a Jesuit parish priest would have had. Once more he stayed with his family in the summer of 1887 (although before agreeing to come, he kicked up a fuss about the difficulty of getting from Haslemere to Guildford for daily Mass), and he made a second visit to Yattendon, where Bridges disapprovingly thought he was 'more of the Jesuit priest than ever'.[17]

Each year he made short trips to stay with friends living around Dublin, such as Judge O'Hagan and his family near at hand in Howth, in a handsome house looking south over Dublin Bay. Most often he was to be found at Monasterevan, where he had a standing invitation from a Miss Cassidy, 'an elderly lady' from a prosperous brewing family who was delighted to put him up for recuperation, leaving him free to read and write, talk to her nephews and nieces, and assist the parish priest.[18]

In trying to reconstruct Hopkins's life in Dublin, one is recurrently struck by how fragmentary it was, with little emotional thread on which to string a series of scarcely connected events. It is hard to believe that the discontinuity of the way he lived was not a reflection of a gradual disintegration of his mental health. His trips became increasingly aimless, the rhythm of his daily life was a boring routine chiefly broken by marking examinations, and few private emotions save complaints that seemed forced out of him found their way into his letters. Although he saw a good many friends and acquaintances, almost none of them fanned him into enthusiasm.

One of the few of his fellow clerics besides Curtis to whom he was fairly close was Fr Matthew Russell, who came to live in St Stephen's Green in 1886 as one of the two priests in charge of students resident in the College. He was an amusing, eccentric, bookish man, and it is probable that he and Hopkins got to know each other moderately well within a short time. Since 1873 Russell had been editor of the *Irish Monthly* and was thus more or less in the middle of the Irish literary revival. There was little else in the way of an artistic group in Dublin, since religious differences prevented most of those so inclined from seeing each other regularly. Fr Russell was much more interested in the accomplishments of young writers and painters than he was in whether they were Catholic or Protestant, and he became something of a non-partisan centre for the diffuse group. He was a minor poet himself, and he admired the poetry of Bridges, for whom Hopkins had constituted himself a promoter, with the mission of introducing his work to Ireland.

In 1886 Russell introduced Hopkins and Katharine Tynan, who had been a contributor to the *Irish Monthly* and was eventually to become well known as a poet and novelist. She had recently published a book of devotional poems which Hopkins said was 'highly and indeed somewhat too highly praised by a wonderful, perhaps alarming, unanimity of the critics'. He described her to Patmore as 'a simple brightlooking Biddy with glossy very pretty red hair, a farmer's daughter in the County Dublin. She knows and deeply admires your Muse.' They met in the Stephen's Green studio of J.B. Yeats, where Miss Tynan was sitting for her portrait.

When Hopkins came into the studio, she thought he brought an air of Oxford with him. 'He was not unlike Lionel Johnson, being small and childish-looking, yet like a child-sage, nervous too and very sensitive, with a small ivory-pale face.' Overcoming his nervousness, Hopkins talked a great deal about Bridges that afternoon, and he stayed on in the studio after Miss Tynan had gone, discussing with his host the question of how much finish a work of art needed. Yeats was immensely pleased with the visit, but he lamented that Hopkins, with all his gifts for art and literature, should have become a priest. When Katharine Tynan mentioned this to Hopkins later, he said simply, 'You wouldn't give only the dull ones to Almighty God.'

Russell was proud of having coaxed Hopkins to accompany him, since he was 'not always to be trusted to make friends'. Partly because she took the initiative, Katharine Tynan saw a good deal of Hopkins for a year or two, and with Russell he visited her farmhouse in Clondalkin at least once.

Either at this first meeting or at a subsequent one, J.B. Yeats spoke to Hopkins about the poems of his son, William Butler Yeats, who had published 'some striking verses' in a Trinity College publication that Hopkins had read. He considered that the younger Yeats had 'been perhaps unduly pushed by the late Sir Samuel Ferguson', an older Dublin poet. With 'some emphasis of manner' Yeats presented Hopkins with a copy of his son's first separate publication, *Mosada: A Dramatic Poem*, containing as frontispiece his father's portrait of him, 'having finely cut intellectual features'. Dryly Hopkins commented that for 'a young man's pamphlet this was something too much; but you will understand a father's feeling'. When he read it, he could not think highly of the poem, but he acknowledged that the young Yeats had some fine lines and vivid imagery, even if he lacked common sense.

When Hopkins had already formed this somewhat unenthusiastic opinion of Yeats and his poetry, there was little probability of anything but anti-climax when the two greatest poets of the age, both still unknown, finally met face to face. A dozen years later Yeats recalled to Bridges that he had just been reading Bridges's *Prometheus the Firegiver* in 1886: 'I remember talking about it with your friend Father Hopkins, and discussing your metrical theories.' But even at the time Yeats wrote this, Hopkins was still completely unknown as a poet, so that there was little reason for Yeats to remember the occasion closely. He said that he and Hopkins had come across each other several times in his father's studio, but that he was too young and too taken up with romantic poetry to be interested in the querulous Hopkins.[19] Years later he admitted the embarrassing truth to Humphry House, that he had no memory of ever meeting Hopkins; it is improbable that what they said to each other would have changed literary history or was even worth preserving for posterity.

Several persons have left records of trying to get to know Hopkins in Dublin, without any real success because of his shyness or reclusiveness. As Fr Russell indicated, his insistence on going to bed at 10 p.m. made evening engagements almost impossible. Even when he did go out, his manner was often peculiar. At one house he was left alone for a few minutes before his hostess appeared, and when she walked into the drawing room he was seated before the fire with his coat off, sewing up a rent in his waistcoat. At the College his behaviour became increasingly odd: once he was discovered blowing pepper through a keyhole to interrupt a meeting within the room by making the occupants sneeze. Even on his deathbed he wrote to Bridges about a joke that had gone wrong: 'I have it now down in my tablets that a man may joke and joke and be offensive; I have had several warnings lately leading me to make the entry, tho' goodness knows the joke that gave most offence was harmless enough and even kind.'[20] The echo of Hamlet is appropriate enough, for his wild and whirling words often seemed quite mad.

Curtis remained friendly with him until the end of his life, but even for such a good companion intimacy was not always easy when Hopkins kept putting obstacles in its way. They tried in 1888 to recreate the mood of their trip to Wales two years earlier by going to Scotland for a fortnight to bathe in the sea and climb Ben Nevis, but it was not a success. When they arrived, Hopkins found that the highroad was very close to the place where they wanted to swim, and presumably out of modesty they had to give that up. In spite of much exercise he was unable to sleep, and he saw the end of the fortnight approaching without much caring:

> I have leave to prolong it, but it is not very convenient to do so and I scarcely care. It appears I want not scenery but friends. My companion is not quite himself or he verges towards his duller self and so no doubt do I too, and we have met few people to be pleasant with.

With no concrete evidence to support the opinion, one suspects that it was not Curtis who was proving to be a bad companion. The result of the deflating trip was that Hopkins became unpleasantly aware of his age: 'I am feeling very old and looking very wrinkled.'[21]

After this his friendship with Curtis dwindled, in part because of Hopkins's tetchiness but more because of the younger man's increasingly bad health. At one time, in the intervals between his epileptic attacks, he had been so adept at leaping fences that Hopkins said there must be a hare in the man's pedigree, but for the last two years of Hopkins's life his friend was often confined to a couch in the College, and though he still taught and was studying theology in preparation for ordination, it had become increasingly clear that his health would preclude his ever becoming a priest. Once, when he ventured out, he hurt himself badly by falling on his face on the spikes of the railings. It meant that the two men could not take trips together, could hardly take walks, and their intimacy naturally became less fervent. Curtis survived Hopkins by only four years; for some time before his death he had to give up teaching and any hope of ordination. He is buried in the same corner of the Jesuit plot in the Glasnevin cemetery as Hopkins.

It was no pleasure to return to the College after the Scottish trip, for Hopkins was convinced that examining was largely useless, Ireland a mess, and the College on a downhill path. When he arrived back in Dublin, he had to begin setting another examination, which was the last straw for him. Ever since he had come to Ireland, he had been complaining about his eyes, saying they were almost out of his head, particularly when he was examining. It was natural enough for them to be fatigued by such intense strain, but he worried that he was going blind, without taking such elementary steps as being examined for glasses, which suggests that more than physical difficulties were bothering him. For years before this time, his eyes had been of prime concern to him as the agents of carnal temptation, so that his almost automatic reaction to feeling that he was in a sinful state was to mortify himself by the 'discipline of the eyes'. There is no way of guessing what kind of self-accusation he was going through in the last year of his life, but even if we knew, we should only be privy to an aberration, for his judgement by now was not to be trusted.

During this year the masochistic cast of his personality became more exaggerated. In August 1888 his hidden obsession with the punishment of sin surfaced in a letter to Bridges describing his reactions to Dana's *Two Years Before the Mast*, which bristled with technicalities of seamanship he could not follow. There were other parts of the book, however, that he felt he could understand only too well, 'as a flogging, which is terrible and instructive *and it happened* – ah, that is the charm and the main point'. Exactly what occasioned his outburst is not clear, but it was obviously related to his own cancerous sense of punishment deserved.

In September 1888, less than a fortnight after his return from the Scottish trip, he had been reduced to a pitiable state; his horrible stories about eyes are clear enough surrogate manifestations of his condition. *Lear* and *Oedipus* probably lie only a short distance beneath the surface of his feelings here. 'It seems to me I can not always last like this: in mind or body or both I shall give way,' he told Bridges. That was enough provocation to launch into a horrible story of a young man known to his community who had put out his own eyes. 'He was a medical student and probably understood how to proceed, which was nevertheless barbarously done with a stick and some wire. The eyes were found among nettles in a field.' He groped his way to a cottage and said, 'I am blind; please let me rest for an hour.' In hospital he would not say 'what was the reason, and this and other circumstances wear the look of sanity; but it is said he was lately subject to delusions. I mention the case because it is extraordinary: suicide is common.'

After the last chilling words, Hopkins told Bridges that he had spent the afternoon in Phoenix Park: 'It did me good, but my eyes are very, very sore.' Later in the same letter he interrupts himself to ask Bridges's medical opinion: 'Can there be gout or rheumatism in the eyes? If there can I have it.' When he was more in control of himself, he would say that the pain in his eyes was merely unpleasant: 'The feeling is like soap or lemon.' At last, in October 1888, he was examined by a competent oculist, who prescribed glasses but told him his sight was very good and that nothing was the matter with him save the onset of middle age. Yet he had gone through a period of torment over a largely imaginary malady, which he had been using as a substitute for more deep-seated matters troubling his conscience.[22] Reading his letters today is like listening to a series of cries for help, in their own way as lacerating as the Terrible Sonnets.

Hundreds of miles away, across the Irish Sea, Bridges received pages of Hopkins's complaint; for his own sanity he had to insulate himself against the pain in his friend's life, and it is understandable why he came to believe that Hopkins's symptoms were exaggerated if not imaginary. He occasionally seems a shade unsympathetic to Hopkins's mental troubles, but his imperturbability may have helped provide the stability Hopkins needed in his friends.

Hopkins had a perfect excuse for not going to Haslemere for Christmas 1888. On the first day of the New Year he had to make his annual retreat, since he had been unable to do so the previous summer when he was busy with examinations. He went to Miss Cassidy for Christmas, then on from Monasterevan to St Stanislaus's College, Tullamore, where the retreat was held.

We are fortunate to have Hopkins's notes from the retreat; a copy of them made by Bridges is now in the Bodleian Library. Reading it today is to feel that Hopkins's heart is on view as it is not even in the greatest of his poetry, and certainly not in his letters, exposed though both those are. All the attempts he made at absolute honesty are here, so desperate that he often seems almost to have falsified his examination of conscience through trying too scrupulously not to give himself any excuses for transgression or omission. It makes agonizing reading, but one is almost ashamed to admit feeling such pain because his own suffering was so infinitely greater. Only a fairly long excerpt can give any of its flavour.

On the first day of the retreat he considered the morality of doing good for the wrong side, and his thoughts turned to the Irish, who thought that because it was right to be Catholic, anything they did to advance their cause must also be right:

> But how is it with me? I was a Christian from birth or baptism, later I was converted to the Catholic faith, and am enlisted 20 years in the Society of Jesus. I am now 44. I do not waver in my allegiance, I never have since my conversion to the Church. The question is how I advance the side I serve on. This may be inwardly or outwardly. Outwardly I often think I am employed to do what is of little or no use. Something else which I can conceive myself doing might indeed be more useful, but still it is an advantage for there to be a course of higher studies for Catholics in Ireland and that that should be partly in Jesuit hands; and my work and my salary keep that up. Meantime the Catholic Church in Ireland and the Irish Province in it and our College in that are greatly given over to a partly unlawful cause, promoted by partly unlawful means, and against my will my pains, laborious and distasteful, like prisoners made to serve the enemies' gunners, go to help on this cause. I do not feel that outwardly I do much good, much that I care to do or can much wish to prosper; and this is a mournful life to lead . . . Yet it seems to me that I could lead this life well enough if I had bodily energy and cheerful spirits. However these God will not give me.

The worst for him that he was unable to leave off his self-laceration, even when he was not in retreat, and it dragged him closer and closer to the sin of total despair.

> I was continuing this train of thought this evening when I began to enter on that course of loathing and hopelessness which I have so often felt before, which made me fear madness

and led me to give up the practice of meditation except, as now, in retreat and here it is again. I could therefore do no more than repeat *Justus es, Domine, et rectum judicium tuum* and the like, and then being tired I nodded and woke with a start. What is my wretched life? Five wasted years almost have passed in Ireland. I am ashamed of the little I have done, of my waste of time, although my helplessness and weakness is such that I could scarcely do otherwise . . . All my undertakings miscarry: I am like a straining eunuch. I wish then for death: yet if I died now I should die imperfect, no master of myself, and that is the worst failure of all. O my God, look down on me . . .

The following morning he could feel nothing in his meditation but loathing of his sins and 'a barren submission to God's will'. Even on the third day of the retreat he could only report, 'Helpless loathing'. One feels that he might with reason have quoted his own sonnet: 'No worst, there is none'. The intensity of his introspection is indicated by Bridges's note at the end of the document: 'I have seen nothing else written by Gerard so small in size of script.'[23]

Two months after the retreat its beneficial effects seemed to have evaporated when Hopkins wrote one of his most gravely beautiful sonnets, 'Thou art indeed just', taking its epigraph and opening lines from Jeremiah xii, 1, which he had quoted in his retreat notes:

> . . . See, banks and brakes
> Now, leavèd how thick! lacèd they are again
> With fretty chervil, look, and fresh wind shakes
>
> Them; birds build – but not I build; no, but strain,
> Time's eunuch, and not breed one work that wakes.
> Mine, O thou lord of life, send my roots rain.

The persistence of Hopkins's imagination and the recurring under-thought of his poetry are indicated by the insistently familiar echo in this work, written in Dublin in 1889, of 'Trees by their yield', composed twenty-three years earlier in Oxford, in which he had used much of the same imagery of sexual sterility to lament his grief over his separation from Dolben (see p. 110).

Word of Hopkins's condition had spread among his friends. In April, 'for a few days, before Easter', his old friend Francis de Paravicini was in Dublin and saw him a time or two, including an evening together. Paravicini 'thought him looking very ill then, & said that he was much depressed. That day or two seemed to bring back all the old friendship, & give it, as it were, new life.'

Although Mrs de Paravicini was a Catholic convert and her husband a Fellow of Balliol, it is not clear precisely what kinds of influence they wielded in demanding that the Society of Jesus bring Hopkins home, but they were too worried by his mental state to be diplomatic about the matter. According to Mrs de Paravicini, they had just spoken 'of Father Gerard to others; & we had just managed that he should be sent for – back to England – when we heard of his illness. We were hoping to have him in Oxford for some time this summer.'[24]

One of the great 'if but . . .' postulations of Victorian poetry is what Hopkins's fate might have been had Paravicini made his Dublin trip a few weeks earlier. The truth is that it was already probably too late, for what Paravicini took as further depression, to be treated by convalescence in Oxford, was the onset of serious physical illness.

The bitter, mocking tone that Hopkins occasionally allowed to soak into his letters to Bridges when he was at his most depressed had been only too evident that spring, and two letters that he wrote in late March and early April seemed so offensive that Bridges put them in the fire: the only letters from Hopkins, he said, that he had ever deliberately destroyed. It was 'very like a sort of quarrel'.[25]

Without knowing of the destruction of the letters, Hopkins was aware that he had presumed too much on a long-suffering friend. On Easter Monday he wrote a sonnet to Bridges 'in explanation' of his own behaviour, tacitly suggesting that it sprang from his despair at the absence of the Divine flame of inspiration which impregnates the poet's mind. He was relying on Bridges's understanding of him to make the connection between artistic dryness and apparent unfriendliness. Not the least of the sonnet's power to move us is that he was thinking so intimately of Bridges that he almost assumed his personality; his diction in the poem is often more like that of his friend than of his own works. In his anxiety to set matters right, he kept the sonnet only a week before sending it off without the usual polishing that would have taken away many of its rough spots: the sacrifice of craftsmanship to affection makes it a particularly touching farewell to his friend of longest standing. It was the last poem he ever wrote, and on the 29th of April he sent it to Bridges in a letter signed only, 'your affectionate friend Gerard':

> Sweet fire the sire of muse, my soul needs this;
> I want the one rapture of an inspiration.
> O then if in my lagging lines you miss
> The roll, the rise, the carol, the creation,
> My winter world, that scarcely breathes that bliss
> Now, yields you, with some sighs, our explanation.

Almost in passing, he had begun the accompanying letter with the brief statement that 'I am ill to-day, but no matter for that as my spirits are good.' Two days later he told his mother that he was suffering from an attack of rheumatic fever, which he found a nuisance because it interfered with setting papers for an examination. If he did not improve, he promised to see a doctor.

When he was unable to sleep and felt some pain, he took to his bed for the first time, and he did see a doctor, who 'treated my complaint as a fleabite, a treatment which begets confidence but not gratitude'. The following day, the 5th of May, he was no better and had 'suspended digestion', which had proved painful but was now almost cured. He still felt well enough to be ironically amused that his illness at least relieved him of the duties of examining in the busiest part of the University term, although he knew that 'there will be the devil to pay'.

On the 8th of May he told his mother that his complaint had been diagnosed as 'a sort of typhoid', but not severe enough to be worrying. By now the attentions of Fr Wheeler, who had been superintending his care, were supplemented by those of a nurse. He was moved into a lighter and less draughty ground-floor room in the adjoining house, where the nurse could come and go without disturbing the other priests. With reason he was tired of beef tea and chicken jelly, and his only complaint was that food and medicine kept 'coming in like cricket balls'. What was most discouraging for his parents was that he was so weak he had to dictate his letter. However, by the 14th of May he seemed so improved that Fr Wheeler notified his family and Bridges that he was on the road to recovery.

Hopkins was ill for nearly six weeks before his death; the length of his illness suggests that the typhoid he had contracted was not the most virulent sort possible. It has usually been accepted that it was caused by the leaky drains of which he had complained when he first came to Stephens's Green, but there is, of course, no way of proving that a century later. Whatever the disease, he was the only resident of the house to contract it. According to those around him, he was conscious to the end and almost never wandering or delirious. Although he had spoken often enough of his illness when it was more psychosomatic than physical, now he became quiet and uncomplaining, 'the placidest soul in the world'.

The improvement Fr Wheeler had reported seems to have lasted a fortnight or more. On the night of Wednesday, the 5th of June, he took a serious turn for the worse, and Fr Wheeler had to tell him it was improbable he would recover. Previously, he had not wanted his parents brought to Dublin 'because of the pain it would give them to see him so prostrate', but now he agreed to have them summoned, and when the first visit was over, he said he was happy they had come. He asked for the Viaticum after he knew he was dying, and received it for the last time on the morning of the 8th of June. According to the members of the College community, he was heard two or three times to say, 'I am so happy, I am so happy' before he became too weak to speak, and even then he appeared to follow the prayers for the dying that Fr Wheeler said at noon. He retained his consciousness until half past one, when he died peacefully.[26]

Hopkins's parents naturally stayed in Dublin for the funeral in St Francis Xavier's, Upper Gardiner Street. Women did not customarily attend funerals then, and Mrs Hopkins was not at the requiem Mass, but her husband was chief mourner at the church, and afterwards he watched his son's body lowered into the earth of Glasnevin cemetery. Probably for the first time Manley Hopkins began to comprehend what it was for which Gerard had given up family, boyhood religion, and country. In reply to condolences from one of Gerard's school friends, he wrote how much he had prized the letter:

> It adds another testimony as to the love Gerard had obtained. In Dublin we found golden opinions on all sides, & devoted friends. All the comfort that such outpourings can give we have, thankfully, received. The funeral services were truly grand. Seventy ecclesiastics & an immense congregation assisted at them. I know that you will rejoice at hearing that your old friend was honoured as well as loved.'[27]

Perhaps some measure of the pride he had come to feel in his son is his understandable but exaggerated estimate of the number of clerics present, which is approximately three times as great as that recorded in other sources. It is sometimes easier to appreciate those near us when we hear them praised by others.

As one enters the main gate of the cemetery at Glasnevin, to the north of Dublin, directly ahead stands the assertive great shaft to O'Connell and his fellow Irish patriots. A hundred yards or so down the walk to the left, which leads through the proud monuments of prelates and country monsignors, is the unassuming burial ground of the Society of Jesus.

It is a ferociously clean, pebbled plot surrounded by a white iron picket fence lined with trees; facing the gate is a looming granite crucifix, the plinth covered with some two hundred carved names of those Jesuits remembered here, their records added in order of their deaths. Hopkins is buried to the left of the entrance in an unmarked grave. When one walks across the pebbles, they give beneath the feet in an unnerving manner, reminding the visitor that those here named are also buried underfoot. The plot is like a religious community with a vengeance, created from the bodies pressed upon each other. It seems oddly fitting for Hopkins, who was so essentially private in his life at the very time he felt his duty to be part of the community: it is easy to imagine him passing eternity in suppressing his unworthy disinclination to share his last resting place as if it were the Great Bed of Ware.

On the base of the crucifix the curious visitor can find the inscription P. GERARDUS HOPKINS OBIIT JUN.8 1889 ÆTAT.

AN. 44. The English version of the notice of his death in the official *Register of the English Province* reads, '1889. On the eighth day of June, the vigil of Pentecost, weakened by a fever, he rested. May he rest in peace. He had a most subtle mind, which too quickly wore out the fragile strength of his body.'[28]

APPENDIX

It is perhaps best to consign to the relative obscurity of an Appendix one's doubts about the reliability of a witness to Hopkins's life, particularly one who has left us with so much information about the dark years in Dublin and who has been the source of information for many Hopkins scholars. Probably most of the facts he provided are accurate at least in part, and there is no reason to think that he ever intended to mislead anyone about Hopkins, but his opinions were so biassed that it is prudent nonetheless to be cautious about accepting either the written or the spoken testimony of Fr Joseph Darlington, who came to teach at University College a year after Hopkins had arrived there.

Darlington, the only Englishman in the house besides Hopkins, was also an Oxford man and had been ordained in the Church of England before his conversion. He too was swayed by admiration for Newman, who instructed him. After Hopkins's death Darlington remembered that he had known him 'so well, and intimately', and he liked to emphasize their closeness by his reminiscences of what he implied they had shared: 'I went to Oxford in the year *1868*, & my Tutor at B.N.C. was also Hopkins' – though of Baliol.'[1] Perhaps his memory was already beginning to fail, for despite his emphasis of the date, it is not in agreement with that recorded in *Alumni Oxonienses*, which is 1869. In any case, what he failed to mention was that though Pater had taught them both, Hopkins had left Oxford in 1867, which was at least one year, and more probably two, before he arrived there himself. Nor is their closeness made more credible by his belief that Hopkins's Christian name was Gerald, which he used more than once, or by the curious fact that his own name occurs nowhere in Hopkins's surviving correspondence from the four years when they were both in St Stephen's Green, living in the same house. Yet as the decades passed after Hopkins's death, his memory of their friendship became increasingly vivid. Between 1889, when he seems to have contributed to the obituary of Hopkins in *Letters and Notices*, and 1933, when he offered to help Humphry House with material for a biography, he wrote several times of his knowledge of Hopkins, and he supplied recollections of him to a number of other writers.

Many – perhaps most – of us exaggerate in our memories our intimacy with famous persons we have met or known. What is surely unusual about Darlington's recollections is that the better he claimed to have known Hopkins, and the longer he did so, the less pleasant the memory became for him.

Darlington, who was himself remembered with devotion by men who had worked with him, had little claim to intellectual distinction, but he was nonetheless 'in many ways the pivot of the college'. He was a man of great organizational abilities and 'almost alarming energy', which he bent to establishing the reputation of the College by beating the Queen's College in Belfast at examinations. If he were to succeed, he needed absolute agreement about his own goals with his superior, Fr Delany, and all the rest of the faculty of the College. 'In such a state of things', wrote Darlington, 'Gerald Hopkins was at an opposite pole to every thing around him: literary, political, social &c (a thorough John Bull incapable of understanding Rebel Ireland).' It was hard for Darlington to comprehend why Hopkins was unwilling to set aside his own standards and ideals temporarily in order to achieve administrative success for the College.

It is easy for us, however, to understand why Darlington's disapproval only provoked Hopkins into further alienation from the College, which in turn so angered Darlington that he supplied increasingly bitter information to anyone writing about either the history of the College or Hopkins himself. He was apparently the source of the stories about Hopkins's blowing pepper through the keyhole at a meeting, of how Hopkins was dragged around the classroom by his students, of how Hopkins marked examination papers in agony with a towel wrapped around his head, and he seems to have supplied most of the ammunition for the charge that Hopkins was underworked and that he was very effeminate in manner. Hopkins himself might not be expected to mention these stories, but it is curious that there is no other authority for any of them that does not seem to lead back directly to Darlington.

When Fr Joseph Keating in 1910 first floated the scheme of writing Hopkins's biography, he turned to Darlington for help and received in return a mass of information, in which Darlington began with tributes to Hopkins's originality and 'sublimest purity of mind' but finally decided that 'G.H. was a merely beautifully painted sea-shell. I never found any mollusc inside it of human *substance*.'

The publication in 1918 of Bridges's edition of Hopkins's poetry turned Fr Darlington's attention to the consideration of 'his poetry-so-called!', and his letters and writings are often severe judgements of his work.

About 1923 Darlington decided to record his own opinions of Hopkins, and the result was 'Gerard Hopkins in Ireland, 1883–1889', of which the erroneous date was later corrected. As it now exists it is an unpublished typescript of some eighteen pages, of which the central section has clearly been lost. It is a rambling, inaccurate account of the founding of University College by 'Father Delaney and his College of "first-class fighting men"', and of Newman's influence, but in spite of the title there is little about Hopkins except the reiteration of their shared experience of Oxford. In the essay there is almost no mention of Hopkins's poems, but Darlington includes one of his own, presumably to indicate how Hopkins should have gone about writing them.

In part because of the opposition of Bridges, Keating's biography was never written, and the first short life of Hopkins was that in 1930 by Fr Lahey, on which Darlington was consulted. Lahey quoted some of Darlington's contentions, such as 'It has been rumoured that he was unhappy in Ireland. This is not the case.' It was presumably Darlington who made it clear to Lahey that Hopkins's work in Dublin was 'interesting and consoling'. Lahey, who had no access to most of Hopkins's letters, therefore concluded that there was no truth in the picture of his 'loneliness, drudgery, and despair'.

Subsequently, Fr Darlington was to provide anecdotes and opinions for the works of Phillipson, the 'Fathers of the Society of Jesus', and Tierney, as well as more recent scholars of Hopkins's last years, who have drawn their material from the earlier works. Few of the statements about Hopkins enhance his reputation.

The subject of Hopkins had clearly become something like an obsession to Darlington at the end of his life. As one of his colleagues said, 'his memory is unreliable for details', but he clung to his opinion of the poet with all the tenacity of a man of eighty who was largely distinguished by his intimacy with a man he had never known very well.

In 1933, when Humphry House visited Dublin to collect material for a biography of Hopkins, he found Darlington 'over-agreeable' about volunteering information. It was probably the loneliness of an old man rather than a desire to harm Hopkins's reputation that prompted his repeated invitations to House, offering still more information. But it was too late, so that what he had to say no longer seemed worth recording, and the only note of any real interest that House made tells us more about Darlington than about Hopkins. When he was saying that he believed the filth of the drains and the rats had caused Hopkins's death, Darlington described how the cook had found the rats in the food he was preparing, and, according to House, 'He roared with laughter again and again telling about the rats in the stew-pot.'

It is probably more important to realize how untrustworthy his evidence is than to know the reasons for his feelings about Hopkins, whom so many other friends seem to have loved, but it is perhaps worth a guess or two. Did they come of an old jealousy over Hopkins's much greater success at Oxford? Certainly, part of his feelings sprang from the traditional antipathy of the scholar and the militantly active academic administrator. Since he and Hopkins were the only Englishmen in the College for most of the years 1884–9, he may also have felt some of that annoyed embarrassment we have all known when we were abroad and have seen our own countrymen behaving badly. But there may have been something deeper in Darlington's feelings that he perhaps was unaware of himself, a kind of sexual antipathy that comes out in his descriptions of Hopkins. Two decades after the poet's death, he still remembered 'the very slippers he wore: the kind little girls of 10 or 12 used then to wear; with ancle straps!!' He spoke of Hopkins's delicacy and how he was too good 'for the *pioneer* roughness' of the College, and he recorded that his fascination was extraordinary, so that 'no one could treat him otherwise than as some delicate, highborn, fastidious lady might be treated.'

Whatever the cause, one can only feel sympathy for a man who nourished for so long what he regarded as causes for grievance. What is important is that they must not cloud our perception of Hopkins.

ACKNOWLEDGEMENTS

My primary obligation is for the permission of the Oxford University Press, granted on behalf of the Society of Jesus, to quote from the writings of Gerard Manley Hopkins that remain in copyright, including both those published by Oxford University Press and *The Early Poetic Manuscripts and Notebooks of Gerard Manley Hopkins in Facsimile*, published by Garland Publishing, Inc.; the latter is quoted with the additional permission of its editor, Norman H. MacKenzie, who has generously helped me in many other ways. I am also grateful to individual members of the Society of Jesus for special help, notably Fr Michael Ashworth, Fr Thomas Conlan, Fr Paul Edwards, Fr Philip Endean, and Fr Peter Hackett. For permission to publish from their holdings I am grateful to the Master and Fellows of Balliol College; the Master of Campion Hall; the President and Fellows of Corpus Christi College, Oxford; the Warden and Fellows of Keble College; the Master of St Benet's Hall; the Governors of Liddon House; the Bodleian Library and staff, in particular J.A. Priestman and Colin Harris.

Lord Bridges and John House have generously let me examine and quote from family papers, and Lord Bridges, Donald E. Stanford and Associated University Presses have allowed me to quote from *The Selected Letters of Robert Bridges*. Quotations from *The Letters of Thomas Arnold the Younger, 1850–1900* are made with the permission of the Auckland University Press. I apologize to any copyright owner whose permission I have inadvertently failed to secure.

Much of this book was written during the year-long pleasure of a Mellon Fellowship at the National Humanities Center. I am also grateful for the generosity of the University of Hawaii Foundation.

It is impossible to mention all those who have helped me, but for assistance too various to specify I must single out Pauline Adams, Vance Allen, Derek Auger, Michael Bampton, Jerome Bump, L.M. Chapman, Michael Dunham, William Foltz, Lesley Higgins, Billie Inman, David Johnson, J. Kastely, A.W. Marks, Lynne Munro, Jude V. Nixon, Cormac ó Gráda, John Shelton Reed, John Roberts, Ruth Seelhammer, Graham Storey, and J.M. Walker.

There are so many excellent articles and books written about Hopkins each year, often fifty or more, that space prohibits mentioning all of them that I have used, but their authors and other scholars will recognize my indebtedness.

ABBREVIATIONS USED IN NOTES

Balliol	Balliol College Library, Oxford; Balliol College Archives, English Register, 1784–1875.
Bodleian	Bodleian Library, Oxford.
Bridges Dep.	Papers of RB, deposited Bodleian.
Brooke Diaries	Ms diaries of Samuel Brooke, 1860–65, 6 v., Corpus Christi College, Oxford.
Facs	*The Early Poetic Manuscripts and Note-Books of Gerard Manley Hopkins in Facsimile*, ed. Norman H. MacKenzie, 1989.
GMH	Gerard Manley Hopkins.
H&D	*Hopkins & Dublin; The Man & the City*, ed. Richard F. Giles, special issue *Hopkins Quarterly*, XIV, 1–4, April 1987 – January 1988.
House	Documents and papers collected by the late Humphry House in preparation for writing biography of GMH.
HQ	*The Hopkins Quarterly*.
HRB	*The Hopkins Research Bulletin*.
J	*The Journals and Papers of Gerard Manley Hopkins*, ed. Humphry House and Graham Storey, 1959.
L&N	*Letters and Notices*, the private quarterly of the English Province of the Society of Jesus.
LI	*The Letters of Gerard Manley Hopkins to Robert Bridges*, ed. C.C. Abbott, 1970.
LII	*The Correspondence of Gerard Manley Hopkins and Richard Watson Dixon*, ed. C.C. Abbott, 1970.

LIII	*Further Letters of Gerard Manley Hopkins, Including His Correspondence with Coventry Patmore*, ed. C.C. Abbott, 2nd ed., 1970.
Liddon Diaries	Ms diaries of H.P. Liddon, 1858–90, Liddon House, London.
Liddon Papers	Miscellaneous Letters, 1860–90, Papers of H.P. Liddon, Keble College, Oxford.
PLDD	*The Poems and Letters of Digby Mackworth Dolben, 1848–1867*, ed. Martin Cohen, Avebury, 1981.
Poems	*The Poems of Gerard Manley Hopkins*, ed. W.H. Gardner and N.H. MacKenzie, 4th ed., 1984.
RB	Robert Bridges.
S	*The Sermons and Devotional Writings of Gerard Manley Hopkins*, ed. Christopher Devlin, 1967.
Thomas MS	Typescript of uncompleted study of background of GMH by the late Fr Alfred Thomas, S.J., in Archives of the British Province of the Society of Jesus.

NOTES

CHAPTER I

1. Thomas MS, to which I am much indebted in this chapter, particularly for information about Hopkins's father.

   A great deal more material about the whole family is to be found in the papers of Humphry House; for part of this information see Norman White, 'Hopkins, Boy and Man. Kate, Manley, and Gerard: Hopkins and His Parents', *Critical Essays on Gerard Manley Hopkins*, ed. Alison G. Sulloway, Boston, 1990.
2. Curiously, Felix Hopkins is buried in Hampstead, next to the grave of someone named Randall (Wade, pp. 71–2). It would be very easy to make too much of the coincidence with the title of Hopkins's poem 'Felix Randal'.
3. *J*, 369–70.
4. Lahey, p. 1.
5. P. 122.
6. Thomas MS.
7. 'The Poetry of Sorrow', *The Times*, 28.11.51.
8. Korn, p. 217.
9. Lahey, p. 3.
10. Facing *LIII*, 68.
11. At the Ransom Humanities Research Center of the University of Texas. See also Skarda, 'Juvenilia'.
12. Kate Hopkins to RB, 7.1.20, Bridges Dep. 62, fol. 84.
13. *LIII*, 68.
14. See Thomas MS; Allsopp, pp. 4–6.
15. Elliott, p. 255.
16. Kate Hopkins to RB, 7.1.20, Bridges Dep. 62, fol. 84.
17. Lahey, p. 6.
18. For the Luxmoore letters, see *LIII*, 1–4, 394–6.

CHAPTER II

1. *LII*, 12.
2. To RB, 23.12.18, Bridges Dep. 62, fol. 64.
3. Liddell, p. 65.
4. Except where otherwise indicated, information about GMH's first term at Oxford is taken from *LIII*, 68–81.
5. Liddell, p. 58.
6. 'University Life', p. 224.
7. *Loss and Gain*, chapter 1.
8. 'West-Running Brook'.
9. Brooke, *Journal*, p. 131.
10. *J*, 133.
11. *Balliol Studies*, p. 161.
12. Davis, p. 200.
13. 'University Life', p. 225.
14. Davis, p. 217.
15. *Letters*, p. 239.
16. XX, 1889–90, 174.
17. *LIII*, 16–17.
18. Lahey, p. 18.
19. Liddon, p. 3.
20. Liddon Diaries, 3.5.63.

CHAPTER III

1. Reed, 'Giddy Young Men'.
2. Brooke Diaries, 13.12.62.
3. *LIII*, 16–17.
4. Liddell, p. 69.
5. *LIII*, 207.
6. Lahey, p. 19.
7. Hilliard, p. 185.
8. Quoted, Reed, 'Giddy Young Men'.
9. *LI*, 194, 198.
10. *Facs*, 182.
11. Symonds, p. 94.
12. P. 39.
13. *Facs*, 126, 32.
14. 'Giddy Young Men'.
15. Pp. 7–8.
16. *LIII*, 83.
17. Paget, p. 29.
18. *LIII*, 249.
19. P. 53.
20. *Balliol Studies*, p. 166.
21. *Balliol Studies*, p. 181.
22. *LIII*, 200.
23. *LIII*, 200–1.
24. See in particular *J*, plates 10–16, and *All My Eyes*, pp. 116–23.
25. *LIII*, 202.

CHAPTER IV

1. *Remains*, quoted by Seccombe and Scott, p. 318.
2. *LIII*, 87.
3. Meyrick, p. 173.
4. 28.1.63.
5. Quoted, Ritz, *Bridges and Hopkins*, p. 19.
6. *LI*, 95.
7. P. 109.
8. Diaries, 10.12.62.
9. *Facs*, 195.
10. *LII*, 20.
11. *J*, 19.
12. *J*, 5.
13. *J*, 24.
14. *J*, 23.
15. *J*, 48.
16. *J*, 37.
17. *J*, 50.

18. *LIII*, 215–23.
19. *J*, 38, 49.
20. *LIII*, 204.
21. *LIII*, 221.
22. *J*, 30; *LIII*, 214.
23. *LIII*, 119.
24. Diaries, 20.2.64, 29.2.64.
25. *LIII*, 213.
26. *LIII*, 212–13.
27. *LIII*, 207.
28. *LIII*, 223.
29. *LIII*, 231.
30. *LIII*, 17–18, 224. For more on Hopkins and Savonarola, see Bump, 'Art and Religion'.
31. *LIII*, 225.

CHAPTER V

1. James, II, 337–8.
2. This and most of the information about Dolben is taken from RB's introductory Memoir in his edition of Dolben's poems; other information *passim* from *PLDD*; Bailey; Cornish; [Devas]; [Harting]; Watkin; Bodleian Library; Dolben family papers, Northamptonshire County Record Office, Delapre Abbey.
3. Bailey, p. 54.
4. Coles to Liddon, 22.1.66, Liddon Papers.
5. *Letters*, II, 338.
6. *Letters*, II, 342.
7. Bridges Dep. 54, fol. 70.
8. Eric Barrington to RB, 22.7.10, Bridges Dep. 54, fol. 9.
9. Bridges Dep. 54, fols. 6, 10, 27.
10. See Liddon's diary, 10.2.64. Ruggles (p. 55) says his first confession had been made three months before he met Dolben, but the source of her information is not given. House (*J*, 325) says that his confession on 25.3.65 was his first recorded one.
11. Sulloway, p. 50.
12. *PLDD*, 149.
13. *PLDD*, 159.

CHAPTER VI

1. To RB, 30.12.18, Bridges Dep. 62, fol. 64.
2. One writer claims that Hopkins recorded 1564 sins in ten months, averaging five a day, and that 'Of these, 238 were sexual sins' (Norman White, 'Hopkins: Problems in the Biography', *Studies in the Literary Imagination*, Spring 1988, XXI, 1, 115). This may well be true.
3. *Facs*, 192, 194.
4. *LI*, 1.
5. *PLDD*, 166.
6. *Facs*, 194.
7. For a reasoned but (to me) not persuasive argument that 'Where art thou friend' is addressed to some ideal future reader, not Dolben, see Bremer, 'Where Art Thou Friend'.
8. *Poems*, 250.
9. E.g., MacKenzie, *Reader's Guide*, p. 24.
10. Brooke Diaries.
11. Brooke Diaries, 30.9.64.
12. Lechmere, p. 96.
13. *Facs*, 156, 191, 169, 161, 168, 169.
14. *LI*, 1.
15. *PLDD*, 159.
16. *Facs*, 177.
17. *LIII*, 89–90.
18. Korn, p. 232.
19. *Facs*, 194, 197, 196. MacKenzie transcribes the last name as 'Rosseti' but questions the reading.
20. *Letters*, pp. 153–4.
21. *LIII*, 226–7.
22. *Facs*, 190.
23. *J*, 71.

CHAPTER VII

1. Brooke Diaries, 29.4.65, 31.12.64; McClelland, *English Roman Catholics*, p. 20; Leslie, p. 180.
2. To Liddon, 19.10.71, Liddon Papers.

3. *LIII*, 434.
4. Pusey to Liddon, 17.11.68, Liddon Papers.
5. Blair, pp. 41–7, 68; Norman, p. 271.
6. For the decisions of the governing body of the College, see Balliol, fols. 184, 185, 213, 222.
7. Faber, p. 137.
8. *J*, 72.
9. *LIII*, 30.
10. *LIII*, 99.
11. Bischoff, p. 6; Bywater, p. 313; Martindale, p. 11.
12. Kilbracken, p. 49.
13. *LIII*, 220, 227.
14. *J*, 134.
15. Suggested in Higgins, 'Essaying Mr Pater'.
16. *J*, 133, 138.
17. Seiler, p. 87.
18. *J*, 141, 143, 144, 146.
19. *J*, 139.
20. *J*, 138.

CHAPTER VIII

1. *J*, 141, 358.
2. Storey, 'Three New Letters', p. 4.
3. *J*, 146.
4. Storey, 'Three New Letters', p. 5.
5. *LIII*, 397.
6. *J*, 146.
7. *LIII*, 397.
8. *LIII*, 26.
9. *LI*, 3.
10. *PLDD*, 163.
11. *PLDD*, 78.
12. 14.9.85, Bodleian, Don. e.656.
13. Cornish, p. 127.
14. *PLDD*, 168–9.
15. *LI*, 7.
16. Newman, *Letters*, XXIII, 313, n.1.
17. Bridges, *Letters*, I, 81.
18. Lahey, p. 18.
19. Bridges Dep. 53, fol. 107.
20. *LI*, 6.
21. *LI*, 5–7.
22. *LIII*, 26.
23. *LIII*, 29–30.

24. *LIII*, 435.
25. *LIII*, 29.
26. *LIII*, 404.
27. *LIII*, 91, 404.
28. *LIII*, 91–5.
29. *LIII*, 96–7.
30. *LIII*, 400.
31. Liddon Papers, 15.10.[66].
32. *LIII*, 401.
33. *LIII*, 97.
34. *LIII*, 31–4.
35. *LIII*, 99–100.
36. Lahey, p. 43.
37. *LIII*, 94.
38. *J*, 310.
39. Crehan, p. 209.
40. *LIII*, 405.
41. *Balliol Studies*, p. 182.

CHAPTER IX
1. *LIII*, 405–6.
2. *LI*, 21–2.
3. *LI*, 15.
4. *PLDD*, 171.
5. *LIII*, 101.
6. Lahey, p. 18.
7. *LI*, 20.
8. *LI*, 19.
9. *LIII*, 406.
10. *J*, 147–9.
11. To Mr Mackworth Dolben, 14.6.67, Northamptonshire County Record Office.
12. W.H. Prichard to RB, Bridges Dep. 54, fol. 110.
13. *LI*, 16–17.
14. Bridges, *Letters*, I, 88.
15. Bridges, *Letters*, I, 88.
16. *LI*, 18.
17. Newman, *Letters*, XXIII, 313; XXV, 358.
18. *J*, 152.
19. *LIII*, 40, 47, 41.
20. *J*, 157.
21. Arnold, xxiv.
22. For GMH's first term, see *LI*, 18; *LIII*, 42–8; *J*, 158–9.
23. *LI*, 22.

24. *LIII*, 408.
25. *LI*, 22.

CHAPTER X
1. *LIII*, 231–2.
2. Quoted, *J*, 381–2.
3. *J*, 165.
4. *J*, 164–5.
5. *LI*, 24.
6. *LIII*, 408.
7. *L&N*, 1891–2, XXI, 24.
8. *J*, 166.
9. *LIII*, 49.
10. 5.6.68, Balliol.
11. *LIII*, 52.
12. *LI*, 12.
13. *J*, 169.
14. *J*, 180, 182.
15. *J*, 187.
16. *J*, 189. Passionate railway lovers may follow the route his train took by consulting *J*, 401.

CHAPTER XI
1. *L&N*, 1932, XL, 9.
2. *LIII*, 104.
3. Meadows, p. 14.
4. *LIII*, 105.
5. Clarke, p. 216.
6. *L&N*, 1863, I, 10.
7. Alcock, p. 106.
8. Maxwell-Scott, p. 76.
9. December 1975, CXXXVI, no. 1299, 339.
10. Steinmetz, p. 189.
11. Meadows, p. 94.
12. *J*, 192.
13. *J*, 196.
14. 'T', pp. 24, 27.
15. *J*, 195.
16. *LIII*, 106.
17. *J*, 194.
18. *LI*, 23.
19. *LI*, 23.
20. *LIII*, 107–8.
21. *LI*, 27.
22. *LIII*, 233.
23. Paget, pp. 29–30.
24. Anson, p. 200.

25. Maison, p. 293.
26. 'T', pp. 20, 18, 32, 39.
27. Steinmetz, p. 209.
28. 'T', p. 39.
29. *LIII*, 106; *J*, 193.
30. *J*, 191, 190.
31. *J*, 200.

CHAPTER XII
1. *LIII*, 112–13.
2. For GMH's impressions of Stonyhurst, see *LIII*, 112–17; *LI*, 151.
3. Meadows, p. 138.
4. *J*, 200.
5. *J*, 201.
6. *J*, 408.
7. *J*, 204.
8. *J*, 216.
9. *J*, 200; italics mine.
10. MacKenzie, *Reader's Guide*, p. 233.
11. *J*, 221.
12. Pick, 'The Growth of a Poet', p. 43. My treatment of Duns Scotus is necessarily quite inadequate except as an indication of Hopkins's attraction to him. For guidance to a great deal more information, see this article as well as Fr Pick's *Gerard Manley Hopkins*, and Zaniello, 'The Stonyhurst Philosophers'.
13. *J*, 233.
14. Thomas, p. 105.
15. *LIII*, 235.
16. Thomas, pp. 105–10.
17. *J*, 213–14.
18. *J*, 221–5.
19. Clarke, p. 221.
20. *LIII*, 115.
21. Thomas, p. 127.
22. *LIII*, 117.
23. *J*, 218.
24. *J*, 230.
25. *J*, 234.
26. 'Expectation of Life in the Society', IV, 41–3.
27. *J*, 202, 409, 220.

28. *J*, 227.
29. *J*, 229.
30. Bump, 'Hopkins at Stonyhurst', pp. 47–50.
31. *J*, 217, 231, 227.
32. *LI*, 27–8.
33. *LII*, 97.
34. Bergonzi, p. 71.
35. P. 47.
36. Quoted, Edwards, p. 65.
37. von Hönsbröch, I, 240–1.
38. *LI*, 28–9.
39. Bridges, *Letters*, II, 628.
40. *J*, 234–6.
41. *LIII*, 122–3.
42. *J*, 236.

CHAPTER XIII
1. *J*, 236.
2. *LIII*, 147–8.
3. *LII*, 147.
4. *S*, 264.
5. *S*, 253–4.
6. *J*, 252.
7. *J*, 238.
8. *LIII*, 60–1.
9. *LI*, 30.
10. *J*, 254.
11. *LIII*, 119.
12. *J*, 237.
13. *J*, 240.
14. Phillipson, p. 339.
15. Mariani, 'Hopkins' "Harry Ploughman"', p. 44.
16. *J*, 249.
17. *J*, 241–3.
18. *J*, 249–50.
19. *LIII*, 142.
20. *LIII*, 126; *J*, 260.
21. *LIII*, 124–5.
22. *LIII*, 126–7.
23. *J*, 258.
24. *LIII*, 127.
25. *J*, 258.
26. *J*, 259.
27. *LI*, 40.
28. *J*, 261.
29. *LIII*, 132.
30. *J*, 263.

CHAPTER XIV
1. Pp. 223–4.
2. *LIII*, 132.
3. *J*, 442.
4. *LII*, 14–15.
5. *LIII*, 135.
6. *LIII*, 138–41.
7. *J*, 382.
8. *LI*, 47.
9. *LII*, 14.
10. *LI*, 46.
11. *LI*, 32.
12. *LI*, 34.
13. *LI*, 38.
14. *LI*, 44–7.
15. Bridges, *Letters*, II, 726.

CHAPTER XV
1. *LIII*, 140.
2. *LIII*, 137.
3. This has customarily been put among those poems written in 1881–2, but Catherine Phillips assigns it a place with the other St Beuno's poems (p. 129).
4. Sprinker, p. 120.
5. *S*, 225–33.
6. See Feeney, 'Grades, Academic Reform, and Manpower' and 'Hopkins' "Failure" in Theology'.
7. *LI*, 43.
8. *LIII*, 146.
9. Thomas, pp. 185–6.
10. For Mt St Mary's, see *LIII*, 149–51; McClelland, *English Roman Catholics*, pp. 40–1; Keegan, *passim*.
11. P. 13.
12. Fr Keegan strongly believes that the models for the characters in this poem were Henry and James Broadbent, which seems probable. Unfortunately, the fact that they were 'real' people is not sufficient to make their reactions believable, or even interesting, within the context of the poem.
13. *LI*, 54.

14. *LII*, 1–2.
15. *LII*, 3–4.
16. *LII*, 6–8.
17. *LII*, xviii.
18. *LI*, 57.
19. Bridges, *Letters*, I, 127.
20. *LI*, 55, 58.
21. For a well-documented argument that the number of his changes was completely normal in the Society at the time, see Feeney, 'Hopkins' Frequent Reassignments'.

CHAPTER XVI
1. *LII*, 12.
2. Paget, p. 50.
3. *LI*, 61.
4. Ward, II, 55.
5. Bywater, p. 300.
6. *L&N*, 1878–9, XII, 112–14; reprinted without comment.
7. *L&N*, 1903–4, XXVII, 556.
8. Vassall-Phillips, pp. 72–3.
9. Ellmann, *Oscar Wilde*, pp. 55–6.
10. *LI*, 68.
11. *L&N*, 1903–4, XXVII, 563.
12. Adams, pp. ii, 95.
13. P. 41.
14. Personal information.
15. *LIII*, 93.
16. Quoted, Thomas, p. 7.
17. *LIII*, 151–2.
18. Vassall-Phillips, p. 81.
19. Ward, II, 57.
20. *LI*, 92.
21. *LI*, 86.
22. *LI*, 92.
23. *LI*, 75, 81.
24. Paget, p. 33.
25. *LIII*, 249.
26. Paget, p. 30.
27. Bridges, *Letters*, II, 927.
28. *LIII*, 62–3.
29. See Ellmann, 'Oscar at Oxford'; Inman, 'Estrangement'.
30. *LI*, 58.
31. *LIII*, 151.
32. *LIII*, 246.

33. Bridges, *Letters*, I, 128.
34. S, 235.
35. Feeney, 'Hopkins, the Fussy Worrier', p. 156.
36. LIII, 63.
37. LIII, 151.
38. LII, 20–6.
39. Taunt, p. 11.
40. LI, 80.
41. 'Hopkins' Frequent Reassignments', p. 112.
42. LI, 97.
43. LIII, 244–5.
44. LIII, 244.
45. LI, 97.

CHAPTER XVII

1. LIII, 243.
2. LI, 90.
3. S, 35, 42.
4. LIII, 245.
5. LI, 93–6.
6. LII, 26–7.
7. LII, 26–31.
8. An admirable exception to this certitude is Alison Sulloway, who writes that 'Hopkins's attitudes towards fame and towards his own aesthetic creations . . . were always openly and frankly ambivalent, rather than secretly or dishonestly so' (p. 102).
9. LI, 66.
10. LI, 231.
11. LII, 93–5.
12. LII, 88, 90.
13. LI, 66.
14. S, 253–4.
15. LIII, 154.
16. For this and much succeeding information on St Francis Xavier's I have relied on the parish history by Fr Nicholas Ryan.
17. Information about Hopkins's preaching comes chiefly from *Sermons*, particularly 5, 8, 9, 50, 53, 62, 68, 79, 80, 81, 83, 89.
18. LIII, 162.
19. S, 9.

20. LIII, 245.
21. LI, 99–100.
22. S, 249.
23. LI, 299.
24. Told me by Fr Thomas Conlan, S.J.
25. LI, 127–8.
26. LI, 126.
27. LI, 110.
28. Bridges, *Letters*, I, 127.
29. LII, 33, 42.
30. For the factual background, see Thomas, 'Hopkins's "Felix Randal"'.
31. LII, 46–9; LI, 127–9, 134.
32. LI, 126, 136.
33. LI, 283.
34. LIII, 157; LI, 104.
35. LI, 264.
36. LIII, 248–9.
37. LI, 135.

CHAPTER XVIII

1. LI, 136; LIII, 288.
2. LI, 135.
3. According to Thomas, p. 192, there were only nine; occasionally the facts he quotes differ from records in the Provincial archives, Mount Street.
4. LII, 70, 75–6.
5. LI, 139.
6. LII, 88–9.
7. LII, 74.
8. LI, 137.
9. LIII, 161.
10. LI, 138.
11. J, 423.
12. LIII, 162.
13. LI, 143.
14. LII, 104.
15. Sambrook, pp. 65–6.
16. LI, 145.
17. J, 296.
18. LI, 147–9.
19. Bridges, *Letters*, I, 134.
20. LI, 150.
21. Thomas, p. 209.
22. Quoted, Roberts, p. 44.

23. *LI*, 151.
24. *LI*, 150.
25. *LIII*, 251–2.
26. Quoted, *H&D*, 196.
27. *LII*, 119.
28. *LI*, 179; *LII*, 110.
29. *LI*, 155.
30. Bergonzi, p. 113.
31. *LI*, 312–13.
32. *LI*, 262.
33. *LI*, 178.
34. *LI*, 183.
35. *S*, 253–4.
36. *LI*, 185.
37. *LIII*, 342.
38. *LIII*, 319, 324.
39. *LIII*, 349, 351.
40. *LIII*, 352–3.
41. Quoted, *LIII*, 391.
42. *LI*, 153.
43. *LII*, 163–4.

CHAPTER XIX
1. Arnold, p. 205.
2. White, p. 94.
3. *H&D*, 195–6.
4. Tierney, p. 32.
5. White, p. 98.
6. *H&D*, p. 197. Delany's point seems to suggest that many more of Hopkins's fellow Jesuits knew about his poetry than we are normally told.
7. *H&D*, p. 220.
8. *H&D*, 20.
9. *LIII*, 63.
10. Arnold, xxxi.
11. *LI*, 190.
12. *H&D*, 102. In what I have to say of the city, I feel particularly indebted to this concise, illuminating article by Mary Daly, 'Dublin in the 1880s'.
13. Arnold, pp. 92–3.
14. Kate Hopkins to RB, 7.1.20, Bridges Dep. 62, fol. 84.
15. *H&D*, 98, 96.
16. *LIII*, 63.
17. *LIII*, 164–5.

18. *LIII*, 64–5.
19. *H&D*, 176.
20. *LIII*, 164.
21. P. 69.
22. *LII*, 123; *LI*, 236.
23. *LIII*, 173.
24. *LIII*, 184–5.
25. *LIII*, 193.
26. Phillipson, pp. 336–7; *LI*, xxxii; Lahey, pp. 139–40. Most of the interviews with those who remembered Hopkins are recorded in a file marked 'Dublin Essay' in the House papers.
27. Litzinger, pp. 41–2.
28. It is an attitude that has not died in the course of a century. See, for example, Gráinne O'Flynne, 'Hopkins's Teaching', *H&D*, pp. 174–5.
29. Fathers of the S.J., p. 106.
30. Tierney, 32.
31. Sambrook, pp. 96–7.
32. Tynan, *Memories*, p. 156.
33. *LIII*, 164.
34. Fathers of the S.J., p. 104.
35. *LI*, 192–3.
36. *LI*, 193–4.
37. Bridges, *Letters*, I, 201.
38. *LI*, 216–19.
39. *LI*, 221.
40. *LI*, 272.
41. *LI*, 222.

CHAPTER XX
1. *LI*, 221.
2. *LI*, 292.
3. *LIII*, 256.
4. *LI*, 270.
5. *LII*, 154.
6. *LIII*, 427.
7. *LI*, 250.
8. Bridges, *Letters*, I, 164; *LI*, 253.
9. Bridges, *Letters*, I, 186.
10. To RB, 12.9.[90], Bridges Dep. 62.
11. *L&N*, XX, 1889–90, 176.
12. Storey, 'Six New Letters', pp. 265–6.

13. *LIII*, 163.
14. *LIII*, 240.
15. *LI*, 225.
16. For Welsh trip see *LI*, 226–8; *LII*, 142–3; *LIII*, 176–8.
17. Bridges, *Letters*, I, 171.
18. *LIII*, 183.
19. For Tynan, Russell, Yeats, see *LII*, 151; *LIII*, 373, 430–1; Tynan, 'Russell', pp. 553–5; *Memories*, pp. 14, 155; Yeats, p. 281.
20. *LI*, 303.
21. *LI*, 278.
22. For his eyes, see *LI*, 282–3, 290, 296.
23. *S*, 261–3; Bridges Dep. 62, fols. 8–11.
24. Frances de Paravicini to Mrs Hopkins, 14.6.89, Bodleian, MS. Eng. Misc. a8, fol. 46.
25. Bridges, *Letters*, I, 188.
26. For Hopkins's last days, see *LIII*, 195–8; *L&N*, 1889–90, XX, 178–9.
27. To E.H. Coleridge, 15.6.89, House.
28. Feeney, 'Hopkins' Earliest Memorial', p. 59.

APPENDIX

1. For sources of this Appendix, apart from those mentioned in the text, see *H&D*, 200–2; House, particularly the folder marked 'Dublin Essay'.

SELECT BIBLIOGRAPHY

(unless otherwise stated, place of publication is London)

Adams, Pauline Ann, *Converts to the Roman Catholic Church in England circa 1830–1870*, unpublished dissertation, Oxford, 1977.
Adlard, John, *Stenbock, Yeats and the Nineties*, 1969.
Alcock, Joan P., *Where Generations Have Trod*, 1979.
All My Eyes See: the Visual World of Gerard Manley Hopkins, ed. R.K.R. Thornton, Sunderland, 1975.
Allies, Mary H., *Thomas William Allies*, 1907.
Allison, William, *My Kingdom for a Horse*, 1919.
Allsopp, Michael, 'Hopkins at Highgate: Biographical Fragments', *HQ*, Spring 1979, VI, 1, 3–10.
Anson: *Memoir of Sir William Anson*, ed. H.H. Henson, 1920.
Arnold, Thomas, *Letters of Thomas Arnold the Younger, 1850–1900*, ed. James Bertram, 1980.
August, Eugene R., 'A Checklist of Materials Relating to the Hopkins Family in the State Archives of Hawaii', *HQ*, Summer 1979, VI, 2, 61–83.
Bailey, John L.H., *Finedon, Otherwise Thingdon*, Finedon, 1975.
Balliol Studies, ed. John Prest, 1982.
Bassett, Arthur Tilney, *S. Barnabas' Oxford: a Record of Fifty Years*, Oxford, 1919.
Baumann, A.A., *Personalities*, 1936.
Bentley, James, *Ritualism and Politics in Victorian Britain*, 1978.
Bergonzi, Bernard, *Gerard Manley Hopkins*, 1977.
Bischoff, D. Anthony, *St. Aloysius: the First Eighty Years, 1875–1955*, Oxford, 1955.
Blair, David Hunter, *John Patrick, Third Marquess of Bute, K.T.*, 1921.
Brandreth, H.R.T., *Dr Lee of Lambeth*, 1951.
Bremer, Rudy, 'Where Art Thou Friend, Whom I shall Never See', *HQ*, Spring 1980, VII, 1, 9–14.

435

Bridges, Robert: *Selected Letters of Robert Bridges*, ed. Donald E. Stanford, 2 v., 1983–4.

Brooke, Samuel, *Sam Brooke's Journal: the Diary of a Lancing Schoolboy, 1860–65*, ed. Peter Hadley, Reading, 1953.

Bump, Jerome, 'Art and Religion: Hopkins and Savonarola', *Thought*, June 1975, L, 197, 132–47.

Bump, Jerome, 'Hopkins at Stonyhurst: a Letter to His Father', *Library Chronicle of the University of Texas at Austin*, Fall 1974, 8, 47–51.

Bump, Jerome, *Gerard Manley Hopkins*, Boston, 1982.

Bywater, Vincent et al., 'Jesuits' Pastoral Work in Oxford, Article I', *L&N*, Christmas 1983, LXXXV, 385, 297–309.

Clarke, R.F., 'The Training of a Jesuit', *Nineteenth Century*, August 1896, XL, 234, 211–25.

Coles, V.S.S., *Letters, Papers, Addresses, Hymns and Verses*, ed. J.F. Briscoe, 1930.

Cornish Blanche Warre, 'Digby Dolben', *Dublin Review*, January 1913, CLII, 304, 111–31.

Crehan, J.H., 'More Light on Gerard Hopkins', *Month*, October 1953, X, 4, 205–14.

Dacey, Philip, *Gerard Manley Hopkins meets Walt Whitman in Heaven, and Other Poems*, Gt. Barrington, Mass., 1982.

Daly, Mary E., *Dublin, the Deposed Capital: a Social and Economic History, 1860–1914*, Cork, 1984.

Davis, H.W. Carless, *A History of Balliol College*, rev. R.H.C. Davis, Richard Hunt, Oxford, 1963.

[Devas, Francis Charles], *The History of St. Stanislaus' College, Beaumont*, 1911.

Dolben, Digby: *The Poems and Letters of Digby Mackworth Dolben, 1848–1867*, ed. Martin Cohen, Avebury, 1981.

Dolben, Digby: *The Poems of Digby Mackworth Dolben*, ed. Robert Bridges, 1915.

Dolben, Digby: *Uncollected Poems of Digby Mackworth Dolben*, ed. Martin Cohen, Reading, 1973.

Downes, David A., 'The Hopkins Enigma', *Thought*, Winter 1961, XXXVI, 143.

Edwards, Owen Dudley, *The Quest for Sherlock Holmes; a Biographical Study of Arthur Conan Doyle*, Edinburgh, 1983.

Elliott, Brian, *Marcus Clarke*, Oxford, 1958.

Ellmann, Richard, 'Oscar at Oxford', *New York Review of Books*, 29.3.84, pp. 23–8.

Ellmann, Richard, *Oscar Wilde*, 1987.

Faber, Geoffrey, *Jowett: a Portrait with Background*, 1957.

BIBLIOGRAPHY

Fathers of the Society of Jesus, *A Page of Irish History: Story of University College, Dublin, 1882–1909*, Dublin, 1930.

Feeney, Joseph J., 'Grades, Academic Reform, and Manpower: Why Hopkins Never Completed His Course in Theology', *HQ*, Spring 1982, IX, 121–31.

Feeney, Joseph J., 'Hopkins, the Fussy Worrier', *Victorians Institute Journal*, 1988, pp. 151–8.

Feeney, Joseph J., 'Hopkins' "Failure" in Theology: Some New Archival Data and a Reevaluation', *HQ*, October 1986–January 1987, XIII, 3 and 4, 99–115.

Feeney, Joseph J., 'Hopkins' Earliest Memorial: the Jesuit Obituary of 1890', *HQ*, Summer 1981, VIII, 2, 53–62.

Feeney, Joseph J. 'Hopkins' Frequent Reassignments as a Priest', *HQ*, Fall 1984, XI, 3, 101–18.

Fitzgerald, Percy, *Father Gallwey: a Sketch*, 1906.

Gardner, W.H., *Gerard Manley Hopkins, 1844–89; a Study of Poetic Idiosyncracy in Relation to Poetic Tradition*, 2 v., 1966.

Gavin, M., *Memoirs of Father P. Gallwey, S.J.*, 1913.

Geldart, E.M. ['Nitram Tradleg'], *A Son of Belial*, 1882.

Green, V.H.H., *Religion at Oxford and Cambridge*, 1964.

Harting, E.M., 'Gerard Hopkins and Digby Dolben', *Month*, April 1919, pp. 285–9.

Higgins, Lesley, 'Essaying Mr. Pater: New Perspectives on the Tutor/Student Relationship between Walter Pater and Gerald Hopkins', unpublished typescript.

Hilliard, David, 'UnEnglish and Unmanly: Anglo-Catholicism and Homosexuality', *Victorian Studies*, Winter 1982, XXV, 2, 181–210.

Hönsbröch, Paul von, *Fourteen Years a Jesuit: a Record of Personal Experience and a Criticism*, 2 v., 1911.

Hopkins, Manley, *Hawaii: the Past, Present, and Future of Its Island-Kingdom*, 1862.

Inman, Billie A., 'The Estrangement between Walter Pater and Benjamin Jowett and Its Connection to the Relationship Between Pater and William M. Hardinge', unpublished typescript.

James: *The Letters of Henry James*, ed. Percy Lubbock, 2 v., New York, 1920.

Johnston, John Octavius, *Life and Letters of Henry Parry Liddon*, 1904.

Keegan, Francis, 'Gerard Manley Hopkins at Mount St. Mary's College, Spinkhill, 1877–1878', *HQ*, Spring 1979, VI, 1, 11–34.

Kilbracken, Lord [John Arthur Godley], *Reminiscences of Lord Kilbracken*, 1931.

Korn, Alfons L., *The Victorian Visitors*, Honolulu, 1958.

437

Lahey, G.F., *Gerard Manley Hopkins*, 1930.

Lechmere, W.L., 'Oxford: 1863–1867', *Oxford and Cambridge Review*, May 1912, 19, 78–118.

Leslie, Shane, *Henry Edward Manning: His Life and Labours*, 1921.

Liddell, A.G.C., *Notes from the Life of an Ordinary Mortal*, 1911.

Liddon: *Henry Parry Liddon, 1829–1890. A centenary Memoir*, 1929.

Litzinger, Boyd, 'To Seem the Stranger . . .', *HQ*, April 1974, I, 1, 41–2.

MacKenzie, Norman H., 'Gerard Manley Hopkins – an Unrecognized Translation: "Not Kind! to Freeze me with Forecast"', *Classical and Modern Literature*, Fall 1984, V, 1, 7–11.

MacKenzie, Norman H., *A Reader's Guide to Gerard Manley Hopkins*, 1981.

Maison, Margaret, *Search Your Soul, Eustace: a Survey of the Religious Novel in the Victorian Age*, 1961.

Mallock, W.H., *Memoirs of Life and Literature*, 1920.

Mariani, Paul L., 'Hopkins' "Harry Ploughman" and Frederick Walker's "The Plough"', *Month*, July–August 1968, CCXXVI, 1211–12, 37–44.

Mariani, Paul L., *A Commentary on the Complete Poems of Gerard Manley Hopkins*, Cornell, 1969.

Marks, J.G., *Life and Letters of Frederick Walker, ARA*, 1896.

Martin, Robert Bernard, 'The Poet, the Nun, and the Daring Young Man', in *Leon Edel and Literary Art*, ed. Lyall H. Powers, 1988, pp. 29–42.

Martindale, C.C., *Catholics in Oxford*, Oxford, 1925.

Maxwell-Scott, Hon. Mrs [M.M.C.], *Henry Schomberg Kerr, Sailor and Jesuit*, 1901.

McClelland, Vincent Alan, *Cardinal Manning*, 1962.

McClelland, Vincent Alan, *English Roman Catholics and Higher Education, 1830–1903*, Oxford, 1973.

Meadows, Denis, *Obedient Men*, 1954.

Meyrick, Frederick, *Memories of Life at Oxford*, New York, 1905.

Morrissey, Thomas J., *Towards a National University: William Delany SJ (1835–1924)*, Dublin 1983.

Newman, J.H., *Loss and Gain*, 1848.

Newman: *Letters and Diaries of John Henry Newman*, ed. C.S. Dessain and Thomas Gornall, 31 v., Oxford, 1961–84.

Newsome, David, *On the Edge of Paradise*, 1980.

Norman, Edward, *The English Catholic Church in the Nineteenth Century*, Oxford, 1984.

Oxford University Catholic Club, [Oxford, 1878?].

Paget, Stephen, *Henry Scott Holland*, 1921.

Phillips, Catherine, ed., *Gerard Manley Hopkins*, Oxford, 1986.

Phillipson, Wulstan, 'Gerard Manley Hopkins', *Downside Review*, April 1933, LI, 146, 339.

Pick, John, 'The Growth of a Poet: Gerard Manley Hopkins, S.J.', *Month*, January 1940, CLXXV, 39–46.

Pick, John, *Gerard Manley Hopkins: Priest and Poet*, 1942.

Purcell, E.S., *The Life of Cardinal Manning*, 2 v., 1895.

Reed, John Shelton, ' "A Female Movement": The Feminization of Nineteenth-Century Anglo-Catholicism', *Anglican and Episcopal History*, June 1988, LVII, 2, 199–238.

Reed, John Shelton, ' "Giddy Young Men": a Counter-Cultural Aspect of Victorian Anglo-Catholicism', unpublished typescript.

Ritz, Jean-Georges, *Le poète Gérard Manley Hopkins, S.J.: Sa vie et son oeuvre*, Paris, 1963.

Ritz, Jean-Georges, *Robert Bridges and Gerard Hopkins, 1863–1889: a Literary Friendship*, 1960.

Roberts, Gerald, 'The Jaded Muse: Hopkins at Stonyhurst', *HQ*, Spring 1979, VI, 1, 35–47.

Ruggles, Eleanor, *Gerard Manley Hopkins: a Life*, 1947.

Ryan, Nicholas, *St. Francis Xavier's Church Centenary, 1848–1948*, [Liverpool], n.d.

Sambrook, James, *A Poet Hidden: the Life of Richard Watson Dixon, 1833–1900*, 1962.

Seccombe, Thomas, and Scott, H. Spencer, *In Praise of Oxford*, 1910.

Seiler, R.M., ed., *Walter Pater: a Life Remembered*, Calgary, 1987.

Sieveking, Lance, 'Remembering Gerard Manley Hopkins', *Listener*, 24.1.57, pp. 151–2.

Skarda, Patricia L., 'Juvenilia of the Family of Gerard Manley Hopkins', *HQ*, Summer 1977, IV, 2, 39–54.

Sprinker, Michael, *'A Counterpoint of Dissonance'; The Aesthetics and Poetry of Gerard Manley Hopkins*, 1980.

Steinmetz, Andrew, *The Novitiate: or, A Year Among the English Jesuits*, New York, 1846.

Storey, Graham, 'Six New Letters of Gerard Manley Hopkins', *Month*, May 1958, XIX, 5, 262–70.

Storey, Graham, 'Three New Letters from G.M. Hopkins to W.A. Comyn Macfarlane', *HRB*, 1975, 6, 3–7.

Sulloway, Alison G., *Gerard Manley Hopkins and the Victorian Temper*, 1972.

Symonds: *Memoirs of John Addington Symonds*, ed. Phyllis Grosskurth, 1984.

'T' [Joseph Peter Thorp], *Friends and Adventures*, 1931.

Taunt, Henry W., *Godstow, Medley, Wytham, and Binsey*, Oxford, ca. 1900.

Thomas, Alfred, 'Hopkins's "Felix Randal": the Man and the Poem', *TLS*, 19.3.71, pp. 331–2.

Thomas, Alfred, *Hopkins the Jesuit: the Years of Training*, 1969.

Tierney, Michael, *Struggle with Fortune*, 1954.

Tynan, Katharine, 'Father Matthew Russell, S.J., Dearest of Friends', *Irish Monthly*, October 1912, XL, 472, 551–8.

Tynan, Katharine, *Memories*, 1924.

'University Life', *Cornhill*, 1865, 11, 223–32.

Vassall-Phillips, O.R., *After Fifty Years*, 1928.

Wade, Christopher, and Nunn, Terence, *Buried in Hampstead*, 1986.

Ward, Wilfrid, *The Life of John Henry Cardinal Newman*, 2 v., 1912.

Watkin, Aelred, 'Digby Mackworth Dolben and the Catholic Church: Some Fresh Evidence', *Dublin Review*, 1951, 453, 65–70.

Whaley, Buck: *Buck Whaley's Memoirs*, ed. Edward Sullivan, 1906.

White, Norman, 'Gerard Manley Hopkins and the Irish Row', *HQ*, Fall 1982, IX, 3, 91–107.

Yeats: *The Letters of W.B. Yeats*, ed. Allan Wade, 1954.

Zaniello, Thomas, 'The Stonyhurst Philosophers', *HQ*, Winter 1983, IX, 133–59.

Zonneveld, Sjaak, 'Hopkins and Newman's Oxford Oratory', *HQ*, Fall 1984–Winter 1985, XI, 4, 119–23.

INDEX